Restoring the Reformation

British Evangelicalism and the Francophone 'Réveil' 1816–1849

STUDIES IN EVANGELICAL HISTORY AND THOUGHT

A full listing of all titles in this series
appears at the close of this book

Rev. Mark Wilks   Rev. César Malan

Rev. Clement Perrot   Rev. David Bogue

Restoring the Reformation

British Evangelicalism and the Francophone 'Réveil' 1816–1849

Kenneth J. Stewart

First published 2006 by Paternoster

Paternoster is an imprint of Authentic Media
9 Holdom Avenue, Bletchley, Milton Keynes, MK1 1QR, UK
and
PO Box 1047, Waynesboro, GA 30830–2047, USA

12 11 10 09 08 07 06   7 6 5 4 3 2 1

British Library Cataloguing in Publication Data
A catalogue record for this book is available from the British Library

ISBN 1–84227–392-2

Typeset by A.R. Cross
Printed and bound in Great Britain
for Paternoster

STUDIES IN EVANGELICAL HISTORY AND THOUGHT

Series Preface

The Evangelical movement has been marked by its union of four emphases: on the Bible, on the cross of Christ, on conversion as the entry to the Christian life and on the responsibility of the believer to be active. The present series is designed to publish scholarly studies of any aspect of this movement in Britain or overseas. Its volumes include social analysis as well as exploration of Evangelical ideas. The books in the series consider aspects of the movement shaped by the Evangelical Revival of the eighteenth century, when the impetus to mission began to turn the popular Protestantism of the British Isles and North America into a global phenomenon. The series aims to reap some of the rich harvest of academic research about those who, over the centuries, have believed that they had a gospel to tell to the nations.

Series Editors

David Bebbington, Professor of History, University of Stirling, Stirling, Scotland, UK

John H.Y. Briggs, Senior Research Fellow in Ecclesiastical History and Director of the Centre for Baptist History and Heritage, Regent's Park College, Oxford, UK

Timothy Larsen, Associate Professor of Theology, Wheaton College, Illinois, USA

Mark A. Noll, McManis Professor of Christian Thought, Wheaton College, Wheaton, Illinois, USA

Ian M. Randall, Deputy Principal and Lecturer in Church History and Spirituality, Spurgeon's College, London, UK, and a Senior Research Fellow, International Baptist Theological Seminary, Prague, Czech Republic

To Dr Ian S. Rennie
who first taught me Church History

Contents

Preface

When I began my réveil researches in 1988, I took as my points of departure the *Lives of the Haldanes*,[1] that nineteenth-century biography which as much as anything has fixed this story in the evangelical Protestant mind, A.L. Drummond's suggestive *The Kirk and the Continent*,[2] and Timothy Stunt's horizon-widening article, 'Geneva and the British Evangelicals in the Early Nineteenth Century'.[3] I had been made curious about the subject of the réveil at Geneva because it constituted a part of the early origins of the strain of pietistic evangelicalism in which I had been raised and part of the on-going story of the churches of the Reformation which had latterly captured my affection.

I was sure that there was more to the story than the Haldane biography, largely followed by Drummond, had disclosed; I was also sure that Timothy Stunt was pointing in the right direction by his investigation of a wider Francophone-British circle of persons who had as definite a part in the story as had Robert Haldane, the Scot who went to Geneva in 1816. I could not initially have known that there was then already in progress a very substantial international discussion of this period of nineteenth-century religious history. I can still remember my consternation upon locating in the bowels of New College's library the astringent treatment of the réveil provided in Alice Wemyss' *Le Réveil: 1790-1849*.[4] According to this author, the British evangelicals had been a nuisance factor, and the réveil movement much ado about nothing. Was this to be the end of my road? An existing doctoral dissertation which was drawn to my attention, Robert Evans', 'The Contribution of Foreigners in the French Réveil' (Manchester, 1977), left me wondering what stone had still been left unturned! To crown it all, I then learned that a lecturer in a neighboring university, Dr Deryck Lovegrove, was himself engaged in Haldane research.[5] And so it went on.

---

[1] Alexander Haldane, *The Lives of Robert Haldane of Airthrey and of his brother, James Alexander Haldane*, (Edinburgh: 1855).

[2] (Edinburgh: 1956).

[3] *Journal of Ecclesiastical History*, 32.1 (1981), 35-46.

[4] (Toulouse: 1977).

[5] Deryck Lovegrove has contributed two important studies to the quest to understand Robert Haldane and his European labours. These are 'Unity and Separation: Contrasting Elements in the Thought and Practice of Robert and James Haldane', in Keith Robbins, ed., *Studies in Church History*, Subsidia 7, (1990), 153-77, and 'The Voice of Reproach and Outrage: The Impact of Robert Haldane on French-speaking Protestantism', in D.W.D. Shaw, ed., *In Divers Manners*, (St. Andrews: 1990), 74-84.

But gradually, I gained the confidence that instead of being only an outsider looking in, I in fact had come to occupy a chair at an ongoing roundtable discussion on this fascinating subject. I learned of others, such as John Roney, working on a related aspect of this subject at Toronto, and of James Deming, pursuing yet another aspect at Notre Dame. I learned of senior scholars, Elizabeth Kluit and Johannes Van den Berg, who had been in the field for decades, and finally of those writers, Jean Cadier and Leon Maury, for example, who had provided remarkably balanced perspectives decades before I began, and gone on to their rewards. Finally, there was the thrill of reading the memoirs and histories, the letters and articles composed by the contemporary réveil participants in that era of amazing Christian internationalism.

And so, eventually, I became convinced that some of the earliest questions I had posed about Haldane and the réveil, instead of being already answered, were still awaiting proper treatment. Thus, I offer here my answers to such questions as, 'What did British evangelicals other than Haldane think about Francophone Europe in this period?', 'What was the actual state of Francophone Protestantism in those decades, following the Revolution, when British evangelicals grew so concerned for the state of Europe?', 'What baggage, besides the essentials of the Christian gospel, did British evangelicals carry with them to Europe?', and, finally, 'How did the European evangelicals with whom the British collaborated, reciprocally force changes in British evangelical thinking in this period of Christian co-operation?'.

I have come to see that, on the larger canvas of Christian history, what we have in the réveil period is a chapter of European mission history, involving the communication of the gospel cross-culturally, with all the dangers and all the unforeseen developments which that can bring in its train. I have aimed not simply to chronicle, but to draw out meaning and significance. I cannot disguise my having reached the conviction that there are certain 'legendary' and hagiographic aspects of this story which are best left behind; I hope that it is just as clear that I find in this story many striking and admirable Christians, characterized by ambition, readiness to trust, and adventurousness in the best sense. There is an astonishing international Christian solidarity shown in this period that is unlike anything I have witnessed in my own time.

This is the place to record gratitude to a number of key individuals. Professor Stewart J. Brown was a steady advisor, who helped me ride out those periods when I feared, like the explorer Robert Scott, that some Amundsen had reached the pole first! Professor Donald Meek, though working in another discipline, was a most helpful guide in all matters pertaining to Robert Haldane. Professor David Bebbington, though of another university, then and since has given helpful suggestions about my topic.

As to the revising of this material, I owe special thanks to Covenant College librarians John Holberg and Tom Horner, who have been unstinting in securing materials through Inter Library Loan. I owe the same thanks to New College, Edinburgh, which showed me new kindnesses in the summer of 2005.

Covenant College's Kaleo Center, funded by the Lilly Foundation, has been most supportive in granting me assistance relative to the revision and publication of this work.

Kenneth J. Stewart

Introduction

Britain's ecclesiastical relations with the Continent in the first half of the nineteenth century constitute a subject which has been little explored. Yet this was a period when the initiatives of British Christianity in Europe were numerous and powerful. By contrast, such relations in the Reformation and post-Reformation era continue to be the subject of fruitful study.[1]

As to the nineteenth century, we have been furnished to date mainly with the histories of major Christian institutions, such as the British and Foreign Bible Society, which were active in Europe (among other places) in the period.[2] General surveys of the period have been far too broad to be truly helpful.[3] There has also been a persistent tendency to treat British Christians, active in Europe in this half-century, as so many 'great men' of history; their personal activity on the Continent is implied to have provided the mainspring for considerable subsequent development.[4] Writers who have approached this subject from a strictly nationalistic perspective have in effect also pursued the 'great man' approach, but

---

[1] So, for instance, the volume edited by Derek Baker, *Reform and Reformation: England and the Continent 1500-1750*, Studies in Church History, Subsidia 2, (Oxford: 1979). Also Menna Prestwich, ed., *International Calvinism 1541-1715*, (Oxford: 1985). Such international links have been helpfully elaborated by Philip Benedict, *Christ's Churches Purely Reformed: A Social History of Calvinism,* (New Haven, CT: 2002); and Graeme Murdock, *Beyond Calvin: The Intellectual, Political and Cultural World of Europe's Reformed Churches*, (London: 2004).

[2] E.g., William Canton, History of the British and Foreign Bible Society, (London: 1904); William Jones, Jubilee Memorial of the Religious Tract Society 1799-1849, (London: 1849).

[3] H.M. Waddams, 'The Nineteenth and Twentieth Centuries', in C.R. Dodwell, ed., *The English Church and the Continent*, (London: 1959), 95-117; Max Warren, *The Missionary Movement from Britain in Modern History,* (London: 1965).

[4] The principle is illustrated supremely by the biographer of Robert Haldane, active in Francophone Europe 1816-19. See A. Haldane, *The Lives of the Haldanes.* The assertion of pivotal influence has been taken up in such works as A.L. Drummond, 'Robert Haldane at Geneva', *Records of the Scottish Church History Society*, 9 (1947), 69-82; John T. McNeill, *The History and Character of Calvinism*, (New York: 1954), 369; and James H. Nichols, *History of Christianity 1650-1950*, (New York: 1956), 140. Recently the focus has been turned on this solitary individual; cf. Deryck Lovegrove, 'The Voice of Reproach and Outrage: The Impact of Robert Haldane on French-Speaking Protestantism', in D.W.D. Shaw, ed., *In Divers Manners*, (St. Andrews: 1990), 74-84; and Alan P.F. Sell, 'Revival and Secession in Early Nineteenth Century Geneva', in *Commemorations: Studies in Christian Thought and History*, (Cardiff,: 1994), 183-209.

emphasized the aggregate influence of persons of a single nation upon continental Christianity.[5]

All of this is due for review. Britain's position in the world of the early nineteenth century both facilitated such bold initiatives in continental Europe (whether institutional or personal) and gave rise to the somewhat ethnocentric records of them passed down to us. The latter have proved very potent in the shaping of ideas about Europe in the English-speaking Christian Church even in the present era. The British missionary movement originating in the last decade of the eighteenth century surveyed the needs of Europe with those of China, Africa and the south Pacific; that movement is now much reduced.

Not only has the world order changed in the last 150 years, but thoughts about the expansion of Christianity. It has become common to appraise whether missionary enterprise has shown sufficient respect to local culture and custom and to ask to what extent Christian expansion has followed on the heels of military and economic initiative. Were the initiatives of British Christianity in nineteenth-century Europe simply part of that current British cultural ascendancy? Was the British Christian estimate of European Christianity at the time of this expansion just and fair? And was British Christianity a purely 'active' agent in Europe in this era, or was there a reciprocity by which European Christianity was also active upon Britain?

The British involvement in the Francophone religious awakening ('le Réveil') emanating from Geneva after 1816 provides an instance of Christian initiative awaiting appraisal along such lines. The natural vantage point from which to begin a survey of this era is that of Britain's eighteenth-century Evangelical Revival. To this we now turn.

---

[5] E.g., Henry M. Cowan, *The Influence of the Scottish Church in Christendom*, (London: 1896), e.g., 128, 129; A.L. Drummond, *The Kirk and the Continent*, (Edinburgh: 1956), e.g., 180, 203.

CHAPTER 1

The Evangelical Revival in Retrospect

Edward Bickersteth (1786-1850), Anglican rector of Watton, Hertfordshire, and William Jay (1764-1853), minister of Argyle Chapel, Bath, were virtual contemporaries and had many things in common.[1] Both had entered the Christian ministry without a university education, both had gained great renown as preachers and devotional authors, both were indefatigable advocates of Protestant foreign missions (the Church Missionary Society and London Missionary Society respectively) and both were exponents of the evangelical Calvinism which had been the underpinning of the Evangelical Revival. Further, both were men of pan-Protestant sympathies; Bickersteth poured his final years into the formation of the Evangelical Alliance, while Jay recalled in his old age that he had long regarded the Anglican periodical, the *Christian Observer*, as part of his standard reading. Yet for all this, Bickersteth and Jay could hardly have differed more in their estimations of where British Protestantism stood as they surveyed it late in their lives.

Bickersteth, notwithstanding the insatiable public demand for his devotional writings and collections of hymnody, and irrespective of the dramatic advance of his beloved CMS, could still claim in 1836,

> even in Great Britain, while the confessions of faith are retained, there has been a grievous departure from those confessions and we have to mourn in all our churches that the great mass have the form of godliness but are denying the power... On the Continent, the true Protestant faith, whether in Lutheran or Reformed Churches, has been almost uprooted.[2]

Jay on the other hand, reminiscing in the 1840s over a long, busy career, could opine,

> I do not believe that in this earth misery preponderates over good. I have a better opinion of mankind than I had when I began my public life. I cannot ask 'what is the cause that the former days were better than these?' The state of the world has been improved and is improving... We also rejoice in hope. We have many and

---

[1] T.R. Birks, *Memoir of Edward Bickersteth*, 2 vols, (London: 1851); William Jay, *Autobiography*, (London: 1854).

[2] Edward Bickersteth, *The Religious State of Europe Considered*, (Glasgow: 1836), 6.

express assurances in the Scriptures, which cannot be broken, of the general and universal spread and reign of Christianity.[3]

The fact that these two contemporaries, both sons of the Evangelical Revival, could differ so markedly about the religious prospects of Britain and the world surely demands explanation. Surely there must have existed a common appreciation that the United Kingdom's churches were aggregately stronger in the 1830s and 1840s than a century before? But, in fact, there was no such common perception.

The Anglican Establishment of Edward Bickersteth had reaped a very inequitable portion of the spiritual harvest taking place in the preceding decades precisely because it had never (with some local exceptions) institutionally embraced the Evangelical Revival. Conversely, Nonconformity (Independent, Baptist or Wesleyan) had proliferated dramatically in direct proportion to the adoption of methods aimed at the re-Christianization of Britain's masses. The methods adopted to this end had been itinerant preaching (often beyond the bounds of stated places of worship), a conscious directing of the Christian gospel to the burgeoning segments of society which had hitherto received scant notice, and the proclamation of an aggressively conversionist message emphasizing the need for personal repentance and faith in the Son of God.

How was it that the Evangelical Revival, which in its early days had had so much to do with Oxford college life, Establishment-approved praying societies in London, and the High Church piety of William Law,[4] tended in the end to serve the interests not of the Establishment but of Nonconformity?

English Religion in Decline

It has become commonplace to view English religion, whether Anglican, Dissenting, or Catholic, as largely moribund in the decade of the 1730s. Political changes in the preceding decades had contributed materially to the decline. Dissent and Catholicism had suffered disintegration and disorientation after the restoration of Stuart rule in 1660. Charles II's earlier affectations of sympathy for Presbyterianism and assurances of forthcoming religious liberty showed themselves to be insincere when he consented to the 1662 Act of Uniformity. More than 2,000 ministers of the English Establishment resigned their livings rather than subscribe to the legislation.

---

[3] Jay, *Autobiography*, 159.

[4] J.D. Walsh, 'The Origins of the Evangelical Revival', in G.V. Bennett and J.D. Walsh, eds., *Essays in Modern English Church History,* (London: 1966), 138ff.

This development meant that these numerous clergymen of Puritan outlook were thereafter looked upon as potentially seditious. Ministers and congregations which only a few years before had found themselves in the religious mainstream were now marginalized and rendered sectarian. English Catholics had still cherished the hope that royal policy might yet return England to Rome. They saw their final hopes dashed when James II fled to France in 1688, thus making way for the unambiguously Protestant William of Orange. Puritan Dissent and Catholic Recusancy therefore had come to share the fate of social marginalization; there had come to be a clear 'stigma' attached to the practice of religion outside the Establishment.[5] The bearing of this stigma was a thing made all the more unpalatable in view of the grand aspirations both had so recently held.

The Church of England, which might have reasserted itself as a pastoral and societal force after the Restoration, was inhibited from responding as it might by the endemic shortage of clergy and the malady of unevenly distributed church revenues. The latter two factors combined to make clerical pluralism and non-residency necessary evils. The removal of some 2,000 clergy had merely exacerbated an already tenuous situation.

The national Church entered the Restoration not only deficient in manpower, but deficient in facilities and accommodation as well. The deficiency was most apparent in the metropolis, where if the parish of St. Martin in the Fields may be taken as representative, there was in 1660 one place in the church pews for each 100 persons in the parish.[6] Although by 1680 three subsidiary parishes had been formed in the area, what were these among some 40,000 inhabitants? There was in fact very little church-building in the eighteenth-century Establishment despite that fact that the population of England and Wales expanded during the century from five and a half to nine million.[7]

The chronic shortage of accommodation in the Establishment may not have been readily seen in its full proportions in the decades immediately following the Restoration period because of a temporary dramatic upsurge in the activity of Dissenters; these had stood apart since 1662. The latter development provided a convenient explanation for the observable decline in attendance at Establishment services. Indeed, following the provisions granted by the Toleration Act of 1689, Dissenters proceeded to obtain licenses for 2,356 places of worship in the capital before the year 1710.[8] Yet the Establishment's fixation on the unsettling tendencies of urban Dissent only served to divert it from facing

---

[5] A.D. Gilbert, *Religion and Society in Industrial England,* (London: 1976), 15.

[6] E.G. Rupp, *Religion in England,* (Oxford: 1986), 41.

[7] T.S. Ashton, *The Industrial Revolution 1760-1830,* (Oxford: 1948), 2.

[8] Rupp, *Religion,* 55.

one harsh reality: the number of citizens attending Christian worship in any form was declining relative to a rising population.

The Establishment's capacity to adapt to the changing society was actually hampered by its state connection. When the minor alteration of parish boundaries required a parliamentary act preceded by many preliminary rounds of consultation, there was clearly no manner by which the Establishment could expand promptly in response to the new social trends. The government's suspension of the Convocations of Canterbury and York in 1717 meant that even consultation by clergy within the Establishment was irreparably hampered. Thus, upon entering the second quarter of the eighteenth century, English religion in general was characterized by numerical decline relative to the population. Over and above the socio-political and demographic factors alluded to, additional contributory causes for the decline included the increase in moral permissiveness in the decades following the Restoration, the unforeseen license given to utter irreligion by the liberties granted under the Act of Toleration, and the effects of current rationalism and deism upon the Christian pulpit.[9] What could not be denied was that Christian belief and practice were waning.

A study of attendance at the sacrament of the Lord's Supper in Oxfordshire parish churches during the period 1738-1810 has shown a steady decline of 25% to the year 1802 and only a slight recovery between 1802 and 1810.[10] In rural areas the Established Church did tend to remain in a position of ascendancy and retain its hold on the community. This was often because of a tacit alliance between clergy, local landowners and magistracy, through which pressure was exerted on tenants and labourers to attend the parish church.[11] Very often, the clergyman himself was the local magistrate,[12] but this combination of religious leadership and social control carried with it many negative implications in an era when the lower classes were growing more assertive. The national Church was not alone in its growing inability to retain the allegiance of the lower orders. In *An Inquiry Into the Reasons For the Decline In The Dissenting Interest* (1731), the Dissenting leader, Philip Doddridge (1702-1751), pinpointed Nonconformity's lack of influence upon these same segments of the population as a major failing.

---

[9] T.S. Ashton, *Industrial Revolution*, 3; Basil Williams, *The Whig Supremacy,* (Oxford: 1962), 133.

[10] Gilbert, *Religion and Society*, 27.

[11] Gilbert, *Religion and Society*, 12. Elie Halévy, *A History of the English People in 1815,* (London: 1924), 392.

[12] Halévy, *A History*, 41.

Sources of the Evangelical Revival

The Evangelical Revival, far from being a merely localized upsurge in religious interest, was international in scope. The dramatic response of churchgoers in Bristol and London (1737) and of the colliers at Kingswood (1739) to the preaching of George Whitefield (1714-1770) is usually reckoned as marking the genesis of the English awakening. But in fact these events had been preceded by similar developments in Wales some years earlier. These Welsh developments (of which Whitefield was fully cognizant) had themselves been anticipated by religious stirrings in the colony of New Jersey in 1719 and 1726[13] and in Easter Ross, Scotland, in 1724.[14] The first 'surprising conversions' of which the Massachusetts preacher, Jonathan Edwards (1703-1758), would write, had occurred in the period 1734-35. The English manifestations of this awakening did not emanate exclusively from the Oxford 'Holy Club' circle which had provided an early link between John (1703-1791) and Charles Wesley (1707-1788) and Whitefield. Quite independently of the Oxford circle, there were persons engaged in pastoral ministries in such disparate areas as Cornwall and Yorkshire for whom evangelical conversion proved the great catalyst in attaining pastoral usefulness.[15] It is significant that the principal leaders of the religious awakening in England, Wales, and New England had all had extensive exposure to the pastoral ideals and writings of August Hermann Francke (1633-1727), the German Lutheran pietist, who had visited England and dealt extensively with the Society for Promoting Christian Knowledge in preceding decades.[16] Also, there had come into the United Kingdom some thousands of Protestant refugees from the central European Hapsburg lands where the Catholic Counter Reformation was proceeding with full force. These refugees brought with them to Britain and New England a familiarity with practices such as field preaching, camp

---

[13] M.R. Watts, *The Dissenters*, I, (Oxford: 1978), 394. The present writer has enumerated evidences of evangelical activity prior to this period in his, 'Did Evangelicalism Predate the Eighteenth Century?' *Evangelical Quarterly*, 77.2 (2005), 135-154.

[14] J.S. Wood, *The Inextinguishable Blaze*, (London:1960), 117; John MacInnes, *The Evangelical Movement in the Highlands of Scotland*, (Aberdeen: 1951), 156ff.

[15] G.C.B. Davies, *The Early Cornish Evangelicals, 1735-1760*, (London: 1951), 58ff; Frank Baker, *William Grimshaw*, (London, 1963), 43ff; Walsh, 'Origins of the Evangelical Revival', 134, 135.

[16] Geoffrey Nuttall, 'Continental Pietism and the Evangelical Movement in Britain', in J. Van Den Berg and J.P. Van Dooren, eds., *Pietismus und Reveil*, (Leiden: 1978), 208ff.

meetings and home gatherings for prayer which would later characterize the whole evangelical movement.[17]

For some time, one school of historians has argued for a distinction between the early Methodist itinerant movement centering around George Whitefield and John and Charles Wesley and another more 'churchly' evangelical movement. The latter is said to be distinguishable not along denominational lines (inasmuch as the three Methodists named had received episcopal ordination) but by the latter movement's observance of the Establishment's regulations against itineration and lay preaching.[18] The distinction is overdrawn, at least in the earliest decades of the Revival period, and is only transparently evident by late century. Such 'churchly' evangelicals there certainly were and they existed quite independently of the Methodists. Yet they were subject to the same formative influences as those less fastidious than themselves; they were also well acquainted with each other.

Any fair comparison between Whitefield, the Wesley brothers and more 'regular' clergy in the early period must give weight to the fact that Whitefield and the Wesleys, though episcopally-ordained, were without fixed pastoral charges and therefore were free to circulate in Britain and abroad in a way quite impossible for a parish minister. Their itinerant preaching, often in the open air, had certainly been preceded by some years by that of Griffith Jones, Anglican rector of Llanddowror, Carmarthenshire, whose example in so doing much encouraged Whitefield.[19] Whether knowingly or unknowingly, this pattern had certainly been followed by William Grimshaw of Haworth, an alleged example of independence from Methodist patterns. The procedure of organizing zealous converts into societies or bands seems to have been universal among the circle of Revival leaders in the early period, in keeping with the noble pre-history of the practice which extended back to post-Restoration London.[20] Pre-existent societies often formed the settings in which the spiritual awakening took hold. If a difference of practice existed with regard to the regulation of these societies, this was

---

[17] W.R. Ward, 'Power and Piety: The origins of religious revival in the early eighteenth century', *Bulletin of the John Rylands University Library of Manchester*, 63 (1980), 239, 248. Ward revisited these themes in *The Protestant Evangelical Awakening* (Cambridge, 1992).

[18] Michael Hennell, *John Venn and the Clapham Sect*, (London: 1957), 16, 17. Walsh, 'Origins of the Evangelical Revival', 134, 135. Kenneth Hylson-Smith, *Evangelicals in the Church of England*, (Edinburgh: 1989), 13.

[19] Nuttall, 'Continental Pietism', 213, 214.

[20] Rupp, *Religion in England,* 327; E. Halévy, *The Birth of Methodism in England*, (Chicago: 1971), 41; Walsh, 'Origins of the Evangelical Revival', 138; Davies, *Early Cornish Evangelicals,* 66.

shown in the reluctance of some clergymen, such as Walker of Truro, to surrender direct supervision of the gatherings into the hands of laymen.[21]

Having recalled the antecedents of the Revival in America, Scotland and Wales, the activity of roaming clergymen as well as those who nurtured evangelical piety within the strict boundaries of their parishes, we may ask whether the existing Protestant Nonconformity had any contribution to offer the cause of religious awakening. It has grown fashionable to depict Nonconformity as being anaemic, demoralized, and in retreat during that period and to draw the conclusion that it too staggered on until provided with the tonic that the Revival furnished.[22] Yet, while allowing for the colossal numerical decline of English Presbyterianism in that century from two-thirds to one twentieth of all Protestant Dissent,[23] we may note that the churches of both Independent and Particular Baptist orientation resisted numerical decline on this scale in part because they resisted the theological decline which underlay the Presbyterian demise.

Even if so socially marginalized as to be incapable of serving as catalysts for the Revival,[24] some Dissenters were at least labouring to that end before the awakening was considered to have dawned. Isaac Watts (1674-1748), minister of the church at Mark Lane, London, from 1702, was a correspondent with Jonathan Edwards and the encourager of George Whitefield. Thomas Cole (1672-1740), the Gloucester Independent pastor and itinerant evangelist, had preached through the countryside after 1716 and had been the butt of Whitefield's disruptive boyish pranks. In the late 1730s, Whitefield's own itineration in the area enabled the aged Cole to gather groups of persons whose newly aroused spiritual concern found no welcome in local parish churches. After Cole's death his place was filled by the like-minded John Oldring who came recommended for the task by his theological mentor at Northampton Academy, Philip Doddridge.[25]

While it is too much to claim that Doddridge's arrival at Northampton in 1729 in the dual capacity of pastor to Castle Hill Chapel and Academy

---

[21] Davies, *Cornish Evangelicals,* 69.

[22] Compare on this point, J.D. Walsh 'Methodism at the End of the Eighteenth Century', in R.E. Davies and E.G. Rupp, *History of the Methodist Church in Great Britain,* Vol. 1, (London: 1965), 263, with Rupp, *Religion in England,* 486. The clearest available summary of Nonconformist vitality in this period is that of Geoffrey Nuttall, 'Methodism and the Older Dissent', in *Journal of the United Reformed Church History Society,* 2.8 (1981), 259-74.

[23] Halévy, *Birth of Methodism* 48; Gilbert, *Religion in Industrial Society,* 36.

[24] *The Dissenters,* 438, 439.

[25] Geoffrey Nuttall, 'George Whitefield's Curate: Gloucester Dissent and the Evangelical Revival', *Journal of Ecclesiastical History,* 27 (1976), 369, 375, 381.

tutor marked 'the beginning of the Evangelical Movement',[26] his importance as a bridge-builder cannot be overestimated. His devotional work, *The Rise and Progress of Religion in the Soul* (1745), was standard fare for evangelical converts in the period.[27] He wrote to the Oxford undergraduate, Whitefield, to assure him of his prayers on his behalf, and welcomed both Whitefield and John Wesley to address his ministerial students. The case of Doddridge demonstrates clearly that some Dissenters saw in the Revival's dawn that for which they had prayed and laboured. While the whole question of the relation of Dissent to the Revival has been too little understood,[28] it is plain that the Revival's numerical impact upon the Independent and Baptist communions was only discernible after mid-century.

Upon reflection, therefore, we should conceive the origins of the Revival not in terms of denominational influences, but in terms of a milieu of beliefs and ideas commonly accessible to those who sought a recovery from the religious decline affecting all churches in a rapidly expanding society. Such a common milieu of influences understandably made for a largely coherent proclamation. The awfulness of sin, the wonder of the cross of Christ, the possibility of present forgiveness of sins through the placing of faith in Christ who suffered and rose—these were the common themes of the preaching.[29] The personal enjoyment of these realities was inextricably connected with a renewed emphasis upon the experience of the new birth, a scriptural teaching earlier recovered for English theology by John Colet (1466-1519).[30] Though this characteristic emphasis of the Revival has usually been attributed to John Wesley and the Moravians who influenced him so deeply at a critical stage in the late 1730s, the earliest and most persistent herald of the teaching seems to have been Whitefield.

---

[26] A. Everett, *The Pattern of Rural Dissent: The Nineteenth Century*, (London: 1972), 16, quoted in Malcolm Deacon, *Philip Doddridge*, (Northampton: 1980), 14.

[27] Frank Baker has, for instance, noted the extensive use made of the work by William Grimshaw, *Grimshaw*, 81. Also note A.S. Wood, *Thomas Haweis*, (London: 1957) 36. Ernest A. Payne, *The Free Church Tradition in the life of England*, (London: 1944), 69, provides still additional examples.

[28] Nuttall, 'George Whitefield's Curate', 370.

[29] There is a helpful discussion of the commonality of these themes in David Bebbington, *Evangelicalism in Modern Britain*, (London: 1989), 42ff.

[30] Rupp, *Religion in England*, 419-20.

Calvinism and the Evangelical Revival

If the Revival had a common theology, it may be said to have been overwhelmingly Calvinistic.[31] But even this assertion must at once be qualified. Walsh[32] has correctly emphasized that many of the early leaders of the Revival had, at the time of their conversions, really no sense of theological identity and were in need of finding a doctrinal framework. For very many this framework was provided by the Calvinist system. But in what forms was Calvinist doctrine available in the early eighteenth century?

One must look very hard and long to find an eighteenth-century figure who could claim to have read the writings of the Genevan reformer. Whitefield, whose painful differences with John Wesley over the doctrine of predestination precipitated a permanent breach in the Methodist movement, had not. John Wesley's own convictions on the question had never been illuminated by reading continental Reformation theology at first hand, but were an amalgam of ideas worked out in exchanges with his mother, Susannah. He had also gained a familiarity with the early writings of John Gill (1697-1771), the Baptist theologian whose supralapsarian views would inhibit the free preaching of the gospel in his own circles for decades.[33]

That Calvin's writings were neglected in eighteenth-century England was not simply part of the reaction against things Puritan. Calvin's influence had not been predominant among the English Puritans of the seventeenth century or English Reformers of the sixteenth. The names of Martyr and Bullinger evidently carried more weight in the century of the Reformation and gave way in the next to Beza, Junius, Danaeus, Ursinus and above all Zanchius.[34] In that same seventeenth century, William Perkins and William Ames, native theologians, had taken their places among the European Reformed theologians reckoned as of the front

---

[31] Rupp, *Religion in England*, 325, speaks of Wesley's Arminian theology as being 'plainly the odd one out' in light of the overwhelming Puritan and Calvinist orientation of the awakening. Mark Noll has addressed this theme in a helpful section of his *The Rise of Evangelicalism: The Age of Edwards, Whitefield and the Wesleys*, (Leicester and Downers Grove: 2004), 53-60.

[32] J.D. Walsh, 'The Cambridge Methodists', in Peter Brook, ed., *Christian Spirituality: Essays for E.G. Rupp*, (London: 1975), 261.

[33] George Whitefield, *Works*, I, 205, 442, 495, quoted in Wood, *Inextinguishable Blaze*, 180. Rupp, introduction to *History of the Methodist Church in Great Britain*, I. xxxi, and *Religion in England*, 371. One of the few 'fathers' of the revival known to have read Calvin was the Welsh preacher, Griffith Jones (1683-1761). See R. Tudur Jones, 'The Evangelical Revival in Wales', in James P. Mackey, ed., *Introduction to Celtic Christianity*, (Edinburgh: 1990), 242.

[34] Patrick Collinson, 'England and International Calvinism 1558-1640', in Menna Prestwich, ed., *International Calvinism 1541-1715*, (Oxford: 1986), 214, 215.

rank. Thus any discussion regarding the influence of Calvinist theology in eighteenth-century England must reckon with the fact that the use of such a term may not be understood to imply a predominance of the Genevan reformer's own distinctive thought. 'Calvinist theology' had become a generic term descriptive of all European Protestant theology emanating from the South German and Swiss Reformation. English participation in this trans-national work of formulating a Protestant dogmatics had in fact produced a definable hybrid strain of thought which one perceptive modern writer has termed 'Anglo-Calvinism', and another has found distinctively displayed in the writings of John Bunyan.[35]

In late-seventeenth and early-eighteenth-century England, there is evidence that such international Reformed theology had fallen distinctly out of favour within the Anglican Establishment. John Edwards (1637-1716), said to have been the last Calvinist don at Cambridge, had found it necessary to retire from both college life and the pastoral ministry by 1683, so unpopular were his views. His extensive polemical writings, composed in this subsequent period of withdrawal, were of use to friends of the Revival after 1740.[36] Bebbington[37] has surely been correct to insist that the hypothesis of an unbroken Calvinistic succession within the English Establishment fails for lack of evidence.

The Calvinistic theology taught in the Nonconformist Academies in the early eighteenth century seems to have been a blend of the writings of seventeenth-century continental dogmaticians such as Johannes Wollebius (1586-1629) of Basel, Francois Turretin (1623-1687) and his son Jean Alphonse Turretin (1671-1737) of Geneva, Benedict Pictet (1655-1724) of Geneva, John Marck (1655-1731) of Leyden, and of native writers such as William Ames (1576-1633) and Richard Baxter (1615-1691).[38] Links were maintained with the continental faculties of theology and it was not uncommon for ministerial students in English academies to spend a year or more at Leyden or Geneva. In the latter location they encountered what was termed the 'sane orthodoxy' of the younger Turretin.[39] A major innovation within the academies was the move by Philip Doddridge of Northampton to use English rather than Latin as the language of theological instruction. This move paved the way for the use

---

[35] Rupp, *Religion in England*, 325, 483; Richard Greaves, *John Bunyan*, (Appleford: 1969).

[36] s.v. 'John Edwards', in J.D. Douglas, ed., *The New International Dictionary of the Christian Church*, (Grand Rapids: 1974), 334; Rupp, *Religion*, 326.

[37] Bebbington, *Evangelicalism*, 36.

[38] H. McLachlan, *English Education Under the Test Acts*, (Manchester: 1931), 22, 300, 302, 303.

[39] McLachlan, *English Education*, 29. David Bogue and James Bennett, *History of Dissenters*, III, (London: 1808), 333, 361.

of English texts, among which were Doddridge's own *Lectures on Pneumatology, Ethics, and Theology* (published posthumously in 1763) and the Baptist, John Gill's *Body of Divinity* (1767).

Yet, even when allowance has been made for the individual efforts of a Thomas Cole or a Doddridge, it is apparent that Nonconformist theology was in a doldrum period. The Salters' Hall Synod controversy (1719), which failed to resolve a growing crisis over the doctrine of the Trinity and the person of Christ, indicated a growing theological polarization with Nonconformity.[40] Independency seemed to offer more doctrinal stability than Presbyterianism in this period and so there were some 'theological refugees' from the latter to the former. But Independency was clearly no uniform force for the spiritual recovery of the nation.[41] Moreover, we seem to look in vain within England in the 1730s for any indigenous Calvinism which can explain the pervasive influence the theology exercised once the movement was in progress.

Having noted earlier that the Revival leaders seem to have acquired a doctrinal framework subsequent to the experience of conversion, it is fascinating to note the sources relied upon for this purpose. Whitefield had early been given the writings of August Francke by John Wesley, but seemed to benefit most of all by a reading of the devotional work of the Scottish theologian, Henry Scougal (1650-1678), *The Life of God in the Soul of Man* (1677). In his biography of Whitefield, Arnold Dallimore has also drawn attention to the evangelist's additional indebtedness to Scots divinity, especially Thomas Boston's *Human Nature in Its Fourfold State* and Ralph Erskine's *Sermons*.[42] Walker of Truro placed into the hands of the young convert, Thomas Haweis, Boston's *Fourfold State* as well as the sermons of Ralph and Ebenezer Erskine. These were no doubt familiar to him through the offices of the Aberdeen schoolmaster, George Conon, who had recently been transferred to Cornwall. Grimshaw of Haworth, under deep impressions of sin late in his first pastoral charge, found great relief upon reading the Puritan John Owen's *Justification by Faith* (1677).[43] Calvinistic writings of an earlier generation seem to have been standard fare among the awakened.

---

[40] Payne, *The Free Church Tradition,* 63. See also Peter Toon, 'The Lime Street Lectures 1730-31 and their Significance', *Evangelical Quarterly,* 41.1 (1969), 42-49.

[41] Geoffrey Nuttall, 'Calvinism in Free Church History', *Baptist Quarterly,* 22.8 (1968), 421.

[42] Arnold Dallimore, *George Whitefield,* 2 vols, (Edinburgh: 1970, 1978), I, 405.

[43] Wood, *Haweis,* 36; Baker, *Grimshaw,* 44. Such proofs of indebtedness provide interesting corroboration for an assertion made by High Churchman E.B. Pusey in the next century. Speaking of evangelicalism within his communion, he complained in his *Letter to the Archbishop of Canterbury,* (Oxford, 1842), 50, that it had borrowed its theology in the previous century from Nonconformity.

In this situation in which the Puritan theology of the previous century had largely fallen into disrepute, appeals to the Thirty-Nine Articles of Religion also seem to have fallen on deaf ears. It is not, therefore, surprising that the Calvinism connected with the Revival should be found to be somewhat unsystematic and piecemeal in its initial period. Such Calvinism as was found in the Thirty-Nine Articles had always been recognized as being modestly expressed, lacking (for good or for ill) the elaboration of the consolidative Protestant creeds and confessions of the seventeenth century. There was in fact nothing to be gained by the generation of Whitefield in espousing a Calvinism any loftier than that which could be defended out of the Establishment's neglected articles.

A similar factor served to exercise restraint over the direction Calvinism would take among Dissenters during this period: these were granted license to assemble under the provisions of the Toleration Act (1689) provided their preachers maintained conformity of teaching to the Thirty-Nine Articles (articles 34-36, excepted).[44] While the Establishment itself seems to have been remarkably lax in enforcing internal conformity to the Articles and with Nonconformity following suit, the Articles may be said nonetheless to have served the purpose of setting some boundaries for theological discussion in an age when the more elaborate Calvinist creeds of the seventeenth century had fallen into neglect.[45]

Against such a backdrop we may reconsider the familiar assertion that the predominant theological tendency of the Revival was one of moderate Calvinism.[46] The inherent difficulty with such terminology is that the

---

[44] H. Gee and W.J. Hardy, *Documents Illustrative of English Church History*, (London: 1896), 654; Deacon, *Philip Doddridge*, 150, n.27. An interesting study of the conserving influence of the Anglican liturgy upon Nonconformity through this era is found in A.E. Peaston, *The Prayer Book Tradition in the Free Churches*, (London: 1964).

[45] See the Westminster Confession of Faith, the Savoy Declaration, the London Baptist Confession. The latter two represent minor modifications of the former.

[46] J.S. Reynolds, *The Early Oxford Evangelicals*, (Oxford: 1953), 3; Davies, *Early Cornish Evangelicals*, 154-156. Davies uses the term as an apt designation of a view which held that saving grace, though sovereignly and discriminatingly given to sinners, also provided for the consent of an enabled human will. Moderate Calvinism this may be; it is also the teaching of the Westminster Confession of Faith, X. i. A.S. Wood, *Inextinguishable Blaze*, 176, contrasts the moderate Calvinism of the regular Church evangelicals with the 'more emphatically Calvinist postion of the party of Whitefield and the Countess of Huntingdon'. This is judiciously said. Walsh, 'Methodism at the End of the Eighteenth Century', 289, contrasts the moderate Calvinist clergy who held to predestined election with 'others' (e.g. Toplady) who did not hesitate to affirm reprobation. This makes one valid distinction while skirting the more basic and fundamental one posited by Wood, above. Bebbington, *Evangelicalism*, 63, utilizes the 'moderate' terminology emphasizing the eighteenth-century determination to weigh Calvin's teaching carefully—a definition which means relatively little given both the inaccessibility of Calvin's writings and the practical displacement of Calvin in English

meaning of the term 'moderate' must always be determined by the extremes it seeks to avoid. A refined terminology is needed both to encompass the different denominational settings in which these questions were agitated and the various controversies which surfaced during this Revival of religion.

The creeds of England's seventeenth century, while certainly more elaborate and detailed than the Thirty-Nine Articles, were themselves moderate statements of the international Reformed dogmatics current in the mid- to late-seventeenth century. A close comparison of the seventeenth-century confessions of Presbyterian, Congregational and Baptist churches with the Articles of the Synod of Dort (1618) indicates that the English confessions show restraint where that Synod was expansive. A close study of the minutes of the Westminster Assembly (1643-47) reveals that there were speculative Calvinist views aired in that gathering which were never incorporated into the Confession of Faith.[47]

In post-Restoration England, these confessions became the legacy of minority parties, while the Articles of the Established Church received only minimal attention. Perhaps as a reflection of their minority status, some Dissenting Calvinists (both Baptist and Independent) were evidently moved to hold what one historian has called 'a doctrine of the salvation of the few'.[48] By 1737, the idea had gained currency among such 'high-Calvinists' that if Christ had died for the elect alone, then only the elect had the power to repent and believe.[49] This view, so restrictive to the free preaching of the gospel, had by the eighteenth century come to be known as hyper-, high-, or false-Calvinism. But not all Calvinists concurred. Such men as John Ryland, Jr, and Andrew Fuller affirmed that Christ's atoning death implemented a particularistic design, but they insisted that free offers of salvation should not be restricted on account of this particularism.

If some Baptists and Independents in the 1730s embraced this strain of dogmatic thought which was so inhibitive of unfettered gospel preaching, there also existed in the West of England and Wales a wide grouping of those whom Rupp has called 'aggressive predestinarians'; these

---

Reformed theology. R.H. Martin, *Evangelicals United*, (Metuchen: 1983), 17ff, uses the term to describe Charles Simeon, Andrew Fuller and Edward Williams, when Fuller himself indicated his distaste for the position implied by the term moderate. Fuller styled himself a 'strict Calvinist'; see John Ryland, *Life and Death of Andrew Fuller*, (London: 1816), 56. Hylson-Smith, *Evangelicals in the Church of England*, 52, uses the moderate terminology without any serious attempt to define more extreme views.

[47] A.F. Mitchell and J. Struthers, *Minutes of the Sessions of the Westminster Assembly*, (Edinburgh: 1890).

[48] Nuttall, 'Calvinism in Free Church History', 418.

[49] Geoffrey Nuttall, 'Northamptonshire and *The Modern Question*: A Turning Point in Eighteenth-Century Dissent', *Journal of Theological Studies*, 16.1 (1965), 102.

combined close belief in the doctrine of election with an aggressive evangelism.[50] It was such listeners as these who took immediate and strong offence when John Wesley challenged their views in 1739. This constituency, which had been rallied by such ministers as Thomas Cole (d.1742) Howell Harris (1714-1773), Griffith Jones (1683-1761) and Daniel Rowland (1713-1790) held to the Calvinism of the previous century. Philip Doddridge's Northampton Academy, often criticized for the proportion of graduates forfeited to rational Dissent, still provided a number of students such as Risdon Darracott who perpetuated this emphasis.[51]

Just as there were such discernible strands of Calvinist emphasis within Nonconformity, so these were also to be found within that element of the Establishment energised by the Revival. While there were those like Walker of Truro whose concern was to maintain the Reformation doctrines without regard to 'system' and then only as the doctrines emerged from the consecutive study of the Bible, there were also not lacking more militant persons such as William Romaine, Martin Madan and Thomas Haweis who were quite unafraid to contend for Calvinist doctrine as the system taught in the Thirty-Nine Articles of the Church.[52] Yet another stance was taken by the polemicist and hymnwriter, Augustus Toplady (1740-1778). Converted under the labours of a Methodist lay-preacher, Toplady became John Wesley's greatest detractor. Responsible for the translation of sixteenth-century dogmatician, Girolamo Zanchius' tract, *Absolute Predestination* (E.T. 1769), Toplady contended for a rigorous Calvinist reading of the Thirty-Nine Articles of the Church of England.

What then was the 'moderate' Calvinism that typified so much of the preaching and teaching of the Revival? It emphasized the doctrines of humanity's utterly depraved nature and need of divine mercy, the cross of Christ as the divine provision for human sinfulness, the sovereign operation of the divine mercy in keeping with an eternal election of grace, and the preserving power of this grace upon the believer. If this Calvinism was often presented as Scripture truth rather than as systematic dogma, this should be understood as the strategy for an age when all systems and articles of faith had fallen into oblivion or contempt. If this approach to dogma did not treat as equally important every detail of the high orthodoxy of the preceding century, this may simply be understood as a strategy based upon the new pastoral realities. John Wesley's determination to know and teach the 'way to heaven' was, in reality, the objective of many other preachers. Anglican friends of the Revival had

---

[50] Rupp, *Religion in England,* 370.
[51] Davies, *Cornish Evangelicals,* 171; Bebbington, *Evangelicalism,* 32.
[52] Wood, *Haweis,* 240; Rupp, *Religion in England,* 483.

no dogmatician of their own and at the century's end were still depending heavily upon Doddridge's *Lectures*.[53]

All this being said, it seems that recent efforts to portray the Evangelical Revival's legacy as one of a dampened concern for doctrinal distinction involve a serious oversimplification.[54] Even leaving the polemical writers aside, there is not lacking abundant evidence of tenacious doctrinal concern. But this tenacious advocacy is, given the circumstances of the period, offered on behalf of central matters of the Christian faith. It is somewhat paradoxical that such contenders as there were for creedal Calvinism in the decades following the advent of the Revival were Anglican and not Nonconformist.[55]

Subscription under the Toleration Act to the modified Thirty-Nine Articles suggested to some Nonconformists (who could not be unaware of the disparagement of these Articles within the Establishment) that creedal subscription was utterly futile. They were certain they could maintain their Calvinism without formulas.[56] Even without creeds to contend for, the non-Wesleyan supporters of the Revival, whether inside or outside the Establishment, shared a common sense of theological direction. Stoughton, the nineteenth-century Nonconformist historian, justifiably wrote:

> they leaped back over a hundred years to get at the time of Goodwin and Owen, Baxter and Howe, Bates and Charnock, Gurnall and Flavel... The wells whence the Evangelicals drew their inspiration were not Patristic, not Anglo-Catholic, but they were Protestant works of the sixteenth and Nonconformist works of the seventeenth century.[57]

The Transmission of the Evangelical Impetus

We have noted already the insufficient response offered by the Church of England to the challenge offered by an expanding London metropolis. Yet it would be misleading to assume that this metropolitan situation pinpoints correctly the setting in which the Evangelical Revival helped to address England's social and spiritual need. In point of fact, the cause of the Revival was not warmly taken up by the London Establishment, and

---

[53] Bebbington, *Evangelicalism*, 87.

[54] Martin, *Evangelicals United*, 10.

[55] Augustus Toplady, *Historic Proof of the Doctrinal Calvinism of the Church of England*, (London: 1774); Thomas Haweis, *The Church of England Vindicated*, (London: 1801).

[56] Bogue and Bennett, *History of Dissenters*, II, 26.

[57] John Stoughton, *Religion in England Under Queen Anne and the Georges*, (London: 1878), 93.

were it not for the early existence of societies there (such as the Moravian society meeting at Aldersgate Street or the society organized by John Wesley at the Foundry) the Revival might not have gained a foothold in that city.

William Romaine (1714-1795) is generally recognized to have been the first beneficed Establishment evangelical in the city. But this appointment as rector of St. Anne's, Blackfriars, in 1766 came only after Romaine had held lectureships in the city since 1748. Patronage arrangements in the Establishment made it initially very difficult for any ordinand known to be supportive of 'enthusiasm' to gain nomination to a pastoral vacancy. This difficulty, especially in the capital, had several significant consequences. The major of these was that various private initiatives were resorted to in order to ensure that 'Gospel' clergy would gain a hearing in the city. Whitefield himself, finding preaching venues in the city increasingly hard to come by, used the Moorfields 'Tabernacle' (a wooden structure erected for his use by Dissenters) regularly from 1741 and had another facility, Tottenham Road Chapel, erected in 1756.[58] The chapel at Lock Hospital, itself the creation of a Christian philanthropist, became the venue for the city ministries of Martin Madan and Thomas Haweis. The same problem of access to city pulpits for evangelicals in the Establishment would eventually lead the Countess of Huntingdon to open chapels in London and elsewhere in order that the message of the awakening might be heard from Church of England preachers. This urban difficulty goes far to explain why many prominent father figures in the move for spiritual renewal in the Established Church did their work in rustic or isolated settings.

These pioneers may have gathered young candidates for the ministry, but it was completely beyond their power to ensure safe passage through an Oxford or Cambridge college and beyond for such hopeful young men. When the Methodist sympathies and associations of six young Oxford men became known in 1768, they were sent down from the University. Aspiring men who sought ordination without university education invariably faced the same obstacles if it became known that they were sympathetic to the Revival. John Newton of Liverpool (1725-1807), dramatically converted from a life of slave-trading, had after his private preparation for ordination seriously to consider ministry with various Dissenting groups when it appeared that no bishop would ordain him. Cornelius Winter (1742-1807), privately trained for the ministry by Whitefield, met with a simple flat refusal from the Bishop of London when he sought ordination for continued service in the Georgia

---

[58] Dallimore, *Whitefield,* II, 49, 280.

orphanage his late mentor had begun.[59] This episcopal recalcitrance in the face of what Walsh[60] has termed the problem of the 'eloquent convert' ensured that twenty candidates were inadvertently provided for the ministry of the Dissenting churches by three evangelical clergymen who could not obtain Episcopal ordination for them.[61]

Members of the Established Church sympathizing with the Revival faced similar difficulties. An evangelical Churchman's removal to another charge could allow unsympathetic patrons to choose a successor-minister of very different sympathies. As well, an evangelical Churchman's itineration around his broad parish could create the nuclei of future congregations for which an evangelical ministry could not be ensured. Both tendencies were illustrated in the case of the energetic Grimshaw of Haworth; at his removal from his initial charge of Todmorden, five-sixths of those who had gathered to hear his preaching declined to support the ministrations of his otherwise-minded successor. Grimshaw's own extensive itineration in the massive parish of Haworth led to the eventual founding of five Nonconformist congregations.[62] The Yorkshire ministry of Henry Venn produced the nuclei of four Congregational churches. The preaching labours of John Berridge of Everton, both within his own parish and beyond, served to found or revive thirteen Dissenting churches.[63]

By the close of the eighteenth century, Establishment friends of the Revival came to take great umbrage at such tendencies. Charles Simeon, for one, lamented, 'the Clergyman beats the bushes and the Dissenter catches the game'.[64] But in point of fact, Church of England evangelicals were quite impotent to overcome these difficulties and the resolution of them awaited such early nineteenth-century developments as the consecration of the first evangelical bishop, Henry Ryder (1777-1836), to the see of Gloucester in 1818, and the purchase of advowsons by the patronage trust established by Charles Simeon.[65] But improvement of the situation came with time. By 1800 it was estimated that evangelical clergy

---

[59] D. Bruce Hindmarsh, *John Newton and the English Evangelical Tradition*, (Oxford: 1996); Wood, *Haweis*, 98ff; William Jay, ed., *Memoir of Cornelius Winter*, (London: 1809), 134, 135.

[60] Walsh, 'Methodism at the End of the Eighteenth Century', 294.

[61] Watts, *Dissenters*, 452.

[62] Baker, *Grimshaw*, 51; Martin, *Evangelicals United*, 7.

[63] Watts, *Dissenters*, 452; C.H. Smyth, *Simeon and Church Order*, (Cambridge: 1940), 266.

[64] W. Carus, *Memoirs of the Life of the Rev. Charles Simeon*, (Cambridge: 1847), 139, quoted in Martin, *Evangelicals United*, 7.

[65] Hylson-Smith, *Evangelicals in the Church of England*, 69, 75.

in the Establishment numbered 500; by 1830 they were thought to comprise between one eighth and one quarter of the entire ministry.[66]

However, for the eighteenth century this aggregation of difficulties—limited access to the major cities, the difficulty of training future ministers and the uncertainty of satisfactory ministerial succession—definitely limited the contribution of evangelicalism in a time of great stress and upheaval. England's population was shifting gradually from the lowland south to the highland zone of the west Midlands, Lancashire and Yorkshire—a shift related to the availability of coal, metals and waterpower there. Yet the national Church was both insufficiently attuned to the country's demographic upheaval and resistant to the efforts of this energetic party whose contribution might have been much larger.

The genuine gulf which gradually opened between friends of the Revival within the Establishment had nothing to do with differences of conviction on the doctrines of salvation (though these did exist) but with differences of attitude regarding the excusability or inexcusability of crossing parish boundaries in order to preach the gospel.[67] To be sure, there were those, such as Joseph Jane of Oxford, who shared Wesley's Arminianism but not his zeal for itineration. There were as well, on the other hand, those like Henry Venn, John Berridge and Thomas Haweis, who distanced themselves from Wesley's doctrinal position, yet joined him in preaching the gospel without geographical limit.

But in point of fact, the itineration of the Wesleys was a slightly different item than the itineration of the others. Both the Wesleys had begun the practice with considerable misgivings over its irregularity (and 'vulgarity' when out of doors), but soon devised a legitimation for it based upon liberties they believed to be inherent in their status as fellows of an Oxford college. Parish ministers who crossed parish boundaries to preach could hide behind no such arguments. Thus the number of Establishment clergymen who would do so was strictly limited. The Wesleys, having made the decision to itinerate, were soon forced to make another expedient decision; they came to rely on lay preachers to assist them in what rapidly became an expanding movement.

John Wesley is reputed to have claimed the world as his parish. In fact, his massive itineration throughout England seems to have been concentrated in the areas of the west and north. It is hardly coincidental that this region was the one undergoing rapid industrialization and a resultant influx of population.[68] While it may have been believed that Wesley's movement was primarily comprised of miners and menial

---

[66] Hylson-Smith, *Evangelicals in the Church of England*, 68.
[67] Wood, *Haweis*, xv.
[68] Williams, *Whig Supremacy*, 92-97.

labourers, in fact the mainstream of the movement also included artisans, shopkeepers, and small manufacturers.[69] The fact that Wesley's 'helpers' (preaching laymen of whom he expected five hours' study per day) were drawn from these same classes illustrates that Wesley understood his constituency well. The principle of selection also demonstrates his realism in assessing what type of leadership might be recruitable for a Christian movement cut from a coarser social fabric[70] than that of the Establishment. This corps of preachers included masons, soldiers, apprentices from the building trades, schoolteachers, textile workers, clay china factory employees and a tin miner.[71]

The first membership statistics available, those of 1767, indicate a following of 22,410 persons; the numbers grew to 56,605 by the year of Wesley's death (1791).[72] A movement which multiplied so rapidly had surely done something right, even if its relationship to the Establishment was lichen-like. From 1744, an annual conference of supporting preachers (ordained Anglicans and lay) was held under Wesley's presidency. From 1746, Wesley's scattered societies were arranged in circuits under the supervision of the carefully chosen 'helpers'.

By 1755, the founder had to respond to an undertow of interest among these 'helpers' in ending the dependency upon the Church of England with a declaration of separation. This tendency Wesley resisted with very mixed emotions, knowing that the possibility of his lay preachers ever being granted ordination by the Establishment was highly unlikely. In the same period, he also resisted an appeal from Establishment clergy in Cornwall, friendly to the Revival, asking that any Methodist societies lying in their parishes be placed under their own direction. This proposal Wesley rejected as it opened the possibility that at some future date a change of local clergy would place his converts under unsympathetic pastoral direction. Though Wesley's societies and their meeting houses were not licensed under the Toleration Act until 1787 and the administration of both sacraments not permitted within the societies until 1795, it is plain that the founder had early on come to settled conclusions about the dangers awaiting his societies through any process of comprehension within the Establishment.[73]

---

[69] Rupp, *Religion,* 446; Gilbert, *Religion and Society,* 59ff.

[70] The felicitous phrase is that of Rupp, *Religion in England,* 391.

[71] Watts, *Dissenters,* 408.

[72] Gilbert, *Religion and Society,* 31. This numerical growth, though notable, is still so far short of nation-shaking, that John Kent has recently questioned the propriety of continuing to speak of the Evangelical Revival as an event of national significance. See his *Wesley and the Wesleyans,* (Cambridge: 2002).

[73] See the Walker of Truro and Wesley correspondence of 1757 published in Davies, *Early Cornish Evangelicals,* 126.

Meanwhile, the prolific growth of the Wesleyan movement held out lessons which were not missed by some of the Dissenting bodies. In 1773 the aggregate number of Dissenting congregations in England (Presbyterians included) totalled 1,080—over 100 fewer than half a century earlier. Yet a recovery of Independent fortunes was plainly underway in the period beginning 1750, for between that year and 1799 269 new meeting places were registered. Among the Baptists, there was an increase of 532 registrations in the period 1751-1808.[74]

The explanation for this reversal is manifold, yet reducible to a neat summary provided by Gilbert, who spoke of the sections of Dissent 'metamorphosed by the Methodist revival'.[75] It is important to note the benefit bestowed by Whitefield upon Dissent in general. First and foremost, many leaders of the renewed Dissent had come to evangelical conversion under Whitefield's preaching. Second, Whitefield had taken the step of registering both Moorfields Tabernacle and his Tottenham Road Chapel as Independent Meeting Houses as early as 1764; the step was taken subsequently in his other preaching stations. And this cementing of a cordial, though unofficial link between Whitefield and Dissent was far from unusual. From 1742, Calvinistic Methodist societies in Wales, standing in the same relationship to the Establishment as Wesley's societies, began to register themselves as Independent Dissenting chapels.[76]

Shortly, Independency was active in utilizing this external assistance. Bogue and Bennett, writing in 1808, believed that the phenomenal growth of Independency in their lifetime was due to an appropriation of Methodism's style of preaching, worship, and hymnody; the judgment was shared by their contemporary, William Jay of Bath.[77] Such chroniclers wrote in retrospect; but, long before such recollections were ever penned, it was plain that Dissent had fresh wind in its sails.

The evidence of this change was at least three-fold. There was first, for Independents and Particular Baptists, a decidedly different theological strategy followed in the articulation of the gospel message. Before 1750 there had been hesitation by many Calvinist preachers in commending the offer of divine mercy and pardon through Christ due to a combination of factors including a Dissenting remnant-psychology and the mistaken inference that human sinfulness freed all but elect sinners from the responsibility of responding to the gospel. Welsh, American, and Scottish awakening preaching early demonstrated its freedom from such mistaken constraints. The unfettered offers of the gospel regularly made

---

[74] Gilbert, *Religion and Society*, 35, 36.

[75] Gilbert, *Religion and Society*, 36.

[76] Walsh, 'Methodism at the End of the Eighteenth Century', 293; Dallimore, *Whitefield*, II, 49; Watts, *Dissenters,* 452.

[77] Bogue and Bennett, *History of Dissenters*, II, 355; Jay, *Autobiography,* 141.

by John Wesley and Whitefield, while proceeding from non-identical theological premises, were at least seen to share in common the confidence that Christ's death for sin was of inexhaustible worth and therefore the warrant for a bold request for divine forgiveness.[78]

Moreover, a theology which addressed directly one of these major theological hindrances to evangelization was shortly available in the pages of Jonathan Edwards' *Freedom of the Will* (1754). The latter argued that a sinful person's moral responsibility to respond to the Christian gospel remained undiminished even while thier natural ability to do so was grossly impaired. Ministerial biographies from the latter half of the eighteenth century repeatedly attest the significance of this volume.[79]

A second hallmark of the expansion of Dissent was the extension of itinerant preaching. Such was the concern to see it take place on the widest possible scale as the means of gospel extension that co-operative interdenominational organizations, such as the 'Societas Evangelica', which was founded in 1776, in order to promote and extend it. It is difficult to determine which came first in order of time: the itinerant movement or the rise of the new preparatory academies—the third feature of the 'new Dissent'. It seems safe to say that the growth of the movement required the creation of these academies and that the enlarged supply of preachers through the academies further spurred on the itinerant movement.

Of course, some prominent itinerants entered the work without the benefit of any formal ministerial training. George Burder (1752-1832), later to figure so prominently in London Missionary Society and *Evangelical Magazine* circles, had begun preaching to farm workers in 1775-76 and was so well received that he was soon preaching twice each Sunday. 'Thus I began my ministerial career in the methodistical way', he later recorded. The 'methodistical way' meant for Burder that simple preaching would first be learned in rustic settings with the study of theology and biblical languages only coming later.[80] Cornelius Winter, who later maintained a small academy of his own, had begun his own work as an itinerant in the 1760s, combining his trade as a metal worker with occasional forays to rural churches in need of pulpit supply. On the basis of such efforts, John Berridge of Everton wrote a commendatory

---

[78] That the unrestricted offer of the gospel based on the inestimable value of Christ's atonement for sin was clearly recognized in seventeenth-century Calvinism is evident even in the Canons of Dordt (1618), Head II, Articles 3, 4. The entire text is found in P.Y. DeJong, ed. *Crisis in the Reformed Churches*, (Grand Rapids: 1968), 240. Thus restrictions of the gospel based on supposed Calvinist inferences have a most uncertain pedigree.

[79] E.g., Ryland, *Life of Andrew Fuller*, 58ff; James Bennett, *Life of David Bogue*, (London: 1825), 124.

[80] Henry F. Burder, *Memoir of George Burder*, (London: 1833), 23-30.

letter on his behalf to Whitefield, who thereafter retained him as secretary
and ministerial understudy. Entirely self-educated, Winter gathered
remarkable learning and at his death left, from his small academy at
Painswick, Gloucestershire, a library of 850 books to the existing
academy of David Bogue.[81]

Such academies had been in existence ever since the two universities
had been closed to Dissenters in connection with the Act of Uniformity
(1662). Many of the earliest academies had operated as true alternatives
to the universities, offering not only instruction in the classics, philosophy
and theology, but also mathematics and the physical sciences. In this
latter respect, such institutions broke new educational ground and
contributed materially to the industrial and scientific advance of England
in the eighteenth century. However, both because of their impermanent
existence (subject to the migratory careers of their tutors, who were most
often Dissenting ministers) and the tendencies of very many academies'
theological instruction to foster the 'rational' forms of Dissent, the older
academies tended after mid-century to give way to new foundations. The
latter were specifically inaugurated to train itinerant preachers for the
expanding Independent and Baptist forms of Dissent. Such academies
usually enrolled fewer students and, as they aimed exclusively at the
preparation of preachers, placed much less emphasis upon the sciences
and mathematics and much more upon theology and pastoral
preparation.[82] The tutors of such academies, quite naturally, were not
expected to be the polymaths so often in evidence in the older
institutions, but primarily exemplary preachers renowned also for their
theological stature.[83] Most importantly, the practice and conduct of
preaching in the surrounding towns and villages was very much
encouraged among the students early in the shortened curriculum of two
or three years.

The new trend in the preparation of preachers seems to have been set
in motion by the foundation in 1768 of Trevecca College by Selina,
Countess of Huntingdon.[84] Though ostensibly created to prepare

---

[81] Jay, ed. *Memoir of Winter,* 52, 62, 249; Chester Terpstra, 'David Bogue, D.D.
1750-1825: Pioneer and Missionary Educator', (Edinburgh University Ph.D thesis,
1959), 60.

[82] So, for instance, the Academy at Newport Pagnell, cf. McLachlan, *Education Under
the Test Acts,* 242. Deryck Lovegrove, *Established Church, Sectarian People,*
(Cambridge: 1988), 69.

[83] It is evident that the small academies operated by Independents such as David
Bogue, Cornelius Winter, and William Bull, derived their reputations from the orthodoxy
and usefulness of their tutors.

[84] Lovegrove, *Established Church,* 69. The role of Selina, Countess of Huntingdon, in
relation to other wealthy Christian patronesses of the eighteenth century is investigated
by Helen M. Jones, 'A Spiritual Aristocracy: Female Patrons of Religion in Eighteenth-

preachers for Welsh Calvinistic Methodism, the college in time contributed many preachers both to the Countess of Huntingdon's own connexion of chapels and wider Independency.[85] In the wake of the founding of Trevecca, there can be observed the emergence of similar institutions from about the year 1782.

The itinerating movement, aided and abetted by the new academies, spread dramatically in the period 1750-1840. Regional examples make this growth evident. The Independent churches within Hampshire formed themselves into a county association in 1781 and shortly thereafter founded an affiliate 'Society for Propagating the Gospel in Hampshire'. Before the death of David Bogue, the instigator of the scheme in 1825, the original ten congregations of the county association had been supplemented by twenty-one new chapels and three congregations meeting in renovated buildings.[86] David Bogue and James Bennett, writing in 1808, were personally aware of 500 Dissenting congregations which did not exist thirty-five years before.[87]

National statistics tell a similar story. The Independent churches are reckoned to have had a membership of a mere 15,000 in 1750; this had increased to 26,000 in 1790, and 35,000 in 1800. Particular Baptists grew from 10,000 to 24,000 in the same fifty year period. It was in the same era that other connexions also grew dramatically. Selina, Countess of Huntingdon, left at her death in 1791 a loose-knit connexion variously numbered at between fifty-five and eighty chapels, with a further seven under direct control of her executors. Whitefield similarly established a loose-knit connexion of congregations in London, Bristol and Gloucestershire.[88] The majority of Independent and Baptist churches had truly been quickened by the Evangelical Revival. By the 1790s, it was plain that these churches were comprised chiefly of the very artisan classes which had found a home in the Wesleyan societies.[89] Increasingly English Dissenters sang the Wesley hymns (though sometimes with suitably altered lyrics) along with the hymns and paraphrases of Watts and Doddridge.[90]

Century Britain', in Deryck W. Lovegrove, ed., *The Rise of the Laity in Evangelical Protestantism*, (London: 2002), 85-94.

[85] Watts, *Dissenters*, 453.

[86] Terpstra, 'Bogue', 197ff.

[87] Bogue and Bennett, *History of Dissenters*, IV, 327, 328.

[88] Walsh, 'Methodism at the End of the Eighteenth Century', 292.

[89] Gilbert, *Religion and Society*, 61, 62.

[90] Note the splendid essay 'The Hymnody of the Evangelical Revival', in Louis F. Benson, *The English Hymn*, (Atlanta: 1964), 315ff.

Scotland and the Evangelical Revival

One writer has remarked that the decade of the 1790s found Scotland's evangelical movement far behind the corresponding movement in England.[91] This opinion, which is almost certainly mistaken, nevertheless highlights the difficulty inherent in any attempt to correlate the ecclesiastical life of the two nations in that age when contacts between the two were sporadic and made difficult by virtue of the rigours of travel.

The distinctiveness of the two nations must be recognized. Eighteenth-century English visitors to Scotland too often made this recognition belatedly. George Whitefield is said to have been taken aback at the great rustle generated by the turning of Bible pages once his text was announced in a Dunfermline congregation in 1741.[92] John Wesley is said to have been surprised at the biblical literacy of his hearers in Scotland, a circumstance which made it difficult for him to teach them anything new.[93]

In point of fact, the visits of the two celebrated English itinerants to Scotland (Wesley making twenty-two visits and Whitefield fifteen) provided a factor of commonality and a basis for attempted correlations between religious developments in the two nations in the period. But it is important to note that religious awakening in Scotland preceded that in England.[94] Whitefield's first visit to Scotland in 1741 preceded but was in no evident way connected with the great religious awakening at Cambuslang (1742), which came in the aftermath of long activity by local ministers and parish prayer societies.

The very rapturous welcomes which Whitefield received bears important testimony to the continued existence in the 1740s of a virile evangelicalism native to Scotland. This is not to say that the spiritual fortunes of Scotland were enviable. In fact, among men like James Robe of Kilsyth and William McCulloch of Cambuslang there was a very clear perception of religious decline in the society of their day. But their very determination to overcome this decline indicates their solidarity with an older Christian outlook. And that this outlook had in fact persisted is not a matter of conjecture at all.[95] We have already noted the pervasive

---

[91] J.H.S. Burleigh, *A Church History of Scotland*, (Oxford: 1960), 310. Recently, John R. McIntosh has taken a distinct view that the Evangelical or 'popular' party of the Church of Scotland began to be numerically significant in the 1760s. See his *Church and Theology in Enlightenment Scotland: The Popular Party 1740-1800*, (East Linton: 1998).

[92] Dallimore, *Whitefield*, II, 88.

[93] A.S. Wood, 'Methodism in Scotland', in Davies and Rupp, eds., *History of the Methodist Church in Great Britain*, III, 266ff.

[94] A point we have made in this chapter p. 5.

[95] Stewart Mechie, 'The Theological Climate in Early Eighteenth Century Scotland', in Duncan Shaw, ed., *Reformation and Revolution*, (Edinburgh: 1967), 258-272, has

influence in southern England of the doctrinal and devotional writings of Thomas Boston and the brothers, Ralph and Ebenezer Erskine.

What is more, the state of the Church of Scotland in this period bore mottled testimony to the continuance of an older Puritan evangelicalism in the Kirk. While distancing ourselves from any simplistic suggestion that the Secession movement of 1740 led by Ebenezer Erskine was motivated purely out of a concern for the preservation and continuation of the Christian gospel, we may still recognize that some of the aggregate concerns behind the Secession stood in clear connection with that great end. Full satisfaction had never been granted in the controversy over the Christological views of Professor John Simson of Glasgow. There was a similar sense of grievance at the General Assembly's repudiation of the sentiments of *The Marrow of Modern Divinity* (1645) that Puritan work, reprinted in 1726, advocating an unrestrained offer of the gospel. Of greater importance had been the Seceders' resolute opposition to the abuses reintroduced with the restoration of patronage to the Kirk.

The Secession Church movement was not simply a manifestation of the new evangelical impulse of the eighteenth century. After all, the Secession castigated Whitefield for his consorting with the Kirk in his Scottish visits and even attributed some of the manifestations which had appeared at Cambuslang to the work of the devil.[96] Yet having said this, it is necessary at once to stress that there existed certain continuities between the Secession and the rising movement of evangelical Dissent in England.

First, in spite of its emphasis upon a continuing role for the National Covenant of 1638 and its insistence upon the obligation of government to support the Protestant religion, the Secession in reality took up a position of 'de facto' voluntarism and existed without state aid and jurisdiction. This was the position of all English Nonconformity, though without any of the limitations imposed upon the English by the Toleration Act legislation of 1689. Second, as to theology, the Secession stood in relation to the prevailing theological and philosophical climate of the eighteenth century approximately where English evangelical Dissent stood; this involved holding fast to the Puritan divinity of the late-seventeenth century. By a process of self-imposed distancing from the Scottish university faculties of Divinity, the Secession began to rely upon the 'academy' system of ministerial preparation.[97]

---

indicated that an evangelical Calvinism was one of four distinguishable Presbyterian outlooks in this era. See also Leigh Eric Schmidt, *Holy Fairs: Scotland and the Making of the American Revolution*, (Princeton: 1989), 21-32; and MacInnis, *Evangelical Movement*, ch. 2, for evidence of the persistence of evangelicalism in Scotland from the seventeenth century onwards.

[96] Dallimore, *Whitefield*, II, 131.

[97] One distinction, however, was that Seceding Scots continued to take a university Arts degree preliminary to the study of theology in an Academy setting.

The points of similarity between the Relief Presbytery (founded 1761) and English evangelical Dissent are plainer still. Thomas Gillespie, former Kirk minister of Carnock and leader of the 'Relief', had attended Philip Doddridge's Northampton Academy and had brought with him not a few ideas current among the English Nonconformists. Hardly coincidentally, Relief Synod folk were the first Presbyterians in Scotland to enjoy the use of hymns; a 1794 ruling of their Synod regularized a practice already instituted in its Anderston congregation.[98]

The Secession and Relief Churches experienced phenomenal growth. In a 1766 appeal to the Church of Scotland General Assembly termed the 'Overture on Schism' it was estimated that divisions of congregations over church patronage had alienated, to date, 100,000 persons now organized into 120 congregations.[99] Champions of conformity to the law of patronage argued that a variety of religious organization and expression was a desirable thing. Yet it is difficult to believe that such a position could have been long maintained if the true costs of the patronage policy were computed. Relief and Secession growth, to be sure, had not been solely by evangelistic ingathering but also by a regrouping of the previously affiliated. Yet it took dramatic action, nearly on the scale of the then-current itineration in England, to accomplish what was by 1820 the ingathering of 29% of the national and 32% of the lowland population into Presbyterian Dissent in its various forms.[100] This growth rate far surpassed that of English evangelical Dissent in the same period.

As in England, this ingathering had a marked class orientation about it. In the eighteenth century, the Secession in its Anti-Burgher manifestation was predominantly rural. Yet the Burgher Secession groups and the Relief Synod were largely comprised of tradesmen such as masons, wrights, and butchers along with some groups of textile workers.[101]

Burleigh's suggestion that the decade of the 1790s found Scottish evangelicalism in a position behind that seen in the nation to the south is not only called into question by an examination of the proliferation of Presbyterian Dissent, but by an appraisal of the constituency of the Kirk, *vis-à-vis* the Church of England. Evangelicalism in the Kirk—its struggles with ascendant moderatism and defections to Presbyterian Dissent notwithstanding—was never reduced to the position of weakness

---

[98] The basic details of Gillespie and the origins of the Relief are found in Hugh Watt, 'Thomas Gillespie', *Records of the Scottish Church History Society*, 15 (1964), 89ff. The present author notes how a significant lacuna regarding Scottish Dissent in this period has been filled by Kenneth B.E. Roxburgh's *Thomas Gillespie and the Origins of the Relief Church in Eighteenth Century Scotland*, (Bern: 1999). On Gillespie at Northampton, see 14-24; Benson, *The English Hymn*, 155.

[99] MacInnes, *The Evangelical Movement in the Highlands of Scotland,* 83.

[100] Calum Brown, *A Social History of Religion in Scotland*, (London: 1987), 31.

[101] Brown, *A Social History of Religion in Scotland*, 4.

experienced by its counter-part in the southern Establishment in the same period.

One of the major reasons for this evangelical resiliency in the eighteenth century is that the Scottish Kirk, while also a territorial establishment, assumed a different posture towards seventeenth-century theology from that of Church of England. In Scotland, the Westminster Confession of Faith and other theological literature of the preceding century continued to exercise an immense influence—never suffering by association the supposed connection with regicide and social disruption which haunted Puritan theology in England after the Restoration. Appeals even to the thus unstained Thirty-Nine Articles may have been in vain in England's early-eighteenth century; not so in Scotland where debates took place as to what the Confession of Faith taught, rather than as to its authority in the Church.

When seen in this light, the Scottish Kirk's ongoing links with the theology of the preceding century indicate that Scotland's theological affinity continued to be with the international Calvinist world. Moreover, from the 1662 Act of Uniformity onwards, the Scottish university faculties of divinity had become a major force in the shaping of English Nonconformity and this role continued until well into the nineteenth century.

It was common for English academy students to complete their study with a year at a Scottish university (most often Glasgow or Edinburgh) so as to take a degree; a good proportion of those who obtained this certification later occupied English academy lectureships themselves. Furthermore, the Scottish faculties of divinity plainly kept abreast with the published works of the leading English Nonconformists and were ready at regular intervals to recognize excellence with the award of the DD degree. King's College, Aberdeen, awarded the degree in 1728 to Thomas Ridgely, tutor in theology at Hoxton Academy. The same college similarly honored Philip Doddridge in 1737—but it had been preceded by one year by its cross-town rival, Marischal College. Edward Williams, tutor in theology at Rotherham Academy, received the honour in 1791 from the University of Edinburgh. A myriad of examples might be given, but these suffice to demonstrate the common bond in operation during the century.[102]

Within the international Calvinist 'orbit' then, of which Scotland never ceased to be a part, Calvinistic evangelicalism continued to be a defensible and formidable theological position. In Scotland, as elsewhere, however, there were varieties of Calvinistic thinking to be found. The biographer of the evangelically-minded John Erskine (1721-1803) of Greyfriars Church, Edinburgh (the 'doyen' of his party in the late-eighteenth

---

[102] McLachlan, *Education Under the Test Acts,* 30, 33, 118, 149, 199.

century) remarked of him that 'while Calvinistical, his was not the vulgar Calvinism which exhausts itself in intricate and mysterious dogmas'.[103]

In sum, we may say that Scottish evangelicalism cannot in any sweeping sense be described as lagging behind that in England in the last decade of the eighteenth century. With respect to the growth of evangelical Dissent, numbers of evangelical clergy, and its size in proportion to the national population, it may well have surpassed that of England. Conversely, it trailed its southern counterpart in its demonstration of hearty co-operation across denominational lines; Presbyterian divisions in the 1740s and 1760s (with eventual re-divisions) meant that mistrust would characterize the relations of these churches for decades to come. The founding of the Edinburgh Missionary Society in 1796 marked a partial reversing of this tide; it was a cause involving both Establishment and Dissenting supporters.[104] Apart from this, Scottish evangelicals were often left to demonstrate their solidarity by supporting schemes which had originated south of the border.[105]

Pan-Evangelicalism in England and Scotland

Writing in 1830 of the late Alexander Waugh (1754-1827), the long-time minister of the Wells Street Presbyterian (Seceding) Chapel in London, his biographers recalled a period in the 1790s when evangelical Dissenters had begun to form voluntary associations for the extension of the evangelical movement throughout England.[106] Of greatest import to our present concern was the formation of four enterprises: the *Evangelical Magazine* (1793), the London Missionary Society (1795), the Religious Tract Society (1796), and the British and Foreign Bible Society (1804). Such enterprises would never have been launched without the existence of a 'common front' evangelicalism spanning a considerable range of Protestant opinion. Waugh's biographers detailed Episcopalian, Presbyterian, Baptist, Independent and Calvinistic Methodist

---

[103] Henry Moncrieff Wellwood, *Account of the Life and Writings of John Erskine*, (Edinburgh: 1816), 380. Evidently, such vulgar Calvinism was not hard to locate in this epoch.

[104] Dudley Reeves, 'The Interaction of Scottish and English Evangelicals, 1790-1810', (Glasgow University MLitt thesis, 1973), 69; John Kilpatrick, 'The Records of the Scottish Missionary Society (1796-1848)', *Records of the Scottish Church History Society*, 10 (1950), 196ff.

[105] Thus the Missionary Societies of Edinburgh and Stirling forwarded funds for the support of William Carey, Baptist Missionary Society worker in Bengal. The Scottish visits of the BMS representative, Andrew Fuller, from 1799 regularly gathered similar support, cf. Reeves, 'Interaction', 26, 28.

[106] James Hay and Henry Belfrage, *Memoir of the Rev. Alexander Waugh, D.D.*, (Edinburgh: 1830, reprinted 1839), 150.

participation in the founding of the magazine.[107] A substantial Scottish involvement was also integral to the origins of each. The creation of the 'common front', contrary to some suggestions, did not indicate the increasing sway of a reductionist evangelical theology, but instead a willingness to work together as co-belligerents.[108] The Scottish involvement, while capable of being given an exaggerated importance, was nonetheless real. In the launch of the *Evangelical Magazine*, two of nine original trustees (Robert Simpson and David Bogue) were of Scottish birth; both, as it happened, were tutors in English Independent academies. In the case of the London Missionary Society, no fewer than ten of an original thirty-six 'fathers' of the society had Scottish links.[109]

While this pan-evangelicalism must be seen as a direct outgrowth of the Evangelical Revival, embodying most particularly the ideals of Whitefield,[110] it is also necessary to say that in the unfolding of its missionary and publishing aspirations outside Britain, it very much reflected the broad horizons provided by the expansion of British investment, technology and trade. A great stimulus to missionary aspirations for the South Pacific had been provided by the publication of the nautical journals of Captain James Cook. Thomas Haweis, a 'father'

---

[107] Hay and Belfrage, *Memoir of the Rev. Alexander Waugh*, 150.

[108] Both Martin, *Evangelicals United*, 17ff, and Walsh, 'Methodism at the End of the Eighteenth Century', 298, have argued that the Calvinism of this pan-evangelical era was increasingly undogmatic. It is so very easy to show this to be untrue even among the inner circle of pan-evangelical leaders that the assertions must be weighed very carefully. Andrew Fuller, (see note 46 above), spoke of moderate Calvinism with obvious disdain, yet is named as a representative of this very tendency. Thomas Haweis, also a central figure, upon learning of the suspicion that his commentary, the *Evangelical Expositor*, had been modeled rather too extensively on the famous commentary of the Presbyterian, Matthew Henry, retorted, 'I am no Baxterian [i.e. he believed Henry to be a 'low' Calvinist] but decidedly and consistently Calvinist'. Cf. Wood, *Haweis*, 116. Again, David Bogue, source of the famous 'death of bigotry' oration of 1795, had held to a very strict Calvinism from his Edinburgh university days and this he evidently communicated to his Gosport pupils without reliance on creeds. Cf. Bennett, *Life of Bogue*, 17. It is not necessary to maintain that all or even most leading pan-evangelicals held to such strict views in order to demonstrate the unfairness of the sweeping generalizations about Calvinism's supposed 'decomposition' (Walsh, 'Methodism at the End of the Eighteenth Century', 298). The judgment of Waugh's biographers (Hay and Belfrage, *Memoir of the Rev. Alexander Waugh*, 150) that this co- operation among leading ministers took place 'without compromising their peculiar principles' is a more trustworthy assessment of the mind of pan-evangelicalism.

[109] Cf. Martin, *Evangelicals United*, 42, 43; and John Morison, *Fathers and Founders of the London Missionary Society*, (London: 1844). The ten, among thirty-six described by Morison, were Bogue, Waugh, Love, Simpson, J. Steven, Hunter, Jerment, Graham, Smith and R. Steven.

[110] Martin, *Evangelicals United*, 9.

of the London Missionary Society, had privately pursued the idea of a mission to Tahiti as early as 1791; in that year he had met Captain Bligh who had returned to England after the famous mutiny on the Bounty.[111] The continent of Europe itself, which would figure largely in the schemes of both the Missionary Society and Bible Society, was increasingly the theatre of growing British economic and diplomatic activity. Missionary activity in India, Africa, and Asia, equally followed the contours of this expansion, though at times over the objections of powers such as the East India Company.

It was in this very decade of pan-evangelical enthusiasm that a key figure in our narrative, Robert Haldane (1764-1842), first crosses the stage. Like his younger brother, James Alexander Haldane (1768-1851), he had made a career at sea. Robert had served in the Royal Navy while his brother had risen to the rank of captain in the service of the East India Company. Through periodic calls at the naval base in Southampton, Robert gained the acquaintance of David Bogue at nearby Gosport. Haldane received some tutoring in theology in Bogue's ministerial academy during shore leaves after 1782. Only in the year 1795, however, did Robert Haldane believe himself to be a converted man. Yet, by the following year we find that Haldane had sold his sizeable estate at Airthrey, Stirlingshire, with a view to utilizing the proceeds in Christian enterprises. With Bogue's assistance, he had also joined the circle of pan-evangelical leaders; from 1796 he was listed among the directors of the fledgling London Missionary Society.[112]

Moving regularly in the overlapping circles of the supporters of the latter society, the *Evangelical Magazine*, and the Religious Tract Society, Haldane was introduced to prominent men such as George Burder (1752-1832), Rowland Hill (1744-1833) and Andrew Fuller (1754-1815). All of these would eventually fill the pulpit of the Tabernacle he would erect on Edinburgh's Leith Walk. In this same period, Haldane became known as the benefactor of the ministerial academies directed by David Bogue and Cornelius Winter.[113] A Scots acquaintance of Haldane, John Campbell (1766-1840), was then also moving in these same London circles. This Edinburgh ironmonger came away from London especially impressed with what he had seen; he shortly thereafter undertook major initiatives in tract distribution and Sunday School organization.[114]

A Haldane 'circle' was in process of formation. Two young Church of Scotland ministers, William Innes of Stirling and his brother-in-law

---

[111] Wood, *Haweis*, 177.

[112] *Reports of the London Missionary Society*, (London: 1796-98). Martin, *Evangelicals United*, 210. Haldane continued as a director until 1804.

[113] Bennett, *Bogue*, 119. Terpstra, 'Bogue', 106.

[114] J.A. Haldane, *Lives of Robert and James Haldane*, (Edinburgh: 1855), 190-91, 230-233; Reeves, *Interaction*, 118.

Greville Ewing of Lady Glenorchy's Chapel, Edinburgh, shared the missionary concerns of Robert Haldane and John Campbell. Influenced by reports of what William Carey was accomplishing in Bengal by the divine blessing, they—in company with David Bogue—proposed in 1796 to go to Bengal on a missionary enterprise; the venture was to be funded 'in toto' by Robert Haldane. Opposition within the East India Company and government combined to ensure that permission to enter the region was never be given.[115]

This rebuff in an attempted foreign mission caused the same energies to be focused upon the homeland. A successful itinerant preaching tour through Scotland by the Cambridge clergyman, Charles Simeon, in 1796 suggested interesting possibilities. The Haldane 'circle' formed itself into the 'Society for the Propagation of the Gospel at Home' in 1797 and there followed a flurry of itinerant preaching and launching of Sunday Schools. James Haldane, brother to Robert, conducted his own extensive preaching tours of the Highlands from that year and in his train went out forty catechists who were assigned to distinct districts for summer seasons.[116]

Acting on a suggestion of John Campbell, the Edinburgh merchant, Robert Haldane in 1798 rented the Edinburgh 'Circus'; the building had then recently been put to temporary use as home of a Relief Presbyterian congregation.[117] He then called on the services of the preachers whose acquaintance he had made in London pan-evangelical circles; in short order David Bogue, Andrew Fuller, James Bennett, Rowland Hill and Matthew Wilks[118] could each be heard preaching the gospel for a series of Sundays to the poor and curious—for the 'Circus' charged no pew rents. The 'Circus' ministry drew crowds of 2,000 and more and soon shifted to a permanent building, the Tabernacle at the head of Leith Walk. Purpose built, it was at completion Scotland's most capacious church building. This success, like that encountered by the catechists and traveling evangelists of the Society for the Propagation of the Gospel at Home, raised the question of what was to be done with the converts. The question had not been wrestled with in advance.

---

[115] Robert Haldane's known lack of enthusiasm for the proposal to raise local militia to guard against invasion by France's revolutionary armies lay behind this combined opposition.

[116] Reeves, 'Interaction', 107, 144. See also Donald Meek, 'Evangelical Missionaries in the Early Nineteenth Century Highlands', *Scottish Studies*, 28 (1987), 1-34; and A. MacWhirter, 'Early Days of the Independents and Congregationalists in the Northern Isles', *Records of the Scottish Church History Society*, 16 (1966), 63-87.

[117] Robert Philip, *The Life, Times and Missionary Enterprises of John Campbell*, (London: 1841), 164.

[118] See for instance, Robert Kinniburgh, *Fathers of Independency in Scotland*, (Edinburgh: 1851) 101, 275, 363, 364.

Robert Haldane, the financial mainstay of the SPGH, had originally aimed only to supplement the efforts of the Church of Scotland, whose services of worship he still attended.[119] As he financed the summer labour of untrained catechists and English preachers and erected halls for the use of Sunday Schools and preaching services, he likely envisioned nothing more than a connexion of meeting houses in an informal relationship to the national Church.[120] But his brother's tendency to denounce Kirk ministers unsupportive of his own itinerant preaching only fuelled a growing undertow of Kirk concern at the size of this Haldane 'home missionary movement'. The result was a pronouncement by the General Assembly of 1798 warning against 'itinerant preachers from England'.[121]

Any notions the SPGH may have cherished about their simply supplementing the efforts of the national Church were now shattered. With the national Church now closing her pulpits to itinerants, the Haldane connexion had come to occupy a kind of ecclesiastical 'no man's land'. But simultaneous with these developments, and largely through the personal influence of the English preachers relied upon for the supplying of the Edinburgh Tabernacle, the ideas of congregational Independency began to take hold. The General Assembly's recent display of hostility to the work of itineration gave the anti-hierarchical polity of Independency particular appeal. Greville Ewing, who as a member of the SPGH then resigned both his position as assistant minister at Lady Glenorchy's Chapel, Edinburgh, and his status as a Kirk minister, came particularly under the influence of these ideas. He now advocated that the Edinburgh Tabernacle be organized into a church on congregational principles. This in fact occurred in 1799; James Haldane was chosen as pastor.

Yet, there was nothing inherent in the Haldanite movement which necessitated its moving in a congregational direction. In fact, there was one sizeable obstacle in the path of such a development; this was nothing other than Robert Haldane's own utter domination. He seemed incapable

---

[119] Philip, *John Campbell*, 280.

[120] This, after all, had been the original plan of Selina, Countess of Huntingdon (1707-1791), until she had been forced to register her various English chapels as Dissenting meeting houses under the Toleration Act. Willielma, Lady Glenorchy, had pursued just the same aim in Edinburgh, first sponsoring services in the former St. Mary's Chapel, Niddry Wynd, in 1770, and later in her own chapel. Cf. T.S. Jones, *The Life of the Right Honourable Willielma Viscountess Glenorchy*, (Edinburgh: 1824), 131.

[121] The measure of the General Assembly not only closed Church of Scotland pulpits to the preachers associated with the SPGH, but also to the formerly well-received representatives of the Baptist and London Missionary Societies. Note the discriminating discussion of the Church of Scotland's 1798 prohibition against English preachers in John R. MacIntosh, *Church and Theology in Enlightenment Scotland: The Popular Party, 1740-1800* (East Linton: 1998), 207-210.

of operating at arm's length and habitually took direct intervening action as the major donor of the Society.

The deleterious effects of such dominance, perhaps only vaguely apparent earlier, would become plain as day in 1808. Then, both Haldane brothers made public their changed views on the doctrine and practice of baptism (they abandoned paedobaptism) and the need for multiple lay homilies (a practice they termed 'mutual exhortation') in church services. The largesse which had subsidized preachers and catechists and erected church buidlings across Scotland was now cut off where their new views were not adopted.[122] Workers whose paedobaptist convictions had not changed were left destitute. Similarly-minded congregations forfeited places of meeting as buildings reverted to the possession of the philanthropist who held their title deeds.[123] But in 1799, this crisis was not foreseen. The Haldane connexion, now congregational in tendency, continued to grow. By 1805 there were twenty-five congregations in existence; by 1808 the number had grown to eighty-five.[124]

If itinerant preaching was a first indicator of the arrival of a 'new evangelicalism'[125] in Scotland, there was also a second: the employment of the 'Academy' system of ministerial training on a hitherto unknown scale. The Haldanite movement did not introduce the concept to Scotland; we have noticed that Secession and Relief Presbyterian churches had employed it beforehand, though as a supplement to rather than as a substitute for university education.

Robert Haldane's first plan was evidently to sponsor up to twenty students for study at the Gosport Academy under his old acquaintance, David Bogue. He aimed to utilize these students as summer catechists in the schemes of the SPGH. However, he did not follow through on this intention. Instead, because of the joint concern of Greville Ewing and James Garie (preacher in the Haldane connexion at Perth) regarding

---

[122] Terpstra, 'Bogue', 223, lists Edinburgh, Glasgow, Dundee, Elgin, Dumfries, Perth, Dunkeld, Aberdeen, Helensburgh, Thurso and Wick as sites of Haldane-financed buildngs.

[123] Examples of this hardship are detailed in Kinniburgh, *Fathers of Independency*, 127, 301, 416, 435. Here, without investigating it, we temporarily leave the question of from where Robert and James Haldanes' revisionist ideas about congregational life may be traced. It was generally suspected at the time that Robert, through his brother James, had been influenced by the teaching of the Scot, John Glas and his son-in-law, Robert Sandeman—by whom his teaching was transmitted to England. A helpful introduction to the thought of Glas and Sandeman with allusions to their influence on the brothers Haldane is provided in Derek B. Murray, 'The Influence of John Glas', *Records of the Scottish Church History Society*, 22.1 (1984), 45-56. We will return to the question of the sources of Robert Haldane's ideas, transmitted to Francophone Europe, in our second chapter.

[124] Reeves, 'Interaction', 107, 144.

[125] The description is justly employed by MacInnes, *Evangelical Movement in the Highlands*, 128.

Bogue's then-notorious republican sympathies and the cultural differences a Hampshire education would entail, Haldane financed academy-style instruction in various Scottish centres under able ministers.[126]

Between 1798 and 1808 (the year in which the Haldane connexion foundered) 300 men received two years of theological education in classes offered at Glasgow, Edinburgh, and Dundee. Classes preparatory to the study of theology were also offered to students in need of preliminary training; these were available in Armagh, Ireland, and Elgin. Twenty thousand pounds were expended in the ten years of the scheme's existence.[127] Haldane both gave his own *imprimatur* to the enrolment of each student (whose costs he paid in full) and monitored all behaviour and manners through student 'censors'.[128]

The Perceived Dangers of Evangelical Dissent

It is worthy of note that evangelical Dissent met considerable opposition in both its northern and southern manifestations. Yet the opposition encountered was not entirely identical by reason of the fact that the English Toleration Act (1689), which regulated the licensing of Nonconformist ministers and meeting houses in the southern kingdom, applied only there. Opposition met by evangelical Dissent in England may be said to have been both legal and religious and that of the Scottish variety religious alone.

The arrival of evangelical Dissent in the form of the Haldane movement raised many apprehensions. That it should have done so in a land whose indigenous evangelicalism had first nourished and then welcomed English representatives of the Revival, had found expression in both Secession and Relief churches, and continued amidst some difficulty in the Kirk, requires explanation.

The rise of foreign missionary interest after 1794-95 received cross-denominational support in Scotland. The founding of the London Missionary Society had a most beneficial effect, according to John Philip, biographer of John Campbell:

> It had a most electrifying effect on the Christians of the north. We were like men who dreamed. From the days of George Whitefield until then, the Christians on both sides of the Tweed had been fast asleep. The Christians of different names were busy repairing and adding to their walls of separation and now and then throwing squibs

---

[126] Terpstra, 'Bogue', 222; R.F. Calder, 'Robert Haldane's Theological Seminary', *Transactions of the Congregational Historical Society*, 13 (1937-1939), 60.

[127] Calder, 'Haldane's Seminary', 62, 63.

[128] Calder, 'Haldane's Seminary', 63.

at each other...but the news of the above Society was like the bursting forth of a bright meteor in a dark night.[129]

Yet the subsequent campaign to establish Sabbath evening schools led first by Campbell and then by the SPGH, received a very different reception because they provided venues for a flurry of lay-preaching. It is not self-evident why this opposition should have been shown. Both the era of the Cambuslang-Kilsyth awakening and the Highland regional practice of 'the men', circulating in broad parishes to assist the minister in catechising, had modestly approximated the lay-preaching of 1797-98.[130] Yet there were differences as well; earlier lay preaching had been carried out inside parish boundaries and under the jurisdiction of the minister. The new movement sent lay-preachers across parish boundaries to wherever the SPGH deemed best.

If the Kirk's opposition was only rooted in moderate party dismay at the denunciatory tendencies of the Haldane itinerants, it is not transparently clear why Secession and Relief churches should have joined in the opposition. Such evidence as we have suggests that Anti-Burgher Secession opposition in 1796 and 1798 was motivated by deep fears about cross-denominational missionary activity in general and the increased scope given for lay leadership in prayer and preaching. The Burgher Synod in the same period had no scope for preaching by the unordained and looked askance at Sabbath evening schools.[131] The Relief Church had warmly embraced the coming of the missionary movement and endorsed the concept of foreign mission in 1796 but may have been moved to resent Haldane activity in the Highlands given their own missionary efforts there.[132] Presbyterian solidarity temporarily triumphed over longstanding differences in the face of the new itinerant movement.

This posture seems to have been the clear counterpart to that of the Church of England towards evangelical Dissent in its various forms; as well there was always a measure of disdain by an Establishment towards other churches which were merely tolerated by statute. Throughout the eighteenth century, Nonconformity in England had laboured under this disadvantage and sought to remove its handicap by seizing opportunities to reassure the sovereign and government of the day of its fidelity.

Questions were raised regarding the political loyalty of Nonconformists in connection with the outbreak of the French

---

[129] Philip, *John Campbell*, 23, 24.

[130] A. Fawcett, 'Scottish Lay Preachers in the Eighteenth Century', *Records of the Scottish Church History Society*, 12 (1955), 97-119; MacInnes, *Evangelical Movement in the Highlands*, 197.

[131] Kinniburgh, *Fathers of Independency*, 18, 19, 225, 355; John McKerrow, *History of the Secession Church*, (Glasgow: 1841), 393.

[132] Reeves,' Interaction', 8; MacInnes, *Evangelical Movement in the Highlands*, 94.

Revolution. While we shall return later to consider more extensively the ramifications of the French Revolution for British religious thought, we may here consider just how disruptive the Revolution and the response drawn by it were to the pan-evangelical spirit. The mere fact that prominent Dissenters expressed initial delight in the French events of 1789, and saw in them a portent of the longed-for elimination of domestic disabilities based on religion[133] was enough to send shock waves through government and the Established Churches.

David Bogue, a man of wide evangelical influence, clearly espoused such hopes both at the time and subsequently when he came to write with James Bennett their *History of Dissenters*. The latter chronicle claimed that 'Multitudes of Dissenters entered, with peculiar ardour into the French Revolution as an event pregnant with happiness to the people of France'.[134] The stream of Dissent which had ceased to be Trinitarian and was now termed 'rational' Dissent was even more forward in extolling the virtues of the Revolution. Richard Price delivered his famous *Discourse on the Love of our Country* (1789), drawing out the implications from France for Britain a bare four months after the fall of the Bastille.[135] While sympathetic to the achievements of the young Revolution, the evangelical Dissenter, George Burder, came away dissatisfied from a 1790 meeting of Dissenters. Gathered from the nine Midland counties, delegates sought a repeal of the Corporation and Test Acts in the light of the Revolution. Alarmed at the violent approach taken by Unitarians present, Burder withdrew from the association shortly thereafter. Yet the consequences of this agitation, when they came, imperiled not only the Richard Prices and Joseph Priestleys of the day, but Dissenters of all kinds.[136]

The enthusiasm of many evangelical Dissenters for the French Revolution caused a chill in their recently more cordial relationships with their Establishment counterparts. A monthly fraternal meeting of ministers at Hull, embracing persons from the Establishment, Dissent, and Methodism was terminated in 1792.[137] The latter year marked the transition of the Revolution from its more moderate to its more radical republican phase characterized by the 'Reign of Terror'. When evangelical Dissenters such as David Bogue continued to support the revolution after 1792 (in his own case with a speech delivered at Salters' Hall) Establishment clergy believed this was confirmation of an alliance between Dissent and forces working for England's destabilization. Even the pan-evangelical John Newton, the strong supporter of the Newport Pagnell Academy for the training of itinerant preachers (founded 1782),

---

[133] Martin, *Evangelicals United*, 27.
[134] Bogue and Bennett, *History*, III, 483.
[135] Watts, *Dissenters*, 481.
[136] Burder, *Memoir*, 145, 146, 148.
[137] Walsh, 'Methodism at the End of the Eighteenth Century', 291, 301.

exclaimed in 1793 that 'all the Dissenters, even the orthodox not excepted, are republicans and enemies to government'.[138]

Of course, many persons not numbered among the Dissenters raised their own hue and cry on behalf of events in France. Social historian E.P. Thompson has demonstrated the strength of the 'Libertarian' tradition in this period as reflected in the Sheffield weekly press and popular street demonstrations in support of French developments.[139] Abortive French attempts at landing troops in Wales and Western Ireland, the latter in conjunction with Wolfe Tone and the United Irishmen,[140] ensured that many quite harmless persons would be held suspect in that uncertain decade.

Quite apart from any political remarks or involvement, evangelical Dissenters found themselves more politically suspect than earlier because the 1790s was for them a period of rapid growth and impressive organization. The founding of a national *Evangelical Magazine*, a well-funded international missionary organization (the LMS) and an affiliated publishing concern (the Religious Tract Society) made the pan-evangelical movement cause for no small concern.[141]

Under such circumstances, only a quite militant breed of Establishment evangelicals chose to be associated with the above-named three enterprises in the decade of their formation. It was understandable that such persons in the Establishment would show a heightened preference for their own kind, demonstrated in the existence of such ministerial fraternals as the 'Eclectic Society of London'. The published notes of the discussions held within this society afford a rich glimpse into the theological and political views of participating members in the years 1798-1814.[142]

William Wilberforce, parliamentarian and Anglican, in keeping with this heightened distrust of Dissent, worked in 1796 to obstruct the

---

[138] Josiah Bull, *Memorials of W. Bull*, (London:1864), 221, quoted in Walsh, 'Methodism at the End of the Eighteenth Century', 303.

[139] E.P. Thompson, *The Making of the English Working Class*, (Harmondsworth: 1963), 111-113.

[140] R.F.G. Holmes, 'United Irishmen and Unionists', in W. J. Shiels and Diana Wood, eds., *Studies in Church History*, 25, (Oxford: 1988), 184.

[141] Deryck Lovegrove, 'English Evangelical Dissent and the European Conflict', in W.J. Shiels, ed., *Studies in Church History*, 20, (Oxford: 1983), 263.

[142] John Pratt, *Notes of the Discussions of the Eclectic Society*, (London: 1856, reprint edition 1978). Some interesting topics discussed in the period include: 'What can be done at the present moment to counteract the designs of infidels?', 'How shall a minister best preserve his people from the influence of Sectarian teachers?', 'By what arguments shall we plead with God to deliver us from the French?', 'What is the duty of a member of the Established Church if the preaching of the Gospel is occasionally suspended or altogether ceases in his parish church?'.

application of a group (alluded to above) to enter India. David Bogue, Robert Haldane, Greville Ewing and John Campbell seemed to be associated with this tendency to disloyalty and thus Wilberforce recorded in his diary that the men were 'perfect democrats'. John Newton, who knew of the proposal through his close acquaintance with John Campbell, also laboured to obstruct it. Yet he simultaneously sought to have chaplains or missionaries of his Established Church introduced to that region.[143]

That the latter aspiration came to fruition with the foundation in 1799 of the Church Missionary Society cannot be attributed chiefly to the fact that the Rev. Joseph Jane, vicar of St. Mary Magdalen Church, Oxford, provided a bequest of some £4,000 for the purpose. The question must still be asked why Jane and others such as John Venn, William Goode and Charles Simeon could not support the existing missionary society founded in 1795. Any explanation would need to include the fear of the 'republicanism' with which the Dissenting supporters of the London Society were thought to be tainted, reservations over that Society's commitment to an undenominational 'fundamental principle', and the lack of unanimity among the London Society's directors as to what type of missionary preparation was in order.[144]

Even with the cause of wider pan-evangelicalism suffering a setback under the pressures of hostility with France, evangelical Dissent grew by great leaps and bounds. The county associations of Baptist and Independent churches, as well as the itinerant societies, maintained an impressive growth rate until approximately 1840; the pattern was virtually the same as that experienced by various Methodist bodies.[145]

Divergent Outlooks on the Christian Future

The conclusion of the era of the Napoleonic Wars combined with recognition of the pacific character of evangelical Dissent made the long-awaited repeal of the Corporation and Test Acts possible in 1828. This steadily improving domestic, political and ecclesiastical situation bred the very kind of optimistic Christian futurism which we noted, initially, to have characterized the outlook of evangelical Dissenters such as William Jay.[146] Perhaps best expressed for that generation by Dissenter, David Bogue's book *The Millennium* (1818), the standard Dissenting and Methodist outlook, which may be termed postmillennialism, expected a

---

[143] Terpstra, 'Bogue', 256.

[144] Martin, *Evangelicals United*, 52; Pratt, *Eclectic Society,* 95-102. Hay and Belfrage, *Waugh,* 153, indicate Waugh's key role in encapsulating the 'fundamental principle'.

[145] Gilbert, *Religion and Society,* 39.

[146] Cf. p. 2, fn. 3.

steady, relentless progress of Christianity throughout the world. By the ordinary use of means such as preaching, catechizing and Scripture distribution, and extraordinary means such as revivals, the triumph of the gospel throughout the world was to be expected prior to the Second Advent. This eschatological outlook, which had been powerfully commended by the impetus of the Evangelical Revival, passed through the revolutionary era (1789-1815) without major modification. It was the view of the Christian future in which Edward Bickersteth had early been nurtured. [147]

Yet while Dissent and Methodism continued to find in this system of belief an outlook on the future which squared with what they saw and experienced in their own generation of gospel progress and expanded political liberties, there was an increasing movement among the clergy of the Established Churches of England and Scotland which saw in the upheavals of the Revolutionary and Napoleonic eras portents of the biblical 'last days'.[148] That it was chiefly persons attached to Established Churches who pursued such themes may have indicated that they believed that the sinister spirit of revolution emanating from France must ultimately threaten the stability of their own nation and Church. Similarly, some early Tractarians were developing parallel apocalyptic concerns, concerns fed by what they viewed as a deplorable Erastian domination of the Church by an increasingly secular state.[149] The newer view of the last things, termed premillennialism, centred on the belief that the reign of the gospel over the world could only be secured by the personal and visible return and reign of the Saviour. While it is overly simplistic to describe adherents of the newer view as united in being 'political reactionaries' or sharing 'deeply authoritarian views of society',[150] it remains true that current affairs in Church and state were viewed by them as alarming indeed. Edward Irving (1792-1834) minister of Regent Square Church, London, and a rising star in the new apocalyptic movement, was described as having opposed the abolition of the Test Act (1828), the enactment of Catholic emancipation (1829) and the general spread of democracy.[151]

---

[147] Birks, *Bickersteth*, II, 42

[148] Ernest Sandeen, *The Roots of Fundamentalism*, (Chicago: 1970), 7, 20.

[149] David Newsome, *The Parting of Friends*, (London: 1966), 11. Apocalyptic warnings can be found in the *Sermon on National Apostasy* preached by John Keble at Oxford in 1833. Such an overlap of concern is also discussed in Timothy C.F. Stunt, 'John Henry Newman and the Evangelicals', *Journal of Ecclesiastical History*, 21.1 (1970), 65-74.

[150] Sandeen, *The Roots*, 41. D.N. Hempton, 'Evangelicalism and Eschatology', *Journal of Ecclesiastical History*, 31.2 (1980), 183.

[151] Margaret Oliphant, *The Life of Edward Irving*, II, (London: 1862), 382, 383. Fresh attention has recently been given to Irving's apocalyptic thought by Tim Grass' essay, 'Edward Irving: Eschatology, Ecclesiology, and Spiritual Gifts', in Crawford Gribben and

And yet, to return to our original examples of Bickersteth and Jay, characterized in late life by such contrasting outlooks but shared principles, we may reflect in concluding this survey, that had they had prescience to know what the decades ahead would hold then each might have been given pause. The evangelical Dissent of which Jay was such an illustrious spokesman was gradually losing its power of multiplication, tied as it was (with Methodism) to a process of the social elevation of the artisan classes. The Church of England, which may have seemed so moribund, so enslaved, to critical onlookers in the 1830s, would shortly, through the provisions of Church Reform, outstrip the growth rates of Methodism and Dissent for the balance of the century.[152]

T.C.F. Stunt, eds, *Prisoners of Hope? Aspects of Evangelical Millennialism in Britain and Ireland 1800-1880*, (Carlisle: 2004), 95-121.
  [152] Gilbert, *Religion and Society*, 29, 39.

CHAPTER 2

Decline and Resurgence in French-Speaking Protestantism, 1685–1819

Francophone Protestantism 1685-1819

The eighteenth century, which witnessed a dramatic reversal of the decline of Protestantism in Britain, brought almost unmitigated trouble for the Protestant churches of Francophone Europe. That the eighteenth century was so evidently dominated by the French Protestants' loss of religious and civil liberties should not obscure the fact that there was concurrently a trans-national faltering of confidence among Europe's Protestants. The Swiss pastor and theologian, Jean Frédérick Ostervald of Neuchatel (1663-1747), sounded warnings regarding this state of affairs in his *Treatise Concerning the Causes of the Present Corruption of Christians* (1700).[1] The work was clearly of such wide application that the English SPCK promptly arranged for an English edition within the first year. Evidently the religious and political struggles of the seventeenth century had left the population of Europe feeling sated with religious controversy; the Christian faith was now neglected in consequence.

So convinced is the French historian P. Joutard of the prevalence of French Protestant torpor at the end of the seventeenth century that he has portrayed the terrible oppression following the revocation of the Edict of Nantes (1685) as almost necessary for Protestantism's re-invigoration and survival.[2] Though public assembly was forbidden under the post-1685 regulations, conventicles were assembling in woods and forests within ten days of the rescinding of liberties. Though all children of Protestant families were obliged to receive Catholic baptism and religious instruction, parents of such children frequently redoubled efforts at instilling Protestant principles in the home. Though widespread banishment and emigration rapidly depleted the supply of pastors, the

---

[1] Eamon Duffy, 'Correspondence Fraternelle: the SPCK, the SPG and the Churches of Switzerland in the War of the Spanish Succession', in Derek Baker, ed., *Reform and Reformation: England and the Continent 1500-1750*, (Oxford: 1979), 257.

[2] P. Joutard, 'The Revocation of the Edict of Nantes, End or Renewal?', in Menna Prestwich, ed., *International Calvinism 1541-1715*, (London: 1985), 360.

tasks of exhortation and the administration of the sacraments were soon taken up by pious tradesmen.[3] Synods were held, albeit secretly, from 1715 onwards and the number of provinces in which the church maintained effective organization grew from three in 1715 to ten in 1750.[4]

While it may be true that such extraordinary measures helped to prevent an even more serious decline induced by cultural assimilation, it is at the same time difficult to exaggerate the staggering costs of the era of persecution. Nation as well as church felt this keenly. Most obvious among such costs was that of massive emigration. An estimated 200,000 Protestants left France in the immediate aftermath of the revocation with the northern provinces of the country contributing disproportionately to this exodus. Northern artisans were more likely to emigrate than peasant farmers of the south and urban Protestants more likely than country dwellers.[5]

In their tens of thousands, the refugees, preponderantly male, made their way first into Switzerland, then into various German principalities and the Low Countries, and subsequently into Scandinavia, England and the New World. They enriched industry and craftsmanship where they settled while they impoverished it in the homeland. The very scale of the immigration exacerbated diplomatic relationships between France and her neighbours as well as serving to confirm anti-Catholic prejudice in Protestant states.[6] One unforeseen result of the emigration was the creation of a very substantial French Protestant diaspora from the eastern Baltic to Ireland in the west, a movement that will have significance in the story of the 'Réveil'.

The forced closure of Protestant colleges combined with the noted emigration of ministers guaranteed an uncertain and varied supply of preachers in the Protestant communities remaining in France. In the first years of persecution and uncertainty, the preaching ministry of lay persons sometimes gave way to 'prophetism'—the alleged deliverance of oracles by the Holy Spirit. Such utterances sometimes served to foment armed resistance to royal policies in the period from 1687-1704. Some exponents of this prophetism were transplanted to England where their controversial influence would cast a suspect shadow during the earliest period of Britain's Evangelical Revival.[7]

---

[3] Joutard, 'The Revocation', 361-62.

[4] Bernard Poland, *French Protestantism and the French Revolution,* (Princeton: 1957), 42.

[5] Joutard, 'The Revocation', 346-48.

[6] Joutard, 'The Revocation', 351; and Edgar Bonjour et al., *A Short History of Switzerland,* (Oxford: 1952), 198.

[7] See Joutard, 'The Revocation', 365; and G.R. Balleine, *A History of the Evangelical Party in the Church of England,* (London: 1911), 14.

When it was learned that the various Reformed churches of Switzerland were reluctant to offer ordination to French ministerial candidates from a fear both of offending French royal policy and of appearing to ratify the preparedness of ill-trained persons, the French Protestant communities responded in two ways. First, they utilized what were termed 'écoles ambulantes' in which already active lay preachers might enjoy a modest course of studies with the help of a circulating tutor. Secondly, they employed foreign funds administered by a committee of French persons at Geneva termed 'Le Comité Français' to provide formal theological education at Lausanne for French candidates from 1729. This Academy at Lausanne, which continued in existence until 1809, provided education for the ministry with a curriculum geared to the candidate lacking a rigorous preparatory education.[8] Yet the Lausanne Academy only educated some 300 students in its entire history and the French Protestant churches remained dependent upon persons with only the most rudimentary of training. For upon the eve of the Revolution of 1789, the harassed French Reformed Church still had a following of more than 400,000 persons.[9]

This dearth of theological learning placed the Reformed Churches of France in a doubly vulnerable position during the eighteenth century. On the one hand, they were prone to a creeping religious legalism which attributed to acts of resistance to royal tyranny a kind of merit before God; this legalism bordered on salvation by works. On the other hand, they were less prepared than some European Reformed and Lutheran neighbours to resist the popular tendency to confine the Christian religion's claims to those within a circle bounded by reason. This tendency, which we conveniently call deism, so swept along the prominent pastor Gebelin that he concluded that all religions were the same.[10]

By many accounts, France's European Reformed neighbours were by no means monochrome in their outlook on such questions. Lausanne, in both its university faculty of theology and French academy seems to have maintained the primacy of revelation over reason as the century wore on.

---

[8] See James Good, *History of the Swiss Reformed Church Since the Reformation* (Philadelphia: 1913), 121-25; Poland, *French Protestantism*, 49; and Daniel Robert, *Genève et Les Églises Réformées de France* (Paris: 1961), 9, 19, 204. The latter insists that the Lausanne Academy was closed in 1812.

[9] Daniel Robert, *Les Églises Réformées En France 1800-1830*, (Paris: 1961), 5.

[10] Robert, *Les Églises Réformées*, 17, 19. It would later be reckoned that the last properly 'orthodox' Reformed theologian at Geneva was Benedict Pictet, recently investigated in Martin Klauber's essay, 'Family Loyalty and Theological Transition in Post- Reformation Geneva: The Case of Benedict Pictet (1655-1724)', *Fides et Historia* 24.1 (1992), 54-67. In ch. 5, we will note that the 'réveil's influence on the English-speaking world included the re-introduction of the writings of Pictet to a nineteenth-century reading public.

But the concessive theology of Geneva, personified in Jacob Vernet, professor of theology 1756-1789, was such that it could earn the ridicule of Voltaire and D'Alembert as Socinianism; all religious mystery was eliminated and all theological inquiry was circumscribed by the bounds of reason.[11]

The sceptical outlook on the traditional dogmas of the Christian faith manifested itself in quite different ways. Already by the mid-eighteenth century, the majority of the Protestant Swiss cantons had ceased to require subscription to the Helvetic Consensus of 1675, a creed composed by representatives of Zurich, Geneva and Basel in order to check the spread of liberalized Calvinism from the French academy at Saumur.[12] Religious syncretism received encouragement from the Enlightenment insistence upon the compatibility of the Christian revelation with the fruits of rational inquiry. Attempts to embrace all religions in one system, such as that characterizing the Masonic movement, were highly attractive in France and Switzerland.[13] Many defended the uniqueness of Jesus Christ only with considerable hesitation while there was similar uncertainty concerning the Christian and biblical emphasis upon humanity's innate tendency to wrong.[14]

A pious young Genevan observed the legacy of this century of theological decline when he began his theological course at Geneva in 1809. Ami Bost (1790-1874) later recalled,

> Doctrine, the church, and manners in general had arrived at a laxity not easy to conceive of today. As for the teaching, this laxity was a fact which dominated all others and which now seems incredible. During the four years we spent in the study of theology—over and above the use of the Old Testament required for the learning of a little Hebrew and translating the Psalms—one never opened the Bible in our lecture rooms. The book was unused and unknown. It never entered our course and apart from language studies it was not necessary to possess it. Without doubt, it was

---

[11] Good, *Reformed Church*, 282-92. An extended discussion of the influence of Rousseau and Voltaire upon Swiss Protestantism in this period is provided in Paul Wernle, *Der Schweizerische Protestantismus im 18. Jahrhundert*, 3 vols, (Tubingen: 1923-1924) II, 44-139. Vernet has recently received fresh consideration in the researches of David Sorkin, who has concluded that Vernet 'helped to articulate and popularize a Calvinist version of the moderate or religious Enlightenment that consisted in the effort of theologians to appropriate key Enlightenment ideas to rearticulate and renew belief'. See Sorkin's 'Geneva's "Enlightened Orthodoxy": the Middle Way of Jacob Vernet (1698-1789)', *Church History* 74.2 (2005), 287.

[12] Good, *Reformed Church*, 164-66.

[13] See Hugh McLeod, *Religion and the People of Western Europe* (Oxford: 1981), 44; and Alice Wemyss, *Histoire du Réveil 1790-1849*, (Paris: 1978), 31, 45.

[14] See McLeod, *Religion*, 9; and J. McManners, *The French Revolution and the Church* (London: 1969), 14.

spoken of sometimes in terms of poetics or oratory. Yet natural theology was appealed to in support of dogma. It was pure deism.[15]

The same writer looked back ten years after the commencement of his theological studies and observed that among the clergy a disbelief in the divinity of Jesus Christ was common; so also was it common to deny the necessity for an operation of divine grace in the individual's receiving Christian salvation and to dispute the possibility of miracles.[16] Now what prevailed in such a centre of Francophone theological training in so blatant a form had been diffused from Geneva for decades.

Without internal centres of theological learning to maintain the biblical grounding of the faith, French Protestantism was most vulnerable to such strains of Enlightenment thought. The result was an ever-closer approximation of Protestant preaching to the philosophy of the day. This very process of approximation was ultimately counter-productive as the distinctive message and witness of the church was lost.[17]

The advent of the period of Revolution brought redress of Protestant civil grievances without altering the religious limitations under which they had laboured since 1685. By the royal Edict of Toleration of November 1787, Protestants gained the right to marry and bear legitimate children outside the pale of Catholicism. Yet, the now-permitted alternative to the Catholic solemnization of marriage was not a Protestant, but a civil ceremony before a royal judge. Protestant worship was still not countenanced, nor was any Protestant right to erect schools and colleges.[18] Thus, when in December 1789 the French National Assembly opened all civil and military offices to Protestants, it was widely expected that the young Revolution would enjoy the support of the Protestant population. This support did not imply anti-royal sentiment on the part of French Protestants at this early stage.[19] Only the King's attempted flight in June 1791 to join with the forces of counter revolution served to detach the loyalty of his Protestant subjects. They easily reasoned that the King, if restored at the head of counter-revolutionary forces, could not allow their newly-received liberties to remain. Now it was the turn of Catholic and Royalist sympathizers to depart from the country in flight from the Revolution, much as the Protestants had had to flee from the rise

---

[15] Ami Bost, *Memòires Pouvant Servir a L'Històire du Réveil Religieux*, 3 vols, (Paris: 1854) I, 24,25.

[16] Ami Bost, *Genève Religieux en Mars 1819*, (Geneva: 1819), 23, 25, 40.

[17] Poland, *French Protestantism*, 249.

[18] Poland, *French Protestantism*, 79-80.

[19] See Poland, *French Protestantism*, 105, 175; and Robert, *Les Églises Réformées*, 22.

of absolutism a century before. An estimated 130,000 left for the Low Countries, Rhenish Germany, Switzerland, north Italy and Catalonia.[20]

In November 1790, a Constituent Assembly ushered in the disastrous period of the Constitutional (Catholic) Church. It was so eager to apply the value of the Church's landholdings to the repayment of national debts that it was prepared to issue stipends to clergy and bishops who would swear loyalty to the new regime. This affected Protestants most by its great failure. The armed rebellion of the summer of 1793 against the Constitutional Church scheme, emanating from conservative elements in the Vendée, had the appearance of pitting organized Christianity against the Revolution. It also helped to justify both the Reign of Terror and the official proscription of Christian worship assemblies (both Catholic and Protestant) until 1795. In the interim there flourished an alarming variety of state-sanctioned substitutes for the Christian religion. Until the anti-Revolutionary rising, Protestants made the most of their *de facto* right of assembly and extended their efforts into long-abandoned areas with a steadily expanding number of pastors.[21] But the proscription of all Christian worship found a surprising number of compliant pastors and congregations. The readiness with which many Protestant clergymen formally and publicly abdicated their tasks (in company with numerous Roman Catholic priests) and lent support to the civic worship of reason and the Supreme Being lends confirmation to the supposition that Christian theology had been so assimilated to Enlightenment patterns of thought as to be incapable of self-defence. The proclamation of freedom of worship (without state financial aid) in February 1795 came none too soon.[22] With it came the first state recognition of the equality of Catholic and Protestant Churches.

With the restoration of religious freedom, there is evidence of sustained religious resurgence.[23] Catholics, who from the beginning had been divided over the rightness of the imposition of a Constitutional Church, were now left with the considerable but not insurmountable task of reconciling the Constitutional and nonjuring factions. All state aid to the Roman Catholic Church promised in 1790 had by now ceased, and yet the substantial landholdings and revenues which enabled the Catholic

---

[20] Franklin L. Ford, *Europe 1780-1830*, (London: 1970), 139. Dominic Bellenger, 'The Émigré Clergy and the English Church, 1789-1815', *Journal of Ecclesiastical History*, 34. 3 (1983), 392, indicates that 5,000 Francophone Catholic clergy entered the United Kingdom as political refugees at this time.

[21] Robert, *Les Églises Réformées*, 26.

[22] Robert, *Les Églises Réformées*, 28-31. Interestingly, S. Mours in *Les Églises Réformées En France*, (Paris: 1958), 19, takes the view that the abdication of pastors may be explained in part by the influx of Enlightenment philosophy into the French Academy at Lausanne. So also Poland, *French Protestantism*, 220.

[23] MacLeod, *Religion*, 5.

Church to enjoy financial independence had largely been alienated. Protestant resurgence, though real, was somewhat subdued as the extent of its subservience in the period of proscription had been more complete. Regional synods met only intermittently, if at all, and the perennial shortage of pastors had been exacerbated by the rash of abdications earlier in the decade.

Within the first year of the Directory, Napoleon Bonaparte set in motion plans for government administration of all the religious bodies in France. But these plans were substantially altered, prior to legislation, in light of the Concordat signed with the Pope in 1802. This recognized Catholicism as the religion 'of the great majority of the French people'.[24] The government now granted subsidies in compensation for both the earlier state alienation of Church property and its own new demand that the state would henceforth nominate the principal clergy. When to their surprise the Protestants were offered a similar subsidy in April 1802 by Napoleon, the vast majority fervently welcomed the proposal (with its claim of direct jurisdiction). Rabaut-Depuy, a Protestant legislator, compared the newly-enfranchised Protestants with the children of Israel who, having survived Moses, themselves entered Canaan: 'Alas, those whom we have outlived, ascended the mountain of Nebo, whence they beheld the land of promise—but we alone have gone in to possess it.'[25]

However, within a generation, acute minds recognized that the terms offered by Napoleon in April 1802 within 'Les Articles Organiques des Cultes Protestants'[26] were nothing other than a vice-like bear hug. In return for state recognition and pastoral stipends, three things were required. First of all, the organic articles required the regrouping of France's Protestants into consistorial units of 6,000 persons with administration vested in a body of pastors and wealthy bourgeoisie invariably centred in a major community.[27] Secondly, they required control over the formation, education and accreditation of ministers. None were to enter upon pastoral functions without completion of a five-year course in arts and theology, only theological colleges supported by the state might be relied upon for this preparation, and only professors ratified by the government might teach such subjects. Under no circumstance would foreigners be eligible to serve within the French Protestant churches under the approved framework.[28] Thirdly, the articles

---

[24] Poland, *French Protestantism*, 264.

[25] G. de Felice, *History of the Protestants of France From the Commencement of the Reformation,* (London: 1851), 466.

[26] This was continued after 1815 by the restored monarchy.

[27] 'Les Articles Organiques des Cultes Protestants', nos. 15-18, printed in Daniel Robert, *Textes et Documents relatifs a L'Histoire des Églises Réformées en France: 1800-1830,* (Paris: 1962), 53, 54.

[28] 'Les Articles Organiques', nos. 7-14, in Robert, *Textes*, 53.

required an indefinite moratorium on the Church's former efforts at internal discipline through regional and national synods. They also required that any efforts towards the articulation of a creed or articles of religion be submitted for the approbation of the government.[29]

The first requirement, that referring to the consistorial units, had two immediate effects. On the one hand there was a concentration of regulative power in the hands of the affluent urban bourgeoisie to the detriment of the former influence of pastor and elders of the local congregation. On the other hand, the very employment of a criterion of 6,000 persons as the administrative unit worked decidedly against the interests of that large part of the country in which Protestant adherents were sparsely represented. The only pastoral care the government would permit for such regions would be of the most cursory kind. By implicit design, there was no room in such a scheme for the evangelization of those who made no Christian profession.[30]

By the second requirement, Napoleon's initiatives accomplished without struggle the closing of the semi-clandestine Lausanne Academy by 1809—a thing pre-Revolutionary governments had been unable to do. To say that he did this while in control of the Swiss cantons (amalgamated as the puppet Helvetian Republic) does not in any way diminish the significance of his elimination of Church-controlled theological education. First, Geneva's Academy was appointed from 1802 as the centre for theological education for the Reformed of the Empire. (Strasbourg had similarly been designated as centre for the churches of the Augsburg Confession within the realm.) Subsequently, Montauban would be established as an alternative to Geneva by Napoleon's own personal designation. Lausanne had produced pastoral candidates with rudimentary training in a mere two years (with some beneficial and some undesirable effects). However, by its insistence on the five-year course, the state's ratification of first Geneva and subsequently Montauban may be said to have unduly restricted the supply of pastors at a time when the actual demand was great. While in 1660 (prior to the Revocation), the French Reformed Churches had had 719 pastors, their numbers were reduced to 138 by 1788. In 1806, the number stood at 210 and was only at 214 in 1815 and at 219 in 1820.[31] The frosty receptions experienced by the somewhat rustic French students at Geneva in the years following 1802, and the struggles faced by Montauban in preparing to receive its

---

[29] 'Les Articles Organiques', nos. 25-31, in Robert, *Textes*, 54. See also de Felice, *History of the Protestants,* 467-71; and Poland, *French Revolution*, 264-67.

[30] See de Felice, *History*, 469-70; Robert, *Les Églises Réformées*, 117; and F. Kuhn, 'La Vie Intérieur du Protestantism Sous Le Prémier Empire', *Bulletin de le Société de l'Histoire du Protestantisme Français*, 51 (1902), 59. Hereafter cited as *BSHPF*.

[31] See Mours, *Les Églises*, 191; Poland, *French Revolution*, 270; Robert, *Les Églises Réformées*, 117.

first students in 1810, illustrate this numerical impasse. It is difficult to avoid the conclusion that Napoleon's policies prolonged rather than resolved the problem of pastoral supply.

As for the third requirement, the denial by Napoleon's government of the church's right to gather in deliberative synods, to print and disseminate journals, confessions of faith and theological works, and to enter into relationships with any foreign churches, this ensured that the French Reformed Church would suffer a greater internal and international isolation than it experienced in any period since the total proscription of all Christian worship in the years 1792-95.[32] Thus nineteenth-century French historian de Felice states in summary of the period,

> French Protestantism has, properly speaking, no history during the fourteen years of the Consulate and the Empire... We are not aware of the publication of a single important book upon dogma, ecclesiastical history or sacred eloquence in the course of Napoleon's reign.[33]

The religious policies of Napoleon regarding conquered territories need not detain us here at length, but two points must be made. First, we should note the government-sanctioned extension of religious toleration (albeit within a government-regulated framework, as above). Thus Jewish and Protestant minorities received protection in Belgium, Catholics in the Protestant Swiss cantons, and Jewish populations within the major cities of the Italian peninsula.[34] Second, and of still greater importance for this study, we must note the heightened interaction between Swiss and French Protestantism in the period of the Directory and Empire. Whereas in the previous century there had been one-way traffic of French Protestant refugees into these regions (and across other frontiers), now in the Napoleonic era the theological influences of Geneva and Lausanne were brought to bear in France in a way unequalled since the seventeenth century. The root of this new influence may be located partly in these cities' long-established reputation as centres of Reformed Protestantism, partly in their ongoing eighteenth-century significance as hubs of refugee activity (among which was clandestine theological education) and partly in terms of their inclusion from 1798 in an enlarged France.

Napoleon's decision of 1802 to make Geneva the centre of theological teaching for all the Reformed Churches[35] may be understood as a partly

---

[32] A. Lods, 'Bonaparte et Les Églises Protestantes de France', *BSHPF*, 46 (1897), 401.

[33] de Felice, *History of Protestants*, 471.

[34] Ford, *Europe*, 159-60.

[35] 'Les Articles Organiques', nos. 10, 13, in Robert, *Textes*, 53. A December 1801 proposal emanating from the Reformed consistory at Paris had called for seminaries at

practical measure—simply consolidating and building upon an existing foundation, and partly a calculating and shrewd design which, like his scheme of consistorial church organization, served the interests of containment rather than expansion. Geneva was not strategically located in terms of the geographical distribution of existing French Churches. Its academy could not hope to enrol sufficient candidates to meet the existing need of French pulpits. And this same institution could not be expected to enrol the relatively untutored French candidates in the same curriculum as its own young citizens who were products of the preparatory 'college'.

The Geneva Academy's response to the latter problem was to propose a two-tiered curriculum with only a more elementary curriculum open for French students who arrived less well-prepared than their Swiss counterparts. This proposal, which in effect simply proposed the continuation of a less demanding curriculum such as had been offered earlier in the French Academy of Lausanne, became repugnant and demeaning when proposed by haughty Genevans concerned to shield the reputation of their own theological academy from any diminution. Furthermore, the Geneva Academy proposed to employ no lecturers of French origin. Such delaying tactics on the part of Geneva meant that by 1807 Napoleon's plans for Geneva had still not been implemented and the Lausanne Academy had still not been closed. A governmental insistence upon immediate implementation brought such deep protests from within France that, in the following year, Napoleon had found it politic to personally designate Montauban in the Midi as a second site for Reformed theological education. Instruction began at the chosen site in 1810.

Yet even so, the stature of Geneva in French religious life was scarcely diminished. The most promising French ministerial candidates were still sent there for academic preparation. Montauban unwittingly paid tribute to Geneva's prominence by styling itself 'the Geneva of the Midi' and turned to graduates of the Geneva Academy for two of its original four professors.[36] Montauban's felt rivalry with Geneva was surely a complicating factor in the allegations of heretical teaching levelled in 1812-13 at the Genevan Esaie Gasc, first professor of dogmatics in the new seminary. Orthodox ministers and divinity students in the Midi region detected departures from the Christian doctrine of the Trinity in Gasc's lectures. From whatever mixture of motives, Montauban was consciously delineating a more conservative position than Geneva. In the minds of a concerted minority, Geneva had come to represent the

---

Nîmes, Geneva, Strasbourg and Cleves, see Robert, *Textes*, 47. On the subject, see also Robert, *Les Églises Réformées*, 208-209.

[36] Robert, *Les Églises Réformées*, 219-20, indicates that in fact three Genevans were offered faculty positions, with only two accepting.

fountain of all errors and was spreading 'socinianism which was at bottom nothing more than a deism tinged with Christianity'.[37] It was charged that such views were being popularized not only among theological students but also among the young, who were being trained by use of a catechism prepared by that most concessive of all Genevan dogmaticians, Jacob Vernet (d.1789). Thus it was that as Geneva and the other Swiss cantons were regaining their independence from France in the year 1813, Geneva's influence was both sizeable and controversial in that nation.

In this epoch of widespread difficulty throughout Francophone Europe, there were various forces working for the sustaining of lively Christian faith. In Switzerland as well as in various German domains, we may notice the presence of pietism. Pietism grew up in an era of high orthodoxy characterized by theological disputation. Ministers such as Johann Arndt (1555-1621) and A.H. Francke (1663-1727) promoted inner heart-religion and a Bible-centred faith as a means of redressing the imbalance which followed in the wake of this era of high orthodoxy. Subsequently, such emphases were maintained in the eighteenth century by Nikolaus Ludwig von Zinzendorf (1700-60), a nobleman who became figurehead of the 'Unitas Fratrum', a religious brotherhood which maintained residential colonies and carried out home and foreign evangelization.[38]

It is plain that the thought and writing of Arndt and Francke, though Lutheran, had much about them that was amenable to the Reformed Churches. Zinzendorf travelled extensively within Europe, visiting Geneva and setting up conventicles there.[39] His followers lived within a framework he termed 'diaspora', i.e., they were adherents of the United Brethren movement living at a distance from actual Brethren colonies, yet associating with local National Churches. In the latter settings, they maintained conventicles or cells in private homes for mutual edification.

Lay evangelists travelled, linking such cells or conventicles with one another. By 1737, such evangelists had penetrated France; they itinerated in the regions of Bordeaux, Saintonge, Poitou and Alsace by 1742. Yet greater successes in Protestant Switzerland than in post-Revocation France are signalled by the fact that Switzerland and Holland were named separate districts of endeavour in 1785, while France received no mention. Twenty such Moravian districts had been delineated in that

---

[37] Kuhn, 'La Vie Interieur', 63-65.

[38] The spread of pietism in Switzerland is described in Paul Wernle, *Der Schweizerische Protestantismus im XVII. Jahrhundert*, 5 vols, (Tubingen: 1923), I, 11-77.

[39] The decades following the visit of Zinzendorf to Geneva saw as many as 700 persons involved in Moravian 'cells' there. See Leon Maury, *Le Réveil Religieux*, 2 vols, (Paris: 1898), I, 18.

year.[40] However, the era of the Empire saw a dramatic upsurge in Moravian activity in the south of France, especially around Bordeaux. The leader of the organized community there, J.J. Mérillat, has been shown to have been an intimate friend of Daniel Encontre (1762-1818), an early dean and professor of theology at Montauban. François Bonnard (1776-1838), an early professor of Hebrew at Montauban, has been shown to be a member of a ministers' fraternal with direct links of regular correspondence with the Moravian leadership at Herrnhut.[41]

Quite independent and external corroboration of this Moravian activity in the period of the Empire and Restoration is provided in a short manuscript of sixteen un-numbered folio pages, entitled 'A Memorial on the State of the Protestant Churches in the Kingdom of France'. Its author, Clement Perrot, was an Independent minister from the Channel Island of Jersey, a loyal supporter of the London Missionary Society, and fluent in both French and English. That society requested him, in the period following Napoleon's 'one hundred days', to visit French Protestants and record his impressions as a means of informing its directors on the post-war outlook for the churches. Among other impressions, Perrot recorded that the twenty to thirty most pious and promising French ministers were heavily dependent upon Moravian literature (in French translation) and tended to limit their usefulness 'by their loud declarations of loyalty to the Moravian Brethren'.[42] Significantly, Perrot as visitor was able to identify by name a much more pervasive Moravian following than that established by modern researchers on the basis of scanty remaining records. He also detected a widespread practical (but not theoretical) Arminianism which he believed could only be expunged by the wide circulation of sound theological works, translated, if needs be, from English.

---

[40] See E. Stoeffler, *German Pietism During the Eighteenth Century*, (Leiden: 1973), 160-61; J. Taylor Hamilton, *A History of the Church Known as the Moravian Church*, (Bethlehem, PA: 1900) 235; and F. Hordern, 'Les Moraves En France Sous L'Empire', *BSHPF*, 112 (1966), 49.

[41] Hordern, 'Les Moraves', 50-51.

[42] Clement Perrot, 'A Memorial on the State of the Protestant Churches in the Kingdom of France, 1815', London Missionary Society (now Council for World Mission) Archive, European Correspondance (France) 1799-1849, Box 3, London University School of Oriental and African Studies. French pastors would certainly have had access to the standard text of Moravian theology by C.A. Spangenberg, *Idei Fidei Fratrum Oder Kurzer Begriff der Christlichen Lehre in der Evangelischen Brudergemeine* (Barby: 1779). Spangenberg, successor to Zinzendorf, sought to present Moravian belief in as close as possible a form to that of Protestant orthodoxy. It was promptly translated into English, Danish, French, Swedish, Dutch, Bohemian and Polish. See Hamilton, *Moravian Church*, 232, and Stoeffler, *German Pietism*, 165.

Moravian activity was also very considerable in Alsace, most of all among Lutherans, typified by the justly renowned Jean Frédéric Oberlin of Ban de la Roche (1740-1825).[43] Oberlin combined zeal for pietism, for the French Revolution and for social and educational reforms. In the French-speaking cantons of Switzerland bordering on Alsace, Moravian conventicles persisted, albeit in diminished strength, into the Napoleonic period. At Geneva, the remaining circle was very small indeed by the period 1810-15.[44] Yet it proved the spiritual 'home' for a surprising number of pious theological students who sought more than the meagre fare available elsewhere in the city. The itinerant Moravian evangelists Mérillat and Mettetal still included the Geneva circle in their preaching circuits and in this way were the means of the conversion of students H.L. Empeytaz (1810) and Émile Guers (1812).[45] Fellow students Ami Bost (whose father presided over many of the Moravian gatherings), Henri Pyt, and Charles Rieu were also regular in attendance.[46]

The spiritual sustenance received in the Moravian setting spawned a distinct student-led pietistic circle, existing between 1810 and 1814. This, the 'Société des Amis', included all the above-named students, others such as J.G. Gonthier, Jonathan Devisme, Matthieu Miroglio, César Bonifas, and several pious artisans and tradesmen.[47] This circle had received the welcome visit of Geneva graduate Abraham Lissignol (1784-1851), then minister at Montpellier, in 1814. Though disbanded in that same year at the insistence of the Geneva Company of Pastors, the circle of pious students by no means forfeited one another's friendship.[48]

It is in this context that we are best able to evaluate the Geneva visits of that charismatic and peripatetic exponent of illuminist mysticism, Baroness de Krüdener. Herself a former novelist and the unfaithful wife of a Prussian ambassador, she had undergone Christian conversion upon being introduced to a Moravian circle while visiting Riga, her maternal

---

[43] F.L. Cross, ed., *Oxford Dictionary of the Christian Church*, (2nd ed., Oxford), s.v. 'Oberlin'; and Hordern, 'Les Moraves', 54.

[44] Thus the biographer of César Malan can speak of 'a mere handful' of persons by 1815. C. Malan, *Life of Malan*, (London: 1869), 35.

[45] Émile Guers, *Le Premier Réveil*, (Geneva: 1872), 41, 42.

[46] Guers, *Le Premier*, 41, 42; Timothy C.F. Stunt, quoting Émile Guers, has aptly called this diminished, but remaining Moravian circle at Geneva, the 'cradle' of the impending 'Réveil; *From Awakening to Secession: Radical Evangelicals in Switzerland and Britain 1815-35*, (Edinburgh: 2000), 25.

[47] Guers, *Le Premier*, 43; Stunt, *From Awakening*, 28.

[48] Guers, *Le Premier*, 59, 67. The pietistic 'underground' of post-Revolutionary Geneva is quite complex. Ami Bost, writing in 1819, was able to describe not only the continued existence of the Moravians, but also 'many little churches where pious people meet without causing a disturbance, often meeting for reunions other than on a Saturday or Sunday', and a 'mystical circle, without a name, where those assembled rely on the writings of Jung-Stilllung'. *Genève Religieux*, 67, 71, 73.

home. She subsequently made an extensive tour of Moravian colonies at Bethelsdorf, Kleinwelk and Herrnhut.[49] The Moravian mystic Jung-Stillung influenced her deeply, as did the devotional writings of Fénelon and Madame Guyon.

Her quietistic message was taught in fashionable parlour gatherings at Lausanne, Geneva, Ban de la Roche and Paris. Eventually she was to gain the confidence of Czar Alexander of Russia in the time of sensitive treaty negotiations at both Paris and Vienna.[50] While the Baroness concentrated her efforts upon individuals, she employed as her chaplain and preacher Henri Empeytaz (1790-1861), the zealous Geneva divinity student (described above). The latter, when denied ordination to the ministry by the Geneva Company for his unrepentant zeal in conducting Sunday Schools, had accepted Krüdener's timely offer of employment. Empeytaz was associated with the Baroness between 1814 and 1817.[51] That Empeytaz, the Moravian convert, should have been comfortable in the service of Krüdener is somewhat indicative of the powerful 'brew' of religious influences circulating in Geneva in the final months of the Napoleonic Empire. Empeytaz's own background and outlook would have given him strong convictions about Scripture, the cross of Christ, and the need for personal conversion. The Baroness was by all accounts mystical, given to dreams, determined (though without success) to produce miracles, and dabbling with excessive forms of Roman Catholic devotion which raised the eyebrows of her largely Protestant following.[52]

British Interest in Francophone Europe before and after 1789

As we have observed, the religious cultures of Britain and French-speaking Europe in the eighteenth century were clearly divergent. None the less, the two different religious cultures did intersect one another with fair regularity. Much of this interaction resulted from the waves of French religious persecution which occurred between the 1680s and the 1790s. Aimed first at Protestants and latterly (in the main) against Roman Catholics, state-supported persecution transplanted many tens of thousands of French refugees into Britain where they encountered a combination of official government welcome and local hostility.

Though the renewal of persecution for French Protestants is usually associated with the official Revocation of the Edict of Nantes in 1685, in

---

[49] Clarence Ford, *Madame de Krüdener,* (London: 1893), 91, 96, 102.

[50] Ford, *Madame de Krüdener,* 166.

[51] Ford, *Madame de Krüdener,* 128.

[52] Ami Bost, who visited the Baroness both in Geneva (1813) and Basel (1817), was no cynical observer. Yet he was certain that her efforts were characterized above all by artificial zeal and a mixture of truth and error. Bost, *Mémoires,* I, 29, 62. See also Stunt, *From Awakening,* 30.

fact two decades of steady erosion of religious rights had preceded this official action.[53] The use of 'dragonnades' (forced lodging of military personnel with Protestant households) as a method of coercing conversions to Catholicism, had in fact begun in 1681 and from that year onwards refugees streamed from the country. As such flight was in fact illegal, many were apprehended and consigned to prison or galley service. Yet some 50,000 (out of an approximate total of 200,000 who eluded border patrols) reached British cities ranging from Bristol, Plymouth and Exeter in the southwest to Southampton, Rye, Dover and Canterbury in the south, and London, Colchester, Norwich and Edinburgh in the east. In London, Canterbury and Norwich, refugees of the Revocation joined French Walloon communities and churches which had survived from the Tudor era. The existing community centred upon the French church at Threadneedle Street, London, often took the initiative in organizing the arrivals into new communities dispersed around the coast.[54]

Immigration on such a scale could have occurred only with the sanction and encouragement of the English government. In fact, the monarch, the Privy Council and Parliament were united in viewing the refugees as fit objects for assistance. This was so because of their having experienced dire persecution on account of their Protestantism and because of their promise of bringing with them trades, technical knowledge and investment capital, all highly in demand in the British Isles. Many citizens agreed with the lead taken by their superiors and consequently contributed some £120,000 in church collections in aid of the newcomers.[55] These gifts were nearly doubled by parliamentary grants.

Much has deservedly been written about the Huguenot contribution to British economic, military, and industrial life.[56] Here, however, it is simply our purpose to stress that the Huguenot community made an impact on eighteenth-century British religious life both within the Anglican Communion and in distinct congregations conforming to French forms and discipline. At the end of the seventeenth century there were no fewer than thirty-one separate French Protestant congregations meeting in London.[57] In the final decades of the seventeenth century, the mere

---

[53] Robin D. Gwynn, *Huguenot Heritage: The History and Contribution of the Huguenots in Britain*, (London: 1985), 21.

[54] Gwynn, *Huguenot Heritage*, 38.

[55] Reginald Lane Poole, *A History of the Huguenots of the Dispersion*, (London: 1880), 193.

[56] The reader may consult the appropriate chapters of Robin D. Gwynn and Irene Scouloudi, eds., *Huguenots in Britain and Their French Background*, (London: 1987).

[57] See Gwynn, *Huguenot Heritage*, 166; and John Stoughton, *Religion in England Under Queen Anne and the Georges 1702-1800*, (London: 1878), 366.

presence of such a sizeable refugee community served forcefully to remind Protestant Englishmen of the potential danger posed to them by James II's Catholicism. The Huguenot presence helped to undermine the credibility of James' policies and prepare for the acceptance of William of Orange.[58]

The French Protestant community made other contributions to the religious life of eighteenth-century Britain. Nowhere was this more evident than in the field of Christian homiletics. Jacques Saurin (1677-1730) was briefly minister of a London congregation after a long ministry at The Hague. His sermons, many of which were translated into English, were looked on as models of passionate eloquence and found wide acceptance, especially among Protestant Dissenters.[59] Similarly, the homiletic manual by the popular minister Jean Claude (1619-87), entitled *Essay on the Composition of a Sermon*, proved widely influential and was recommended to the public in editions seen through the press by the Baptist, Robert Robinson (1779), and the Anglican, Charles Simeon (1826).

Further, the gradual assimilation of French refugees into the indigenous churches of their adoptive home meant that in time many persons of Huguenot descent rose to positions of leadership in religious life. Historians have noted the inclusion of many such ministers in the *Dictionary of National Biography*.[60] There was, however a far larger influx of Catholic and Royalist refugees into Britain during the French Revolution, and especially in the period immediately following the abortive flight and arrest of King Louis XVI. Of this mammoth exodus, some 150,000 eventually returned to France under an amnesty proclaimed by Bonaparte.[61] But while in Britain the refugees had been the recipients of £200,000 in parliamentary aid as well as private subscriptions.[62] Spontaneous charity on such a scale to an immigrant Catholic community indicated to some that the time was ripe for Catholic emancipation; in actuality the legislation was delayed until 1829.

Britain received an additional body of French-speaking visitors as a result of the Napoleonic wars. From Edinburgh in the north to

---

[58] Gwynn, *Huguenot Heritage*, 142.

[59] See Stoughton, *Religion*, 365; and Gwynn, *Huguenot Heritage*, 86. David Bogue recommended perusal of Saurin's *Sermons*, 6 vols, (London: 1796), to his Gosport Academy pupils.

[60] See Gwynn, *Huguenot Heritage*, 86.

[61] M.H. Wadams, 'The Nineteenth and Twentieth Centuries', in C.R. Dodwell, ed., *The English Church and the Continent*, (London: 1959), 95.

[62] See Halévy, *A History*, 478; and A. R. Vidler, *The Church in an Age of Revolution* (Harmondsworth: 1981), 43. For the further significance of the Catholic pro-royalist refugees in England, see Dominic Bellenger, 'The Émigré Clergy and the English Church'.

Southampton and Plymouth in the south an estimated 60,000 French prisoners of war were detained. The missionary possibilities of the situation were not lost on those who were concerned to carry forward the impetus of the Evangelical Revival. Thus, Thomas Haweis, Anglican rector of Aldwincle, Northamptonshire, and a future founding father of the London Missionary Society, had journeyed to Brighton in 1793 to distribute French language evangelistic leaflets to the refugees congregated there.[63] John Campbell, the Scottish itinerant and associate of the Haldanes, distributed similar literature to prisoners quartered at Edinburgh Castle and at Penicuik in 1801.[64] The Methodist mission superintendent Thomas Coke, always watchful for new evangelistic opportunities, requisitioned William Toase, a Francophone Channel Island circuit preacher, for the work of ministering to French prisoners on the south coast of England in 1811.[65] Theological students at David Bogue's Gosport Academy visited prisoners equipped with tracts supplied by the London Missionary Society.[66]

Yet British Protestants were by no means content simply to aim at the support and (where possible) the proselytization of the French-speaking refugees and prisoners who had arrived in Britain. On the contrary, British Protestants, having been alerted to the political and spiritual condition of Europe, determined to explore the needs of the Continent itself. One of the pioneers of the Evangelical mission to the Continent was David Bogue of Gosport, who journeyed to Amsterdam and Paris in the year 1784 as a private individual. There he established personal contacts, who later forwarded to him information which he used to urge the LMS in March 1799 to sponsor missionary initiatives in Holland, Belgium and France.[67] In September 1791, Methodist superintendent Thomas Coke journeyed to Paris and negotiated for the purchase of a disused church in the belief that the times were propitious for establishing a Wesleyan mission there. However, he soon discovered that his invitation to Paris had been issued by two cunning English schoolmasters, eager to gather pupils through the influence of a British preacher. This disclosure brought the effort to a prompt conclusion.[68]

---

[63] Wood, *Haweis* , 185.

[64] Kinniburgh, *Fathers of Independency*, 237-39.

[65] See John Vickers, *Thomas Coke, Apostle of Methodism* (London: 1969), 314; and W. Toase, *Memorials of William Toase Illustrative of the Rise and Progress of Methodism in France and the Channel Islands,* (London: 1874), 15-44.

[66] Toase, *Memorials of W. Toase*, 30. Expenses for the colportage are reflected in the ledger, 'Disbursements to France', Europe Handlist, Council for World Mission (LMS) Archive, School of Oriental and African Studies, University of London.

[67] Council for World Mission (LMS), Home Correspondence, 1795-1876, Box 1.

[68] Samuel Drew, *Life of Coke,* (London: 1817), 242.

The century closed with Britain at war with revolutionary France. Contacts with European Protestants were kept up only with the greatest difficulty. It was hardly surprising that British evangelicals in that expansionist missionary era often came to the most severe conclusions about Europe at this time, dominated as it was by militant nationalism, political revolution and the rationalism of the Enlightenment. In his three-volume *An Impartial History of the Church of Christ* (1800), the LMS director, Thomas Haweis, opined regarding Switzerland,

> The information I receive misleads me if through all the Protestant cantons the greatest decays are not visible. The Lord's Day is closed with amusements beyond the others. Those who descend from the pulpits partake of them with their flocks... The arch-infidel Rousseau...spreads his destructive opinions. Voltaire, the high-priest of infidelity...diffused the poison of his scepticism. I doubt if there remains a single professor or pastor at Geneva who adheres to Calvin, either in principle or practice, but the lowest form of moral essay, and Socinian Christianity prevails.[69]

Haweis offered a similar diagnosis of France which had once been

> distinguished for the purity of the reformed faith, and then, as we have seen, reduced to the greatest extremities. I am rather induced to think the Protestants themselves have drank [sic] as deeply as any others into the infidel philosophy... Of living Christianity among the Protestant professors, I can find little evidence.[70]

It was this sombre outlook on Francophone Europe which moved David Bogue in April 1800 to advocate that the LMS circulate a French translation of the New Testament in France and the Belgian provinces. Bogue also proposed the addition of an introduction on Christian evidences.[71] The proposal met with prompt acceptance, but no concrete action could be taken until the Peace of Amiens was signed in March 1802. During the brief interval of peace, the LMS sent four of its directors—Bogue, Joseph Hardcastle, Matthew Wilks and Alexander Waugh—to Paris.[72] The four were to verify the need for a French New Testament, to explore distribution arrangements and to inquire as to what

---

[69] Thomas Haweis, *An Impartial History of the Church of Christ*, 3 vols, (London: 1800), III, 290. We will later have reason to note that this extremely grave outlook on Francophone Europe was shared by Robert Haldane, and yet was opposed by others.

[70] Haweis, *An Impartial History*, 298.

[71] See Bennett, *Bogue*, 225; and Terpstra, 'Bogue', 236.

[72] The journey was to have taken place in August of that year and to have involved Thomas Haweis. The latter received serious injury in a riding accident and after delays, the mission proceeded without him in September. Hay and Belfrage, *Waugh*, 16; Bennett, *Bogue*, 227.

welcome would be given to British ministers who might come to serve in France without state salary.[73]

The visiting delegation was soon able to report that they had found a member of the French National Assembly who would be willing to translate the essay on Christian evidences which was to be bound with the French Testaments. As to the need for a French translation of the Scriptures, four days of exploration among Paris bookshops produced no copy available for sale. However, one bookseller was prepared to order 1,500 copies immediately, preferably in Protestant format. It was found that Piedmont, a Catholic region recently annexed to France, now welcomed Protestant activity and sought unfettered access to the Scriptures.[74] By way of recommendation to the LMS, the delegation urged the following:

1. Printing and circulation of 2,000 New Testaments with preface on Christian evidences;

2. Printing for sale 5,000 Bibles, 5,000 of each of Isaac Watts' first and second catechisms, 5,000 Westminster Shorter Catechisms, 4,000 New Testaments in Italian, and 2,000 separate copies of Bogue's essay (on Christian evidences) at a cost to the LMS of £848;

3. Promotion of a French language magazine equivalent to the *Evangelical Magazine*;

4. Support for the theological education of six French students; and

5. Appointment of an LMS agent for Paris, with the Rev. Samuel Tracy to serve the first six months.

These recommendations, all of which were unanimously adopted,[75] mark a decided escalation of British missionary activity on the Continent. From this juncture, we may note the inclusion of French language instruction as well as the presence of French students in Bogue's theological academy at Gosport.[76] Further, from this time forward the LMS consistently earmarked funds for France. These were used for the support of individual Francophone workers, for the publishing of French literature, and for efforts among the French prisoners before and after the brief peace of 1802.[77]

---

[73] See Hay and Belfrage, *Waugh*, 164; and *Evangelical Magazine*, 10 (1802), 462.

[74] 'Report Concerning the State of Religion in France', *Evangelical Magazine*, 10 (1802), 462-467. This important report is reprinted, in full, in this volume as Appendix A.

[75] *Evangelical Magazine*, 10 (1802), 466-467.

[76] Terpstra, 'Bogue', 41, 207.

[77] Council for World Mission (LMS) Archive, *Europe Handlist*, 'Disbursements to France 1800-1837'. Significant among the literature produced were editions of Philip Doddridge's *Essays* in 1807 and 1812.

As with the LMS, so also was there an orientation to Francophone Europe for the several related agencies it helped to spawn. The Religious Tract Society, formed in London in 1799 primarily to furnish materials for itinerant and colportage work at home, had responded promptly with tracts suited to the needs of interned French prisoners.[78] The success of this venture led the society to adopt foreign objectives in 1805 in addition to its original domestic intention. The historian, Roger Martin, has argued convincingly that it was the clear demonstration by the LMS of French demand for the Scriptures, rather than the crying need for Welsh Bibles personified by the young Mary Jones of County Gwynedd, which summoned the British and Foreign Bible Society into existence in March 1804. That a state of war had existed with France since May of the previous year did not keep the LMS from pursuing its French agenda, albeit discreetly through the war years.[79] However, it printed no more Scriptures in French after 1803, for this task and that of circulating Scriptures in French Europe by way of Basel was rapidly assumed by the Bible Society.[80]

British Protestant missionary zeal for French Europe was not dissipated but only held in partial check in the period of intermittent war ranging from 1792 to 1815. That this was the case surely calls for some explanation. We have seen (*supra* p. 36) that the dawning of the era of revolution had been deeply disruptive of the growing evangelical Protestant unity which was the enduring legacy of the eighteenth-century revival of religion. Church of England evangelicals had reacted with disdain to Dissenters' hopes for their own political rehabilitation modelled on the removal of Protestant disabilities by France's Revolutionary government. Yet the onset of the French 'Reign of Terror' (1792-95), the rise of the deistic civil worship of 'Reason', and the ambitious military campaigns which sent French armies into neighbouring states had a most telling effect on British opinion. What the historian Franklin Ford has called 'the identification of progressivism

---

[78] W. Jones, *The Jubilee Memorial of the Religious Tract Society 1799-1849*, (London: 1850), 282-83.

[79] LMS expenditure for France in the war years is itemized in *Europe Handlist*, 'Disbursements to France', CWM (LMS) Archive. Expenditures amounted to £500 in the period 1803-1815.

[80] R.H. Martin, 'The Bible Society and the French Connection', *Journal of The United Reformed Church History Society*, 3.7 (1985), 278-90. Martin posits the convincing thesis that the clandestine nature of the commitment to the supplying of French Scriptures by the BFBS is to be explained by the war fever of the time in which any seeming gesture of assistance to France would be utterly misconstrued. The genuine scarcity of the Scriptures in Welsh thus served as a genuine though non-exhaustive rationale for the creation of the new society.

with Francophilia'[81] was seriously eroded by such excesses. Not only Protestant Dissenters but also the circle of romantic poets experienced sober second thoughts. William Blake, the poet and illustrator, had proudly worn the symbol of the Revolution, the red bonnet with white cockade. However, upon receiving news of the massacres of September 1792, he tore it off and never wore it again. Another earlier sympathizer with the Revolution, William Wordsworth, found the turning point for his affection in the crowning of Napoleon as emperor in 1804.[82]

Perhaps ironically, this change of heart by Dissenters and literati towards the revolutionary events in France coincided with the introduction of British anti-Jacobin legislation which restricted the right of public meeting and free association.[83] The legislation was a blunt instrument which made no distinction between the now-disenchanted and the still-enamoured who were urged on by the reading of Tom Paine's *Rights of Man* (1791-92).

Evangelical Protestants learned to strike a different posture during the subsequent war years; they concentrated on gospel extension and studiously avoided politics. As the editor of the *Evangelical Magazine* (est. 1793) put it in his year-opening preface for 1802,

> No political sentiment, from any quarter, has ever gained admission to our publication. On the contrary, it has been our invariable study to direct our readers to higher objects and matters of superior consideration... By Divine assistance, we shall always pursue the same course.[84]

Yet as we have seen, a retreat from open sympathy with the direction taken by the French Revolution and the exercise of editorial discretion in refraining from political comment did not mean that British Protestant interest in France suffered any material set-back. Quietly, and at times secretively, the LMS, tract, and Bible societies continued to focus their energies upon the region throughout the entire period of hostilities between the two nations. It is only when this constancy of interest is understood that we can properly interpret the otherwise puzzling record of communication between Protestants in the two countries throughout the war years. By proceeding from this constancy of interest, we are able to understand why both the *Christian Observer* and *Evangelical Magazine* troubled to reprint in full a translation of the 'Organic Articles' for the French Churches (Catholic and Protestant) which

---

[81] Ford, *Europe*, 164.
[82] Stephen Prickett, *England and the French Revolution*, (London: 1989), 62, 131.
[83] Halévy, *A History*, 154.
[84] *Evangelical Magazine*, 10 (1802), 1.

Napoleon introduced in 1802.[85] Even after the resumption of hostilities with France in May 1803, the *Evangelical Magazine* did not hesitate to publish an article by M. Martin, pastor of the Reformed Church at Bordeaux, calling for the soonest possible implementation of the LMS programme for France enunciated in the magazine in the previous year. Evidently the periodical had its avid readers in both countries. Martin had gone so far as to suggest that the LMS grant pecuniary aid to French Protestant pastors with sizeable families who were experiencing hardship due to the consular government's non-payment of promised stipends.[86] The same magazine was able to report in 1807, despite the blockade and war-time conditions, that French Protestantism was undergoing a remarkable resurgence in certain locales and was anticipating the foundation of a new theological seminary (sited by Napoleon's wish in 1808 at Montauban).[87] Similar items of news indicating French Protestant advance were circulated by the magazine in 1811.[88]

In April 1814, the month of Napoleon's abdication and before the signing of the Treaty of Paris, the *Evangelical Magazine* made a public appeal for financial support on behalf of the Rev. G.C. Smith of Plymouth who was shortly to visit France, Spain and Portugal for the purpose of distributing Bibles and tracts. Smith, in turn, forwarded encouraging reports in time for the June and August issues and reflected particular pleasure in having been present at the July ordination of thirteen graduates of the Protestant seminary at Montauban.[89] Contacts established in this tour provided later sobering reports of the 'unhappy insulated state' of French Protestant life under the restored monarchy in early 1815.[90] The *Christian Observer* in the same month could publish a letter from a 'Protestant minister in the south of France' noting similarly trying circumstances yet an encouraging gradual increase in the supply of evangelical ministers.[91]

In summary we may note that the British Protestant missionary interest in Francophone Europe predated the atrocities of the Reign of Terror (which so markedly dampened British enthusiasm for the Revolution),

---

[85] See *Christian Observer*, 1 (1802), 259-65; and *Evangelical Magazine*, 10 (1802), 197-99. The *Observer* editor went on to highlight the insincere motives from which he believed the government of France was proceeding.

[86] *Evangelical Magazine*, 11 (1803), 451.

[87] *Evangelical Magazine*, 14 (1807), 136.

[88] *Evangelical Magazine*, 19 (1811), 318, 349.

[89] *Evangelical Magazine*, 22 (1814), 155, 224, 328. In this same period, the directors of the LMS commissioned the Rev. Clement Perrot of Guernsey to survey the situation of the French churches. His report, 'A Memorial on the State of the Protestant Churches in the Kingdom of France', has been alluded to in footnote 42.

[90] *Evangelical Magazine*, 23 (1815), 170-71.

[91] *Christian Observer*, 14 (1815), 25-6.

and persisted through the first phase of the Revolutionary Wars up to 1802. It flourished openly during the Peace of Amiens (1802-03) and continued under the dramatic wartime conditions 1803-14. The promptness with which personal links between British and French Protestants were re-established after 1814 suggests that the Revolutionary and Napoleonic Wars did not break, but only impeded a growing kinship of feeling between Protestants in the two nations. This spirit of cooperation might have developed much more rapidly had it not been for the French Revolution. Such a steady growth of common interest, despite the devastations of war, transcended the confines of purely national interest.

This Protestant solidarity was shown in its most militant form to date in the period following Napoleon's abortive 'One Hundred Days' in the spring of 1815. The Emperor's crushing defeat at Waterloo left all who had rallied to his cause in positions of extreme vulnerability. Among these were some Protestants in the southern department of Gard. They had found their religious rights rather indifferently upheld by the restored monarchy, and had therefore shown sympathy to the Emperor's forces moving north between Marseilles and Paris. With Napoleon's defeat, all Protestants in the region became vulnerable to accusations of complicity in insurrection. Among those most ready to level such a charge was a vindictive Catholic and royalist element which called all Protestant religious liberties into doubt. There were horrible massacres in some districts; in others, houses and properties were burned. It was only by the eventual intervention of Austrian troops that order was restored. The local courts of justice failed to convict any persons for the atrocities, despite the promises by the central government that the perpetrators would be brought to justice.[92]

Details of these events were slow in reaching the British Protestant public. Nonetheless, there was a sufficiently clear understanding of the situation for two London committees to be summoned to meet on 21 November 1815. These committees were the 'General Body of Ministers of the Three Denominations in the Cities of London and Westminster' (Baptist, Presbyterian and Independent) and the 'Protestant Society for the Protection of Religious Liberty'.[93] The former body sent a deputation of four ministers to confer with the government and heard their report one week later. The conference succeeded in gaining expressions of 'deepest regret' from His Majesty's Government, along with some communication on the subject between Lord Liverpool and the French

---

[92] Daniel Robert, *Les Églises Réformées*, 279-87.

[93] G. Lewis, 'British Nonconformist Reactions to the "Terreur Blanche"', *Proceedings of the Huguenot Society of London*, 20 (1964), 514.

president, Richelieu.[94] The conference also decided to hold collections on behalf of afflicted Protestants and to mount a national effort to publicize their plight. These efforts succeeded in raising and distributing over £6,000 among those most in need.[95] Clement Perrot of Guernsey, already a trusted commentator on French religious affairs, was commissioned by a 'Committee of Inquiry, Superintendence and Distribution for the Relief of the French Protestants' to survey the actual state of things in the south of France. His report, which documented 200 deaths in the city of Nîmes alone and 450 deaths in the department of Gard as a whole, went far to vindicate the efforts of British Nonconformists in the affair. These efforts were portrayed in the *Times* and *Christian Observer* as assisting political dissidents whose Protestantism was largely irrelevant.[96] The *Edinburgh Christian Instructor*, however, pilloried the *Observer* for its jaded effort to secure the stability of the restored French monarchy at the cost of innocent Protestant lives.[97]

Protestants in the south of France did not simply receive substantial British gifts to help them in their time of need. They also learned that once more it was the Nonconformist Protestants and the far-flung constituency supporting the London Missionary Society which cared most for their welfare. French Protestant leaders received copies of the petitions for relief of their grievances which the 'Ministers of the Three Denominations' had placed before the British government. They were consequently led to trust that such a strategy would bring intervention by their own government.[98]

It was but a small step beyond this state of affairs when Pastor Abraham Lissignol of Montpellier, one of that select number of exemplary French pastors earlier commended to the LMS by Clement Perrot, wrote a letter to the *Evangelical Magazine* published in the December 1816 issue:

---

[94] See Lewis, 'British Nonconformist Reactions', 516; and *Edinburgh Christian Instructor*, 11 (1815), 417.

[95] Lewis, 'British Nonconformist Reactions', 525.

[96] See *Christian Observer*, 15 (1816), 65-68; and Lewis, 'British Nonconformist Reactions', 512-13.

[97] *Edinburgh Christian Instructor*, 12 (1816), 127-40, 257-82. The controversy over the true explanation for the persecution spawned considerable literature of its own. Finding a 'religious' basis for the persecution were Ingram Cobbin, *Statements of the Persecution of the Protestants in the South of France*, (London: 1815), and *Summary of the Persecutions of the Reformed Church in France*, (London: 1815); and Mark Wilks, *History of the Persecutions Endured by the Protestants in the South of France...During 1814-16*, 2 vols. (London: 1821).

[98] See Lewis, 'British Nonconformist Reactions', 517; and Robert, *Les Églises Réformées*, 287-88.

We need that you should send over to us some who shall re-animate that faith which is ready to die among us, to give fresh ardour to the few faithful labourers in the fields who have born the burden and the heat of the day.[99]

The records and correspondence of the LMS indicate the prompt but limited response the Society was able to make to such appeals in the financially trying period following the return of peace. Several workers in France received part or full assistance, and a very full exchange of correspondence between French friends of the Society and London indicates an effort at expansion of the work.[100] Yet even as Abraham Lissignol penned his appeal in the autumn of 1816, Britons visiting the Continent were rapidly forming their own conclusions about what response the situation demanded.

One of these was Dr John Pye Smith (1774-1851), theological tutor at Homerton College, London, from 1806. He travelled extensively throughout France and Switzerland in the summer of 1816 in search of improved health. After lingering at Geneva, Smith wrote in his diary,

Geneva stands in need of a reformation and reformer scarcely less than she did in the sixteenth century. The introduction of a suitable minister, if such could be found, who would act on an independent plan appears to be a practical measure... He should be a Swiss or a Frenchman, a scholar and an orator... Oh that the Christians of Great Britain may be honoured as instruments of obtaining and encouraging such a man.[101]

Just then another Briton arrived in France pursuing a missionary resolve he had framed some years previous. That individual was Robert Haldane.

Robert Haldane's Individualistic Mission

Robert Haldane's departure for France on 9 October 1816 represented the culmination of a long-standing desire. In 1839, Haldane, in order to clarify details about his European sojourn for the benefit of Edward Bickersteth, reported,

For many years I had cherished the idea of going to France with a view to doing something to promote the knowledge of the Gospel in a country in which I had been

---

[99] *Evangelical Magazine*, 24 (1816), 521-22.

[100] One worker, Laurent Cadoret, had worked in France with LMS support as early as the 1803-06 period. Unnamed workers received assistance from 1817. See CWM (LMS) Archive *Europe Handlist*, 'Disbursements to France'.

[101] John Medway, *Memoir of the Life and Writings of John Pye Smith, D.D.* (London: 1853), 227.

three times before as a traveller. Accordingly, when the return of peace rendered my design practicable, I went to the continent.[102]

The first of the three previous visits to which he had alluded had almost certainly been in company with David Bogue. That summer visit of 1784, undertaken shortly after a period of tuition under Bogue at Gosport, may well have planted the 'germ' of this later interest. A second and more extended visit followed one year later and included Holland, Germany, Austria, north Italy, southern France, Switzerland and, briefly, Paris.[103] But at this juncture, Robert Haldane made no open profession of the Christian faith; this would follow in 1795. His third continental visit prior to 1816 cannot be pinpointed with accuracy.

Having come to Christian faith, Haldane plainly thought much about Europe. We have noted (p. 31) his suspected sympathy with the early stages of the Revolution. Far more significant for our purposes was his appointment, in the year following his conversion, to the Board of Directors of the London Missionary Society. He cannot have been well known, for the secretary who noted his election entered his name erroneously as the *Rev.* Robert Haldane of Airthrey, although he was never ordained. His service in this capacity ended in 1804; by then the LMS had determined to replace one quarter of its 104 directors each year in the interests of wider participation.[104]

There is ample evidence of Haldane's deep involvement in the Society's affairs during his period of service. A recorded gift of £50 in 1796 may not have been large given his net worth, but it ranked among the largest single donations that year. In 1799, Haldane surpassed all other directors with his gift of £105 towards the costs incurred by the loss of the LMS ship, the 'Duff', to pirates. By 1800, Haldane was one of two directors, each promising £500 towards the creation of a Society seminary for missionary preparation. It so happened that the committee which was struck to pursue the matter recommended that the seminary be conjoined to the academy which was already under David Bogue's care at Gosport, Hampshire. In addition to having personally benefited from Bogue's teaching, Haldane had since 1798 provided £10 per annum support to a maximum of ten Gosport Academy students for three years, thus making

---

[102] Robert Haldane's *Letter to Edward Bickersteth*, (London: 1839), was a pamphlet-style publication of twelve pages reproducing his personal correspondence of 4 September of that year. Published with additional clarifications by the Rev. César Malan of Geneva, the pamphlet's existence indicates the author's deep concern to certify his role in the 'réveil'. Substantial excerpts are found in A. Haldane, *Lives of the Haldanes*, 388-92.

[103] A. Haldane, *Lives of the Haldanes*, 35-36.

[104] *Reports of the L.M.S. 1796-98*, CWM Archive, University of London, XXIII-XXIV, (1797) vii.

up a financial deficit arising from the death of an earlier benefactor, George Welsh.[105]

Haldane's participation as an LMS director in these years would also have provided him with a degree of familiarity with continental Protestant affairs and the Society's various schemes for continental assistance.[106] However, it is significant to note that even during these years of LMS involvement in and orientation towards Europe, Haldane did not operate on any assumption, stated or unstated, that his growing European interests must be restricted to those of the existing mission, tract or Bible societies. Thus in 1803, we learn of his efforts to recruit an Edinburgh businessman named Alexander to serve as an independent Christian literature agent for Leghorn, in northern Italy. He also attempted to recruit an agent for the German port city of Hamburg.[107]

This determination not to be confined to the efforts of the LMS with its sister organizations is reflected as well in his attempt in 1810 to discern from John Campbell of London

> if there be any (scheme for) translation of the Scriptures...not likely to be carried into effect by the societies in London...or of an enlarged distribution of Scriptures which you are not at present able to embrace... I would wish to do it in such a way as would be an addition to what is at present going on. Do you know if anything in this way could be done on the Continent? Can anything more be done for Spain and Portugal? I suppose nothing could be attempted as to France—or would it be possible to send over more copies of the Bible to that country?[108]

Here we see not only the continuation of his long-standing interest in Europe and awareness of what the London-based societies were currently doing under war-time conditions, but also Haldane's characteristic desire to undertake private action. We may say that this is the outlook of the independent-minded Christian philanthropist who had already organized and controlled the 'Society for the Propagation of the Gospel at Home', an organization defunct since 1808. Such an outlook implied no necessary hostility or contempt towards existing societies. Events subsequent to Haldane's 1819 return amply indicate a widespread

---

[105] See Lovett, *History of the L.M.S.*, (London: 1898), I, 63. Terpstra, 'Bogue', 106; and Bennett, *Bogue*, 133. After 1802, the LMS committed itself to preparing a limited number of French preachers at Gosport. See p. 59 *supra*.

[106] It is, therefore, unwarranted to insist, as does A. Wemyss, *Le Réveil*, (Toulouse: 1977), 83, 84, that Haldane's insistence on a personal mission to France indicated his ignorance of LMS activities and David Bogue's decision not to inform him regarding them.

[107] See A. Haldane, *Lives of the Haldanes*, 305; and James Ross, *W.L. Alexander, His Life and Work*, (London: 1877) 3.

[108] Letter of 25 December 1810 printed in A. Haldane, *Lives of the Haldanes*, 360.

community of interest among such groups. But Robert Haldane was always a man of independent action.

Though Robert Haldane now went to Europe at the 'return of the peace',[109] he cannot be said to have been part of the first 'wave' of Britons to cross the Channel in the post-war period. Already in January 1815 (prior to Napoleon's 'One Hundred Days'), the *Christian Observer* could report that the city council of Geneva had allotted a chapel for use of Church of England adherents in the city.[110] By early 1816, Britons could board the wooden steamship *Defiance* at London and travel across the Channel and up the Rhine to Cologne.[111] British 'literati' were drawn to the Continent at this time. The poets Percy Bysshe Shelley (1792-1822) and Lord Byron (1788-1824) were then surveying Alpine scenes and sampling Swiss life. British financiers, engineers and entrepreneurs were also present in numbers, making up, as it were, for the time lost during military hostilities. The half-century after Napoleon's defeat saw continental railway building, river navigation, gasworks, waterworks and textile mills expanded on a massive scale with the aid of British capital.[112] Significantly, Haldane's biographer would record the spiritual influence of a believing textile engineer, the Welshman Richard Wilcox, who met repeatedly with an existing pietist conventicle at Geneva in the months prior to the Scot's arrival. Wilcox was part of this industrial and entrepreneurial 'invasion' by Britons. A British visitor to the city in 1823 remarked on the advances in navigating Lake Leman resulting from a ferry service—with steam engines—of Scots design.[113] Britons were welcome in Europe. It was widely appreciated that British subsidies had enabled impoverished European governments to field and equip their armies for the defeat of Napoleon. These subsidies in cash, armaments and materials had amounted to £10 million in the last year of the war and £52 million between 1793 and 1815 exclusive of Britain's own military expenditure.[114] Switzerland was especially grateful for Britain's efforts at the Congress of Vienna to secure the restoration of her old borders and to maintain the integrity of all nineteen cantons formerly fused in Napoleon's 'Helvetic Republic'.[115]

It is difficult to avoid the conclusion that Robert Haldane went to Europe not only to fulfil a long-standing ambition, but also to escape

---

[109] R. Haldane, *Letter to Chenevière*, (London: 1824), 2.

[110] *Christian Observer*, 14 (1815), 62.

[111] W.O. Henderson, *Britain and Industrial Europe*, (Liverpool: 1957), 51.

[112] Henderson, *Britain*, 7-8.

[113] See A. Haldane, *Lives of the Haldanes,* 397; and Daniel Wilson, *Letters From an Absent Brother*, 2 vols, (London: 1823), I, 296.

[114] See F.L. Ford, *Europe*, 246; and J.M. Sherwig, *Guineas and Gunpowder*, (Boston: 1969), 4.

[115] Bonjour et al., *History of Switzerland*, 242.

from personal difficulties in Britain. His biographer speaks of 'twenty chequered years of failure and success' preceding the journey, a reference no doubt to the dramatic rise and inauspicious disintegration of the Haldane connexion of churches through disputes about the need for multiple pastors in a single congregation, various worship practices, and believers' baptism. Though Robert Haldane 'announced his intention of making a missionary tour of the Continent of Europe', his announcement stirred little public interest. Too many recalled Haldane's failures and controversies of the previous decade.[116]

The Haldane brothers had, no doubt, retained a circle of influential friends despite the demise of their connexion. Rowland Hill of Surrey Chapel, Joseph Hardcastle of the LMS and Bible Society, and Andrew Fuller, the pastor-theologian of Kettering who itinerated so widely on behalf of the Baptist Missionary Society, all continued their friendship with the Haldanes.[117] But the decline of their cause had been apparent to any observer and even their close friends lamented the changes. David Bogue, the spiritual and theological mentor of both brothers, chose to portray them as disciples of the teaching of Robert Sandeman—the divisive proponent of a biblical restorationism involving the upholding of all biblical precepts, in his *History of Dissenters* (1808).[118] Andrew Fuller, though himself a Baptist, had warned the brothers in 1808 that they

---

[116] A. Haldane, *Lives of the Haldanes,* 387. The Haldane biographer's pregnant phrase regarding 'twenty chequered years' is a striking statement, coming from a nephew who, as biographer, regularly shows himself determined to enhance the reputation of his two subjects. The biographer, Alexander Haldane, was—from his transferal from Edinburgh to London—no longer associated with the restorationist Christianity of his upbringing. He was known as a rigorous upholder of the Protestantism of the Church of England through his editorship of the *Record* newspaper; *s.v.* 'Alexander Haldane' in Donald M. Lewis, ed. *Blackwell's Dictionary of Evangelical Biography*, 2 vols, (Oxford: 1996), I. The stance of the *Record*, edited by Haldane, is helpfully portrayed in Joseph L. Altholz, 'Alexander Haldane, the *Record*, and Religious Journalism', *Victorian Periodicals Review*, 20 (1987), 23-31.

[117] The Haldane biographer noted a continuation of their correspondence in the decade following the connexion's demise, A. Haldane, *Lives of the Haldanes,* 363-64.

[118] David Bogue and James Bennett, *The History of Dissenters*, 4 vols, (London: 1808), IV, 124-25. Bogue and Bennett noted, however, that the Haldanes' new position on baptism separated them from Sandeman's continued paedobaptism. James Bennett's 1833 revision of the *History* no longer maintained any Haldane-Sandeman connection. *The History of Dissenters*, 3 vols, (London: 1833), II, 447.

had once been as positive about paedobaptism as (they) now were about exhortation, discipline and the kiss and that he strongly suspected that it was one of Satan's devices to draw attention to those little things.[119]

Fuller's work, *Strictures on Sandemanianism* (1810), addressed directly some of the very tenets being championed at Edinburgh. Young Christopher Anderson (1782-1852), converted under James Haldane's preaching, and by 1806 the pastor of the Baptist congregation meeting at Richmond Court Chapel, Edinburgh (and from 1818 at Charlotte Chapel, Rose Street), spoke plainly to his mentor, reminding him 'of the former days' when the gospel had seemed to be advancing in Edinburgh. Now, Anderson 'conceived that on the whole, religion was in decline, except someone stepped forward'.[120] This was a stern way of speaking; it came from a young man once dismissed from the Tabernacle's membership for a change of conviction on baptism identical to that which his mentor had now himself undergone and was enforcing on others![121]

From the fact that Robert was not the great public figure of the connexion (a role which his brother James filled) and was not the first to submit to a second baptism, some have suggested that Robert was far less erratic than James.[122] But there is little evidence that Robert did not embrace the new views with equal fervour. On the contrary, Robert engaged in a preaching tour to Newcastle and London in 1805 in order to promote the very ideas about congregational order and worship which James was shortly to popularize in his book, *A View of Social Worship*

---

[119] Ryland, *Andrew Fuller*, 326. The remarks were directed primarily to James, yet the memoir makes plain that similar reasonings took place with Robert also.

[120] Hugh Anderson, *The Life and Letters of Christopher Anderson*, (London: 1854), 10, 66.

[121] It must be admitted that no 'straight line' connects the teaching of John Glas, his son-in-law. Robert Sandeman, and that of the Haldane brothers c.1805. While we may speak of affinities in matters such as the conception of the pastoral office as multiple, the place of spontaneous mutual exhortation in church services, etc., there were also disaffinities. Sandemanian congregations, following John Glas, had not repudiated paedobaptism, whereas the Haldanes had. The Sandemanian movement was not overtly evangelistic, whereas the Haldane brothers never ceased to be. The indication that Robert Haldane also encountered several of these same 'restorationist' practices during an 1805 visit to Dublin among the 'Kellyites' suggests that the 'brew' of restorationist ideas then in circulation was not simply equatable with Sandemanianism, however much it may have overlapped with it. For Kellyism in Dublin as encountered by Haldane, see Grayson Carter, *Anglican Evangelicals: Protestant Secessions from the Via Media 1800-1850*, (Oxford: 2002), 71, 72. Therefore, when a long-time acquaintance of the Haldanes like Andrew Fuller believed that perceived Sandemanian tenets in his friends, he was interpreting the less-well known by the better known. As we shall see, this perception of Robert Haldane's stance colored the English perception of his activity on the Continent.

[122] So, for instance, Reeves, 'The Interaction', 147.

(1805). Further, Robert's was the unseen but supporting hand in the publication of associate W. Ballantyne's pamphlet urging a plurality of preaching elders in every congregation.[123] The same brother sorely tested old bonds of friendship with John Campbell, now of Kingsland Chapel, London, by urging weekly communion and a plurality of preaching elders upon him. In 1807 Haldane wrote to his old acquaintance,

> Your situation is highly dangerous. The cry of usefulness drowns every other voice. How much seldomer do we hear of duty? Yet if the former be pursued at the expense of the latter, our efforts must be abominable to God. Are you not doing this in regard to the Lord's Supper?[124]

Public confidence in both of the brothers fell hand in hand with the demise of their connexion. They had claimed only to be encouraging forbearance on the questions of baptism and the ordering of the details of worship. But those who found the Haldane innovations in the ordering of congregational ministry, sacraments and worship to be unconvincing perceived only another instance of what one contemporary observer termed the 'heavy purse and powerful influence of Haldane'.[125] After the break-up of their connexion, there came the unseemly spectacle of divided congregations and property disputes to which we have earlier referred. And, almost inevitably, rumours circulated which showed neither party in a favourable light. The family biographer was still contending against such stories thirty-five years after the spectacle.[126]

The Leith Walk Tabernacle saw its core membership reduced to one third of its former strength and at least eight other derivative new congregations emerged in Edinburgh during these years of instability.[127] James Haldane continued as pastor of the rump congregation at Leith Walk, assisted for a few years by Robert in a makeshift attempt at achieving the ideal of a multiple pastorate.[128] In this capacity, Robert proved himself quite able; his nephew and biographer could vividly recall his exposition of the *Epistles of Peter* at a space of more than forty years. He continued to preach regularly after his removal in 1809 to an estate at Auchingray, Lanarkshire. Both in an Airdrie chapel linked with the Edinburgh Tabernacle and in a small meeting house erected for the

---

[123] A. Haldane, *Lives of the Haldanes*, 333-34.

[124] Philip, *Memoir of John Campbell*, 360, 361.

[125] Anderson, *Christopher Anderson*, 13.

[126] A. Haldane, *Lives of the Haldanes*, 344.

[127] A. Haldane, *Lives of the Haldanes*, 352; Donald Meek, 'The Doctrinal Basis of Christopher Anderson', 2, (privately circulated essay, 1989) states, 'the Tabernacle was the source of at least eight other churches in Edinburgh, most of them owing their origins to troubles within the Tabernacle'.

[128] A. Haldane, *Lives of the Haldanes*, 354.

tenants of his new estate, the older brother regularly gave expositions of the Scriptures.[129] These Lanarkshire years were also filled with efforts towards the supplying of Gaelic-speaking missionaries to the Highlands.[130]

Robert Haldane's trip to France might have proved to be nothing more than a six weeks' grand tour such as he had taken before the years of Revolution. He journeyed 'unacquainted with any individual and therefore unable to arrange any plan of action'.[131] He consequently despaired of finding any usefulness on arrival at Paris as he doubted that much Protestantism would have survived after the long history of persecution and revolutionary upheaval. Yet, unexpectedly, Haldane met an American gentleman named Hillhouse who recommended Geneva as a scene of endeavour and named two pastors in that city as contacts. Hillhouse added something else likely to stir Haldane's interest; in his view 'nearly the whole of Geneva's other pastors were Arians or Socinians'.[132]

Perhaps consistent with such an analysis, the initial visit to Geneva in mid-November was unproductive; it was followed by one to Berne, outside which the younger of the two persons recommended by Hillhouse was now serving as a pastor. This person, A.J. Galland (1792-1862), sought Haldane's teaching twelve hours a day for a week and in turn referred Haldane to a close pastoral acquaintance a short distance from Geneva.[133]

---

[129] A. Haldane, *Lives of the Haldanes*, 358, 360.

[130] David Bebbington, ed., *The Baptists in Scotland*, (Glasgow, 1988), 43.

[131] R. Haldane, *Letter to Bickersteth*, 2. It is highly significant that in 1839, twenty years after his return from the Continent, Haldane was still standing by this 'minimalist' perspective of how much vital Christianity had been remaining in Francophone Europe in the post-Napoleonic years. While noting that his old acquaintance, Thomas Haweis, had set out the same grim prospectus about European Protestantism in his 1801 *Impartial History of the Church of Christ*, and that in this case (in 1816) an American already resident in Paris had confirmed him in this opinion, it is nevertheless remarkable that Haldane never found reason to modify this original grim 'prognosis'. In this respect, Haldane strongly differed with most of his old associates in the London Missionary Society. They looked for and found reasons to expect that the gospel cause in Francophone Europe still had numerous supporters, whom they proposed to assist. Haldane's analysis of Europe, both initially and subsequently, was like the proverbial 'glass half-empty'.

[132] Haldane, *Letter to Bickersteth*, 3.

[133] See Haldane, *Letter to Bickersteth*, 3; and A. Haldane, *Lives of the Haldanes*, 393. Neither Haldane, *Letter*, nor his biographer, A. Haldane, *Lives of the Haldanes*, indicate that Galland had already gained a reputation for preaching the 'new birth' before his departure from Geneva for Berne. See Émile Guers, *Le Premier Réveil et la Premier Église Independante a Genève*, (Geneva: 1872), 61. Here, the present author believes, is evidence of the biographer's tendency to portray Francophone believers as being

Before returning to that city, however, Haldane proceeded to visit other Swiss cantons. He sought out the Englishwoman Miss Anna Greaves at Lausanne, who was rapidly gaining a reputation for her work of literature distribution. He also sought out 'the celebrated Baroness Krüdener' at Basle and found in her 'a spirit of charity but very little knowledge'.[134] He was subsequently preparing to depart from the Swiss cantons for Montauban, the 'Geneva of the Midi', in search of opportunity there.[135] His former involvement with the LMS and his familiarity with the reports furnished by the *Evangelical Magazine* would have made the significance of Montauban plain enough. But a second visit to Geneva set in motion a chain of events which would detain Haldane from his travels to the Midi for half a year.

The return visit was initially no more productive than the first. Two Prussian clergymen, a Professor Sack and his brother travelling homeward from London, provided Haldane with little satisfaction in conversation.[136] A visit with the recent ordinand Louis Gaussen (1790-1863) at the village of Satigny near Geneva was more productive; Gaussen had just recently 'submitted his faith to the great doctrines of the Scriptures' and found in Haldane encouragment for his young faith. Subsequently, Gaussen returned Haldane's visit in response to an invitation relayed by a young theological student, Jules Charles Rieu (1792-1821). A second conference with the senior minister, Moulinié (1757-1836), produced little of substance other than the statement that the city was in 'deplorable darkness'.[137] But the old minister did make a kind offer to show Mrs Haldane a scale model of the surrounding peaks the following morning. It was his inability to make good on this offer on account of physical weakness and his sending of an inquisitive divinity student, G.L. James (1790-1867), as his replacement that led to the deferral of all plans to proceed to Montauban. Haldane, finding the student ignorant concerning the gospel, spoke with him in his hired lodgings late into the night.

The young man was sufficiently intrigued by Haldane's command of biblical teaching that he returned next morning with another theological student. Haldane's opinion of both was that

had they been trained in the schools of Socrates or Plato, and enjoyed no other means of instruction, they could scarcely have been more ignorant of the doctrines

---

maximally dependent on their Scottish visitor. We would suggest that what goes unreported about Galland is as significant as what is reported.

[134] A. Haldane, *Lives of the Haldanes*, 395.
[135] A. Haldane, *Lives of the Haldanes*, 392.
[136] A. Haldane, *Lives of the Haldanes*, 391.
[137] A. Haldane, *Lives of the Haldanes*, 393, 391.

of the Gospel... To the Bible and its contents their studies had never been directed.[138]

These two (James and Rieu) in turn brought six additional students who began to pay return visits at all hours until Haldane proposed stated times of 6 to 8 p.m. three nights per week. Proceeding on this stabilized basis, the Scot was freer both to prepare lectures for the stated sessions and to converse with still additional students who called on him at Place Maurice, No. 19, Promenade St. Antoine. Paul's Epistle to the Romans formed the basis of his lectures to this group of eight for about two weeks, ending in mid-February 1817. At that time he began the lectures afresh due to the enlarged number of students desiring to take part. This course of expositions, delivered through a translator, lasted until May-June. In addition to those attending official lectures, numerous other persons both male and female came for instruction.[139]

It is important to note that Haldane was by no means alone in his endeavours among the students in this period. The two Prussians (with whom Haldane found conversation so unprofitable), the Lutheran minister of Geneva, M. Wendt, and Haldane were all active in a similar way. 'A learned doctor from New York and a faithful young minister' (whom we now know to be Dr John Mitchell Mason and Matthias Bruen) were also active with students and others in Geneva at the commencement of 1817. Student meetings involving up to fourteen students at a time were held in Mason's rooms as late as March 1817. Haldane and the Americans were themselves visitors in one another's apartments.[140]

The Genevan ecclesiastical establishment and the students who frequented Haldane's parlour had been agitated in November 1816 by the publication of H.L. Empeytaz's pamphlet, *Considérationes sur la Divinité de Jésus Christ*. Great sensation was stirred up by the pamphlet's claim—based on a survey of sermons printed in the city over a sixty-year period—that the Genevan pulpit's virtual silence regarding Christ's divinity indicated disbelief in this central affirmation of the faith. While Haldane's entry to Geneva was in fact quite independent of such developments, he was profoundly affected by the aftermath. Only two

---

[138] Haldane, *Letter to Bickersteth*, 4-5.

[139] Haldane, *Letter to Bickersteth*, 5.; and A. Haldane, *Lives of the Haldanes*, 399. Haldane read French fluently but spoke it haltingly. He relied upon students Rieu, Monod and James as translators.

[140] C. Malan, *The Conventicle of Rolle*, (1821, E.T. London: 1865), 109; S.C. Malan, *Life and Labours of C. Malan*, (London, 1869), 44-45; and John M. Mason, *Sermons, Lectures and Orations*, (Edinburgh, 1860); xii. Mason (1770-1829) was in Europe recuperating from an over-active term as New York City pastor of the Associate Reformed Presbyterian Church and Professor in Theology in that city's Columbia College. Mary D. Lundie, *Memoirs of Matthias Bruen*, (Edinburgh: 1832) 32.

theological students, Henri Pyt (1796-1835) and E. Guers (1794-1882), had declined to sign a student petition to the Venerable Company of Pastors protesting against the charges made by Empaytaz. The two, called before the Venerable Company to defend this implicit support for Empaytaz, cited the articles from the French Confession of La Rochelle (1559) bearing on the divinity of Christ. The Company, knowing it would be impolitic to contend against this historic creed, let the matter rest.[141]

This student body, which had in this way recently demonstrated its substantial support for the current teaching in the theological Academy, formed the audiences which waited on Haldane's expositions. The attendance of the students at these sessions was noted by their professors, with J.J.C. Chenevière (1783-1871), professor of dogmatics, taking down the names of participants.[142] Supposing a connection between the November publication of the Empeytaz pamphlet and Haldane's lectures, the Venerable Company responded with denunciatory sermons and the issuing of a pastoral regulation on 3 May 1817. This required that all prospective ordinands ('proposants') sign and all ministers and pastors abide by a promise to abstain from propounding their own opinions as to:

1. the manner in which the divine nature is united to the person of Jesus Christ;
2. original sin;
3. the manner in which grace operates, or efficacious grace; and,
4. predestination.

They also had to promise not to combat the opinion of any pastor or minister on these matters.[143]

But what teaching was it that provoked such restrictive measures as these? Haldane's own well-supported claim is that he took the Epistle to the Romans as his subject, expounded it and dilated on its great doctrines. He did not hesitate to name and confute Geneva's current theological aberrations.[144] However, it is not a simple task to establish the details of Haldane's expositions. The French edition of his Romans exposition, published at Montauban in 1819, was admittedly the product of an additional two years' study and reflection; therefore, it was no mere

---

[141] See Émile Guers, *Vie de Henri Pyt,* (Toulouse: 1850), 17; and Blanche Biéler, *Une Famille de Refuge* (Paris: 1930), 106.

[142] A. Haldane, *Lives of the Haldanes,* 402.

[143] The entire French original is printed in Henri Heyer, *L'Église de Genève: 1555-1909,* (Geneva: 1909), 119. We may note here that in the Genevan context, all ordained clergy were termed ministers. Only those attached to particular congregations were termed pastors.

[144] Haldane, *Letter to Bickersteth,* 5, 6.

transcript of what his Genevan auditors actually heard.[145] We would not go far wrong if we were to understand the notorious 'règlement' (pastoral regulation) of 3 May as summarizing the main thrust of Haldane's teaching, for there is little doubt that the instruction given at No. 19, Promenade St. Antoine, pilloried the current Genevan outlook on each issue.

The theological stance taken was above all biblicistic, with primary authority being attributed to chapter and verse of the biblical text. Bibles in the biblical and modern European languages lay open on the large table around which all gathered and to these the teacher would appeal. Frédéric Monod, an eager student participant in the sessions, would recall almost thirty years later that

> He answered every question by a prompt reference to various passages… He never wasted his time in arguing against our so-called reasonings but at once pointed with his finger to the Bible, adding the simple words, 'Look here—how readest thou? There it stands written with the finger of God'. He was, in the full sense of the word, a living concordance.[146]

In this biblicistic emphasis, Haldane was emulating his own mentor of three decades earlier, David Bogue.[147] In common with many evangelical Nonconformists of the period, Bogue and Haldane were confident that historic Protestant orthodoxy could best be maintained not by appeals to confessional statements but by direct appeal to the scriptural text. Haldane's biblicism, however, may well have advanced beyond that of his mentor. Haldane had recently crystallized his thoughts on the subject of revelation and inspiration in his two-volume *Evidences and Authority of the Divine Revelation* (1816), which he had seen through the press at Edinburgh immediately prior to his European journey. The work was not innovative in its argument for the necessity of a divine revelation committed to writing. In this area he maintained, with a myriad of others of his age, a biblicistic stance; i.e., that 'it is only from the revelation itself that the urgency of that necessity to man can be fully known'.[148] Humanity's estrangement from and way of return to God could only be properly grasped through God's self-communication.

---

[145] A. Haldane, *Lives of the Haldanes*, 450. The 1819 edition has proved unobtainable in the UK. We will refer to the expanded London edition of 1836.

[146] A. Haldane, *Lives of the Haldanes*, 403. The author has drawn on remarks which were given by Monod in the 1845 General Assembly of the Free Church of Scotland. See the *Free Church Assembly Reports*, (Edinburgh: 1845), 128-33.

[147] Terpstra, 'Bogue', 42-43.

[148] R. Haldane, *The Evidences and Authority of the Divine Revelation*, 2 vols. (Edinburgh: 1816) I, 4.

Haldane does seem to have been a trail-blazer, however, in his distancing himself from the widely-popular view held among eighteenth-century evangelicals that the divine revelation committed to Scripture had been written under varying and discernible degrees of inspiration; these were specified to be superintendence, elevation and suggestion.[149] Proceeding from the conviction that 'our knowledge of the inspiration of the Bible, like every other doctrine it contains, must be collected from itself', Haldane went on to argue that such 'degrees' of inspiration were no part of Scripture's self-description, and were, therefore, inadmissible. In fact, he stated,

> the Scriptures uniformly assert the highest degree of inspiration and give no intimation of any part of them being written under an inspiration of any kind but one.[150]

Haldane admitted that the Spirit of God might have communicated the revelation to the human writers in differing manners, yet insisted that inspiration was ultimately uniform.[151] Such views were not characteristic of all British evangelical Protestantism at this period; some proponents of the very notions Haldane repudiated nonetheless joined with him in mission work on behalf of Francophone Europe. But there is little doubt that Haldane communicated his pronounced views on biblical inspiration and authority to his auditors at 19, Promenade St. Antoine.[152] Moving from this foundational aspect of Haldane's theology to his more specific views, we may first consider 'the manner in which the divine nature is united to the person of Jesus Christ'. The latter was the first theological issue over which the 3 May 1817 pastoral regulation sought to bring about a moratorium of debate. We must note that Haldane had almost certainly left Scotland in the conviction that the Protestantism of Francophone Europe had largely lapsed from affirming the full deity of Jesus Christ. This perspective had only been strengthened

---

[149] Such 'degrees' of inspiration were distinguished by Philip Doddridge (1702-1751). Haldane's near contemporary, the Glasgow Secession theologian, John Dick (1764-1833), had used these distinctions circumspectly while attempting to defend a plenary inspiration of Scripture against deist skepticism. See J. Dick, *The Inspiration of Scripture*, (Edinburgh, 1800, 2nd revised edition Glasgow: 1803), 1-24. His own mentor similarly used this framework of 'degrees' in defending plenary inspiration, Bogue, *Lectures*, 370-71. For a vindication, particularly of Dick's use of these distinctions, see Donald Macleod's entry 'Systematic Theology' in Nigel M. de S. Cameron, ed. *Scottish Dictionary of Church History and Theology*, (Edinburgh: 1993), 811.

[150] R. Haldane, *Evidence*, I, 134-35.

[151] R. Haldane, *Evidence*, I, 134-35.

[152] We will turn to the question of the duplication of Haldane's views in some of his soon-prominent auditors in a following chapter.

by his contact with the American whom he had met at Paris. Was the conviction entirely justified? There is strong evidence to suggest that Haldane's 'verdict' on Geneva's theology was highly premature, and hindered him from exercising dispassionate judgement. One year earlier an anonymous correspondent had written to the London-based *Christian Observer* to extol the fervent evangelical preaching which he had heard from two Genevan preachers in a single Sunday. In the year of Haldane's visit, a correspondent to the same periodical reported that at least five of Geneva's twenty-five ministers were orthodox.[153] Furthermore, the biographer of one student (Merle D'Aubigné) who came to know Haldane intimately in early 1817 recorded the existence of four senior pastors known for their orthodoxy and piety serving in the city at that time.[154] Haldane's pre-commitment to independent action seems to have prevented him from either seeking a vital orientation from such sources in preparation, or striving to identify sympathetic ministers in the city on arrival at Geneva. Only from such a stance could he later remark of the students who gathered in his rooms and their preachers that

> While such was the deplorable state of religious instruction in the Theological Academy...nothing was heard from the pulpits of Geneva to compensate the students for this woeful defect.[155]

The effects of such a sweeping dismissal of the entire Company of Pastors were far-reaching. Yet, having admitted this, we must not overlook the kind of evidence which would have warranted wariness on Haldane's part. He claimed to have collected the clergy's arguments against what he taught as scriptural truth; he had certainly heard Professor Chenevière preach.[156] The latter, the professor of dogmatics who later sought to discredit Haldane by publishing 'A Summary of Theological Controversies Which Have Agitated Geneva' in a London periodical in 1824, could even then affirm no more than that 'each one of the pastors confessed that Jesus was a divine being'.[157] Haldane considered this view

---

[153] *Christian Observer* 14 (1815), 800-803. *Christian Observer*, 16 (1817), 713. These impressions were echoed in the *New Evangelical Magazine*, 4 (1818), 297.

[154] Biéler, *Une Famille*, 106, names Peschier of Coligny, Diodati of Cartigny, Naville of Chancy, and Cellérier of Satigny. Moulinié, to whom Haldane had been referred by Hillhouse at Paris, and who twice proved quite unhelpful, does not appear to have been endorsed by D'Aubigné to his daughter-biographer.

[155] R. Haldane, *Letter to Chenevière*, (Edinburgh: 1824), 21. The remark was a sweeping and unjustified generalization.

[156] See Haldane, *Letter to Bickersteth*, 6, and *Letter to Chenevière*, 23.

[157] J.J. Chenevière, 'A Summary of the Theological Controversies Which Have Recently Agitated Geneva', *Monthly Repository of Theological and General Literature*, 19 (London, 1824), 5.

to mean no more than that the Saviour was 'the first of created beings'.[158] In light of such vagaries, Haldane had made it his business while at Geneva to teach a robustly Trinitarian theology which accorded full deity to God the Son. Commenting on Romans 1:4 ('declared to be the Son of God with power'), he would later state,

> This expression, the Son of God, definitely imports Deity, as applied to Jesus Christ. It as properly denotes participation of the Divine nature as the contrasted expression, Son of Man, denotes participation of the human nature... The belief, then, of the import of this term is the substance of Christianity.[159]

In the second main point, the pastoral regulation of May 1817 had singled out the notion of original sin as being one about which contention should be curtailed. Haldane's interviews with various students led him promptly to conclude that they had been taught that men were born pure.[160] Young Merle D'Aubigné, who visited him privately, was for a long time unwilling to renounce the idea of the natural goodness of humanity. Haldane had himself heard Chenevière preach this doctrine.[161]

Commenting on Romans 5:12 ('Wherefore, as by one man sin entered the world, and death by sin and so death passed upon all men, for that all sinned'), Haldane stated,

> It is not that sin merely commenced by one, but that it came upon all the world from one. This is the only point of view in which it can be contrasted with Christ's righteousness. The meaning is that as Adam's sin came upon all men, so Christ's righteousness came upon all his posterity, or his people whom he represented.[162]

Now this, in combination with his emphasis upon sin as a present power within human life would have no doubt sounded novel to students whose ideas of theological anthropology probably owed more to Rousseau's *Émile* and other Enlightenment works than to biblical teaching.[163] Third, the pastoral regulation of May 1817 stipulated the question of 'the manner in which grace operated, or efficacious grace'. At stake here was the question of whether the Christian experience of grace is conscious experience. On such themes, alluded to in the eighth chapter of Romans,

---

[158] Haldane, *Letter to Bickersteth*, 6.

[159] See Haldane, *Letter to Chenevière*, 25, and *The Exposition of Romans*, 3 vols, (London: 1835), I, 37-38.

[160] Haldane, *Letter to Bickersteth*, 6.

[161] See Biéler, *Une Famille*, 111; Haldane, *Letter to Chenevière*, 23.

[162] Haldane, *Romans*, I, 445.

[163] Ami Bost, *Life of Félix Neff*, (London: 1855), 5, reports that Neff, a young convert and preacher of the Réveil period, had found his favourite reading material to be the works of Plutarch and Rousseau.

Haldane confessed to 'having been long detained'.[164] Commenting on Romans 8:28 ('to those who are the called according to his purpose'), he would write,

> This is a further description or characteristic of God's people. They are called not merely outwardly by the preaching of the Gospel, for this is common to them with unbelievers, but called also by the Spirit with an internal and effectual calling, and made willing in the day of God's power. They are called according to God's eternal purpose... It imports that their calling is solely the effect of grace.[165]

The fourth and final doctrine dealt with in the pastoral regulation, predestination, was also one which Haldane had taught with relish. From the ninth chapter of Romans he had taught that divine predestination to eternal life is quite absolute as illustrated in the case of Jacob and Esau. On Romans 9:13 ('Jacob have I loved, but Esau have I hated'), he would write,

> That the Apostle quotes these words in reference to Jacob and Esau personally is clear, since he speaks of the children before they were born. Jacob was loved before he was born, consequently before he was capable of doing good; and Esau was hated before he was born, consequently before he was capable of doing evil.[166]

When Haldane was subsequently upbraided by Professor Chenevière for being a 'rigid Calvinist', the Scot offered the rejoinder,

> What! Sir, are you afraid of Calvinism? Has the ghost of Calvin, whom you thought dead, and buried, and forgotten, appeared among you? Is he again raising his voice from the chair which he once occupied, but from which you had hoped that it would never more be heard, and are you greatly alarmed?[167]

The above is admittedly only our selective representation of Haldane's teaching assembled to demonstrate the essential congruence of the May 1817 regulations with the themes pursued in his lectures. The Scot later provided a summary of his teaching gathered round the foci of the

---

[164] Haldane, *Letter to Chenevière*, 34.

[165] Haldane, *Romans*, II, 345.

[166] Haldane, *Romans*, II, 461-62.

[167] See Chenevière, 'A Summary of Theological Controversies', 4; Haldane, *Letter to Chenevière*, 3. When one realizes that Haldane's published letter was penned as much with a view to influencing British public opinion as to changing the mind of his Genevan alter-ego, Haldane's use of the 'ghost of Calvin' idea is deeply suggestive. At very least it conveys Haldane's serene confidence that his own chequered ecclesiastical past notwithstanding, the position for which he is contending is indistinguishable from that of the late Reformer. Haldane's assumptions here, I suggest, were increasingly shared by the British constituency to whose attention he directed his letter.

charges levelled against him by Chenevière in 1824.[168] These charges were: 1) a preoccupation with the mysterious points of the Christian religion; 2) a diffusion of an exclusive and intolerant spirit; 3) a contempt of reason; and 4) a disparagement of good works.

Haldane indicated that he was unashamed of having taught 'mysterious points of the faith' if by this was meant the vital doctrines omitted from the Genevan pulpit:

> There was little or no allusion to the fall of man or his ruined condition by nature, and nothing of the necessity of the New Birth... The imputation of the Redeemer's righteousness and justification by his blood, were also set aside. The person and work of the Son of God were passed by and the work of the Spirit overlooked.[169]

Haldane had directed the attention of his Genevan hearers to these doctrines 'in the full conviction that they are conducive in the highest degree to the interests of holiness...'[170].

As for the charge that he had encouraged in the students an 'exclusive and intolerant spirit', Haldane was again unembarrassed. On the contrary, he had seen it as his duty to emphasize the exclusive claims of the Christian gospel for Jesus Christ as the only Saviour. Accordingly, Haldane freely admitted to having taught that one who denied the deity of Christ—such as an Arian—could not be Christian.[171] As for 'intolerance', he denied having encouraged any such outlook; he claimed instead to have taught a 'toleration among Christians in articles not fundamental'. Significantly, his imperviousness to the charge indicates that he did not perceive it as a fundamental criticism of his entire Genevan mission.

That he had encouraged the disparagement of reason in religion he partly admitted, insofar as he had consciously stressed the transcendence of God and his ways above the realm of human understanding.

> I can follow him [God] but one or two steps in his lowest and plainest works, till all becomes mystery and a matter of amazement to me. How shall I account for his nature or account for his actions...? The only proper use of our reason in reference to religion is to listen when God speaks.[172]

Had he also 'waged war with good works'? The answer must be 'yes' in settings where Haldane heard it contended that performance of these might contribute to human justification before God. But having shown in his exposition of Romans that this state of justification could be entered

---

[168] Chenevière, 'Summary of Theological Controversies', 4.

[169] Haldane, *Letter to Chenevière*, 22.

[170] Haldane, *Letter to Chenevière*, 39.

[171] Haldane, *Letter to Chenevière*, 41.

[172] Haldane, *Letter to Chenevière*, 45.

only by the exercise of faith in Christ who suffered for our sins, he had also 'urged upon the students and ministers at Geneva the duty of observing the holy precepts contained in the last six chapters of the Epistle to the Romans'.[173] We may, therefore, summarize Haldane's theological teaching at Geneva by saying that it was a presentation of the proven 'ruin and redemption' theology of the Evangelical Revival from a decidedly biblicistic and Calvinistic orientation. In its main essentials, it might have been equally well presented by any number of British preacher-theologians of that era.

It is evident from multiple accounts that what Haldane propounded in his lecture room he also applied in a searching personal manner in private conferences. Merle D'Aubigné, whose attachment to the notion of innate human goodness we have noted, was not only confronted with scriptural evidence to the contrary and made to grant the fact, but was then asked, 'Do you see this in your heart?'[174] Of the approximately twenty-five students who attended Haldane's lectures regularly (this being almost the entire body of local theological students), the greater part were deeply and permanently affected.[175]

Such an overview of his lectures on Romans leaves unexplored, however, the important question of whether Haldane promoted at Geneva the views on which his connexion of Scottish churches had foundered in 1808. This question is inextricably bound up with another: did Haldane promote ecclesiastical separation? As to the first, the family biographer insisted that there had been no such advocacy: 'He was silent in regard to all the questions which had agitated and divided the Congregational Churches of Scotland.'[176] But we must ask for independent testimony on the question.

Some light is shed on the first question through the testimony of Louis Gaussen. Gaussen had been an intimate of Haldane's during the winter of 1817, and was later professor of dogmatics in the alternative school of theology established in the city in 1831. After the death of Haldane in 1842, he recalled,

His wisdom at Geneva was indicated by the sobriety of his language, and by the pre-eminence he assigned to all that was essential. He was himself a Baptist, but never did I hear him utter a word on the subject. I have been told that our brother, M. Guers, at that time also a Baptist, wrote to him, 'We have baptised two persons' and

---

[173] Haldane, *Letter to Chenevière*, 54.

[174] Biéler, *Une Famille*, 111; and Malan, *Conventicle*, 113, 114.

[175] Correspondence of Louis Gaussen, quoted in A. Haldane, *Lives of the Haldanes*, 433. But such a claim may not be construed as meaning that this number of students necessarily dated their Christian conversions to the Haldane lectures. We will consider the diversity which existed in this matter in the following chapter.

[176] A. Haldane, *Lives of the Haldanes*, 425, 429, 431.

that he replied, 'I should have been much better pleased had you written that you had converted two persons'.[177]

As for the second question, the advocacy of ecclesiastical separation, we have the testimony of two Genevans who could hardly have held more varied sentiments about the overall effect of the Scot's visit. Both Professor J.J.C. Chenevière and the Rev. César Malan (1787-1864) portrayed Haldane as standing within their Reformed tradition— Chenevière depicting him as one belonging to a 'sect of the Reformed', and Malan incorrectly describing him as a Scots Presbyterian. The former, despite his intense distaste for Haldane's lecturing, placed blame for the separatist impulse upon his British successor at Geneva, Henry Drummond (1786-1860). It was Drummond, 'of less skill, but greater impetuosity who collected assemblies in which he distributed both instruction and money'.[178] César Malan was also called on to declare whether or not the visitor, Haldane, had shown himself to be a separatist. His questioners at Rolle, mid-way between Geneva and Lausanne, had evidently heard reports to this effect prior to 1821. Malan replied to them that Haldane had never 'advanced a single opinion that could lead me to suppose so. There is no evidence of separationism in his *Evidences* or *Romans.*'[179] Malan's testimony seems trustworthy; Malan did, after all, remain nominally a minister of the Genevan National Church until 1823 and was himself no friend of separatism when he visited Rolle. Is there, then, no basis for a charge of separatism?

The charge of the advocacy of separatism was rooted in the fact that a separatist church, later termed 'Bourg-de-Four', did emerge from Haldane's sojourn at Geneva. Haldane's biographer, cognizant of this fact and its potential for casting an unfavourable reflection upon his

---

[177] Correspondence of Louis Gaussen to Alexander Haldane, quoted in A. Haldane, *Lives of the Haldanes*, 431. The recollections of Gaussen are buttressed by the fact that the *Exposition of Romans* steadfastly avoids comment on the disputed aspects of Christian baptism at Romans 6:1-6, the major 'locus' of the doctrine in the Epistle. R. Haldane, *Romans*, II, 11-27. However, Gaussen, writing at a distance of twenty-five years, seems guilty of faulty memory. Émile Guers, to whom he refers as a Baptist, could not have held such baptismal views in spring 1817 as he was still then a candidate for the Genevan Reformed ministry. That he did hold such view *subsequent* to Haldane's visit and then wrote the Scot with news of baptismal 'successes' would seem to suggest the opposite conclusion than that drawn by Gaussen.

[178] See Chenevière, 'A Summary of Controversies', 1, 4; and Malan, *Conventicle*, 111. It is interesting to note that Chenevière's judgement about the culpability of Drummond, but not Haldane, to the charge of separatism was endorsed by A.L. Drummond in his *The Kirk and the Continent*, (Edinburgh: 1956), 89.

[179] Malan, *Conventicle*, 114-15.

uncle, Robert Haldane,[180] stressed that the latter had departed for and was resident in Montauban when the little separatist congregation assembled for its first formal administration of the Lord's Supper on 21 September 1817. Yet this, while true enough, is hardly the whole story. The biographer, in his determination to clear his uncle of the suspicion of complicity in this development, did not deal even-handedly with the eyewitness accounts on which his own narrative depends.

Émile Guers, author of *La Vie de Henri Pyt* (both author and subject were charter members of the 'Bourg-de-Four' congregation), was commended by the Haldane biographer for having preserved the 'dates and days connected with Robert Haldane with a pious care'.[181] Yet this very Guers, in addition to recording Haldane's departure for Montauban on 20 June 1817, states that the infant church, 'for which they had found a suitable organization', was founded on 18 May 1817 (though not constituted formally until 23 August). To this young church, Guers reported, Haldane had given the parting advice that they 'adopt for their rule nothing besides the Gospel'. Haldane was also credited with bringing union between his student followers and the surviving cell of Moravian believers in the city.[182] Moreover, Henri Pyt, writing to a friend in London in March 1818, reported that the young separatist congregation had received financial aid from Haldane at Montauban.[183] Thus, the very involvement which Haldane's biographer denied was openly acknowledged by Haldane's Genevan followers.

Too much should not be made of Haldane's encouragement to the nascent separatist church, which the family biographer, like Chenevière, was so prepared to attribute to 'the more rash and sanguine...Henry Drummond'.[184] We need not attribute to Haldane the separatist impulse itself. This orientation was plainly present in certain student's minds many months before his arrival. Empeytaz had published his pamphlet, *Considérationes sur la Divinité de Jésus Christ* (1816) after withdrawing from the student body of the faculty of theology. During the late 1816 sojourn of the Welsh artisan, Wilcox, an enlarged circle of seven persons observed the Lord's Supper in the dwelling of J.G. Gonthier (d.1823), another student of theology—all this well before Haldane's arrival.

But we must attribute to Haldane the quickening and strengthening of the impulse. The pastoral regulation of 3 May 1817 requiring a

---

[180] Alexander Haldane, the nephew and biographer, had himself chosen to forsake the legacy of controversy surrounding the Edinburgh Tabernacle at Leith Walk. It was most definitely separatist in tendency.

[181] A. Haldane, *Lives of the Haldanes*, 426,430

[182] Émile Guers, *La Vie de Henri Pyt*, (Toulouse : 1850), 24-25.

[183] Henri Pyt to Mr. A(nderson?), 7 March 1818, printed in *Christian Repository and Religious Register*, 3 (1818), 309-311.

[184] A. Haldane, *Lives of the Haldanes*, 429.

moratorium of preaching on selected doctrines found three of his more earnest pupils (Guers, Pyt and Gonthier) quite unambiguously opposed to the regulations *in toto*; the studies of all three were abruptly terminated.[185] The resolve to found a separate congregation emerged immediately after 3 May and in little more than two weeks the die was cast. It is here that we may justly suppose that Haldane, the somewhat circumspect lecturer, became a frank adviser to those who had drawn their own conclusion that a form of independency was to be pursued.

Where, then, may his hand be discerned? Certainly in the procedure followed in compiling the first membership roll for the young church. In a scene which might have been lifted from an *Evangelical Magazine* account of the constituting of a chapel membership, we read of two believing men, Henri Pyt and Antoine Porchat (1792-1861), accepting the declaration of one another's faith and then, as a committee of two, proceeding to hear declarations of faith made by others.[186] In what seems irrefutably a manifestation of a practice urged on the Scottish Haldane connexion in 1808, we find the new church comprised of not more than ten initial members yet led by three pastors, Méjanel, Gonthier and Pyt.[187]

It is possible that anti-paedobaptist sentiments had come to the fore in the minds of some of Haldane's student auditors quite independently of their teacher. However, the early prevalence of these sentiments among a segment of his auditors and within a segment of the young 'Bourg-de-Four' congregation is most simply explained by Haldane's disseminating of these views through conferences with enquirers.[188] Significantly, such sentiments cannot be attributed to contemporary Moravian thought or the illuminist circles of Madame de Krüdener—the two previous 'streams' on which the young church drew. Moravian theologian, A.G. Spangenberg (1704-1792), had presented a strong biblicist case for paedobaptism in the standard theological compendium, *An Exposition of Christian*

---

[185] Guers, *Vie de Pyt*, 14, 20.

[186] Guers, *Vie de Pyt*, 24.

[187] See A. Haldane, *Lives of the Haldanes*, 430; Guers, *Vie de Pyt*, 26. We may add that both sources report that César Malan, the silenced but not yet divested minister of the National Church, had declined the pastorate when offered to him alone. For a contemporary description of the services and ministry of the 'Bourg-de-Four' congregation, see Appendix B.

[188] British readers were informed of this diversity of baptismal views in the young congregation by Henri Pyt's correspondence of 7 March, 1818 reprinted in the *Christian Repository*, 3 (1818), 310. He indicated that both he and G(uers?) held to baptistic views. Ami Bost (1790-1874), who served the 'Bourg-de-Four' congregation as pastor both in 1821 and 1825-26, recorded in his *Mémoires Pouvant Servir à L'Histoire du Réveil Religieux*, 3 vols, (Paris, 1854), I, 379, that 'Haldane and Drummond had carried baptist views to Geneva'.

Doctrine (1778).[189] H.L. Empeytaz, the travelling chaplain of Krüdener, upon entering the joint pastorate of the 'Bourg-de-Four' church in March 1818, was for a time the solitary pastoral practitioner of paedobaptism in that congregation.[190]

We are also hard pressed to explain two other features of church life at 'Bourg-de-Four' without recourse to the Scottish precedents which the Haldane biographer claims were studiously avoided. These are the practice of mutual exhortation of Christians both on the Lord's Day and at weeknight services and the custom of weekly administration of the Lord's Supper. Both practices had been very much *de rigeur* in the Haldane connexion at 1808.[191] Both relate closely to Haldane's reported parting dictum to the 'Bourg-de-Four' nucleus—'adopt nothing as a rule apart from the gospel'.[192] Thus it would seem that Haldane's old zeal for the imitation of supposed apostolic practices had not been left at home in Scotland.

Contrary to what may be taken as special pleading on the part of the family biographer, then, it seems that Robert Haldane privately counselled and advised those bent on venturing into independency. The end result was a congregation which in its structures, style of worship and sacramental usage, was remarkably similar to those which the brothers Haldane had established in Scotland.[193] The young preachers were decidedly Calvinistic but, like their Scots mentor, ultimately committed to a kind of apostolic 'restoration'. The eyewitness and participant, Émile Guers, asked and then answered his own question:

---

[189] Spangenburg, *An Exposition*, 235. We note below at ch. 3. p. 136 the confessed influence of Spangenburg's published theology for the young students prior to Haldane's arrival.

[190] See Good, *Swiss Reformed Church*, 380-382; and Émile Guers, *Le Premier Réveil à Genève*, (Geneva, 1872), 202; Bost, *Memoires*, I, 379.

[191] Henri Pyt supplied a very full description of the young church's polity and format of worship to British readers within six months of the 18 May decision to form a church. See his letter of 4 November 1818 in *New Evangelical Magazine*, 4 (1818), 96. We reprint this at the end of this volume as Appendix B. T.C.F. Stunt, 'Geneva and the British Evangelicals in the Early Nineteenth Century', *Journal of Ecclesiastical History*, (hereafter *JEH*), 31.1 (1981), 36. It must be admitted that weekly observance of the Lord's Supper was practiced by many early nineteenth-century Congregational Independents whose gatherings would never have had the term 'restorationist' applied to them. It was this weekly observance for which Haldane had been an advocate in 1808 that raises the likelihood of his having passed on peculiar views to the infant congregation.

[192] Guers, *Vie de Pyt*, 24.

[193] In concluding this section, it is interesting to note that the Haldane biographer, while attempting to distance his uncle from the movement of separation, adopts a deeply hostile tone toward the Genevan National Church as soon as the separation has been described. 'Arian' promptly becomes the common adjective used in describing the church left by the separatists. A. Haldane, *Lives of the Haldanes*, 429-30.

Was this a return to Calvin? After falling so far there was needed not a return to Calvin but a return to Jesus and the apostles. They cast away the weight of human traditions, protestant or Roman, and the servile imitation of the churches of the sixteenth century.[194]

In late June during Haldane's final days in Geneva, there occurred a remarkable 'changing of the guard' comparable to that of Haldane's succeeding Wilcox, six months earlier. Henry Drummond, a banker and young convert to the Christian faith, arrived from Genoa to see the religious developments at Geneva for himself. The short overlap between Drummond's arrival and Haldane's departure was filled with hours of intensive reportage of the recent developments.[195] In these sessions, there was laid the basis for more than a decade of further cooperation in aid of Francophone Europe.

The Robert Haldane who reached Montauban in July 1817 was in certain respects an altered man from the one who had left Scotland the preceding October. He had now abandoned all thought of a 'six weeks' tour', he had gained considerable ability in conversational French and had acquired a sense of earnest direction about his work in Europe. He now aimed at the preparation of his *Evidences of Christianity* and *Romans* lectures for publication in the French language. Though ministry among students seems to have been no part of his original design in October 1816, it was now his settled expectation as he arrived in southern France. The attraction of Montauban for Haldane lay not in the city's size but in its school of theology which then had a student body of sixty-four.

He might well have been optimistic concerning the reception he would receive there. Though the theological faculty at Montauban was largely made up of theological graduates from Geneva and Lausanne, it had at the same time manifested an independent spirit. Geneva's own current retreat from trinitarianism had been rebuked when such views had been propounded at Montauban by the Genevan, Esaie Gasc, in 1812-13. British Protestants had received favourable reports of the college through such periodicals as the *Evangelical Magazine*.[196] Yet as one reads the narrative of the Haldane biographer, he encounters only the most begrudging acknowledgement of this improvement of theological climate:

---

[194] Guers, *Vie de Pyt*, 36-37.

[195] A. Haldane, *Lives of the Haldanes*, 426. That Drummond had heard the reverberations of Genevan developments in Genoa is some indication of how the ecclesiastical divisions of Geneva were noised abroad.

[196] E.g., *Evangelical Magazine*, 22 (1814), 328. We may refer also to the generally supportive comments of Clement Perrot, 'Memorial on the State of the Protestant Churches' (1815), n.p..

Nothing could be worse than the state of the Churches throughout France, but at Montauban itself the darkness was not quite so palpable as that which but a little while before had brooded over Geneva.[197]

There is at least an acknowledgement of the piety and orthodoxy of François Bonnard (1776-1838), professor of Hebrew, and Francois-Maurice Marzials (1779-1861), preacher and president of the Montauban consistory. The dean of the seminary, Daniel Encontre (1762-1818), had then recently been warmly commended to the directors of the London Missionary Society by Clement Perrot as

a man of unfeigned devotedness to the Redeemer. He is one of the best mathematicians in France and still more to be respected as one of the best theologians in that vast and demoralized country.[198]

At Encontre's untimely death in 1818, the *Evangelical Magazine* eulogized him as 'distinguished by a firm and enlightened attachment to the doctrines of the gospel (and) by a fervent piety'.[199]

Yet in Haldane's eyes, the professor was little more than 'a strong Arminian and very indistinct in his apprehensions of the truth' and 'enveloped in much of Pelagian or semi-Pelagian darkness, teaching grievous error'.[200] It may be argued that Haldane formed his impression over a protracted period and that he was thus the more perceptive judge; yet this would still not account for an astonishing lack of charity towards a well-meaning Protestant leader in a demanding situation.

Perhaps Haldane's negative impression of Encontre stemmed from Encontre's coolness towards the Scot. There is evidence that Encontre actually discouraged his students from group attendance at Haldane's rented quarters and that he distributed Haldane's reprint of Luther's *Letter to Erasmus on Justification* only after considerable deliberation.[201] Thus we read of no thrice-weekly expositions of Romans to crowded student assemblies at Montauban but of many individual callers, both ministers and students. In a more leisurely atmosphere than he had found in the Swiss city, he prepared his books and tracts for publication and succeeded in seeing an edition of the Bible through the press.[202] Here also

---

[197] A. Haldane, *Lives of the Haldanes*, 444.

[198] Perrot, 'Memorial', n.p..

[199] *Evangelical Magazine* 26 (1818), 574. The British public was able to gauge something of the fervour of Encontre's piety through the publication of a fervent address to his Montauban students in *The Christian Magazine or Evangelical Repository*, 12 (1818), 81-88.

[200] A. Haldane, *Lives of the Haldanes*, 446, 448.

[201] See Robert, *Les Églises Réformées*, 355-56; A. Haldane, *Lives of the Haldanes*, 449.

[202] A. Haldane, *Lives of the Haldanes*, 448.

he began to ponder the application of the methods and strategies utilized in Scotland by the late 'Society for the Propagation of the Gospel at Home' to the challenge of distributing the Scriptures and other religious literature in French Europe.

Robert Haldane departed from Montauban in August 1819. He left behind no cell of separatist Christians, as at Geneva, but a large supply of his *Evidences* and *Exposition of Romans* for distribution to students.[203] The Montauban ministry, though not surrounded by the controversy and notoriety of the earlier sojourn at Geneva, had nevertheless been conducted on the basis of the same two foundational assumptions.

First, Robert Haldane had acted consistently with a presumption that the existing Christian churches of Francophone Europe were guilty of the gravest departures from the historic faith. Admittedly, he shared this outlook with some of his British evangelical associates. Yet, he parted company from a great many of this number in his evident disbelief that a gradual reversal of this state of affairs had been in progress since at least the re-introduction of Christian worship in 1795 and the state recognition of Protestantism in 1802.

He consequently had treated with scepticism reports of the admittedly small yet growing number of orthodox and pious ministers of the gospel. Clement Perrot had informed the LMS that he knew personally of twenty to thirty men worthy of trust and that there were probably many more.[204] Haldane seems to have operated on the assumption that all of France contained a mere 'four or five besides those at Montauban and Toulouse'.[205] Accordingly, he refused to attend the Lord's Supper unless it was to be administered by one of the select group of ministers who enjoyed his personal trust. His lack of confidence in the faculty of theology at Montauban would shortly move him to fund theological training at Paris by tutors wholly responsible to himself.[206]

The difference of perspective is far broader than the differing estimates of evangelical strength would suggest. Robert Haldane, with his new associate Henry Drummond, in all their forthcoming organizational efforts on behalf of Europe, were entirely indisposed to expect their principles and convictions to be affirmed by the institutional church. On such assumptions, private or individual action seemed the only reasonable course.

A second foundational assumption flowed necessarily from the first. If Europe's churches were so far gone and if reports of gradual recovery were to be distrusted, there seemed to follow what we can only term a sense of personal indispensability (or in the case of organizational efforts,

---

[203] A. Haldane, *Lives of the Haldanes*, 436.

[204] Perrot, 'Memorial', n.p..

[205] A. Haldane, *Lives of the Haldanes*, 449.

[206] A. Haldane, *Lives of the Haldanes*, 453, 545.

corporate indispensability). It is evident that both Haldane and his biographer viewed Francophone Europe from this self-referential perspective. It was not the simple self-infatuation of Robert Haldane which led the biographer to write that

> the inanimate condition of the French churches continued, with scarcely a symptom of spiritual life, down to the conclusion of the war and the period when, in July 1817, Robert Haldane...presented himself at Montauban.[207]

The biographer would for identical reasons happily repeat the asssertion of Haldane's Montauban acquaintances that 'they traced the Revival in France to Robert Haldane'.[208] It was, instead, this sense of personal indispensability rooted in a profound mistrust of the institutional church.

British evangelicals after 1815 largely shared Robert Haldane's ethnocentrism. Britain had rescued Europe from Napoleonic despotism; now it was quite reasonably supposed that British endeavour would re-invigorate European Christianity. Yet British evangelicals did not necessarily share Haldane's outlook of utter mistrust of French Europe's churches or his supposition that only Britons and those directly responsible to them would be the means of setting things right. And therein lay the seed of the great tension which would complicate British missionary efforts to the Continent for the next three decades.

---

[207] A. Haldane, *Lives of the Haldanes*, 443.
[208] A. Haldane, *Lives of the Haldanes*, 449.

CHAPTER 3

Geneva's 'Réveil' and the Awakening of Francophone Europe

Geneva's Position of Precedence

Among the various religious awakenings in the Francophone territories formerly comprising the Napoleonic Empire, the precedence belongs to that of Geneva. Writing in 1968, the French historian, Henri Dubief, stated that

> Everyone agrees that the Réveil in French-speaking Europe emerged from Geneva in the years 1816-1820. There had been contributing movements in operation since 1810. From there, the first wave was diffused through French Switzerland and the Protestant Midi on a ground prepared by Quakers and Moravians.[1]

It is not immediately clear why Geneva should have taken the leading role in the 'Réveil'. The events and influences which led to the awakening at Geneva in 1817 (the illuministic teaching of Jung-Stillung, the itineration of Madame de Krüdener, and the fervent evangelization of the Moravians) were widespread throughout the Rhineland, Alsace, Switzerland, the Low Countries and eastern France. Nor was Geneva the only city to receive visits by British evangelicals.[2] Yet contemporary observers as well as modern authors concur in attributing to Geneva's

---

[1] Henri Dubief, 'Réflexions Sur Quelques Aspects du Premier Réveil'. *BSHPF*, 114 (1968), 374-75. That regions such as Belgium and the Netherlands did not make such direct acknowledgement will be noted in due course. A helpful older survey of the spiritual quickening experienced in the various Swiss cantons in the nineteenth century is found in James I. Good, *A History of the Swiss Reformed Church Since the Reformation*, (Philadelphia: 1913).

[2] E.g., the work of Miss Anna Greaves at Lausanne, referred to in ch. 2 and the extended service later rendered in southern France by the English Methodist, Charles Cook, described in Leon Maury, *Le Réveil Religieux dans L'Église Réformée à Genève et en France*, 2 vols, (Paris: 1892), I, 416-442.

'réveil' an influence over similar movements in the region.[3] We may justifiably ask why this should have been so.

We have noted above that the theological pre-eminence of Geneva was greatly enhanced by the decision of Napoleon's government in 1802 to make Geneva's Academy the centre for Reformed theological study in the Empire. This decision provided Swiss graduates of the Geneva Academy with wider opportunities for service than those available prior to Geneva's annexation in 1798. One such graduate was Abraham Lissignol (1784-1851), a Genevan student under Moravian influence, who was called to serve at Montpellier in 1809; he remained there until his death in 1851. By every reckoning, Lissignol was a father figure in the movement for the re-awakening of France. Of precisely the same outlook was Matthieu Miroglio (1792-1866), Genevan-born theological graduate of 1810, who gave long service at Besançon, France, from 1814-65.[4]

This enhanced influence of Geneva survived the restoration of Swiss independence in 1813. Thus from within the circle of students which Robert Haldane gathered in his salon at 19, Promenade St. Antoine, at least two went immediately upon graduation to French pastorates and found wide usefulness.[5]

Yet Geneva's Academy was more than just only the most prestigious place of ministerial preparation for the French Reformed Church; it had also never ceased to be the primary source of ministers for the churches of the Huguenot diaspora, spread across northern Europe.[6] Well prior to the Haldane sojourn at Geneva, theological students under Moravian influence had been called to serve French congregations in this Huguenot diaspora. Thus A.J. Galland (1792-1862), whom Émile Guers recalled as a strong preacher of the need for 'new birth' even prior to Haldane's visit,[7] was first called to a French congregation in the German-speaking Swiss canton of Berne, where he remained until 1824. Ami Bost (1790-

---

[3] E.g., J. Cart, *Histoire du Mouvement Religieux et Ecclesiastique dans le Canton de Vaud*, 3 vols, (Lausanne: 1890) I.i.142, 162, 163, 172, 230. Malan, *Life of Malan*, 284ff. E. Guers, *Le Premier Réveil et la Premier Église Independante à Genève*, (Geneva: 1872) 173, 196, 252, 323 ; Evans, 'The Contribution of Foreigners', 66, 67.

[4] For Lissignol, cf. H. Heyer, *L'Église de Genève*, (Geneva: 1909), 483, and for Miroglio, see pp. 491, 492. Robert, *Les Églises*, 565 ; and Guers, *Le Premier Réveil*, 43.

[5] These were Frédéric Monod (1794-1864) who settled at Paris and helped to found *Les Archives du Christianisme*, and César Bonifas (1794-1856), subsequently minister at Grenoble and later professor of Hebrew at Montauban. The younger brothers of Frédéric Monod, Guillaume and Adolphe, studied subsequently at the Geneva Academy, and were also caught up in the 'réveil'.

[6] Thus Jean Monod (1765-1836), father of Frédéric, Guillaume and Adophe, himself a Geneva graduate, had first served the French Church at Copenhagen (1794-1808) before a long pastorate at Paris.

[7] Guers, *Le Premier Réveil*, 61. We have noted above (p. 72) Haldane's extended consultation with Galland at Berne in autumn 1816.

1874), later the author of the invaluable eyewitness account of the period, *Mémoires Pouvant Servir à L'Histoire du Réveil Religieux* (3 vols, 1854), had secured a first ministerial posting at Moutiers-Grand Val, also in the canton of Berne, in 1816. Bost's contemporary and 'réveil' sympathizer, J.E. Coulin (1792-1869), had in that same year accepted a call to the French congregation at Frederica, Denmark.

This existing pattern of placement was repeated by the non-dissident[8] members of the Haldane circle. Gabriel Louis James (1790-1867), the theological student inadvertently introduced to Haldane because of the illness of the Genevan minister Moulinié,[9] was ordained in 1818 and called to be the minister of the French congregation at Breda, United Netherlands, in 1820. Jules Charles Rieu (1792-1821), who had assisted as a translator in the Haldane 'Romans' expositions, received his first call to the Frederica, Denmark, congregation recently served by J.E. Coulin (*supra*). There Rieu soon succumbed to a fatal illness.[10] Perhaps most striking in this vein is the manner in which a call was issued to the diligent postgraduate student at Berlin, Jean Henri Merle D'Aubigné (1794-1872), by the Huguenot congregation at Hamburg. The young scholar was content to let the matter be adjudicated for him by the Geneva 'Compagnie des Pasteurs' and, on their recommendation, he served the congregation from 1818 to 1823.[11] D'Aubigné's subsequent pastorate at Brussels (1823-30), while not strictly among the Huguenot diaspora, was nevertheless conducted in the French language and on the basis of his close association with Geneva.[12]

It is necessary to stress this diffusion of 'réveil' influence by means of Geneva's established theological dominance in order to show that the movement did not have an intrinsically separatist impulse. Most of the young ministers named above had earlier embraced the Moravian strategy for renewing the Church by gospel preaching combined with

---

[8] I.e., those who refused to adopt the beligerent stance of students H. Pyt, J.G. Gonthier and E. Guers in the face of the infamous 'règlement' of May 1817.

[9] Cf. ch. 2 *supra*, and Heyer, *L'Église de Genève*, 476.

[10] F. Monod, *Memorial of Jules Charlies Rieu* (translated from the French), (Edinburgh: 1854). A printed edition of Rieu's *Lettres* rapidly became staple reading among 'réveil' supporters. The *Memorial* makes plain that 'réveil' emphases were certainly transmitted to Frederica in Rieu's short ministry there.

[11] Biéler, *Une Famille de Refuge*, 137. D'Aubigné had gone from Geneva to Berlin in Autumn 1817. 'Réveil' themes were clearly the subject matter of the young minister's preaching, see pp. 152ff.

[12] The congregation's patron was William, King of the United Netherlands. In the congregation was Groen Van Prinsterer, secretary to the royal cabinet. Biéler, *Une Famille de Refuge*, 159.

careful cultivation of 'réunions', or cell groups of the awakened inside existing parish structures.[13]

If Geneva's theological prestige meant that its theological graduates were welcomed across northern Europe, there was also a second, and more weighty, factor about the city which made it an export centre of 'réveil' teaching and activity. This was the public controversy over the central doctrines of the Christian faith sparked by the 'règlement' of May 1817.[14] No doubt the 'Venerable Compagnie', which drafted the 'règlement', intended to encourage concord by insisting upon the avoidance of unseemly public theological debate. Yet the fruit of the 'règlement' was not concord but division. The historian of the 'réveil' period, Leon Maury, has observed that the 'règlement'

> was the starting point of a twenty-year struggle and its publication served to push the orthodox party on the road to separation... First Émile Guers, then also Henri Pyt and J.G. Gonthier refused to sign... Within the 'Compagnie' Moulinié, Cellérier Sr., and Demellayer refused to give their approbation to the 'règlement'. César Malan prevaricated and finally refused to give his approval and subscription... The practical result was just the opposite of the intended effect. It provoked the foundation of an independent church.[15]

While the conforming ministers and theological students of Geneva still enjoyed opportunities for service at home and elsewhere, those for whom the 'règlement' represented the point of no return as regards theological orthodoxy found themselves with few such opportunities. This fact explains in part why the fledgling independent congregation (later called the 'Bourg-de-Four') had at its earliest period a team of three pastors but only ten members.[16] More important, it explains why so many ordained and lay evangelists, colporteurs and schoolmasters left the community of Genevan evangelical dissidents to be dispersed throughout not only France and Francophone Switzerland, but also the Low Countries.

Because the 'règlement' of 1817 was viewed with hostility in at least the Canton of Vaud and the Reformed Church of France,[17] the Geneva

---

[13] The *ecclesia in ecclesiola* strategy is well described in A.J. Lewis, *Zinzendorf, Ecumenical Pioneer*, (London: 1962), 116ff. Guers *Le Premier Réveil*, 97, indicates that the inability of the Genevan dissidents to employ this strategy any longer after their separation from the National Church was a very major frustration. Bost's reliance on the Moravian strategy at Moutiers-Grand Val is reflected in his *Mémoires*, I, 53.

[14] We have printed the 'règlement' above, see p. 75.

[15] Maury, *Le Réveil Religieux*, I, 56, 57. So also Guers, *Le Premier Réveil*, 90, 91; and Cart, *Histoire*, I, 156.

[16] We have suggested in the previous chapter that the Haldanite practice of encouraging multiple ministry was also a factor.

[17] Maury, *Le Réveil*, I, 61, indicates that 'Orthodox Genevans distributed the règlement to foreign places. The faculty of Montauban, the periodicals of France and

dissidents often found a friendly reception when they ventured out from their canton. Thus, César Malan was active in the canton of Vaud as early as 1819. Henri Pyt terminated a short period of service in the young dissident congregation at Geneva in 1818 in order to accept a position as 'suffragant' (assistant) to the French Reformed pastor of Saverdun, Pierre-Cyprian Verge. Émile Guers, Pyt's biographer and Geneva co-pastor, seriously considered leaving Geneva for the same type of opportunity in France. This pattern of service with non-Genevan National Churches was also followed by the justly-famous Félix Neff (1798-1829), who assisted Reformed ministers at Grenoble and Mens before working alone at Freysinnières and Plombières in the High Alps.[18] This anomaly of persons allied to a dissident church at Geneva but attempting to labour in concert with National Churches beyond their own canton would later become the seedbed of considerable fricton and misunderstanding. The concerted attempt by Geneva's 'Venerable Compagnie' to resist the 'réveil' by the 'règlement' of May 1817 was plainly the largest single contributing factor to Geneva being a 'net exporter' of advocates of religious awakening.[19]

Events in Geneva 1816-1831

We have already had occasion to note that Robert Haldane had seriously underestimated the size of the orthodox minority within the Geneva 'Compagnie'.[20] This mis-appraisal later had very far-reaching implications for the future connection between Haldane's circle of British contacts and the 'réveil'. Yet Haldane's miscalculation notwithstanding, the orthodox minority was substantial in size and already in a process of asserting itself in the period preceding and concurrent with Haldane's visit. Pastor Charles Etienne Francois Moulinié (1757-1836), of whom Haldane had a poor impression even after two encounters, had already gained the admiration of the circle of theological students unsatisfied with the teaching in the Academy; he invited many students to his home for lectures on scriptural topics.[21] Moulinié and a second pastor of Geneva,

---

England all occupied themselves with it. The clergy of Vaud broke off contact with Geneva and the French Reformed Churches refused to receive candidates from Geneva who had signed it.

[18] Guers, *Vie de Pyt*, 41, and *Le Premier Réveil* 97; A. Bost, *Letters and Biography of Félix Neff*, (London: 1843), 57, 68, 171, 348.

[19] A similar but less-extensive dispersion of evangelical dissidents was to take place from Lausanne and the Canton of Vaud following 1821. But we will contend that Lausanne developments were accelerated by events at Geneva.

[20] See Ch. 2

[21] Guers, *Le Premier Réveil*, 49. This recognition of Moulinié's contribution is the more significant as it is from the pen of one driven into dissidence in May 1817. One is

Antoine Paul Pierre Demellayer (1765-1839), had defended H.L. Empeytaz when the 'Compagnie' questioned the correctness of his association with Baroness Krüdener in 1813.[22] A third Genevan pastor of the same generation, J.I.S. Cellérier (1753-1844), had responded to the publication of Empaytaz' explosive tract *Considérations Sur La Divinité de Jésus Christ* in August 1816 by preaching upon the divinity of Christ during the Christmas season of that year.[23] It was then considered unfashionable to do so. His successor in the parish of Satigny, F.S.R.L. Gaussen (1790-1863), though soon to be permanently influenced by the outlook of Haldane, was already in 1816 earning the disfavour of the 'Compagnie' for weekday afternoon expository lectures which drew citizens across parish boundaries.[24] Cellérier and Gaussen responded to the 'règlement' of 3 May 1817 by jointly republishing the *Second Helvetic Confession of Faith* (1566) with a preface on the importance of creeds.[25]

As a lecturer in apologetics and homiletics within the Academy, Jean-Louis Duby (1764-1849) earned the respect of pious theological students. He also served as first secretary of the Geneva Bible Society and supported the Geneva Mission Society from its foundation in 1821.[26] J.F.L. Peschier (1759-1831), pastor of the Genevan village of Cologny, was respected for his encyclopaedic learning, thoughtful lecturing in the Academy, and presidency of the Geneva Mission Society.[27] Alexandre Amedée Edouard Diodati (1787-1860), pastor at Avilly, was recognized as a 'friend of the gospel' though 'slightly tainted with mysticism'.[28] Francois Marc Louis Naville (1784-1846), pastor at Chancy, was also remembered as being 'firm in the faith'.[29]

---

left to wonder whether Haldane's mis-appraisal of the Genevan theological scene was not the combined result of a predisposition to think poorly of Francophone Protestantism, poor counsel received at Paris, and a paltry ability in conversational French. In the pages following, the 'table Biographique' furnished at the close of Heyer's *L'Église de Genève*, has proved invaluable.

[22] Maury, *Le Réveil Religieux*, I, 34. Guers, *Le Réveil*, 20, indicates Demellayer's considerable influence over H.L. Empeytaz.

[23] Maury, *Le Réveil Religieux*, I, 51. The aim of Cellérier in this was evidently that of underlining the essential truthfulness of Empeytaz's charge that most Geneva clergy now doubted Christ's deity. The charge would at least not 'stick' to him.

[24] Bost, *Mémoires*, I, 35. Two hundred persons eventually attended these gatherings before the Compagnie intervened.

[25] Bost, *Mémoires*, I, 35

[26] Guers, *Le Premier Réveil*, 59 ; Maury, *Le Réveil*, I, 27.

[27] Guers, *Le Premier Réveil*, 24 ; Maury, *Le Réveil*, I, 27.

[28] The phrase is that of Guers, *Le Premier Réveil*, 24. Maury, *Le Réveil*, I. 27.

[29] Biéler, *Une Famille*, 106. The recollection was in this instance that of Merle D'Aubigné.

The existence of this sizeable group of pastors sympathetic to orthodox Christianity within the Geneva 'Compagnie' in this period goes far to explain several developments otherwise difficult to account for. First, the majority of that circle of between twenty and thirty theological students who thronged Haldane's apartments for the Romans expositions did find a way to negotiate their way through the 'shoals' presented by the 'règlement' of May 1817 and to be ordained as ministers.[30] That this was a very difficult process for young men with newly-heightened doctrinal sensitivity is plain. Young Merle D'Aubigné confided to his diary at the time, 'After conscientious examination of the issues, I have believed it necessary to make this agreement (to abide by the "règlement")'.[31]

It is difficult to understand how the zealous young ordinand could have consented to abide by the 'règlement' were it not for the encouragement to do so provided by the orthodox minority in the 'Compagnie'.[32] Some of this number worked to soften the terms of subscription in order to stop other candidates from being driven into dissidence.[33] It is against this backdrop that we should understand the prevaricating activity of César Malan (1787-1864). Barred by the 'Compagnie' from preaching in any city pulpit of the National Church after an inflammatory sermon on justification by faith on 8 March, 1817, the young minister's[34] suspension was only compounded by the promulgation of the 'règlement' on 3 May. Refusal to conform to the 'règlement' kept Malan out of city pulpits until May, 1818. Then, in response to the blandishments of J.I.S. Cellérier, he submitted and offered the 'Compagnie' a fawning apology for his earlier extremism. The liberty to preach thus gained was extremely short-lived; further sermons contrary to the taste of the 'Compagnie' meant that an absolute ban was imposed in August 1818 and never lifted.[35] Although Malan preferred to be loyal to the Genevan National Church, he was driven into *de facto* secession in order to maintain a preaching ministry.

---

[30] E.g., James, Rieu, Bonifas, D'Aubigné, Monod, etc. Yet it is perhaps significant that not one of these persons lingered to serve at Geneva, but all dispersed to serve Francophone churches elsewhere. Biéler, *Une Famille,* 115, hints at this deliberate distancing from Geneva.

[31] Biéler, *Une Famille,* 115. The entry indicates a careful weighing of the interpretation of the 'règlement'.

[32] As it was, several of this minority witheld their own consent to abide by the articles. Cf. footnote 15, above.

[33] Biéler, *Une Famille,* 115, names J.I.S. Cellérier and Jean Heyer (1773-1859) as ministers active in this way. See also Malan, *Life of Malan,* 67.

[34] I.e., minister without charge. The title 'pastor' designated a minister linked to a particular congregation.

[35] Malan, *Life,* 67-70.

A Sunday School and Sunday gathering for edification (both outside the stated city hours for church services) soon led to the establishment of a congregation which met in a chapel erected on Malan's own property in the suburb of Pré L'Évêque. The 'Église du Témoignage' was erected in 1820 with the assistance of concerned Christians in Germany, England, Scotland, Ireland, France, America and Switzerland, and it was soon full to capacity. Malan's whole outlook was one of all possible continuity with the Reformed traditions of Geneva and this stance made his chapel an acceptable alternative to the National Church, particularly for persons of means who wished to attend elsewhere.[36]

However, the opening of the chapel and Malan's eventual celebration of marriages and administration of the sacraments there, precipitated the final break between Malan and the canton's 'Compagnie'. In July 1823, the 'Compagnie' suspended him from the ministry and insisted on treating him as an ordinary citizen.[37] With some gallantry, 'Compagnie' member, Louis Gaussen, stood to grasp the hand of Malan as he departed from the awkward scene of the final suspension.[38] Malan's suspension had the dual effect both of making him more dependent upon the moral and financial support of foreign Christians and of narrowing the actual distance between himself and dissidents of 'Bourg-de-Four'.[39]

The total suspension notwithstanding, the gathered congregation at the 'Église du Témoignage' grew steadily until its capacity was taxed to the limit. After 1830, however, the chapel began to experience steady decline; a call by Malan for a vote of confidence from his congregation in that year saw a third of the members and adherents depart; they immediately re-affiliated with the original dissident congregation at 'Bourg-de-Four'. At the root of the separation lay dissatisfaction with Malan's high-Calvinism in the pulpit and his autocratic manner in directing the affairs of an ostensibly Presbyterian congregation. From the year of the rupture, Malan gave himself more fully to itineration outside the borders of canton Geneva.[40]

---

[36] Malan, *Life,* 116, 154; Good, *History,* 389; Maury, *Le Réveil,* I, 122. The American clergyman, W.B. Sprague, visited the chapel in 1828 and found 250 persons in attendance. W.B Sprague, *Letters from Europe,* (New York: 1828), 25.

[37] Malan, *Life,* 100.

[38] Malan, *Life,* 96. Gaussen's role as builder of a Genevan evangelical coalition was here present in germinal form.

[39] This strengthening of foreign ties is elaborated in the following chapter. For the moment, we may simply note the impressive outpouring of financial support directed towards Malan from seven nations. Malan had earlier been offered the founding pastorate of the Bourg-de-Four dissident congregation but declined it, partly due to his hopes of regaining usefulness within the National Church.

[40] Malan, *Life,* 259; Good, *History,* 389.

The suspension of Malan by the 'Compagnie' in the period 1817-23 was, however, not wholly typical of that body's actions before 1831. Responding to the widespread complaint that the curriculum of the Academy paid insufficient attention to biblical study[41] (as opposed to biblical languages) the 'Compagnie' appointed Jacob Elisée Cellérier (1785-1862)[42] as honorary professor of biblical criticism in 1824. The appointment gained widespread approval. National Church ministers Gaussen, Coulin and Diodati were at this time unopposed by the 'Compagnie' in their efforts to inaugurate the Geneva Misssionary Society in 1821. Initially linked to the pioneering Basle Missionary Society, the Genevan society welcomed the support of dissidents as well as National Church members.[43]

Yet these encouraging signs were matched by others of a most unsettling type. J.J.C. Chenevière (1783-1871), the Academy's professor of theology from 1817, chose to counter the efforts of Gaussen and Cellérier, Sr, in republishing the old *Second Helvetic Confession* (1566); his counterblow was a tract entitled *Sur Les Causes Qui Retardent Le Progrès De La Théologie Chez Les Réformés* (1819). In the young professor's view, appeals to the Reformed confessions of the sixteenth century were anachronistic and a definite 'brake' on progress.[44]

Controversy increasingly gathered round Gaussen in the following decade. The city's Mission Society came increasingly under the domination of pastors whom Gaussen, a founder, viewed as unorthodox; in 1828 he departed from the Society with his supporters.[45] About this time, Gaussen (still pastor at Satigny) also fell foul of the 'Compagnie' for his refusal to utilize the revised catechism of 1814 (which he viewed as doctrinally suspect) for the training of children. The dispute had two major consequences. First, Gaussen's refusal to comply with the 'Compagnie's' directives regarding mandatory use of the catechism and his insistence on appealing to the civil courts in the matter led to his total exclusion from all sessions from that church assembly for one year.

---

[41] This charge was later echoed by Bost, *Mémoires*, I, 25; 'one never opened the bible in our lecture rooms. The book was unused and unknown.'

[42] Cellérier, son of the senior minister of Satigny, was ordained in 1808 and was professor of oriental languages in the college preparatory to the Academy, 1816-54. Heyer, *L'Église de Genève*, 436.

[43] Good, *History*, 384; Maury, *Le Réveil*, I, 149.

[44] Chenevière drew two replies: one was a pacific rejoinder by A.J. Galland (cf. p. 72 *supra*), then French minister at Berne; a second came from the pen of L.A. Curtat, 'doyen' of the company of pastors of Vaud. See Cart, *Histoire*, I, 150.

[45] To this date, the Missionary Society had permitted participation by the dissident Christians of the city. With Gaussen's departure, this participation was halted. Maury, *Le Réveil*, I, 151. Wemyss, *Le Réveil*, 192, indicates that Gaussen was one of four National Church ministers to depart from the society at this point. Names are not supplied.

Secondly, Gaussen and his supporters in the dispute (many of whom were high-placed members of Genevan society) then founded the Evangelical Society of Geneva. A.J. Galland, the Genevan minister at Berne who had since 1824 worked on behalf of the Paris Missionary Society at both Paris and Lausanne, was one of the founding members of the new Evangelical Society. Four other founders were members of the Genevan Council of State.[46]

The Evangelical Society, inaugurated in January, 1831 distributed tracts and Bibles, promoted foreign missions, and carried out evangelization within the canton.[47] The society soon began holding Sunday evening preaching services (conflicting with no stated service in the National Church), a Sunday School, a day school founded on evangelical principles, and a monthly missionary meeting.[48]

The work of the Evangelical Society of Geneva provoked a strong reaction from the 'Compagnie', which now entrusted to its theological professors the launching of a religious periodical, *Le Protestant de Genève*, in 1831. All faculty members, with the exception of J.L. Duby, contributed to this periodical which warned its readership of the dangers of 'methodism' and decried the fixation of 'réveil' supporters with the theology of the sixteenth century. In the same year, Prof. J.J.C. Chenevière published various lectures in theology which many felt substantiated long-standing fears that he had retreated from trinitarianism.[49] Chenevière's lectures provided some justification for the launching of a new Evangelical School of Theology by the Geneva Evangelical Society.[50]

So sizeable and influential was this movement of 1831, that it is now regarded as constituting a second 'wave' of the 'réveil' movement in Geneva and abroad.[51] At Geneva the special meeting place erected in 1834 for the activities of this Society (L'Oratoire) was soon filled to its capacity of 1,000 for Sunday services. The leadership of L'Oratoire maintained a continuity of doctrine, liturgy and ministerial dress with the

---

[46] Maury, *Le Réveil*, I, 158.

[47] Maury, *Le Réveil*, I, 153-58; Good, *History*, 461.

[48] Maury, *Le Réveil*, I, 159. Many of these activities took place in a rented facility on the 'Rue de Chanoines' which was utilized until 1834.

[49] The published lectures were entitled *Essais Théologiques*, (Geneva: 1831-34). The separate published lectures were re-issued together as *Dogmatiques Chrétiennes*, (Geneva: 1840).

[50] Of which more below. Cf. Good, *History*, 461. Involvement in this scheme brought Merle D'Aubigné a total suspension from preaching in Geneva's established pulpits. Gaussen was formally excluded from the Genevan ministry in 1832. Heyer, *L'Église de Genève*, 468, 488.

[51] Guers, *Notice Historique*, 25; Maury, *Le Réveil*, I, 176; Smith, *British Nonconformists and Swiss Dissidents*, 77; Biéler, *Une Famille*, 187, 199.

Genevan National Church's tradition. While at first no sacraments were administered and no gatherings assembled during hours of services in the National Church, by the mid-1830s such restrictions were allowed to lapse and L'Oratoire gradually took on the character of an independent church consciously in the Reformed tradition.[52]

The greatest initial impetus for the 'réveil' at Geneva, however, came from the dissident church initially called 'La Pétite Église', but soon known as 'Bourg-de-Four'.[53] It is not immediately apparent why this dissident church, led by Henri Pyt, J.G. Gonthier and Pierre Méjanel, emerged at all when we remember that the largest portion of the circle of students and other persons who had frequented Robert Haldane's lectures on Romans declined to become separatists.[54] As almost all of these shared an earlier exposure to Moravian influences, we may not attribute the separatist impulse to this source with any degree of certainty. Indeed, the young dissidents themselves soon recognized that their whole prior orientation to the Moravian pattern of church renewal was now of little use to them, determined as they were to stand apart from the National Church on account of the restrictive 'règlement'. Émile Guers later recalled the time of upheaval and wrote,

> We, having withdrawn from the academy, were cast on the way of dissidence. Meanwhile, we knew nothing as of yet of this outlook other than the system of Spener and the Moravians—little churches within large—and we asked nothing more. We were so little inclined towards separation from the national church that I turned my eyes to France thinking I would volunteer to accept a post as pastor or 'suffragant' in a consistorial church; this is what my friend Pyt did the following year. Gonthier stood with us in this.[55]

But separate they did, albeit without the company of most friends in the Haldane circle. Fortified by the Scot's invigorating teaching, they now wished to distance themselves from what they perceived as the open abuses of their National Church. They were repelled 'as much by the communion as by the preaching, for the Supper was most often

---

[52] Maury, *Le Réveil*, I, 176. From 1837, chief minister of the Oratoire congregation was J.A.S. Pilet, a Vaudois, who served until his death in 1861.

[53] This locale of Geneva, from which the congregation took its name, was in fact the fourth venue at which the young church met. It located there in 1818, having assembled earlier in a schoolroom in the section of the city known as 'Croix d'Or, then in an inn called the Écu de France, and in the neighbourhood of Rive. Cart, *Histoire*, I, 160 ; Guers, *Le Premier Réveil*, 107.

[54] See p. 84 above.

[55] Guers, *Le Premier Réveil*, 97, 98 , and *Notice Historique*, 15. By 'consistorial', Guers simply meant the French Reformed Church as locally administered by government-regulated consistories.

distributed by men who did not believe in redemption'.[56] In refusing to
abide by the 'règlement' of 1817, Pyt, Gonthier, and Guers soon found
themselves part of a circle of persons (the majority of whom were not
students) who absented themselves from the stated worship services in
their city's Established Churches. In May 1817, these persons formed
themselves into 'a simple Christian association lacking all ecclesiastical
character'.[57] The association, established on the principle that only
persons of undoubted Christian faith might be admitted, proceeded with
the approbation, though not the involvement, of Robert Haldane; the
latter departed Geneva on 20 June 1817.[58]

This association, now comprised of at least six members, and with the
eager involvement of Henry Drummond,[59] constituted itself into a church
on 23 August. Two days later the membership assembled in
Drummond's lodgings where they were joined by César Malan, Pierre
Méjanel and Marc Dejoux. A multiple pastorate was envisioned from the
first and the unpalatability of this plan was one reason (among others)
why Malan (the first choice of the membership for such a pastoral team)
declined the request.[60] Pierre Méjanel, the Montauban minister who had
recently arrived via London,[61] was then chosen in company with Henri
Pyt and J.G. Gonthier to comprise the multiple pastorate. The multiple
pastorate was no doubt meant to emulate apostolic precedent; it also
enabled the young church to maintain a feverish level of activity with
preaching services daily and three assemblies each Lord's day.

When Méjanel's preaching gifts proved more slender than expected, a
fourth preacher, Henri Empeytaz, was called to assist in November 1817.
Empeytaz, ordained at Ban de la Roche by the renowned Oberlin, while
travelling as chaplain to Madame Krüdener, was returning to Geneva after
an absence of three years. He prudently studied the affairs of the new
church for six months before openly identifying himself with it and
accepting its call in April 1818. By this juncture, Méjanel had been

---

[56] Guers, *Le Premier Réveil*, 97.

[57] Guers, *Notice Historique*, 15 , and *Le Premier Réveil*, 99.

[58] Guers, *Le Premier*, 99, 100. Haldane's non-participation in the fledgling
association did not, however, rule out the supplying of advice both before and after his
departure for Montauban. See also ch. 2, p. 86 *supra*.

[59] Ch. 2. 87 *supra*; Guers, *Le Premier*, 104.

[60] Guers, *Le Premier Réveil*, 108. Malan, though in cordial fellowship with the leaders
of the new church at this stage (labouring as they all were in opposition to the
'règlement'), deeply disagreed with their attempt to found everything on apostolic
precedent.

[61] Pierre Méjanel's allegiance to the new church can only partly be explained by the
French Reformed Church's clear reaction against the 'règlement' of May. His own
separatistic and erratic tendencies became most clear after his expulsion from Geneva and
subsequent residence at Paris.

required to leave Geneva on order of the Council of State, while Henri Pyt had departed to commence a pastoral assistantship at Saverdun; the original pastoral team was reduced to J.G. Gonthier, who was then joined by Émile Guers.[62]

The energetic preaching of the gospel by the team of dissident ministers was by no means the sum total of the young congregation's outreach. The members of the little church engaged in door-to-door visitation on Sunday afternoons and offered literature to interested persons. Initially, the literature distributed consisted simply of translations of available English tracts and booklets. Soon, however, the little church was distributing a journal of its own production, entitled *Le Magazin Évangélique*.[63] It was by design a missionary church which sent out its members into the districts of Geneva and Vaud to carry the evangelical message to places where it seemed to be lacking.[64] Such aggressive measures brought growth which necessitated multiple changes of venue for Sunday assembly. It was just as the young congregation was in process of relocating to the new location in 'Bourg-de-Four' in July, 1818, that violent persecution and harassment broke out against them.[65]

But this persecution at the hands of jeering mobs and in the columns of a hostile press did nothing to halt the growth of the young church. From 1820, the congregation was swelled by the affiliation with them of the entire remaining Moravian circle in Geneva.[66] By the year 1823, 300 were in membership, drawn primarily from the labouring and artisan classes.[67] The accession of numerous persons previously affiliated with Malan's 'Église du Témoignage' to 'Bourg-de-Four' in 1830 soon

---

[62] Guers, *Le Premier*, 139. It is interesting to note that Guers, the dear friend and promoter of Empeytaz as a prospective member of the pastoral team, yet observed (p. 110) that, at his return from touring, 'in Bible knowledge, Empeytaz stood where we had before our exposure to Haldane'.

[63] Guers, *Le Premier*, 231, 222. Among those early translations were Robert Haldane's *Emmanuel, or Scriptural Views of Jesus Christ* (n.d.), and Thomas Scott's *Force of Truth* (1779). From 1819-22, Guers edited *Le Magazin Évangélique*, a missionary magazine modelled on its London namesake. See Guers, *Le Premier*, 139. According to the *New Evangelical Magazine*, 5 (1819), 263, the Geneva-produced counterpart was soon for sale in Lausanne, Yverdon, Berne, Neuchâtel, Basle, Paris, Brussels and London. The magazine reported that the initiative for the launching of the magazine had come from the late renowned Lutheran minister of Ban de la Roche, Jean Frédéric Oberlin.

[64] Guers. *Notice Historique*, 21; Smith, *British Nonconformists*, 46. In time, a daughter congregation was begun in the suburb of Carouge.

[65] Guers, *Le Premier*, 140 ; Wemyss, *Le Réveil*, 90.

[66] Guers, *Le Premier*, 177. The re-affiliation was approved by the Moravian leadership at Herrnhut.

[67] Guers, *Le Premier*, 109, 248; Wemyss, *Le Réveil*, 90

created a situation in which a larger hall was required.[68] Built with substantial British financing and opened in 1839,[69] the congregation was now re-named 'La Pélisserie'.

Steady growth continued until the year 1842, when sixty members withdrew promptly and without warning under the influence of the strident teaching of the Englishman, John Nelson Darby.[70] This unforeseen development so demoralized the congregation that it was rendered instantly more amenable to co-operative evangelical schemes being pursued by the Evangelical Society of Geneva and its congregation meeting in L'Oratoire.

The preceding two decades of steady growth had given this primary dissident congregation of Geneva a considerable influence within Switzerland and eastern France. Initially too poor to underwrite the cost of commissioning its own members as missionaries to the neighbouring regions of Switzerland and France, it co-operated to the full with the London-based Continental Society for the Diffusion of Religious Knowledge for this purpose.[71] Pierre Méjanel, member of the dissident congregation's original pastoral team, was named the Continental Society's first agent in France within two months of his expulsion from Geneva in March 1818.[72] Henri Pyt, a second member of that pastoral team, himself entered the society's service in spring 1819. Émile Guers, who entered the joint pastorate to fill the void created by the departure of the aforementioned duo, served the London Society as general agent for France until the late 1820s. Yet another person, subsequently a member of the 'Bourg-de-Four' pastorate, Ami Bost, served the society as itinerating agent during two separate periods.[73] The congregation's involvement with the Continental Society was not, however, limited to the

---

[68] Good, *History*, 389, estimated this number to have comprised one third of Malan's total congregation.

[69] Guers, *Le Premier*, 330, 333, indicates that £563 towards the cost was collected from a mere handful of concerned women in England.

[70] Darby's destructive Swiss activity is helpfully surveyed in C.S. Smith, 'J.N. Darby in Switzerland', *The Christian Brethren Review Journal*, 34 (1983), 53-94.

[71] The development of which is described in the following chapter.

[72] The society, until then a mere notion which had been taking shape in the minds of Henry Drummond, Robert Haldane and their intimate friends, seems to have been precipitated into existence by Méjanel's banishment from Geneva and return to his native France.

[73] Bost's activity for the society is in many ways instructive. In his *Mémoires* we read of fund-raising itineration in England (I, 310ff), extensive preaching activity among the Moravians of the Rhine region (I, 126), contact with evangelical Catholicism (I, 198) and attempts to set up European affiliates for the Society (I, 206). His second period of service was initiated at his own request (II, 8, 9).

ranks of its ministers; at least six members of that church served as missionaries in France under Continental Society auspices.[74]

As the Bourg-de-Four congregation grew in numbers and influence in its second decade of existence, it began to be less wholly reliant upon the missionary strategies and funding of the London-based society. Thus, by 1829, it took the initiative and called a conference at Lyons for sympathetic ministers and missionaries 'in order to discover the best means of advancing the kingdom in neighbouring places'.[75] Of twenty persons in attendance, only seven were Continental Society agents. In the same year, Bourg-de-Four determined to launch a Missionary Training Institute for preparing its own popular evangelists and missionary schoolmasters.[76]

As in regional evangelization, so also in global missionary efforts, 'Bourg-de-Four' demonstrated a readiness to move from participation in the schemes of others towards launching its own missionary enterprises. Thus, from 1819, the infant congregation heartily supported first the efforts of the Basle Missionary Society and then the Genevan Missionary Society (led by National Church ministers, Gaussen and Coulin). When the latter came under the direction of unsympathetic elements in the National Church in 1829, 'Bourg-de-Four' threw its not inconsiderable weight behind the Paris Missionary Society and substantially assisted the latter to send its first three workers to Basutoland, South Africa. By the mid-1830s, the congregation was commissioning its own members for independent missionary labour abroad.[77]

---

[74] Evans, 'The Contribution of Foreigners', 676. The most illustrious of these, surely, was Félix Neff. The six were engaged in itinerant preaching, literature distribution, and school teaching. When it is noted that the Continental Society never employed more than thirty-one agents at any one time (*infra*, p. 172) the 'Bourg-de-Four' component will be seen in its true significance.

[75] Guers, *Le Premier Réveil*, 323. The host of the conference would seem to have been Adolphe Monod, then serving as a minister of the National Church at Lyons. Guers records his attendance.

[76] Guers, *Le Premier Réveil*, 291. The institute continued in existence until the disruption created by the rise of militant Darbyism. See p. 341.

[77] Guers, *Le Premier Réveil*, 242, 245. Rodolphe de Rodt, formerly of Berne, was thus commissioned to India in 1835 by the congregation. Further information regarding de Rodt is provided by Stunt, *From Awakening*, 87-89, 301, 302. After 1842, the congregation (now La Pélisserie) commissioned three married couples and two single men for missionary work in the region surrounding Montreal, Lower Canada, see p. 341. The 'réveil' missionary concern for Lower Canada (today's Quebec) is described by Robert Merril Black, 'Anglicans and French-Canadian Evangelism 1839-1848', *Journal of the Canadian Church History Society*, 26.1 (1984), 18-33; Randall Balmer and Catherine Randall,'"Her Duty to Canada": Henriette Feller and French Protestantism in Quebec', *Church History,* 70.1, (2001), 49-72; Glenn Scorgie, 'The French Canadian Mission

The same progression may be observed in the congregation's ordering of its internal affairs. Following the advice of Robert Haldane that they 'adopt no rule in anything other than the Word of God', the congregation attempted to make its own way forward with 'no written rules other than the Word of God and no guide except the Spirit'.[78] This policy gave the young congregation little guidance when facing such questions as whether sympathetic members of the National Church (who made no formal identification with the dissident congregation) might join professing members of the young congregation at the Lord's Supper, or whether persons of baptistic outlook could be countenanced in that chiefly paedobaptist congregation. Both issues were eventually resolved in the affirmative, yet the painful process of achieving a consensus on these questions after 1825 required an advance beyond the somewhat fond principles embraced so enthusiastically in 1817.[79]

Over the same first decade there came a gradual but steady recognition by the civil and religious authorities of Geneva that the 'Bourg-de-Four' congregation was a permanent fixture which would not be easily deterred. In the first years of its existence, the congregation had had to endure the ugly threats of street mobs and to see its pastors threatened with conscription for military service (as persons not recognized as cantonal clergymen).[80] The congregation's second decade was free of such external threats; energies and funds were, therefore, freely channelled into extension efforts.

Society: A Study in Evangelistic Zeal and Civic Ambition', *Fides et Historia*, 36.1 (2004), 67-81.

[78] Guers, *Le Premier Réveil*, 100, 109.

[79] The first issue of admission to the Supper had, until it was resolved, left the young church open to the charge of sectarianism. Until December 1824, a distinction was insisted upon between church member and mere communicant. The latter category had somewhat begrudgingly extended the right of participation in the Supper to those National Church members who were able to articulate a principled rationale for their continuance in the Establishment! Plainly, the policy was one of obstruction. From December 1824 onward, the congregation reckoned participation in the Supper (open to all believers) as the basis of a new, widely embracing membership. Paedobaptism alone was permitted in the formal services of worship, yet baptism of adults was permitted outside these services. Guers, *Le Premier Réveil*, 201-208; Bost, *Mémoires*, I, 378.

[80] It was in just this setting that pastors Émile Guers and J.G. Gonthier went to London in May 1821 armed with letters of introduction from orthodox ministers of the National Church of Geneva and Reformed Church of France in order to gain a recognized ordination in Poultry Chapel. Their status as proper ministers was never thereafter challenged in Geneva. Guers, *Le Premier Réveil*, 188. The ordinations were fully reported in the *Evangelical Magazine*, 29 (1821), 339.

The period to 1831 thus saw the preponderance of evangelizing activity from Geneva carried out by Protestant dissidents.[81] With them had lain the initiative in the publishing of tracts and journals for wide distribution, the establishing of a training school for missionary colporteurs and school teachers, and the commissioning of Christian workers for itinerant ministry in neighbouring cantons and the east of France. The same dissidents had worked in closest conjunction with the British evangelical societies and come to enjoy a considerable measure of recognition among the British Protestant public.

Events at Geneva 1831-1849

Yet these considerable developments began to be put in the shade by the flurry of similar activity generated by the newly-founded Genevan Evangelical Society in 1831.[82] If the dissidents had printed tracts and journals, commissioned itinerant Bible agents and evangelists, and promoted foreign mission, the new Society, aided by numerous wealthy patricians of the city,[83] soon surpassed these attainments. Yet we read of not a trace of rivalry in the period of the 1830s between the earlier dissidents and the latter (for that is in fact what supporters of the Society were). The roots of this cordiality lay in the sympathetic posture struck by the continuing orthodox party in the Genevan National Church towards the original dissidents in the entire period 1817-31. For the 'Bourg-de-Four' congregation, this sympathetic posture was personified by Gaussen, minister of Satigny. Of him, 'Bourg-de-Four' minister and later chronicler, Émile Guers, could write,

> He approved of our doctrine, but did not share our thoughts and views on the church. Knowing the grave reasons which had motivated our dissidence and the share of responsibility belonging to the majority of the 'Compagnie', he could not view our efforts for the gospel without interest. From the first day, we were able to count him among our most devoted friends... He possessed all our confidence and we made no important choice or decision without consulting him... We were always warmly received in his home.[84]

It had been Gaussen's circle (including Coulin, Peschier, Cellérier, Sr, and Moulinié) which had provided for dissident involvement in the Genevan Missionary Society until the reverses of 1829 caused the circle

---

[81] Maury, *Le Réveil* I, 150, concludes, 'It seems that it was "Bourg-de-Four" which had harvested most of the results of the first period of the "Réveil"'.

[82] The origin of which has been described above, p. 100.

[83] Maury, *Le Réveil* I, 158 ; Guers, *Notice Historique,* 25.

[84] Guers, *Le Premier Réveil,* 293, 294.

to resign in protest.[85] The same circle had readily penned letters of reference to assist Émile Guers and J.G. Gonthier in obtaining ordination in London in 1821 and shown ready friendship to 'Bourg-de-Four' missionary to the Alps, Félix Neff.[86] It was then a mere extension of this relationship into the changed circumstances of the 1830s which explains the gradual convergence of the earlier and later 'waves' of Genevan dissidence. The participation of Gaussen, a minister of L'Oratoire' and professor of dogmatics in the Evangelical School of Theology, in the March 1839 dedication of 'Bourg-de-Four's' new edifice at 'La Pélisserie' was fully consistent with this convergence.[87] So also was the involvement of past and present 'Bourg-de-Four' ministers Bost and Guers in the affairs of the Genevan Evangelical Society and School of Theology.[88]

The convergence was assisted not only by such bonds of long friendship, but by three additional factors. First was the positive consideration that the Geneva Evangelical Society (of which L'Oratoire and Theological School were but two concerns) made it plain that it was prepared to carry on, on a larger scale, the very type of enterprise pioneered by the 'Bourg-de-Four' congregation in the 1820s. Second, the futility of duplication of any such effort became all the more apparent when both L'Oratoire and 'Bourg-de-Four' congregations found themselves co-beligerents against the common foes of Irvingism and Darbyism in the years following 1835.[89] The 'Bourg-de-Four' congregation's loss of one wealthy supporter and numerous students from its Missionary Institute to Darbyism directly threatened the viability of that college and led to its closure in 1842.

Thirdly, there was a drastically changed political situation within Geneva. Whereas the period through the 1830s had seen the National Church and cantonal government working in tandem to protect mutual interests, the rise of liberal and secularist political strength in the Geneva of the 1840s ended the cantonal regulation of the National Church and made it internally governed.[90] Whereas formerly major changes in the

---

[85] Cf. p. 99 *supra.*

[86] Guers, *Le Premier Réveil*, 188, 300. Cf. ... Bost, *Life of Neff*, (London: 1855), 355, where, in a letter, Neff speaks of Gaussen as 'our dear friend'.

[87] Guers, *Le Premier Réveil*, 333; Biéler, *Une Famille*, 186, speaks of the 'consolidation of an evangelical "bloc"' in Geneva of the 1830s to counter the opposition of the city's liberal 'bloc'.

[88] Bost, *Mémoires*, II, 266 ; Maury, *Le Réveil*, I, 180.

[89] Guers, *Le Premier Réveil*, 341; Smith, *J.N. Darby in Switzerland,* 74, 75.

[90] A new constitution of 1847 decreed these changes. Maury, *Le Réveil*, I, 207-209. Biéler, *Une Famille*, 200, notes that many pious members of the National Church had come to relish this deregulation under the influence of Alexander Vinet's seminal book of 1842, *The Manifestation of Religious Convictions.*

Church had been subject to the review of the Council of State, now devolution of authority to the Church made it master of its own house; the change also served to allow an acceleration of rapid innovation. On the one hand, cantonal congregations were freed to choose as their own ministers any properly qualified person meeting their particular criteria. Yet another feature of this de-regulation was the removal of all former (and merely formal) cantonal obligation that the Church must maintain a fixed creed.

In the 'year of revolutions' (1848) official representatives of the L'Oratoire and 'Pélisserie' (formerly 'Bourg-de-Four') congregations as well as private individuals affiliated both to Malan's 'Église du Témoignage' and the now de-regulated National Church began prolonged conferences about the possibility of union in this new and undefined situation. Their motivations no doubt differed. The thriving L'Oratoire, claiming to represent the true heritage and doctrine of the National Church, found that the de-regulation of the latter called for a complete re-appraisal of its own posture; there was now nothing to be gained by an anachronistic stance towards Genevan creeds and discipline which had been rendered quite irrelevent by the recent upheaval in Church-state relationships. The 'Pélisserie' and 'Église du Témoignage' congregations had already peaked numerically in years prior to the introduction of the new constitution and were motivated primarily by a desire after solidarity in a society which had undergone rapid secularization.

The negotiations were highly difficult and lasted a full year. L'Oratoire representatives desired to maintain continuity with the doctrine, worship, and government of the Reformed tradition. They were especially concerned to preserve the government of churches by elders, the distinct office of the minister and the normativity of paedobaptism in the face of a prolonged relaxing of such standards by 'Bourg-de-Four—Pélisserie'.[91] The concerns of César Malan (who unlike some of the members of his chapel, did not eventually enter the 'Église Libre') centred around the maintenance of high-Calvinism, for which he had long been known.[92]

In 1849, the majority of members of the three dissident congregations and additional persons until then affiliated to the National Church united

---

[91] In this congregation, the long tradition of mutual admonition and exhortation in public services had led to an altered conception of the pastoral office. Always congregationalist in tendency, the church seems to have consciously affirmed such a polity after 1837 when it censured its ministers for Presbyterian tendencies. Guers, *Le Premier Réveil*, 162, 163, 334. We have referred above at p. 106, to the congregation's baptismal tensions.

[92] Maury, *Le Réveil*, I, 210.

to form the 'Église Évangélique Libre de Genève'.[93] In polity, the newly amalgamated body determined to be presbyterian. In doctrine, it adhered to a new confession which while clearly Calvinist 'consolidated the dogmatic divergences which had separated the supporters of the "réveil"'.[94] The two congregations which entered the new body as units (L'Oratoire and 'Pélisserie') were permitted to maintain their distinctive patterns of worship; the former thus continued the style of church service customary in the Genevan Reformed tradition while the latter continued to encourage the extensive lay participation for which it had long been known. Even differences over baptism were accommodated; while paedobaptism was to be normative, it was resolved that 'there would exist no need for division if some brothers believed it necessary to await the arrival of a more advanced age for the ceremony'.[95]

Geneva's 'Réveil' Crosses Borders

Francophone Cantons

We have observed already that the 'réveil' at Geneva took precedence over similar movements in surrounding territories largely on account of the city's tradition of theological pre-eminence and a relative abundance of dissident missionaries.[96] It is appropriate now to pause and consider the precise relation in which Genevan developments stood to those in neighbouring cantons.

The fervour and intensity of Geneva's awakening in the period to 1831 may be understood as a reaction against the pervasiveness of Enlightenment theological thought in the 'Compagnie des Pasteurs' and Academy. Yet the Protestant ministry and colleges of theology in other Francophone Protestant cantons in this period neither exhibited an identical theological tendency nor provoked the reaction which had fragmented Geneva's religious life. The religious tensions which did plague these cantons in the decades following 1820 were highly unique to each.

The Reformed Church of Neuchâtel had enjoyed a high degree of autonomy from the state since Reformation times; it continued to uphold a formal orthodoxy until well into the nineteenth century. This stance was only challenged in mid-century when a new cantonal government,

---

[93] Good, *History*, 462, reports the initial membership by profession to have been 700.

[94] Maury, *Le Réveil*, I, 217. The discipline and doctrine of the new church is printed as an appendix to Guers, *Notice Historique*, 84-94. The articles of doctrine appear in French and English with helpful commentary in P. Schaff, *Creeds of Christendom*, 3 vols, (London: 1877), III, 781-86.

[95] Maury, *Le Réveil*, I, 218 ; Guers, *Notice Historique*, 93.

[96] Cf. pp. 91-95 *supra*.

zealous to limit the church's long-standing freedoms, began to nominate theological scholars of a sceptical outlook to the cantonal university. The Church, long accustomed to appointing all theological professors according to its own criteria, resisted such inroads being made. Additional pressure by the canton upon the Church's long-established prerogatives eventually led to ecclesiastical separation in 1873 and from this sprang 'L'Église Évangélique de Neuchâtel'.[97] The latter established a highly credible faculty of theology from which scholars Frédéric Godet and August Gretillat exercised an influence far beyond the confines of their church and canton.[98]

We may not speak, however, of any clear-cut dependency of these Neuchâtel developments upon Genevan antecedents. It is plain that the Genevan itinerants, Félix Neff, Ami Bost and César Malan had periodic activity in the canton,[99] but such itineration clearly preceded by several decades the polarization and separation of the cantonal Church. It is entirely likely that this activity served to nurture forms of evangelical independency which sprang up in advance of the eventual disruption of the cantonal Church.[100] Yet, as regards the latter, the established Genevan

---

[97] Good, *History*, 494-499. Charles Monvert, *Histoire de la fondation de l'église évangélique Neuchâteloise*, (Neuchâtel: 1898). It is of interest to note that this 'église évangélique' was numbered among the founding members of the 'Alliance of Reformed Churches Throughout the World holding the Presbyterian System' (now World Alliance of Reformed Churches) at its inauguration in 1875. Cf. Marcel Pradervand, *A Century of Service*, (Edinburgh: 1975), 23.

[98] Good, *History*, 497-99. Godet's commentaries on Luke (1871), Romans (1879-80) and 1 Corinthians (1886) have been kept in print almost continuously since their initial release. Gretillat authored an important dogmatics, *Exposé de théologie systematique*, 4 vols, (Paris 1885-92). His historical and theological retrospective of the 'réveil' period, 'Movements of Theological Thought Among French-Speaking Protestants 1820-1891', *Presbyterian and Reformed Review*, 3, (1892), 421-47, will be alluded to below. Significantly numbered among the graduates of Neuchâtel's alternate faculty of theology were two sons of Geneva's J.H. Merle D'Aubigné. See Monvert, *Histoire*, 304.

[99] Cart, *Histoire*, I, 162, 163; Gilly, *Life of Félix Neff*, 47; Bost. *Mémoires*, II, 10, 11. It is plain that the majority of Bost's itinerating efforts in Switzerland and south Germany centred around Moravian communities, however. See Malan, *Life*, 273. The 'Continental Society', described above, had one agent, named Magnin, in the canton of Neuchâtel as late as 1834. Cf. *Appeal of the Continental Society, Dublin Auxilliary*, (Dublin: 1834). Three Neuchâteloise ministers, J.H. Grandpierre (1799-1874), and brothers F.E. Petitpierre (1804-89) and G.A.F. Petitpierre (1801-84), served independent evangelical causes in France in the years to 1836. F.E. Petitpierre was translator of the *Lives of Robert and J.A. Haldane*. See Robert, *Les Églises Réformées*, 557, 568.

[100] The Scottish Congregationalist, W.L. Alexander, witnessed the pervasiveness of this Independent movement during his tour of Switzerland in 1845. In his *Switzerland and the Swiss Churches*, (Edinburgh: 1846), 222-23, he wrote, 'In almost all the Protestant cantons and especially those of French Switzerland, churches of the Independent order have sprung up which stand to the Church of the Pélisserie [formerly 'Bourg-de-Four'] in

pattern of an alternative to the cantonal Church and faculty of theology was no doubt held out as an example when concerned Christians of Neuchâtel asked themselves what was to be done about the unprecedented intrusion of the secular power into the affairs of their Church and academy.

However, we tread on entirely different ground when examining the relationship between developments at Geneva and the canton of Vaud. Vaud's contiguity with the canton of Geneva ensured that its ministers had a high level of awareness of religious currents in the neighbouring region. From their standpoint of formal orthodoxy concerning the doctrine of the Trinity, the two natures of Christ, justification by faith, and biblical authority, Vaud's clergy found much to unsettle them in their annual conferences with their Genevan counterparts (conferences which continued until 1818). Thus, they perused the polemical pamphlet of young Henri Empeytaz, *Considérations Sur La Divinité de Jésus Christ* (1816), with great eagerness and largely sympathized with its primary contentions.[101]

From 1810, the senior minister ('doyen') of the canton, L.A. Curtat (d.1832), had given supplementary lectures in his own home to the theological students of the Lausanne 'Academie'. He chose to dwell especially on subjects of current debate and thus addressed the divinity of Christ and the inspiration of Scripture. He also gave sermon analysis as part of which he showed himself ready to insist that every sermon must speak of Jesus Christ.[102] Yet this man, the chronicler of 'réveil' activity in Vaud termed both 'the first and one of the most powerful advocates' of the upsurge in religious activity within the canton, and (paradoxically) also 'the greatest opponent and adversary of the same'.[103] Curtat harboured an inveterate fear of the pietistic religion which flourished concurrently with his own special efforts at the preparation of ministerial candidates.

The 'doyen' thus looked askance at the rise and prolific activity of the Lausanne Bible Society in 1814; thereafter the society's two divisions for Scripture and tract distribution unwittingly aided pietistic conventicles. Now-plentiful Scriptures and tracts were so much grist for the pietists'

---

the relation of sister churches.' Independency of this type had sprung up in Neuchâtel in 1828. Alexander found fifty such independent churches in the French cantons and ten in the German; see p. 268.

[101] Cart, *Histoire du Mouvement*, I.i.159. The annual conference was terminated in protest by doyen L.A. Curtat in response to the Genevan issuance of the 'règlement' of May 1817.

[102] Cart, *Histoire du Mouvement*, I.i.85.

[103] Cart, *Histoire du Mouvement*, I.i.79.

mill.[104] Curtat was similarly alarmed by the rise of the missionary movement. The wide readership found within Vaud by *Le Magazin Évangélique*,[105] so full of missionary affairs, immediately gave rise to agitation for a mission society at Lausanne. At the centre of this agitation was the Englishwoman, earlier involved equally in the launching of the Lausanne Bible Society, Mary Anna Greaves.[106] By mid-1820, Miss Greaves had summoned the young convert and budding missionary, Félix Neff, from Geneva to assist in the promotion of the mission society cause.[107]

'Doyen' Curtat believed he detected a pietistic conspiracy in all this. He alerted the cantonal council to the financial implications of a substantial outflow of currency from the region in support of foreign missions. The council acted promptly on this warning by publicly discouraging involvement in the missionary cause.[108] Curtat went further still and wrote a series of tracts against the growing tendency towards religious meetings in homes ('conventicules'). The best known of these was *De L'Établissement des Conventicules dans le Canton de Vaud* (Lausanne: 1821). In this, he warned that such non-official religious assemblies were, in effect, 'fronts' for an influx of English religious sentiment, that they used literature printed with English donations, and that they held out the prospect of the cantonal Church rapidly becoming 'a humble auxiliary of one of the two sections of English Methodism'.[109]

Yet it was not merely concerned Britons who took note of this adamant opposition emanating from a hitherto impeccable source.[110] The Genevan, César Malan, who was often in the neighbouring canton of Vaud after 1818 in order to preach in such conventicles and missionary gatherings, wrote in defence of gatherings such as the one at Rolle, Vaud, in 1821. The pamphlet, *Les Conventicules de Rolle par un Témoin digne de Foi*, defended such gatherings against the charge of separatism, counselled

---

[104] Cart, *Histoire du Mouvement*, I.i.102, 103. Prime mover behind the Lausanne Bible Society was Professor David Levade. Initial deliberations leading to the formation of the Lausanne Society also involved representatives from the cantons of Neuchâtel and Geneva.

[105] Published at Geneva from 1819 by the 'Bourg-de-Four' congregation.

[106] Greaves had been made a life member of the Bible Society for her pioneering efforts on its behalf. Cf. Cart, *Histoire du Mouvement*, I.i.105.

[107] Bost, *Life of Neff*, 122. Neff spoke in many small evening gatherings over a two week period in advocacy of a mission society. Cart, *Histoire du Mouvement*, I.i.162-69, outlines the extensive visits of Neff and Bost to Vaud.

[108] Cart, *Histoire du Mouvement*, I.i.191, 204.

[109] L.A. Curtat, *De L'Établissement des Conventicules dans le Canton de Vaud*, (Lausanne: 1821), iv.

[110] Curtat's opposition necessitated the relocation of Miss Greaves to Geneva by early 1822. She there became affiliated with the congregation of Gaussen at Satigny. Wemyss, *Le Réveil*, 155.

prudence in dealing with parish ministers who seemed strangers to the gospel, and related the circumstances of Malan's own post-ordination conversion. All this had been disclosed in response to the questions of three Vaud ministers. The pamphlet then went on, however, to urge that prayer be offered for the obstructive Curtat![111]

Anti-conventicle legislation was promptly enacted by the government of Vaud in 1821. Devotional services in homes involving any persons other than family members were strictly forbidden. There followed a series of resignations by ministers and ordinands who objected to this onslaught against pietist activity and to what they perceived as a drifting of their National Church from close adherence to the *Second Helvetic Confession* (1566) and proper exercise of discipline.[112] With the anti-conventicle legislation in place, there was no legal scope for dissident Protestantism in the canton, and thus, belatedly, Vaud became like Geneva an exporter of preachers and missionaries to other Francophone regions. Yet, in spite of the restrictions, the 'réveil' diffused itself through the canton. By 1824, twenty-six ministers within the National Church petitioned the council of the canton to repeal the anti-conventicle legislation. The following year, an 'Evangelical Society of Vaud' was organized. Shortly thereafter, Alexandre Vinet, who had earlier stood with 'doyen' Curtat against conventicles, reversed his views and made the change of outlook plain by publishing an appeal in favour of religious liberty.[113]

The granting of complete religious liberty in 1834 at the hands of the current secularizing Vaud council of state marked a new chapter in the history of evangelical dissidence. Henceforth, one might hold public or private religious gatherings outside the National Church framework with perfect liberty. But this same secularizing council was simultaneously examining what it viewed as the outdated outlook of the National Church; in 1839 it rendered this church creedless by abolishing the *Second*

---

[111] Malan, *Les Conventicules de Rolle*, (Geneva: 1821). We have utilized the English translation produced at London in 1865. See pp. 16-21, 109-115. The jibe directed towards Curtat drew immediate criticism from young Alexandre Vinet, a loyal supporter of the doyen. But Vinet later defended the religious rights of dissidents. See Laura M. Lane, *Life and Writings of Alexandre Vinet*, (Edinburgh: 1890), 40-41, 121.

[112] Cart, *Histoire du Mouvement*, I.i.301-308. By June 1824, there were at least six dissident ministers and ordinands. Cart also demonstrates (p. 229) that all of the first dissidents had been participants in Malan's conventicles. Louis Barbey, Henri Juvet, Alex Chavannes and F. Olivier were such men.

[113] Good, *History*, 475, 476. Such was the illicit activity of pietistic dissidents that Ami Bost of Geneva records his presence and activity in a 'synod of independents' at Lausanne in November, 1828. See Bost, *Mémoires*, II.90.

Helvetic Confession as the standard of teaching.[114] Now, as in 1824, there was a stream of pastoral resignations from the National Church. In response to the council's reforms, there was growing agitation for the separation of Church and state. No individual did more to further this cause than Vinet, whose treatise on the subject, *Essai sur la manifestation des convictions religieuses et sur la séparation de l'église et de l'état* (Paris: 1842), became influential in Francophone Protestantism far beyond Vaud's boundaries. From 1839, the cantonal government also dismantled the National Church's internal government and administered each parish directly by a ministry of religious affairs,[115] much on the current French model. The cantonal government's insistence in 1845 that National Church ministers read from their pulpits a written declaration indicating support for the new arrangements served as the catalyst for a massive disruption. One hundred and forty ministers departed while only eighty-nine remained in the National Church. The clear majority of theological professors and students also seceded; shortly a 'Free Faculty of Theology' was established. The Free Evangelical Church of Vaud was constituted on 15 December 1845; the abandoning of manses and church buildings in mid-winter was rightly considered an heroic action. The Free Church of Vaud cause was rapidly taken up through the Protestant world.[116]

The disruption of the National Church of Vaud was a clear and conscientious response to the state's invasion of the Church's right to determine her own doctrine and administer her own affairs. It was an occurrence which could never have taken place without the leavening agent of the 'réveil', much of the impetus of which was provided by the dissidents of Geneva.

France

Some contemporary British observers in post-Napoleonic France were easily led to the conclusion that the cause of the gospel had been well-nigh extinguished there. Often relying on patchy religious intelligence,

---

[114] This development moved A. Vinet, by this time professor of practical theology in the Academy of Lausanne, to resign from his post and the ministry. See Lane, *Vinet*, 95. Vinet's ideas on church and state have been set out by Elsie Ann McKee, 'Alexandre Vinet on Religious Liberty and Separation of Church and State', *Journal of Church and State* 28.1 (1986), 95-106.

[115] Good, *History*, 476, 477.

[116] Good, *History*, 480. Over 400 Church of England ministers declared their support. The Free Church of Scotland assisted the Free Church effort in Vaud promptly from 1845. Cf. ch. 4, p. 198. The Free Church of Vaud was a constituting member of the World Alliance of Reformed Churches at the inauguration of that body in 1875. Cf. Pradervand, *A Century of Service*, 22.

they reached conclusions about the extent of orthodox Christian belief and proclamation which bore little relation to the real state of Christianity in France's many 'departements'. Robert Haldane had believed that France contained only four or five ministers of orthodox views outside the Montauban and Toulouse which he claimed to know well. The Methodist missionary, Charles Cook, had asserted in 1818 that he could number all the orthodox ministers in France on the fingers of one hand.[117]

In fact, French Protestantism, while far from robust, was nevertheless showing unmistakeable signs of quickening in the period dating from the decision in 1808 to establish an approved theological college at Montauban. Two early professors there, Daniel Encontre and Jules Bonnard, were participants in a circle of ministers which also included the Moravian evangelist, J.J. Mérillat. The circle maintained official links with the Moravian headquarters at Herrnhut, Saxony.[118] Under the influence of lecturers such as Encontre and Bonnard, Montauban soon sent a steady supply of generally orthodox and Trinitarian ministers into the pulpits of the National Church. We have noted above the posture struck by Montauban and the National Church vis-à-vis the Genevan 'reglement' of May 1817.

Against such a backdrop, we are driven to the conclusion that the historian of the 'réveil', Maury, was substantially correct to claim that

> a judgement describing the French church as utterly fallen in 1815 has little foundation. It is certain that around 1815 there were in our church a number of zealous and faithful pastors who joyfully received the help of foreigners—yet who without and before them laboured with perseverance.[119]

It was as part of this indigenous stirring that the French churches received Genevan graduates who had been touched by Haldane's influence in 1817; it had also welcomed like-minded graduates in preceding years. The Monod brothers and César Bonifas were welcomed every bit as heartily following 1817 as had been Abraham Lissignol in 1809 and Matthieu Miroglio in 1810. In the 1820s there was plainly opportunity in the ministry of the National Church for several men of French citizenship whose studies at the Gosport, Hampshire, academy of

---

[117] A. Haldane, *Lives of the Haldanes*, 449. Maury, *Le Réveil Religieux*, I, 225. Yet Cook, upon undertaking an extensive tour of the south of France, quickly came to see that there were many men with whom he could collaborate.

[118] See ch. 2, p. 52 above.

[119] Maury, *Le Réveil Religieux*, I, 474.

David Bogue had been financed by the London Missionary Society.[120] While full ministerial rank was most difficult to obtain for anyone other than a native (given the governmental insistence upon citizenship as a prerequisite), the National Church nevertheless offered almost unlimited opportunity for those Francophones who, lacking citizenship, were ready to serve as pastoral 'suffragants'.[121] We lay stress on these facts so as to emphasize that the National Church, though beset with difficulties of very long standing, extended an open door of opportunity after 1815 and harboured within it many friends of the 'réveil'.

The 'réveil' at Geneva furnished the National Church of France both with leading personalities of a generation younger than Daniel Encontre and Jules Bonnard and a widened trans-national orbit within which to operate. As regards the first, it is sufficient to note that no names figure so prominently in the affairs of the the French Protestant Church in the period to 1849 as the brothers Frédéric, Adolphe and Guillaume Monod—Genevan graduates all. As regards the second, we can observe that by the 1830s, the seminary at Montauban was attempting to move explicitly in concert with the tendencies of Genevan evangelical theology. Adolphe Monod was offered but declined a post in the new theological school established at Geneva in 1832, preferring to accept a chair in ethics and sacred eloquence at Montauban in 1836.[122] César Bonifas, associated with Haldane in Geneva in 1817, joined the Montauban faculty in the same decade. J.H. Merle D'Aubigné declined the Montauban chair in theology in 1830 in the period of his transition from a Brussels pastorate to a post at the Evangelical School of Theology in Geneva.[123]

Beyond the seminary, we may observe that César Malan of Geneva itinerated extensively in the eastern and southern 'départements' of France between the years 1836 and 1853,[124] while Ami Bost served National Churches at Bourges, Asnieres, Melun, and Paris in the period

---

[120] These were Laurent Cadoret and Gilles Portier. On Cadoret's somewhat stormy relationship with the National Church, cf. Robert, *Les Églises Réformées*, 244-45, and Wemyss, *Le Réveil*, 126ff.

[121] We have noted, p. 95, that Genevan dissidents Henri Pyt and Félix Neff served in this way while their comrade, Émile Guers, at least contemplated the idea.

[122] Monod served the Montauban faculty until 1847. Heyer, *L'Église de Genève*, 493.

[123] Biéler, *Une Famille*, 168.

[124] I.e., in the years 1836, 1841, 1849, 1852, 1853. Cf. Malan, *Life of Malan*, 284. The financial backing for such itineration was often supplied by the New York based 'Foreign Evangelical Society'. The published *Report of the Foreign Evangelical Society* (New York: 1842), 29-30, of this organization for 1842 indicates the funding for such itineration.

1843-52.[125] The 'door' of the National Reformed Church was then definitely open to the influences of the 'réveil'. The growth patterns of the French Reformed Church to the middle of the nineteenth century give the most unambiguous evidence of the movement's quickening effect. Writing in 1854, Ami Bost could recollect that

> in 1814 one could have counted two hundred churches (with pastors) salaried by the state and not one dissident congregation. Presently there are 763 pastors salaried by the state and an indefinite number of independent churches.[126]

The means by which this great change was effected we will shortly consider.

For the moment, it is necessary for us to recollect our earlier contention that at Geneva the momentum of the 'réveil' in the period to 1831 lay primarily with the dissident congregation of 'Bourg-de-Four'.[127] This factor ensured that France—like the canton of Vaud—would initially encounter Geneva's 'reveil' extensively through its dissident representatives. Frédéric Monod, member of the Haldane 'circle' and future assistant to his father, Jean Monod, in the National Church at Paris, was ordained at Geneva in July 1818; he began his Paris ministry in the following year. The young man was the first member of the Haldane 'circle' to attach himself to the National Church in the capital.[128] Yet already in March-April 1818, the Genevan dissidents had, in the person of Pierre Méjanel, their own representative at Paris. By May, Méjanel had been appointed the first agent of the 'Society for the Diffusion of Religious Knowledge On the Continent of Europe', and by April of the following year both Henri Pyt and Ami Bost were similarly employed.[129]

---

[125] Bost, *Mémoires*, II, 297ff. Bost had been re-admitted to the ministry of the Genevan National Church in 1840 and thus became eligible for call to France.

[126] Bost, *Mémoires*, II. 307. His statistics cannot be easily verified. Statistics excerpted from Soulier's *Statistique de 1828* quoted in Gilly's *Life of Félix Neff*, (London: 1832), 140-141, make plain that even by 1828 the number of pastors had increased dramatically to 303. The number of state church buildings in 1828 was reported to be 438. Mours, *L'Église Réformée*, 190, 191, documents an increase from 200 pastors in 1820 to 569 in 1865.

[127] This assertion was made above, p. 94.

[128] Heyer, *L'Église de Genève*, 407. César Bonifas, also of the 'circle', had been ordained in July 1817 in company with Merle D'Aubigné; he then proceeded to serve at Grenoble.

[129] The first annual *Report* of the Continental Society (London: 1819), 9, reported that 'there are now four itinerants serving in France'. The rise and progress of this society is described in detail in the following chapter.

The significance of this lies not so much in the inauguration of a Christian society outside the jurisdiction of the consistories of the National Protestant Church (a thing which we will find, below, to have been commonplace) but in the selection of personnel. Pierre Méjanel was himself a minister of the National Church; yet at this stage of his career he had no thought of resuming pastoral work in that setting. Ami Bost had been ordained in the Genevan National Church in March 1814[130] and served a first pastorate at Moutiers-Grand Val, in the canton of Berne, 1816-18. In early 1819 he had returned to Geneva and allied himself openly with the dissident 'Bourg-de-Four' congregation.[131] Only in 1840 did he return to the fold of the Genevan National Church. Henri Pyt also came to the 'Continental Society' from 'Bourg-de-Four' by way of a short-term as 'suffragant' in the French National Church at Saverdun. His shift of allegiance had been motivated by a desire to 'avoid compromise with the National Church'.[132]

Such agents at best adopted an eclectic attitude to the National Protestant Church of France. Where its pastors and consistories welcomed them they were happy enough to occupy its pulpits. But where this hospitality was not extended they felt free to bypass such churches altogether. Such free-lance preaching, distribution of literature and organization of home gatherings was all the more naturally the pattern followed in the vast tracts of France where Protestantism had long gone under-represented. From the Pyrenees north to Flanders and especially across the whole sweep of northern France, these apostles of independency roamed.

But they were by no means the only advocates of a Protestantism outside the confines of the state Church. The number of such advocates grew steadily through the 1820s in direct proportion to the state's efforts to tether Protestantism.[133] Any direct proselytization of France's nominally Catholic population was severely frowned upon in the period to 1830. The historian Leon Maury records that

in 1825, the consistory of Paris was refused the right to open a church in Ageux simply for those of Protestant birth. The following year, the consistory of Lyons was refused the right to hold religious services in neighbouring communities where curious Catholics requested these. Yet Protestant conversions to Catholicism were

---

[130] Heyer, *L'Église de Genève*, 406.

[131] A change of allegiance announced in his publication of that year, *Genève Religieux*, (Genève: 1819), 2.

[132] Guers, *Vie de Pyt*, 59.

[133] The extent of the state's surveillance of Protestant attempts at proselytization in the period to 1830 is helpfully surveyed in Pierre Genevray, 'L'État Français et la Propagation du Réveil', *BSHFP*, 95-96 (1946-47), 12-39.

highly encouraged. The prince of Salm, who renounced Catholicism at Strasbourg in 1826, was expelled from France by ministerial order.[134]

Such events made some forward-looking persons weigh the benefits of state establishment against the limitations which this status entailed. The latter certainly strengthened the case for the creation of various evangelical societies at Paris, commencing with the 'Société Biblique Protestant' in 1818. A less-regulated National Protestant Church, subsuming as it did in the post-1815 period virtually all French Protestantism, might have been expected to launch such beneficial schemes at its own initiative. But in point of fact, it was restrained from doing so by the terms of the Napoleonic 'concordat' of 1802—now carried forward under the restored monarchy. The Bible Society and its subsequent counterparts[135] were consequently the embodiment of private or individualistic Christian initiative and the substantial successes accomplished by these agencies tended to serve as proof positive of how the interests of evangelical Protestantism could be well served outside the framework of the 'concordat'.[136] Such private initiatives brought together like-minded Lutheran, Reformed and independent Christians in France.[137] Strong support was also given by foreign churchmen, such as the English Independent, Mark Wilks, who served an English-speaking Paris chapel from 1822, British Methodist missionaries John Hawtrey and Charles Cook, and the American merchant, Sampson Wilder.[138] In so far as the Bible, tract and mission societies employed their own agents to traverse the country, we must observe in their efforts the gradual emergence of 'para-church' endeavour as the primary means of Protestant expansion in the 1820s.

This expansion of evangelical endeavour by societies was furthered by two additional factors: the emergence of theological polarization within

---

[134] Maury, *Le Réveil Religieux,* I, 470, 471.

[135] 'Société des Traités Religieux' (1821), 'Société des Missions Évangéliques' (1822) Comité pour l'Encouragement des Écoles du Dimanche' (1826), and 'Société pour l'Encouragement d'Instruction Primaire parmi les Protestants de France' (1829).

[136] While the viability of the principle of such private (rather than ecclesiastical) initiative had been amply demonstrated in Great Britain in the preceding twenty-five years, this private initiative may be said to have been needed to overcome the effects of Protestant pluralism. In France, the obstacle to ecclesiastical initiative was not this pluralism but state regulation.

[137] Churches of the Augsburg (Lutheran) Confession had also been recognized and funded by the state in the 'concordat' of 1802. They were concentrated in north-east France. The cooperation of various Christians is documented in O. Douen, *Histoire de la Société Biblique Protestante de Paris*, (Paris: 1868), 79-83.

[138] Their activity, especially in the organization of the Tract Society, is related in ch. 4, p. 159. Cf. Sampson V.S. Wilder, *Records from the Life of S.V.S.W.* (New York: 1865), 80.

the French Reformed Church and the upsurge of evangelical internationalism. First, during the 1820s there is evidence of theological polarization in the French Reformed Church between friends and foes of the 'réveil'. Samuel Vincent (1787-1837), minister at Nîmes, gave voice to those uneasy with the new strident conversionist emphasis through his editing the periodical *Mélanges de Religion, de Morale et de Critique Sacrée* (1820-24).[139] Adolphe Monod encountered stern opposition from ministers of this outlook from the time of his arrival at Lyons in 1826; his opponents eventually succeeded in gaining his dismissal from his pastorate and obstructing his potential appointment to a chair at the Montauban seminary.[140] The upshot of this altercation at Lyons was the inauguration of the 'Église Évangelique de Lyon' under Monod's leadership. Independent action by societies had initially been justified on the ground that state regulation of the Church inhibited the launching of publishing and proselytizing schemes. Now, if only on a regional basis, it seemed necessary to resort to independent action because of ecclesiastical hostility to the same endeavours.

But secondly, a step like that taken by Monod at Lyons was rendered feasible largely because of the enlarged operation of what can only be called an 'evangelical internationalism'. César Malan's Genevan 'Église du Témoignage' had been erected by an early manifestation of the same generosity, while the 'Bourg-de-Four' congregation of the same city would similarly afford the unaffordable in erecting their new edifice at 'La Pélisserie' after 1839.[141] To just such a constituency at home and abroad Monod appealed for assistance with his *Appel aux Chrétiens de France et de l'Etranger en faveur de l'Église Évangélique de Lyon* (Paris: 1833).[142] The Lyons congregation grew rapidly through an aggressive evangelism and regional itineration and joined an informal network of

---

[139] Robert, *Les Églises Réformées*, 378, typifies the theological outlook of Vincent as being 'pre-liberal' and approximating the thought of Schleiermacher. Two authors have drawn further attention to the theological polarization in French Protestantism at this time. See Lynn J. Osen, 'The Theological Revival in the French Reformed Church, 1830-1852', *Church History*, 37.1 ((1968), 36-49, and James C. Deming, 'The Threat of Revival to a Minority Protestant Community: The French Reformed Church in the Department of the Gard, 1830- 1859', *Fides et Historia*, 21.3 (1989), 68-77.

[140] Robert, *Les Églises Réformées*, 407-409. Monod, the subject of investigation from 1829, was dismissed from his pastorate by the state-regulated consistory of Lyons in March 1832. He gained a chair at Montauban on a second attempt in 1836. It is evident that a certain rigidity on Monod's part exacerbated actual divergences on matters of doctrine. Cf. Maury, *Le Réveil Religieux*, I, 159.

[141] Cf. p. 108 *supra*.

[142] The mere presence of a copy of the pamphlet in the library of New College, Edinburgh, suggests something of the audience to which Monod appealed. That this was far from an isolated occurrence is helpfully documented by Evans, 'The Contribution of Foreigners', 414ff.

other such independent congregations existing at Bordeaux, Castetarbe, Paris, La Nougarède, St. Étienne, Le Havre and Strasbourg.[143]

Paris itself had become the hotbed of evangelical independency largely because it was to this centre that foreign evangelicals gravitated. To the capital came the exiled Vaudois pastors François and Henri Olivier; in 1824, with funding from Robert Haldane, they commenced the private tutoring of men for the ministry outside the National Church. A congregation of independent views sprang up in conjunction with this, 'L'Institut Haldane'.[144] To Paris in 1824 came A.J. Galland, the Genevan-educated minister of the French congregation at Berne;[145] he served as the first director of the Paris Mission Society. Galland, like the brothers Olivier, held preaching services which were boldly evangelical. At his 1826 return to Geneva, Galland was replaced by a citizen of Neuchâtel, J.H. Grandpierre (1799-1874). The latter combined his administrative duties with the Mission Society and the role of preacher in Paris' most prominent independent chapel, 'La Chapel Taitbout'.

The sudden end of the Bourbon monarchy by the forced exile of Charles XII in July 1830, and the rise of the house of Orleans through the reign of Louis Philippe created an atmosphere which was considerably more amenable to French Protestantism in its varied forms.[146] No change was more significant than the relaxation of Bourbon legislation inhibiting the right of assembly for purposes other than worship. Now there could be gatherings for deliberation and for strategy formation. Three major consequences followed from this restored right of free assembly: these were the extension of the Christian society movement; the spread of the 'réveil' among the upper classes of Paris by what is called the 'réunion' movement; and the rise of open debate regarding the suitability of the National Church's linkage to the state.

First, while the Established Church now began to engage, gingerly, in some church extension, the existing pattern of evangelistic initiative by societies meant that it was these (and not the Church) which were poised to exploit the new situation most fully. A cue was taken from the groups of likeminded persons at Lausanne and Geneva who had established 'Evangelical Societies' in 1825 and 1831. By August 1834 there also

---

[143] Maury, *Le Réveil Religieux*, I, 465, 506.

[144] Maury, *Le Réveil*, I, 446; A. Haldane, *Lives of the Haldanes*, 545. After 1831 the direction of school and congregation passed into the hands of Henri Pyt. Guers, *Vie de Pyt*, 262, maintains that Pyt erected a chapel of his own with lavish assistance from an English donor.

[145] We have noted above Galland's exposure to Haldane in autumn 1816 and his eventual cooperation with F.S.L. Gaussen in 1831 in founding the Evangelical Society of Geneva.

[146]Maury, *Le Réveil*, 471. Guers, *Vie de Pyt*, 258: 'the fall of the Bourbon kings created much wider opportunity for the free preaching of the gospel'.

existed at Paris the 'Société Évangélique française'—a new organization which would shortly eclipse the efforts of all foreign bodies working for French evangelization.[147] The foundation of the Paris-based society reflected both the indigenization of home missionary effort and the fact that the internal political climate of France was now more hospitable to such proselytizing efforts among the nominally Catholic population.

Already by 1838 the Paris-based society employed sixteen ministers, ten evangelists, seventeen school teachers, and nine colporteurs. Further, it was assisting seven candidates who were in various stages of preparation for the ministry.[148] The Paris society worked in close conjunction with its Genevan counterpart which was focusing its missionary efforts on the eastern regions of France surrounding Lyons.[149] The co-operation between the two societies, which included the training of French preachers in the Evangelical School of Theology at Geneva for service of the Parisian society,[150] extended also to a shared eclectic attitude towards the French Reformed Church. Both societies aimed not only at the preaching of the gospel, but also at the erection of chapels. Would these or would these not be affiliated to the recognized Protestant Church of the land? The policy of the societies in this regard was one largely determined by the attitude of the regional consistory towards their evangelistic efforts.

When queried on the point for the sake of conscientious Church of England donors (who found the prospect of funding any apparently sectarian endeavour worrisome) the Paris society replied in measured terms:

> In the instruction to the agents of the Society, Article IV, they are told 'to keep in view, not only that there is nothing hostile to the churches legally constituted in France, but on the contrary the committee is anxious to cooperate everywhere,

---

[147] The awkward situation created by this development for the London-based Continental Society is related in the following chapter.

[148] Excerpts from the *Quarterly Report of the Paris Evangelical Society*, (July-October 1838) reprinted in Edward Bickersteth, ed., *A Voice From the Alps*, (London: 1838), 160ff. Those under preparation were almost certainly studying at the Evangelical School of Theology, Geneva.

[149] By the year 1846, the Paris Society would employ 146 agents and the Geneva Society 124. *Sixth Report of the Foreign Aid Society*, (London: 1846), 11, 15. It is the contention of Evans, 'The Contribution of Foreigners', 410, that the two societies were substantially funded to the tune of US $83,340 in the years 1839-49 by the New York 'Foreign Evangelization Society' in which S.V. Wilder was a principal. Evans further alleges that initial American funding was integral to the founding of each society.

[150] Maury, *Le Réveil*, I, 186.

wherever it can be done with the pastors of those churches for the advancement of the church of God by the propagation of the pure gospel'.[151]

But such a policy clearly anticipated numerous situations where co-operation would be unfeasible and independent congregations would spring up. Reservations within the National Church regarding such a policy encouraged the formation in the 1840s of several evangelization societies termed 'Sociétés Protestantes' throughout France.[152] These societies differed from those of Paris and Geneva in professing 'to act consistently with the constitution of the French Reformed Church of 1802 and by virtue of which conforming pastors received government stipends'.[153]

By the mid 1840s, the Evangelical Societies of Geneva and Paris were clearly reflecting current ecclesiastical tensions in France[154] and were now indicating that their posture towards the National Church was so regionally variable as to be one of acting 'either with, or independent of and sometimes opposed to the Consistorial churches'.[155] It is hard to avoid the conclusion that the principle of private or individual action pursued by the societies of Geneva and Paris had ultimately served the interests of ecclesiastical independency.[156]

Second, the right of free assembly now facilitated the gatherings ('réunions') of upper-class Parisian Protestants who met in the drawing rooms ('salons') of influential Christians on week-day evenings. In the homes of Mark Wilks, Frédéric Monod, Thomas Waddington (an English industrialist), Jules Hollard (a Vaud physician), V. de Pressense, and Henri Lutteroth (a Bavarian banker) interested persons from the intellectual, governmental and economic elites assembled for far-ranging discussions bearing on the relation of the Christian faith to modern life. There was in all such gatherings an over-arching concern to

---

[151] Bickersteth, ed., *A Voice,* 158. Bickersteth's English readers were also re-assured that M. Juillerat-Chasseur, an immediate past moderator of the Reformed Church, was a secretary of the 'Société Évangélique'. Yet the fact, while true, was not the ironclad guarantee of denominational loyalty implied.

[152] Branches were located in Paris, Orleans, Normandy and Bordeaux.

[153] *Seventh Report of the Foreign Aid Society,* (London: 1847), 21.

[154] To be detailed below.

[155] *Seventh Report of the Foreign Aid Society,* (London: 1847), 20.

[156] The detailed statistical analysis provided by Mours, *Les Églises Réformées,* 190-191, indicates that by the later date of 1865, the 638 salaried clergy of the National Church had a nationwide counterpart of 218 pastors or evangelists not salaried by the state. This ratio, albeit for a slightly later date, indicates the dramatic growth of independency.

announce the gospel in its simplicity to those of their fellow citizens for whom indifference, doubt, and prejudice combined to keep them far from any sanctuary.[157]

Like the London Clapham circle on which they modelled themselves, this influential Paris group came to be called the 'Saints'. They arranged visits by Thomas Chalmers and Elizabeth Fry, who discussed their Christian approach to social problems.[158] Christian women, including some very highly placed in society such as the Baroness de Stael, hosted distinctive gatherings for women at their own level in society. By October 1830, this influential Parisian circle had opened a small place of worship in 'rue Taitbout' which prospered so much that by 1833 their Sunday assemblies had to be relocated to a concert hall on the same thoroughfare. A National Church minister, Jean-Joel Audebez (1790-1881),[159] was called from Nerac in 1831 and under his ministry (now on an independent footing) a sizeable congregation of influential Parisians was assembled. The 'chapel Taitbout' was essentially an outreach centre for the well-born; only in 1839 did it assume a churchly character by administering the sacraments and solemnizing marriages. From that year, it declared its independence from the state, established a roll of membership for those who made profession of faith and declared its doctrinal basis to be the historic French Reformed Confession of La Rochelle (1559).

The congregation, which moved into a new buidling on the 'rue de Provence' in 1840, shortly initiated six additional congregations by sending out teams of itinerant preachers and colporteurs. One of the six was specifically created for the working classes.[160] What the 'Société Évangélique de France' attempted in the 'départements' of France beginning in 1834 this congregation of affluent individuals attempted simultaneously in Paris. Not animosity towards the National Church, but simple impatience at its corporate lethargy, served as the original impetus.

The third major consequence of the July monarchy for French Protestantism was the new freedom to debate the desirability of the linkage of Church and state. Since the enactment of the 1802 'concordat', the various regimes ruling France had all proven reluctant to fund any sizeable expansion of the Protestant ministry and church

---

[157] Maury, *Le Réveil Religieux,* I, 456, 457.

[158] Wemyss, *Le Réveil,* 187.

[159] Significantly, Audebez, in this para-church post, also became a founding secretary of the eclectic 'Société Évangélique de France'. See Robert, *Les Églises,* 542.

[160] Maury, *Le Réveil,* I, 457-463. The congregation's declared adherence to the historic confession was deeply significant, coming as it did in a period of agitation over the National Church's being left virtually 'creed-less' by the terms of the 'concordat' of 1802.

facilities.[161] The difficulty was partly administrative; under the terms of the 'concordat', the Reformed Church's national synod was forbidden to meet without governmental approval and this was consistently withheld. The debate, which could therefore not take place in a national synod, came to be argued out in the pages of the various Protestant journals. The case for the drastic revision or even repudiation of the 'concordat' was argued in the pages of *Les Archives du Christianisme*, edited by Frédéric Monod. Perhaps the most forceful advocate of this position was the rising young theologian, Edmond Scherer (1815-89).[162] In a series of articles entitled 'L'État actuel de L'Église réformée en France', Scherer argued that a Church deprived of the right to assemble in synod (there to establish and uphold its own doctrine and discipline) had been fatally compromised:

> By lopping off its head, the ecclesiastical constitution that now regulates us has annihilated the Reformed Church amongst us, in so far as it exists in an organization of its own. The Synod was the bond of unity of this church. We had a church, we have now only churches. The proper character of our ecclesiastical system was the association of our churches in opposition to the system of isolation; by the suppression of our Synod, this isolation has become our system. Our regime was presbyterianism, it has lapsed into congregationalism.[163]

Yet this protest was not only about the absence of a national synod, it was also a cry against the operation of the existing consistory system—weighted as was all political life in that era in favour of the upper middle classes. Under the 'concordat' of 1802, the churches had forfeited the right to choose the elders who were to comprise the regional consistories. When such men were no longer chosen on the basis of Christian maturity and knowledge, further ruin resulted.

> Our consistories...instead of being composed of the most experienced Christians of a flock are formed of the most considerable or the most busy among them... Every consistory may choose an infidel or a believing pastor according as the majority in

---

[161] The total number of ministerial graduates produced at Montauban in the years 1815-29 was 144, or an average of 9.6 per year. This could hardly sustain let alone expand a church which, even in 1815, had had 441,890 members. Robert, *Les Églises,* 539; Mours, *Les Églises,* 188, 189.

[162] Scherer, bold champion of ecclesiastical independence from the state, had received the DTh at Strasbourg in 1843. He served the Evangelical School of Theology at Geneva 1845-49 as professor of exegesis, but was dismissed from that institution when he disclosed radical convictions regarding the biblical canon. Heyer, *L'Église de Genève,* 516; Maury, *Le Réveil,* I, 185.

[163] Scherer's *Archives'* articles were subsequently printed separately under the identical title at Paris in 1844. We quote the English edition, *On the Present State of the Reformed Church in France,* (London: 1845), 27.

the consistory may chance to be. In this manner error finds itself placed exactly in the same rank with truth.[164]

Another source of agitation for separation of Church and state was the Paris journal, *Le Semeur*, edited by Alexandre Vinet of Lausanne. But there was also a party in the Church ('réveil' supporters among them) who believed that the best course of action was to seek only a limited modification of the present system and the redress of specific grievances. This substantial segment had as its organ the magazine called *L'Espérance*. The agitation of the Church-state question continued until the 'year of revolutions' (1848). Following the fall of the July monarchy, the Reformed Church, capitalizing on the temporary disarray in government, summoned an irregular synod.[165] Three major issues were addressed in this gathering. The first was the place of confessional statements in the Reformed Church. Opposition to all confessions of faith by one party led to a stalemate, and the synod failed to resolve the matter. Second, the synod considered ending the present system of regional consistories and returning actual authority to the local congregation and its elected officers. Third, the synod debated the practicability of returning to the historic pattern of regional and national synods.[166]

The failure to secure immediate satisfaction regarding restoration of fixed doctrinal articles in the sessions of the irregular synod of 1848 was utilized by forces centring around Frédéric Monod and Agenor Louis Gasparin as legitimation for withdrawal from the National Church and the founding, in the following August, of 'L'Union des Églises Évangéliques de France'.[167] 'L'Union' began with thirteen existing congregations and eighteen in formation.[168] This union invited to its inaugural synod

---

[164] Scherer, *On the Present State*, 37, 51. Ami Bost, *Mémoires*, II, 328, 329, records how just such an unsatisfactory pastoral choice at La Force in 1844 resulted in the dissatisfied members (who had no right of call in the matter) departing to form an independent church with his son, John, as pastor.

[165] Under the 'concordat' of 1802, state approval was required for a synod to meet.

[166] Maury, *Le Réveil*, I, 510, 511. Each of the three issues would eventually be resolved in favour of the church's historic Reformed practice. The state-supervised consistories were terminated in 1852 while the recovery of recognized articles of doctrine and the reconstitution of regional and national synods was accomplished in 1872.

[167] Maury, *Le Réveil*, I, 514; Wemyss, *Le Réveil*, 215. This union had actually been preceded by an informal association of independent congregations existing since 1847.

[168] Maury, *Le Réveil*, I, 514. Wemyss, *Le Réveil*, 215, suggests these numbers to have been fourteen and sixteen respectively. By 1899, the jubilee, the 'Union' still comprised only thirty-six churches, but sixty-one had been admitted at various stages in the preceding years. Cf. *L'Union des Églises évangéliques libres de France, Ses Origines, Son Histoire, Son Oeuvre* (Paris: 1899), 215. Evans, 'The Influence of Foreigners', 535, indicates that none of the thirty-one congregations had been in existence for more than twenty-five years, all being the products of the 'réveil'.

representatives of the Free Church and United Presbyterian Church of Scotland, the Free Churches of Vaud and Geneva, and the Congregational Union of England and Wales.[169] The Scottish Free Church delegates were unsuccessful in urging that the establishment principle (as distinguished from current abuses of it) should be maintained. English Congregationalists returned home confident that a posture towards the state similar to their own had been adopted.[170]

The formation of 'L'Union' was not without stresses and strains for the National Church; there was no clear consensus among 'réveil' supporters as to what course of action to follow. Brothers Frédéric and Guillaume Monod supported the creation of 'L'Union' while brother Adolphe stood firm in the National Church. The prestigious Paris pastorate, L'Oratoire, vacated by Frédéric when he withdrew from the National Church, was shortly filled by his brother, Adolphe. This Monod had turned decisively against the independency he himself had temporarily adopted in the crush of events at Lyons in the years 1832-36. The younger brother now supplied the basis for his continuance in the Establishment by penning *Pourquoi Je Demeure dans L'Église Établié* (Paris: 1849). It is plain that the majority of the 'réveil's' supporters continued within the Establishment as did Adolphe Monod.[171] The new 'Union des Églises Évangéliques' was primarily composed of individuals and congregations which had long existed outside the Establishment and been assisted by either the Continental Society, Evangelical Society of France, or Evangelical Society of Geneva; it did not by any means embrace the whole evangelical movement outside the National Church.[172]

---

[169] *L'Union des Églises*, 69ff; Wemyss, *Le Réveil*, 215. The Free Church of Scotland delegated Dr Patrick Clason (Edinburgh) and Dr David Brown (Aberdeen). The United Presbyterian Church was represented by Dr Gavin Struthers (Glasgow) and Dr Andrew Thompson (Edinburgh). Both the French Reformed Church and the Union of Evangelical Churches were among the founding members of the World Alliance of Reformed Churches at its organization in 1875. Pradervand, *A Century of Service*, 23.

[170] Mark Wilks of Paris had kept readers of *Les Archives du Christianisme* abreast of the Scottish developments of 1843 with a series of articles subsequently published as *Précis de l'histoire de l'Église Libre d'Écosse*, (Paris: 1844). Cf. the report of Congregational historian, John Waddington, in the *Evangelical Magazine*, 28 n.s. (1850), 38. The articles of doctrine and constitution of the church had appeared in the same magazine in English translation in the December issue of the preceding year. See *Evangelical Magazine*, 27 n.s. (1849), 654-656. The magazine, for its own ideological reasons, chose to call the new body the 'Evangelical Anti-State Church of France'.

[171] This is the interpretation supported by statistics provided by Mours, *Les Églises Réformées*, 189. Rapid growth continued in the Establishment until 1862 and then gave way to decline in the period to 1895.

[172] Mours, *Les Églises Réformées*, 189, reports that there were 180 non-state supported Protestant clergy in France in 1865. The 'Union', even by 1899, was served by

The Low Countries

It is necessary to observe, albeit briefly, that the impetus of the Genevan 'réveil' was quickly transmitted beyond purely Francophone regions. The United Netherlands, formed in 1815 at the Congress of Vienna by the union of the Netherlands and Belgium, was one such region. We have noted already the presence of some members of the Haldane circle, namely members G.L. James and J.H. Merle D'Aubigné at Breda and Brussels from 1820 and 1823 respectively.[173] D'Aubigné's ministry proved especially significant, for in the period from 1823 to 1830 (when revolution severed the kingdom into the Netherlands and Belgium of today) he exercised a significant ministry as court preacher to King William I. In the same pastorate, D'Aubigné exercised a profound influence over Groen Van Prinsterer, a recent Leiden University graduate now attached to the royal court. Van Prinsterer was subsequently secretary to the Cabinet and royal archivist.[174] From Geneva, there were also in this period evangelists and colporteurs sent out by the 'Bourg-de-Four' congregation.[175] Émile Guers, 'Bourg-de-Four' minister and central agent of the Continental Society, visited the United Provinces on that society's behalf in early 1823.[176]

Yet such data, while worthy of consideration, ought not to obscure the fact that there had been earlier and (sometimes) indigenous forces at work for spiritual renewal. The historian, M. Elisabeth Kluit, has documented the significance for the Netherlands of the visit of John Wesley in 1783, the influence of the translated writings of John Newton and James Hervey, and the assistance of the London Missionary Society in the inauguration of a Dutch counterpart in 1797; all were examples of British evangelical influence preceding the post-Napoleonic 'réveil'. The same writer observed a significant Moravian influence in the region flowing from the educational institution of Montmirail (in the French

---

only forty-five pastors and fifteen evangelists. See *L'Union des Églises*, 230. Evans, 'The Influence of Foreigners', 414, reports that by 1848, the Evangelical Society of France had been sustaining 200 churches alone.

[173] See p. 93 *supra*.

[174] The significance of D'Aubigné's years in Brussels is stressed in Michael Wintle, *Pillars of Piety*, (Hull: 1987), 22, and Gerrit J. tenZythoff, *Sources of Secession: The Netherlands Hervormde Kerk On the Eve of the Dutch Immigration to the Midwest*, (Grand Rapids: 1987), 109. Biéler, daughter and biographer to D'Aubigné, indicates in *Une Famille*, 159, that her father 'had the joy of propagating the "réveil" in Holland' and (p. 170) had the offer of a call from the French church at Rotterdam when the Revolution required his removal from Brussels.

[175] Bost, *Mémoires*, II, 98 ; and Guers, *Le Premier Réveil*, 287.

[176] Guers, *Le Premier Réveil*, 252. The Continental Society had a least one pastor-evangelist in this region from 1820. See the second *Report of the Continental Society*, (London: 1820), 4.

Jura region) as well as the diffusion of the Reformed pietism of Johan
Caspar Lavater (1741-1801), preacher of St. Peter's Church, Zurich.[177]
Along similar lines, the Belgian historian, H.R. Boudin, has
demonstrated that activity by agents of the Netherlands Missionary
Society (f.1797), the Basel Missionary Society (f.1815), and the British
and Foreign Bible Society substantially predated the labour of the better-
known Swiss evangelicals in the region of the United Provinces which
would once more be identified as Belgium after 1830.[178]

After acknowledging this pre-history, we may note that certain
Protestants in the Netherlands observed developments at Geneva after
1816 with keen interest. One such group of observers was a patrician and
intellectual circle of persons gathered around the Leiden historian,
William Bilderdijk; the circle was characterized by deep piety, loyalty to
the House of Orange (now restored in the person of William I) and a
loathing of the atheism and disorder of the French Revolution. Groen
Van Prinsterer, to whom we have referred above in connection with the
Brussels pastorate of Merle D'Aubigné, was part of this circle; he had
been one of Bilderdijk's Leiden pupils.[179] From 1816, this circle kept
abreast of Genevan developments; it was fully conversant with the
explosive Genevan pamphlet of that year, *Considérationes Sur La Divinité
de Jésus Christ*. One member of the circle, Cornelis Baron van Zuylen van
Nijeveldt, subsequently translated for local consumption the similarly
potent treatise of 1819, *Genève Religieux en Mars 1819*, by Ami Bost.[180]

The Bilderdijk circle saw in the vigorous activity of the young
orthodox ministers of Geneva a pattern worthy of emulation in their own
national and ecclesiastical situation. Van Prinsterer himself visited Geneva
in 1833 to meet with his former minister, D'Aubigné, as well as César
Malan and Louis Gaussen. He also made it his business to consult the
increasingly influential Alexandre Vinet of Lausanne.[181]

Similarly, the Bilderdijk circle rapidly developed affinities with the
patrician evangelicalism of Paris. There were comparable efforts to

---

[177] M. Elisabeth Kluit, 'Internationale Invloeding in de Voorgeschiedenis van het
Réveil in Nederland', *Nederlands Archief Voor Kerkgeschiedenis*, 44-45 n.s. (1961-63),
37-45.

[178] H.R. Boudin, 'Einige Aspekte des Reveils in Belgien', in J. Van den Berg and J.P.
Van Dooren, eds., *Pietismus und Reveil*, (Leiden: 1978), 289, 298.

[179] tenZythoff, *Sources of Secession*, 59, 109.

[180] M. Elisabeth Kluit, 'Wenselijkheden Voor de Studie Van Het Réveil', *Nederlands
Theologisch Tijdschrift*, 11 (1956-57), 360; tenZythoff, *Sources of Secession*, 62.

[181] Perhaps it was Van Prinsterer who brought to the fledgling Evangelical Society of
Geneva the donation from King William alluded to in Bickersteth, *Voice From the Alps*,
4.

resolve current social ills by the application of Christian principles.[182] A periodical, *De Vereeniging Christelijke Stemmen* (*The Society of Christian Voices*) sought to keep sympathizers of the movement abreast of developments akin to their own in England, France and the Rhineland.[183] Such patrician and intellectual evangelicalism would seem to have provided the setting for the extended preaching tours of César Malan through the Netherlands and Belgium during 1842 and 1845.[184] Yet this movement in Holland, even at its zenith, is said to have embraced not more than 3,000 persons.[185]

A second and more expansive movement of Dutch Protestantism, also characterized by intense opposition to the tendencies introduced during the period of French domination, was similarly cognizant of developments at Geneva. This grouping, which left the National Reformed Church of the Netherlands in 1834, and was then termed the 'Afscheiding', had its origin in the royal imposition of a new church order in 1816. King William's government, then apparently enamoured with the efficiencies of the consistorial system introduced in Napoleonic France, determined in 1816 to administer Church affairs through representatives of its own choosing, and to impose new and ambiguous formulas of subscription to the Reformed confessions of faith for use by candidates seeking ordination.

Such measures understandably antagonized the representatives of this outlook, characterized as they were by adherence to the high-Calvinism of the pre-Revolutionary period. This theological outlook was then experiencing something of a resurgence. Unlike the patrician constituency of the Bilderdijk movement, these supporters of a rigorous confessional theology in the Netherlands were predominantly provincial, lower middle class, and long accustomed to attendance at conventicles supplementary to stated religious services.

This movement, though similar to others we have considered both in its resistance to state intrusion in church affairs and use of home gatherings, nevertheless stands apart. The movement was not markedly 'conversionist' and was largely content to repeat Reformed theology as it had been handed down; the popularized Calvinism of the Francophone

---

[182] Cf. pp. 124, 125 *supra*. Wintle, *Pillars of Piety*, 23, describes the activities of W. de Clerq, who deliberately sited the industries of the Dutch East Indies Trading Company so as to alleviate chronic unemployment.

[183] Wintle, *Pillars*, 22.

[184] Malan, *Life*, 284. In Belgium, Malan would certainly have connected his labours with those of the 'Belgian Evangelical Society', described below. His 1842 trip was underwritten with the aid of the 'Foreign Evangelical Society' of New York. See their *Report*, (New York: 1843), 33.

[185] Wintle, *Pillars*, 22.

'réveil' was not the note being sounded within the 'Afscheiding'.[186] At first, the declarations of secession from the National Reformed Church brought rigorous military and governmental harassment. This continued until, in the 1840s, it was recognized that the seceders harboured no intention of promoting political upheaval.[187]

In 1830, Belgium had broken away from the control of the Netherlands. Belgium was almost exclusively Roman Catholic, with a Catholicism that had scarcely been challenged by the Reformation of the sixteenth century. Such enclaves of Protestantism as did emerge had very often been 'colonies' of French Huguenots. There had also been some colonies of Hollanders, though most of these withdrew in 1830. By 1837, only seven Protestant churches were still in existence; all were state-supported under the constitution of 1831. All seven congregations were served by foreign pastors and four of the seven were comprised exclusively of foreigners—many recently arrived from various German states to pursue business or establish industry. The three indigenous congregations had no more than 800 members and adherents among them.[188]

The situation began to change when a Scripture distribution committee was established in Brussels in 1834 with assistance from the British and Foreign Bible Society. The latter supplied a resident agent, William Pascoe Tiddy, in the following year. The widespread diffusion of Scriptures by colporteurs greatly assisted the Protestant Churches in the task of evangelization. A second significant development was the visit in 1836 of the American minister, Dr Robert Baird, who was touring in Europe as the representative of a New York based 'French Committee'. Through Baird's influence, the American 'French Committee' assisted in the cost of construction of a second Protestant place of worship in Brussels.[189]

With such encouragements as these, W.P. Tiddy of the British and Foreign Bible Society began to make special efforts to secure the services

---

[186] Yet the magazine of the Christlijke Gereformeerde Kerken (which arose from the 'Afschieding' or secession), *Die Reformatie*, reflected a healthy interest in the unfolding of religious affairs at Geneva from its inauguration in 1837. See, e.g., 'Berigt van de Evangelische Maatschaapij te Geneve', *Die Reformatie*, 1 (1837), 124.

[187] tenZythoff, *Sources*, 61ff; J.D. Bratt, *Dutch Calvinism in Modern America*, 6ff.

[188] Leonard Anet, *Histoire des Trente Premières Années de la Société Évangélique ou Église Chrétienne Missionaire Belge*, (Bruxelles: 1875), 14, 18, 20. One of these seven foreign pastors was J. Devisme, serving a church at Dour. He had been a close acquaintance of Émile Guers since their days together in the University of Geneva. Cf. Guers, *Le Premier Réveil*, 43.

[189] Anet, *Histoire*, 23. Wilder, *Records from the Life of S.V.S. Wilder*, (New York: 1865), 273, indicates that this 'French Committee' subsequently became the 'Foreign Evangelical Society'.

of Francophone evangelists. It was in these circumstances that Louis Vierne, a 'Bourg-de-Four' missionary to France, was invited to assist the Belgian Protestant movement in 1837.[190] In the same year, Tiddy's enquiries secured the services of a M. Girod, a recent graduate of the Evangelical School of Theology at Geneva. Shortly thereafter, a third new worker was secured, a M. Maton who had been assisting an independent church at Leme, France, as an agent of the Continental Society. The latter organization re-assigned Maton to La Bouverie, Belgium, in response the entreaties of Tiddy.[191] But further expansion seemed problematic. Three of the seven long-established churches, with their ministers, stood opposed to all such aggressive efforts at evangelization as were underway. Further, all new missionary labourers (such as the three named) were dependent not on state subsidy, but private (and largely foreign) support.

Such circumstances commended the pattern of missionary endeavour being followed at Lausanne, Geneva and Paris. The Bible Society agent, Tiddy, joined forces with the four supportive National Church pastors and other concerned individuals to found the Belgian Evangelical Society in November 1837.[192] The immediate direction taken was one of making the three privately supported missionaries the initial agents of the new society. That the initial three agents were all dissident Protestants seems to have been incidental. In fact, most of the leading figures in the society favoured the state support of Protestantism; both Lutheran and Reformed sympathies were evenly represented.

The foundation of the Belgian society was warmly acclaimed in Geneva, Paris, Holland and London; financial aid was soon forthcoming. Belgian ministers of Lutheran outlook travelled to Cologne, Frankfurt, Berne, and Basle to gather support for the new enterprise.[193] But there were soon political difficulties. In May 1839, the Belgian government determined to place supervisory responsibility for all Protestant religious affairs in a newly-created synod of the seven established Belgian

---

[190] Anet, *Histoire*, 25. Vierne is mentioned in Bost, *Mémoires*, II, 98, as being somewhat problematic for the 'Bourg-de-Four' congregation as he belonged to its Baptistic minority. Cf. also Guers, *Le Premier Réveil*, 287.

[191] Anet, *Histoire*, 29, 30. The printed *Appeal of the Continental Society, (Dublin Auxilliary)*, (Dublin: 1834), n.p., identifies Maton as an agent in the north of France. Another graduate, besides Girod, of the Evangelical School of Theology at Geneva, Louis Durand, was pastor at Liege, Belgium, in this period. Cf. Guers *Le Premier Réveil*, 253. The first native of Belgium to enrol at the Evangelical School of Geneva did so in 1838. Bickersteth, *A Voice*, 177.

[192] Anet, *Histoire*, 35

[193] Anet, *Histoire*, 143. The contributions to the Society in the period 1837-44 with their sources were (in Belgian francs): Belgium (32,282), Great Britain (152,131), Holland (37,679), Germany (7,311), France (515), Switzerland (11,090), America (9,781).

Protestant Churches. A powerful element in the Established Churches had consistently opposed the work of evangelization as then conducted.[194] The government's move left the society, with its five agents and mission stations, liable to the unfriendly control it had sought to avert by its independent organization.

In response, the society re-organized its affairs in such a way as to again side-step this unfriendly jurisdiction and by 1842 could begin once more to expand. This expansion led to the creation of a new denomination, 'L'Église Chretienne Missionaire Belge', in March 1849.[195] Organized along presbyterian lines and adhering to _The Belgic Confession_ of 1561, the fledgling body rapidly took its place in an orbit of like-minded European Churches.[196] Fourteen congregations or preaching stations existed in 1858.[197]

We may note finally, in passing that the influence of the Genevan 'réveil' passed to other regions in Western Europe. A consciously related movement taking the name 'Freie Evangelisch Kirche' arose at Wuppertal-Elberfeld in the German Rhine region in 1854. The principal proponent of the cause, a businessman named H.H. Grafe (d.1869), had been a member of the Reformed congregation at Elberfeld. While on business in Lyons, France, in 1841-42, he had encountered and come to admire the Evangelical Church of Lyons—founded a decade earlier. Grafe assisted in the formation of a congregation at Wuppertal in 1854; the articles of faith adopted were those of the Free Evangelical Church of Geneva. This movement, motivated in part by displeasure at government encroachment in Church affairs, soon spread into the Rhineland, Westfalen and Hesse.[198]

Moreover, we may observe the influence of Geneva in the strengthening of evangelical life among the Italian Waldensians. Lacking any theological faculty of their own, the Italian churches entered into an

---

[194] Anet, _Histoire_, 72.

[195] Anet, _Histoire_, 159.

[196] Anet, _Histoire_, 172, cites the Presbyterian Church of England, United Presbyterian Church of Scotland, Free Church of Scotland, and Free Evangelical Churches of Geneva and Vaud as early fraternal churches. Consistent with this configuration, the Belgian Church was a founding member of the World Alliance of Reformed Churches in 1875. Cf. Pradervand, _A Century_, 22.

[197] Anet, _Histoire_, 278. An interesting account of the Belgian Evangelical Society's labour in the 1840s is provided in Hugh Heugh, _Notices of the State of Religion in Geneva and Belgium_, (Glasgow: 1844).

[198] Gunnar Westin, _The Free Church Through the Ages_, (Nashville: 1958), 296. We may assume that the visit of the Genevan preacher, César Malan, to this region in 1856 was in some way connected with this movement. Malan, _Life_, 284. The 'Freie Evangelische Kirche' was a founding member of the World Alliance of Reformed Churches. Cf. Pradervand, _A Century_, 23.

agreement with the Evangelical School of Theology at Geneva and sent a steady stream of students there until 1855. At the opening of the Waldensian College at Florence in that year, Merle D'Aubigné was present to give an inaugural address.[199]

The 'Réveil' and Theology

'The "reveil" was before all else a doctrinal affair', observed the historian of the movement, Maury, in 1892.[200] This observation has never been seriously questioned, not even by those contemporary critics of the movement who either dismissed it as 'Methodism' or faulted it for an obsession with the theology of the sixteenth century. More recently, the French historian, Jean Cadier, has written that 'the orthodoxy of the nineteenth century was born in the réveil'.[201]

Yet the claim of theological importance for the 'réveil' is extremely problematic for two reasons. First, while the movement clearly generated or stimulated theological writing (Vinet on Church and state, for example), no such treatise ever represented the thought or conviction of the international 'réveil' as a whole.[202] Thus, we cannot attribute the particular views of any single writer of the period to the movement as a whole. Second, and inseparable from the first, is the fact that no work of Protestant dogmatics was published by any participant in the 'réveil' movement during the period in question. Indeed, the great opponent of the movement, the Geneva theologian, J.J.C. Chenevière, stood quite alone in this respect, for in publishing his *Dogmatique Chrétienne* (Geneva: 1840) he offered the Francophone public the only Protestant systematic theology of the nineteenth century before the year 1885.[203] With these

---

[199] Good, *History,* 465; *Facolta Valdese di Teologica, 1855-1955,* (Florence: 1955), 70ff. This volume makes plain that it was the spread of the Genevan 'réveil' which led to the heightened vitality of the Waldensian movement and, ultimately, the foundation of the faculty of theology at Florence. The presence of Hungarian, Spanish and Canadian students in the Evangelical School at Geneva would suggest a similar diffusion of the 'réveil' in those regions. Cf. Biéler, *Une Famille,* 194.

[200] Maury, *Le Réveil Religieux,* II. 7. A quite different opinion was held by Jacques Cart. *Histoire du Mouvement,* I. ii. 342 ; the latter spoke of réveil theology as being 'a reaction, an accentuation of certain doctrines'.

[201] Jean Cadier, 'La Tradition Calviniste Dans Le Réveil du XIX Siècle', *Études Théologiques et Religieux,* 27 (1952), 9.

[202] Vinet's *Essai sur la manifestation des convictions religieux et sur la séparation de l'église et de l'état,* (Paris : 1842), cannot be said to have convinced the majority of French 'réveil' supporters for whom Adolphe Monod was speaking when he wrote *Pourquoi Je Demeure dans L'Église Établie,* (Paris: 1849).

[203] A. Gretillat, 'Movements of Theological Thought Among French-Speaking Protestants From the Revival of 1820 to the end of 1891', *Presbyterian and Reformed Review,* 3 (1892), 422. We may note in passing that the libraries of the University of

boundaries to our discussion in mind, however, we may still discover suggestive facts about the theology of the 'reveil'.

About Books

We may first ask, what the early preachers of this movement read, over and above the Scriptures. Émile Guers, separatist and later pastor of the 'Bourg-de-Four' congregation, has left a very clear record of what his circle of friends read in the years and months prior to the visit of Haldane to Geneva:

> We relied on religious books such as à Kempis' *Imitation of Christ*—which dwelt exclusively on sanctification. A corrective to it was needed—or a complement. We found this in David Hollaz' *L'Ordre de la Grace dans L'Economie du Salut*—a work translated from the German. Lissignol of Montpellier reprinted this later in 1825. The *Heidelberg Catechism* became very important as did *L'Exposition de la Doctrine des Frères du l'Unité* by their Bishop Spangenberg. The *Sermons* of Nardin and of Jean Daillé were also read.[204]

During this period, César Malan (who was not part of Guers' circle) had been ruminating on *L'Abrogé des Doctrines* of Benedict Pictet (1655-1724), a writer regarded as the last orthodox dogmatician at Geneva, as well as upon the *Belgic Confession of Faith* (1561).[205] The writings of Calvin receive no mention among the recollections of the 'réveil' men for this period. It was to rectify this neglect that the English banker, Henry Drummond, personally financed two printings of the *Institutes*.[206] There was, however, no lack of interest in Calvin at Lausanne, where doyen L.A. Curtat made readings from Calvin the basis of his special lectures to ministerial students.[207] In France, Calvin and other theologians of the Reformation and post-Reformation era were neglected

---

Geneva and Princeton Theological Seminary contain hand-copied versions of Louis Gaussen's theological lectures. There is no evidence suggesting that these were put into print. The Princeton copy is dated 1851-52.

[204] Guers, *Le Premier Réveil*, 50. This is a highly significant list. David Hollaz (1648-1713) was, according to John MacPherson, *Christian Dogmatics*, (Edinburgh: 1898), 61, 'a strict Lutheran on whom pietism has a powerful silent influence. His writing, characterized by great precision of definition, marks the transition from the severely scholastic formalism of the seventeenth century to the pietism of the eighteenth century'. We have referred already to this text of Spangenberg at ch. 2, p. 86 *supra*. Nardin and Daillé were popular seventeenth-century preachers.

[205] Malan, *Life*, 44. Guers obviously knew of and appreciated Pictet's writings, cf. *Le Premier Réveil*, 10.

[206] Guers, *Le Premier Réveil*, 223. Guers himself supervised the re-issue.

[207] Cart, *Histoire du Mouvement*, I.i.83. Cart notes the consequences, unforeseen by Curtat, of this re-exposure to Calvin.

as at Geneva. Yet in France the neglect was the direct consequence of the 'enforced theological silence following the Revocation of the Edict of Nantes (1685)'.[208] In the United Netherlands, a future leader of the secession ('Afscheiding') of 1834, Hendrik de Cock, encountered the *Institutes* for the first time in another minister's library in 1829.[209]

What did 'réveil' leaders make available for others to read—either by their own translation or simple distribution? Ami Bost translated into French John Bunyan's *Pilgrim's Progress* as well as the *Life* of the late John Newton (1725-1807). Bost also translated into German Haldane's *Exposition of Romans* and assisted in the French translation of Charles Finney's *Lectures on Revival* (New York: 1835).[210] Edouard Petitpierre (1804-89), the Neuchâtel-born and Geneva-trained evangelist in the east of France and his own canton, translated Alexander Haldane's *Lives of Robert and J.A. Haldane* and the *Life of George Müller of Bristol*.[211] Félix Neff, whose literary labours did not extend to the translation of foreign works, was nonetheless active in urging his parishioners of the High Alps to read them, when available. Bunyan's *Life* and *Pilgrim's Progress*, Edwards' *Life of David Brainerd* and the early 'réveil' classic, *Letters of Charles Rieu* (late of Frederica, Denmark) were the titles he recommended most often.[212]

Quite apart from the labours of 'réveil' leaders in translating and distributing such literature, we may note the substantial endeavour for the printing of evangelical literature operated by the Courtois brothers at Toulouse. This concern, 'La Société de Livres Religieux', was responsible for the production of a large proportion of French evangelical literature in the period following the revolution of 1830.[213]

The works that the men of the 'réveil' read or recommended to others reflects a Protestant eclecticism quite in step with the evangelical theological outlook then current in Britain and America. One can readily

[208] Cadier, 'La Tradition Calviniste', 10.

[209] tenZythoff, *Sources of Secession,* 111. We have maintained above that this secession of 1834 was not organically related to the Genevan 'réveil'.

[210] Bost, *Mémoires,* I, 267, 306, 291. Guers, *Le Premier Réveil,* 225.

[211] Guers, *Le Premier Réveil,* 286

[212] Stephen Gilly, *Memoir of Neff,* (London: 1832), 301.

[213] Among the titles produced at Toulouse were the following of American origin: Archibald Alexander, *The Canon of Sacred Scripture* (1835); Gardiner Spring, *The Distinguishing Traits of Christian Character* (1824); W.B. Sprague, *Lively Oracles* (1829); Charles Hodge, *Romans* (1837), and *The Way of Life* (1844). The following were of British origin: Richard Baxter, *Call to the Unconverted* (1657) and *The Saints' Everlasting Rest* (1650); John Bunyan, *The Pilgrim's Progress* (1678); John Newton, *Life* (1827), and *Cardiphonia* (1780); Philip Doddridge, *Proofs Which Establish the Truth of Christianity* (1763). This is a compilation of titles drawn from Evans, 'The Contribution of Foreigners', 417, 564, and the *Third Report of the Foreign Evangelical Society* (1842) 34, 35.

understand how it is that Francophone historians, noting these similarities and the free flow of translated literature, would readily attribute all to foreign rather than native influence. Thus, Alice Wemyss has written of 'this massive importation of English civilization'[214] in this period, while Jean Cadier has described how a

> French Protestantism which had been (by persecution and Revolution) cut off from its origins, received from outsiders powerful new influences in its theological culture.[215]

But the suggestion of Wemyss—that theology of the 'réveil' is only the theology of the late Evangelical Revival transposed into another tongue—is unconvincing for several reasons. First, virtually all of the leading personalities, preachers and missionary agents of the period were Francophone and not foreign. Secondly, the majority of France's Protestants would probably never have met a missionary agent or owned a translation of a British or American evangelical work. Third, leading participants in the 'réveil' insisted that they were influenced by continental Moravianism before any pronounced British influences were brought to bear after Napoleon's fall.[216] Yet, after observing that the basic theological thought of the 'réveil' was formed first by European and only subsequently by British or American forces, we can still recognize that Francophone evangelical theology in our period was not strikingly different from what one would have found in Britain or America.

In point of fact, Reformed preaching and theology in Britain and America in this period had itself undergone some simplification of presentation and argument through contact with Methodism.[217] It is now commonplace to speak of the 'moderation' of British Calvinism through

---

[214] Wemyss, *Le Réveil*, 143.

[215] Cadier, 'La Tradition Calviniste', 12. It should be noted that Cadier's reasons for acknowledging foreign theological influences are quite different from those of Wemyss. Cadier, a twentieth-century neo-Calvinist, was concerned to recover and emphasize a 'pristine' French Reformed Theology; yet he writes of the 'réveil' period with clear affection. Wemyss wrote from a stance which was clearly dismissive of religious enthusiasm.

[216] Guers, whom we have already quoted at fn. 205 acknowledging theological indebtedness to the Moravian Bishop Spangenberg, was always at pains to emphasize that 'Moravianism was the "cradle" of the 'réveil'"; cf. *Le Premier Réveil*, 40, 41; and Cart, *Histoire du Mouvement*, I.i.140.

[217] We have noted in ch. 1 the observations of David Bogue and William Jay on the modification of Nonconformist Reformed theology and preaching by contact with Methodism, both in its Whitefieldian and Wesleyan forms.

this interaction.[218] We will do well to consider the evangelical theology of the 'réveil' as having gone through a similar 'modification'—its Reformed theology having been 'nursed' through a century of persecution and rationalism by Moravianism and the Continental pietist tradition and then only latterly influenced by British evangelicalism.[219] It is to this sometimes ragged amalgam of views that Cadier was referring when he maintained that

> while the 'réveil' missionary-evangelists were not theologians, had not studied theology and had no proper regard for theology, such theologians as the 'réveil' had were Calvinists.[220]

About Doctrines

Maury, who provided a thorough treatment of the question of what the men of the 'réveil' believed and taught, wrote,

> The 'réveil' had at its base the dogmatic truths which have served since the Reformation as the foundations of evangelical theology: the authority of Scripture, the divinity of Christ, expiation, grace, regeneration by the Holy Spirit, and sanctification.[221]

Affirming the accuracy of these sentiments, we wish here to consider briefly only three questions, each of which have a bearing on the issue of whether the 'réveil' introduced new doctrinal formulations. The first is the question of the understanding of 'regeneration by the Holy Spirit'. Understanding regeneration to be that divine quickening of the hearer of the gospel necessary to the active acceptance of the message about Christ, (conversion), it is plain that the 'réveil' men did not stand on the same ground as did their respected senior ministerial friends. Émile Guers, who in his early student days had incurred parental disapproval for his frequenting of Moravian gatherings, received surprising though qualified

---

[218] The terminology is imprecise and unhelpful in that it gratuitously assumes a pervasiveness and fixity of British Calvinism prior to the rise of Methodism—yet useful in designating the adjustment which Bogue and Jay observed.

[219] It is here significant to note the warm praise of Guers not only for Zinzendorf but for pietists such as Jean de Labadie and Spener and mystic-contemplatives such as Madame Guyon. See *Le Premier Réveil*, 6.

[220] Cadier, 'La Tradition', 27. An earlier twentieth-century French Reformed writer, also neo-Calvinist, Auguste Lecerf, was willing to allow that the réveil preachers were Calvinist only in a popular sense, and he used Whitefield as an exemplar of their approach. See Lecerf's 'The Reformed Faith in France', *Evangelical Quarterly*, 4.4 (1932), 395.

[221] Maury, *Le Réveil Religieux*, II, 12.

support for his attendance at such assemblies when the senior minister of Satigny, J.I.S. Cellérier, told his father that the Moravians

> were excellent Christians and that they would be a good influence on me. Cellérier senior, did object, however, to the Moravian distinction of people into Christian and non-Christian.[222]

Cellérier, then, was in the view of Guers orthodox and even pietistic in outlook; but he was not 'conversionist'. Young Guers was decidedly so. His own conversion had come about by means of a personal interview with the Moravian evangelist, J.N. Mettetal.[223] Jacques Cart, the chronicler of 'réveil' activity in the canton of Vaud, had similar recollections of his mentor, L.A. Curtat, who was impeccably orthodox on major doctrines but seemed to lack an appreciation for conversion. In Cart's view, Curtat was lacking

> a clear understanding of the work of the Holy Spirit, the appropriation of salvation and Christian assurance. In his thought, the Holy Spirit works in all. All are considered by him [Curtat] as Christians. He insists strongly on the redemption wrought by Christ, but he considers it essentially as an objective fact.[224]

We are not able here to explore the question of whether Reformed ministers such as Cellérier and Curtat represented their theological traditions well in looking askance at 'conversionism'.[225] What is beyond doubt is that a younger generation of students and ministers imbibed this from the Moravians, were schooled in it further by Haldane and other British evangelicals and then came to consider its absence in the older generation to be a grave omission. This issue had, in fact, been one on which the promulgators of the Genevan 'règlement' of May 1817 had sought to enforce a cessation of debate.[226] We may simply note that the preachers and evangelists of the period were careful not to embrace the facile notion that conversion would necessarily be experienced in some standardized manner.[227]

Second, we must note that the evangelical theologians of Geneva—and in particular Malan, Gaussen, and D'Aubigné—were charged by some contemporaries and some members of the succeeding generation with

---

[222] Guers, *Le Premier Réveil,* 21.

[223] Guers, *Le Premier Réveil,* 41.

[224] Cart, *Histoire du Mouvement,* I.i.80-82.

[225] Maury in the above quotation is endorsing the view that 'réveil' convictions about regeneration were anticipated by the Reformation.

[226] The third of four topics itemized in the 'règlement' had been 'the manner in which grace operates, or efficacious grace'; cf. ch. 2, p. 75 *supra.*

[227]César Malan, e.g., recorded that his own conversion to Christ had been 'rather like the rousing of an infant by a mother's kiss'. Malan, *Life,* 38.

theological extremism. The espousal of high predestinarianism by Malan and the embracing of the doctrine of the verbal inspiration of Scripture by Gaussen and D'Aubigné drew this censure.[228] In considering this accusation of theological extremism, we must first note that evangelical theologians at Geneva exercised considerable influence 'on the coat-tails' of the long-established and long-influential Geneva Academy. Much Genevan evangelical theology was the theology of rejoinder. Second, the struggle for theological the 'high ground' which developed between the Academy and the Evangelical School of Theology after the latter's foundation in 1832 was initially fought along the lines of which institution stood in clearest continuity with the sixteenth-century Reformation. As the Academy was determined to distance itself from the theology of the sixteenth and seventeenth centuries,[229] it was very soon the case that the new college had established for itself an essentially conservative and retrospective posture which was far happier in emphasizing the abiding truths of the older orthodoxy than in engaging in creative theological writing for the nineteenth century.

This retrospective posture cannot be said to have ever embraced the entire faculty. Samuel Preiswerk, the New Testament lecturer from 1834, defected to Irvingism by 1838, while Edmond Scherer, who joined the faculty as lecturer in exegesis in 1844, was dismissed by 1849 for making concessions to German criticism.[230] Yet Louis Gaussen and Merle D'Aubigné[231] seem to have felt obliged to uphold a high orthodoxy consistent with the Reformed confessions. Included in this high orthodoxy were the doctrines of absolute predestination and the verbal inspiration of Scripture. Outside the polemical context of the rival Genevan faculties of theology—whether among the theologians of Montauban or the pastor-evangelists of 'Bourg-de-Four'—'réveil' supporters pursued a more practical and less retrospective theological

---

[228] Cf. the disapproving attitude of Alexandre Vinet in Laura M. Lane, *Vinet*, 7; of Adolphe Monod (then of Montauban) in Maury, *Le Réveil*, II, 35; of Gretillat, 'Movements of Theological Thought', 423. Biéler, daughter of D'Aubigné, exempted her father from the criticism, but laid the charge at the feet of Malan and Gaussen; *Une Famille*, 112.

[229] A determination signalled, for instance, by the 1819 publication by Chenevière of the tract *Sur Les Causes Qui Retardent Le Progrès de La Théologie Chez Les Réformés*; the tract singled out the current upswing in attention to the Reformed Confessions as one such 'check' on progress.

[230] Maury, *Le Réveil Religieux*, I, 185

[231] César Malan, a non-faculty member, shared this retrospective approach to theology in general and predestination in particular. It must be remembered in all this that the 'agenda' for theology was largely pre-determined for the evangelical theologians of Geneva by the 'règlement' of 1817 and the publication of Chenevière's lectures in 1831.

line. Biblical authority was a constant for the 'réveil', but the Gaussen-D'Aubigné approach to biblical inspiration was not embraced by all 'réveil' supporters.[232] The same point could be made about the doctrines of election and predestination. All Genevan evangelicals of the period had had these doctrines forcibly placed at the forefront of their thinking by the dual fact that Robert Haldane had emphasized them in his exposition of Romans and the 'Compagnie' had proscribed debate over them by the 'règlement' of May 1817. Thus, not only César Malan, but also the young preachers of 'Bourg-de-Four' and Gaussen of Satigny were busy in defending and propagating these doctrines from 1817, perhaps in the belief that since the doctrines had been challenged it was now necessary to give them prominence. By contrast, the Genevan graduate Abraham Lissignol of Montpellier—on meeting the English Methodist (and anti-predestinarian) missionary, Charles Cook in 1819—cordially agreed to overlook their undoubted differences over this matter in the interests of a wider co-operation.[233]

It was to this more pragmatic stance that the 'Bourg-de-Four' preachers eventually came. They realized that their early months of preaching on these doctrines, immediately subsequent to the departure of Haldane in June 1817, had been unbalanced and had constituted an actual obstacle to evangelization. Having been warned by the visiting London Scot, William Anderson, in late 1818 'not to be so foolish as to place the doctrine of election between the sinner and Christ',[234] they thereafter came to see the doctrines of election and predestination primarily as consolatory truths. Félix Neff, the 'Bourg-de-Four' convert who went on to evangelize in the High Alps, undoubtedly believed these doctrines firmly, but censured a young preacher under the influence of César Malan for his seeming obsession with them.[235] Ami Bost similarly believed these doctrines firmly, but insisted that a complementary doctrine—the personal responsibility of the sinner for his own destiny—be equally emphasized.[236] It is significant that when the Free

---

[232] In 1842, Gaussen published his *Théopneustie* at Paris. D'Aubigné in 1850 published *L'Autorité des Écritures Inspirées de Dieu* at Toulouse. Both were characterized by an indebtedness to the high orthodoxy of the seventeenth century and an affinity with the position taken by Robert Haldane in his *The Evidence and Authority of Divine Revelation* (Edinburgh: 1816). We discuss the international impact of Gaussen's views in the following chapter.

[233] Maury, *Le Réveil*, II, 121.

[234] Guers, *Vie de Pyt*, 28.

[235] Bost, *Letters and Biography of Félix Neff*, 326-33.

[236] Bost, *Mémoires*, I, 200-201, and II, 457, 458. Bost, in composing his *Mémoires*, was gratified to find that Thomas Chalmers had insisted on the same equilibrium between these doctrines.

Churches of Geneva and France (both established in 1849) set out their doctrinal articles, election and predestination were dealt with in this restrained manner.[237]

About Confessions of Faith

What has just been demonstrated in the particular instance of the doctrines of election and predestination holds equally true in the matter of attitudes towards the historic Reformed confessions of the sixteenth and seventeenth centuries. In the Francophone regions we have surveyed, the 'réveil' preceded concern for confessional integrity rather than the reverse. It was because they had been awakened and desired systematic biblical instruction that Émile Guers and his friends began to seek assistance from the *Heidelberg Catechism* (1563).[238] Gaussen and Cellérier reprinted the *Second Helvetic Confession* (1566) in 1819 because they were committed to evangelical renewal in the face of their canton's moratorium on the discussion of central Christian doctrines. The confessions were viewed almost as an armoury—from which clear definitions could be drawn, like so much weaponry, as the need arose. There is nothing to suggest that the 'réveil' men were advocating a return to the more strict confessional subscription of a previous era.

Laurent Cadoret, 1804 graduate of David Bogue's Gosport Academy serving the National Church of France at Luneray, successfully appealed to the *French Confession of Faith* (1559) when charged in 1809 with preaching on abstruse doctrinal questions. The mere fact that the doctrines in question were included in the confession told in favour of Cadoret.[239] Similarly, Daniel Encontre, dean of the seminary at Montauban, acted in concert with concerned ministers of his region and appealed to the same confession for clear definitions of trinitarian orthodoxy in an attempt to check the anti-trinitarian teaching of their Genevan theological professor, Esaie Gasc in 1813.[240] Young Henri Pyt and Émile Guers also appealed to this confession in autumn 1816 when challenged by their Genevan professors to justify their sympathy for the provocative pamphlet of Henri Empeytaz.[241]

But this is not to say that such 'réveil' men were theological precisionists. They were in fact as much indebted to the Moravian-Pietist

---

[237] See the Geneva article number ten in Guers, *Notice Historique*, 88, or Schaff, *Creeds of Christendom*, III, 781ff. For the French articles, see the *Evangelical Magazine*, 27 n.s. (1849), 654.

[238] Cf. the quotation from Guers, *Le Premier Réveil*, at p. 136 above.

[239] Robert, *Les Églises Réformées*, 245.

[240] Robert, *Les Églises Réformées*, 221.

[241] Guers, *Vie de Pyt*, 17. The pamphlet was *Considérations Sur la Divinité de Jésus Christ* (1816).

tradition as to the Calvinist; yet without insincerity they made use of the Reformed confessions as honoured guardians of the great doctrines of the faith. It was for these reasons that the Alpine missionary, Félix Neff, was able in all good conscience to tell his London theological examiners, met at the Poultry Chapel in May 1823, that he 'subscribed both in matters of faith and practice, to the confessions of faith of the Reformed Churches of France and Switzerland'.[242]

Such appeals to the confessions did not, however, always mean the same thing. At Geneva, César Malan certainly aspired to conform his teaching and preaching in every respect to the ancient formularies.[243] Louis Gaussen, when admonished by the 'Compagnie' of Geneva for refusing to utilize the catechism of 1814 in the training of parish children, threatened legal action to prove that the old catechism of Geneva had never been officially set aside by constitutional authority.[244] With this somewhat 'constitutionalist' approach may be contrasted the attitude of the dissidents of 'Bourg-de-Four' and their associates in other cantons and in France. For them, the sixteenth-century Reformation had been compromised by its embracing of the National Church idea while the scholasticizing theology of the seventeenth century had, in their view, substituted frigid formulae for the religion of the heart. Émile Guers, speaking for those who combined this outlook with adherence to central Calvinist teachings, had no patience with the idea of

> the servile imitation of the churches of the sixteenth century... After falling so far there was needed not a return to Calvin, but a return to Jesus Christ and the apostles.[245]

This was the circle which Haldane had admonished to 'take no rule but the Gospel'. For persons of this outlook, a revived adherence to Reformation confessions was less to be desired than a recovery of apostolic teaching and example.

The year 1832 brought the inauguration of the Evangelical School of Theology at Geneva. What posture did it strike as to historic doctrinal formularies? It was a harbinger of things to come in that it adhered to no single existing confession but selected articles on

> the state of man and the grace of God; the nature of Christ; the work which he has done, and that which he is still doing for the salvation of his people,—the

---

[242] Gilly, *Neff*, 91; Bost, *Neff*, 114.

[243] His son and biographer went so far as to cite his father's readiness to emphasize even the British (not Continental) confessional teaching regarding Sabbath observance. *Life of Malan*, 241, 338, 345.

[244] Maury, *Le Réveil Religieux*, I, 156-59.

[245] Guers, *Le Premier Réveil*, 3, 4 ; *Vie de Pyt*, 36, 37.

doctrines which the Protestant churches proclaim with one accord in their confessions of faith.[246]

The articles in question were selected from the *French Confession* (1559), *The Thirty-Nine Articles of the Church of England* (1571), the *Augsburg Confession* (1530), the *Westminster Confession of Faith* (1647) and the *Second Helvetic Confession* (1566). Why, we may ask, this deliberate eclecticism?

Perhaps it was a gesture to the international Protestant community which stood by, with wallets open, to assist the Geneva Evangelical Society and its daughter School of Theology. Anglican and Presbyterian supporters were certainly involved to a large degree.[247] A second hypothesis is that the Geneva school was aiming from the outset to meet an international and inter-confessional need for preachers and Christian workers. Strong appeals had come from ministers in France for the creation of the school, while dissident Protestant Churches in the other Swiss cantons and the existing Reformed Churches of Belgium and the south German Rhine had at this stage no reliable source of ministerial supply.[248] Whatever may be the full reason for its eclectic posture, the college's confessional stance marked a major innovation and set an important precedent for the international co-operative schemes of the following decade, as well as for the creation (also in the following decade) of abbreviated confessions for 'L'Église Évangélique Libre de Genève' and 'L'Union des Églises Évangéliques de France'.

Finally, we should note briefly that the 'réveil' made a significant contribution to theological literature. Having drawn attention already to the writings of Vinet of Lausanne and Gaussen of Geneva, we may here simply observe that the international reputation of Merle D'Aubigné was established with the publication of his multi-volume *History of the Reformation of the Sixteenth Century* (1835 and 1853).[249] Another historian and preacher, Edmond de Pressense (1796-1871) was the disciple of Alexandre Vinet of Lausanne. Minister of 'La Chapelle

---

[246] J.H. Merle D'Aubigné, 'An Account of the Geneva School of Evangelical Theology', in Edward Bickersteth, ed., *A Voice From the Alps*, (London: 1838), 49.

[247] We will note in the following chapter that the very creation of the Geneva Society called into being a 'Central Committee in Aid' of it at London, supported by Church of England persons. Evans, 'The Contribution of Foreigners', 402, alleges that American finance was critical to the launching of both Genevan enterprises. This, while interesting, still does not account for the multi-confessional approach.

[248] D'Aubigné, 'An Account of the Geneva School', 47, 48.

[249] A multi-volume sequel, *History of the Reformation in Europe in the Time of Calvin*, 8 vols, (1863-78), did not enjoy the same widespread acclaim. Two modern studies of D'Aubigné are those of Jochen Winkler, *Der Kirchenhistoriker Jean Henri Merle D'Aubigne*, (Zurich: 1968), and John B. Roney, *The Inside of History: Jean Henri Merle d'Aubigné and Romantic Historiography,* (Westport, CT: 1996).

Taitbout', in Paris from 1847 and supporter of 'L'Union des Églises Évangéliques de France', he was the author of the still-useful *History of the First Three Centuries of the Christian Church,* (Paris: 1858).

Early Calvin scholarship was given impetus by the 'réveil'. The first major biography of the reformer in the nineteenth century was the work of Paul Henry (2 vols, 1825-44), minister of the French church at Berlin. Henry moved freely in the Geneva 'réveil' circle and was numbered among the close friends of César Malan. Jules Bonnet, historian of the French Reformation and friend of Merle D'Aubigné, was the collator and editor of the standard nineteenth-century edition of the *Letters of John Calvin,* (3 vols; 1855-58). Though of a subsequent generation, the massive researches of the Montauban historian, Émile Doumergue, *Jean Calvin, Les hommes et les choses de son temps,* (2 vols, 1899 and 1902) built upon the renewed interest in Calvin generated by the 'réveil'.

Having said this, it must also be observed that the theological legacy of the 'réveil' was all but dissipated by 1900. Largely because the evangelical theology taught at Geneva was, as we have intimated above, retrospective and somewhat pre-critical, 'réveil' sympathizers were not well prepared by it for the coming dominance of German critical theology. Maury insisted that the Free Theological Academy of Lausanne had far excelled its Genevan counterpart in intellectual and theological rigour.[250] By 1907, the Geneva school stood in need of a thorough re-organization and by 1922 it had ceased operation altogether.[251] So unsettling were the theological currents of the late nineteenth century that the Free Church-National Church divide had virtually ceased to be determinative of theological outlook.[252]

---

[250] Maury, *Le Réveil Religieux,* I, 186. Maury, while sympathetic to the Geneva school, faulted it for failing to insist upon the entrance prerequisite of a university diploma. Without this standard, its graduates were never eligible for service in the National Church of France or for postgraduate study. Maury's esteem for the Free Academy of Lausanne is open to question. Gretillat, 'Movements of Theological Thought', 442, indicates that the orthodoxy of the Lausanne Free Academy had waned considerably by the 1880s.

[251] Heyer, *L'Église de Genève,* 242; Biéler, *Une Famille,* 194.

[252] Gretillat, 'Movements of Theological Thought', 445-447.

CHAPTER 4

The British Response to the 'Réveil' at Geneva

The Formation of a British Outlook on the 'Réveil'

Journalistic Reports of Developments at Geneva

The foregoing discussion regarding the spread of the 'réveil' from Geneva and its theological development has carried us forward in time considerably from the years most closely connected with the period of the awakening. It is now fitting to consider both how nineteenth-century Britons learned of the 'réveil' and assisted its progress.

By August of 1817, Robert Haldane had settled comfortably at Montauban and the young convert, Henry Drummond, had succeeded him at Geneva as advisor to the young dissidents. Though there is no evidence to indicate that either individual publicized his activities for the benefit of the British religious public, that public nonetheless learned of Genevan developments remarkably soon from other sources.

For example, readers of the *Christian Observer* for November 1817 could peruse a report of late summer events at Geneva by an anonymous Anglican correspondent who described the theological division within the city's Company of Pastors, the activities of 'two Scotch gentlemen' (Drummond's nationality was misconstrued), and the baneful effects of the pastoral regulation of 3 May.[1] However, the *Observer* then maintained a studied silence until May 1819, when it announced that

> the difficulty of obtaining the whole truth...is almost insurmountable as the facts of the case, even if clearly ascertained are not absolutely necessary to be known by our readers... We think we shall stand excused to the majority of our readers (notwithstanding the eagerness of some of our correspondents) for not particularly meddling with a topic of so much irritation.[2]

The periodical did not mean to minimize at all the degenerative trend in Genevan theology. On the contrary, it maintained that this degeneracy

---

[1] *Christian Observer*, 16 (1817), 712-14.

[2] *Christian Observer*, 18 (1819), 310, 311. It is perhaps significant that the *Observer*'s comments came in the immediate aftermath of César Malan's first visit to England in April 1819.

now made imprudent the custom of sending promising young students to Geneva for studies preparatory to university entrance. Yet in keeping with the details supplied by its correspondents of November 1817, the *Observer* recognized that the Genevan Church had an orthodox minority fully deserving of support.[3] In so recommending, the periodical was carefully following a policy suited to the English religious situation. After all, the *Observer*'s own readership formed a party of small and humble origin now growing within the National Church; it would, therefore, scrupulously insist on the validity and propriety of the efforts of this Swiss orthodox minority. If the position of one minority within a foreign establishment should be depicted as untenable, what would be the domestic implications?

This same outlook was reflected in an extended *Observer* review of four volumes of sermons and prayers published in 1818 and 1819 by J.I.S. Cellérier, one of the orthodox senior ministers of Geneva's Company of Pastors.[4] The reviewer, after offering what was to date Britain's most judicious and well-informed account of the conflict underway at Geneva, proceeded to contend that Cellérier's orthodox preaching exemplified the kind of edifying and faithful ministry still permissible within the constraints in operation at Geneva.[5] The reviewer also commended Cellérier for his co-operating with Louis Gaussen, his ministerial successor at the cantonal village of Satigny, in republishing the *Second Helvetic Confession* (1566).

The *Observer* minced no words in laying central blame for the hostilities in Geneva at the door of the Company of Pastors. They had departed from the doctrines of the Reformation and had dismissed César Malan in a highly arbitrary way. However, the reviewer took a kind of gleeful delight in highlighting one edifying sermon of Cellérier on Luke 19.10. The text was, in fact, one of two on which Malan had preached with great offence; this preaching had led to his dismissal. Thus, opined the writer,

> It becomes M. Malan to consider whether the inconveniences he has incurred and the dissensions which have unhappily arisen between him and the Company of Pastors might not have been obviated by closely imitating that meekness of Christian wisdom which shines so conspicuously in M. Cellérier.[6]

As for the Genevan dissidents now established at 'Bourg-de-Four', their conduct

---

[3] *Christian Observer*, 18 (1819), 311. The November 1817 writer had found five orthodox ministers in a Company of twenty-five.

[4] *Christian Observer*, 19 (1820), 399-415, 469-78, 546-54.

[5] *Christian Observer*, 19 (1820), 407.

[6] *Christian Observer*, 19 (1820), 415.

has become in some respects unadvised and precipitate, and their accusations against the Company of Pastors far too unmeasured and exaggerated.[7]

The Nonconformist evangelical press was soon vying with the Anglican *Observer* in press coverage, although initially it seemed to lack for informed correspondents. The *Evangelical Magazine* for December 1817 responded to 'various misrepresentations in the public papers respecting a Mr. Drummond who lately resided some months in Geneva' by rushing to his defence, as well as to that of Robert Haldane.[8] The two gentlemen were to be commended for their travel 'not only for amusement...but nobler purposes'. This periodical seems to have been unaware that the activity of Haldane and Drummond had contributed to the founding of a new church. The disclosure of this fact, as well as the earliest lengthy appraisal of recent theological developments at Geneva, was provided by the Nonconformist *Eclectic Review* in January 1818, which provided an extensive analysis of two recent publications emanating from Geneva—H.L. Empeytaz's *Considérations sur la Divinité de Jésus Christ* (1816) and the Company of Pastors' *Catechism* (1814). The reviewer observed that readers might wonder at the need to concern themselves in the theological affairs of European neighbours. Such involvement, the writer believed, was demanded of Britain by the prominence she had come to enjoy:

> As a commercial nation not only are our sympathies in great measure governed by our commercial relations, but our opportunities of beneficence, and the power attaching to national influence are chiefly confined to the same channels... It is to her commercial character that England is, under Providence, mainly indebted for that high distinction which it is her noblest prerogative to enjoy, as the Evangelist of nations.[9]

The writer then proceeded, by a telling comparison of Geneva's new and old catechisms, to demonstrate the retreat from trinitarian orthodoxy currently in vogue there. In this light, the controversial pamphlet by H.L. Empeytaz, which decried this trend and purported to demonstrate the anti-trinitarianism of the city's current and recent ministers, was shown to be substantially correct.[10] The author then related the story of the founding of the separatist congregation there. Sharing the *Christian Observer*'s tendency to construe the Genevan events according to

---

[7] *Christian Observer*, 19 (1820), 404, 405
[8] *Evangelical Magazine*, 25 (1817), 489. It is significant that Henry Drummond was not known to the editors at this date.
[9] *Eclectic Review*, 27 (1818), 2. The editor at this time was Josiah Conder.
[10] *Eclectic Review*, 27 (1818), 10, 11.

contemporary British categories, the *Review* writer spoke of the new church as being formed 'on the plan of the English nonconformists'.[11] Having just made such an identification of British and Genevan religious tendencies, the writer spoke of the important contribution of Mr Haldane, 'from whose design nothing seems to have been more remote than any project of a sectarian character'.[12] As if to qualify his quite total exoneration of Robert Haldane from any meddlesome activity, the writer then proceeded to utter the hope that the church would show no predilection for the 'Sandemanian hypothesis' that Haldane had earlier championed with chilling effects![13] The writer closed his essay by warning his readers that there was no intrinsic obstacle to the plagues of Geneva being rained down upon Britain insofar as these errors found their source in 'a learned ministry destitute of the genuine spirit of piety'.[14]

Within a month, the *New Evangelical Magazine* could identify the hitherto little-known Henry Drummond as 'the banker of London' and print a letter from dissident Genevan pastor, Henri Pyt, giving a quite fulsome description of the polity and worship of that young church. The congregation was plainly a stronghold of apostolic 'primitivism' as well as being earnestly evangelistic.[15] The same periodical subsequently printed correspondence (likely supplied by the same London source) from J.G. Gonthier, another of the separatist pastors. Gonthier indicated that the young cause had received moral support from orthodox ministers within the Company of Pastors. He reported public puzzlement over their use of mutual exhortation[16] in worship, and gave news of a general religious stirring across Switzerland. The editor noted that Christian churches in both England and Scotland had already supplied more than £100 for the young congregation.[17]

The same journal, which had by now established itself as the best source of Genevan news, reprinted further correspondence from Henri Pyt, indicating his itinerant preaching forays from Geneva into the mountainous French region of the Jura and his forthcoming relocation to

---

[11] *Eclectic Review*, 27 (1818), 12. The *Eclectic* writer had in fairness acknowledged 'honourable exceptions to the general defection from Christianity among the pastors'. So also the *Evangelical Magazine*, 26 (1818), 122.

[12] *Eclectic Review*, 27 (1818), 13.

[13] *Eclectic Review*, 27 (1818), 16. The reviewer thus knew well Haldane's past. See the discussion in ch. 2, p. 150 *supra*.

[14] *Eclectic Review*, 27 (1818), 18.

[15] *New Evangelical Magazine*, 4 (1818), 96. The letter was dated 4 November 1817. We believe that the London recipient of the letter, one 'lately returned from Geneva', was the merchant, W. Anderson, referred to in Guers' *Vie de Pyt*, 28. The letter is printed in full at the end of this volume as Appendix B.

[16] I.e., a spontaneous admonition or homily by lay members.

[17] *New Evangelical Magazine*, 4 (1818), 274, 275. The letter was dated 20 April 1818.

assist a French minister at Saverdun.[18] An anonymous member of the remaining pastoral team supplied the same magazine with the first details of the outbreak of persecution in July 1818.[19]

Concerned Protestants in Scotland were not well served by their local publications. The *Edinburgh Christian Instructor* took no notice of the evangelical resurgence at Geneva, though this had been widely reported in London periodicals. The Seceding Presbyterian (Anti-Burgher) *Christian Magazine or Evangelical Repository* could do better; the March 1818 issue surveyed the Genevan theological landscape, reported the establishment of the separatist congregation 'on congregational principles', and told of the approach of persecution.[20] Yet the Seceding Presbyterian (Burgher) *Christian Repository and Religious Register* of May 1818, apparently relying on the same London sources as the *New Evangelical Magazine*, was able to publish the correspondence of Henri Pyt to Mr A(nderson?), who had not long since visited Geneva, in which Pyt reported all recent developments. A new place of worship had become necessary as attendances had surpassed one hundred. Quantities of the Scriptures (in reliable translation) were now required for distribution, and financial support was needed desperately.[21]

The troubles experienced by the fledgling Genevan congregation in its first year were fully reported in the London religious press. The *Evangelical Magazine* reported the January 1818 enunciation of an edict of deportation against the French-born dissident pastor, Pierre Méjanel; the implementation of the edict on 4 March was also reported.[22] The same journal took pleasure in providing a translation of a pamphlet produced by the young congregation at Geneva in an effort to end the violent and abusive molestation of their assemblies which began in July 1818.[23] As Nonconformist English Protestants still experienced such intermittent

---

[18] *New Evangelical Magazine*, 4 (1818), 276, 277. The letter was dated 27 June 1818.

[19] *New Evangelical Magazine*, 4 (1818), 310, 311. On the basis of so many publishing 'firsts', the magazine editor would boast in his preface to volume 5 (1819), 'for the last several months of 1818, we have been the exclusive source of Genevan news'. This was an exaggerated claim, no doubt; yet the editor's wanting to stake such a claim is deeply significant.

[20] *Christian Magazine or Evangelical Repository*, 12 (1818), 88-94.

[21] *Christian Repository and Religious Register*, 3 (1818), 309-311. The supply of Pyt-Anderson correspondence to this journal suggests that Anderson was a Scots Seceding Presbyterian residing in London. The magazine supplied two Glasgow and two London names and addresses (Anderson's being one of the latter) to which donations for Geneva might be sent.

[22] *Evangelical Magazine*, 26 (1818), 121, 211.

[23] *Evangelical Magazine*, 26 (1818), 391-93, 438. See also the *London Christian Instructor*, 1 (1818), 555.

harassment themselves, they would have been capable of feeling considerable solidarity with their Genevan comrades.[24]

In 1819, the *New Evangelical Magazine* heralded the inauguration of a sister periodical, *Le Magazin Évangélique*, in Geneva at the commencement of the year. It also supplied an extensive coverage of the Genevan debate over the right of religious dissent between an advocate, M. Grenus (in support) and an academy professor of homiletics, M. Duby (in opposition).[25]

The Emergence of César Malan

The distinct phase of developments at Geneva marked by the suspension of César Malan from ministerial and teaching duties in August 1818 was closely reported in British periodicals. A correspondent to the *Evangelical Magazine* in November 1818, identified simply as 'an English lady at Geneva', extolled Malan by exclaiming

> I often think that if the Christians in England were but to witness the utter destitution of such a man as this, they would rise up with the same zeal as they did for the persecuted Protestants of France.[26]

That such ideas as these were already occurring to others in Britain is plain; as we have seen, financial assistance was already being gathered in both England and Scotland.

The same number of the *Evangelical Magazine* provided a full letter of explanation regarding Malan's plight from the Rev. Mark Wilks of Peckham, just returned from the Continent. He was an eyewitness of the events he described.[27] That the Genevan preacher was not then lacking in London supporters who were his intimate friends was illustrated by letters to the same magazine from correspondents 'Cosmopolite' and J. Pye Smith.[28] The former related that the deprived Malan had been actively supported before the Company of Pastors by pastors Gaussen and Moulinié. The latter related his personal introduction to Malan in August 1816 and his lofty estimate of his worth. We need not doubt that Smith

---

[24] The *Evangelical Magazine*, 26 (1818), 211, reported just such an outbreak at East Coker, Somerset, and the successful prosecution of the disturbers.

[25] *New Evangelical Magazine*, 5 (1819), 263, 67-72, 148-151. Professor Duby, not utterly without sympathy for the dissidents, was also secretary to the Geneva Bible Society.

[26] *Evangelical Magazine*, 27 (1819), 28. We have already noted the attitude of the *Christian Observer* towards Malan (pp. 147, 148) in the interest of demonstrating that journal's early and settled coolness towards him.

[27] *Evangelical Magazine*, 27 (1819), 27, 28. This concern for French Europe would take Wilks to Paris for an extended pastorate. See p. 158 below.

[28] *Evangelical Magazine*, 26 (1818), 526, 527.

saw in Malan the true embodiment of his longing for a preacher-evangelist to arise from within the city of Calvin.[29] Given that Malan's most enthusiastic supporters were so evidently Nonconformists, there was some chagrin that the Genevan's brief visit to England in April 1819 (ostensibly to gather pupils to receive his instruction) was spent so substantially in the company of Church of England ministers. The *New Evangelical Magazine* complained of Malan's partiality for the Established Church only to be rebuked by Malan who denied the charge. Nonetheless, the editor insisted that the Anglicans had unfairly 'embargoed' Malan during his brief stay.[30] From the episode we may infer that there were many Church of England clergy and laity who did not share the coolness of the *Christian Observer* toward the separatist side of Genevan religious affairs. We may also note the manifestation of Nonconformist-Established Church rivalry, each group being determined to claim Genevan developments as falling within their own bailiwick. There is evidence to suggest that Malan, for all his generosity of time with sympathetic Anglicans, still knew that sympathetic Nonconformists were most likely to provide financial backing for the erection of his proposed chapel. He sent the *Evangelical* and *New Evangelical* magazines identical copies of a diplomatic letter acknowledging gifts already received and indicating the outstanding balance still needed.[31]

One other consequence of Malan's April 1819 trip to England was the inauguration of a series of publications thrusting him still more directly into the public eye. Those who wished to do so could read Malan's *Sermons Translated From the French* (1819) with accompanying commentary upon religious developments at Geneva.[32] It was in fact these sermons which had brought about the preacher's deposition by the Company of Pastors. His subsequent removal from his teaching post was then followed by the publication of *Documents Relative to the Deposition of the Rev. Caesar Malan From His Office In the College of Geneva* (1820). The purpose of the book's release was to familiarize the British public with Malan's present plight. Not only were gifts forthcoming; English families were also eager to place their adolescent children under

---

[29] Cf. *supra* p. 65.

[30] *New Evangelical Magazine*, 5 (1819), 152, 178.

[31] The *Evangelical Magazine*, 28 (1820), 241, had reported that £600 in all would be needed. The *Evangelical Magazine*, 29 (1821), 114, and *New Evangelical Magazine*, 7 (1821), 59, both printed his letter indicating progress made and outstanding balance required.

[32] For an extended review of the sermons, cf. *New Evangelical Magazine*, 5 1819), 105-108. The reviewer could state that 'Malan's name had presented itself repeatedly to the eye of the reader of our magazine during the last six months'.

Malan's tutelage, thus providing Malan with needed income.[33] By April 1822, Malan's renown was such that the *Evangelical Magazine* included him among its notable ministers whose engraved likenesses graced its inside covers.[34]

In summary, we may say that the religious developments at Geneva and the leading Swiss personalities involved had assumed a considerable importance in the eye of the British Protestant public prior to the return of Henry Drummond in mid-1818 and of Robert Haldane in August 1819. This extensive coverage, whether from the deliberately 'cool' perspective of the *Christian Observer* or the unabatedly zealous outlook of such periodicals as the *Evangelical Magazine*, reflected the frequent comings and goings of other interested Britons to Geneva in the initial two years following Haldane's lectures there. By 1819, British concern for Geneva had developed a momentum of its own. Against this backdrop we can understand the vying of Anglicans and Nonconformists for the attention of Malan at his 1819 visit and the readiness of London Nonconformist ministers to ordain the dissident ministers of Geneva, J.G. Gonthier and E. Guers, in June 1821.[35]

Additional British Visitors to Geneva

Against this backdrop, we may also properly construe the recorded impressions of additional British visitors to Geneva in the period following 1817. It would seem that anyone who ventured there with any ecclesiastical interest felt compelled to comment on these matters which had so stirred the interest of the British religious public.

The Rev. John Owen, Anglican rector of Paglesham, Essex, and secretary to the British and Foreign Bible Society, visited many continental cities between 25 August and 14 November 1818. In travelling, he sought both to recover his broken health and to encourage the European Bible societies affiliated with his own. After visiting the Bible societies in some fifteen cities (where he distributed more than £1,500 in aid) he came to Geneva on 31 October with great apprehension. He recorded that

> The information I possessed convinced me...that I should contend there with difficulties of a peculiar nature... It is well known that for a long time past there

---

[33] The anonymous biographer of John Adam, LMS missionary to India, indicates that Adam's family placed him as Malan's student in 1821 as 'the privations of Malan had excited peculiar interest and sympathy in the minds of English Christians'. See, *Memoir of John Adam*, (London: 1833), 5.

[34] *Evangelical Magazine*, 30 (1822), facing p. 133.

[35] *Evangelical Magazine*, 29 (1821), 339. Presbyterian and Congregational ministers presided.

have been very serious discussions in matters of theological doctrine among the pastors and professors of Geneva and that these divisions have given occasion to many contentions.[36]

Owen's mission was indeed a delicate one. He represented a pan-evangelical society whose supporters were responding to Genevan developments according to their varied denominational outlooks. He found to his utter chagrin that the Genevans themselves held wildly differing expectations regarding his visit. Would Owen support the dissidents or the establishment? He carefully determined to do neither and acted in a manner which he calculated would best preserve the Bible Society's independence. He worked to assure members of the Geneva Bible Society that the institution he represented was not simply a vehicle of advancing Methodism (of which they considered their own dissidents to be a distasteful manifestation) by emphasizing the affiliation to his own society of bishops and nobility. He did nothing to openly identify with the religious dissidents of Geneva and preached only in the Sunday services of the congregation of the Church of England in that city.[37]

Five years later, Daniel Wilson, Anglican rector of St. John's Chapel, Bedford Row, London, also visited the major centres of Europe and included Geneva among his points of call. He entered that city full of reverence for its past:

I approach Geneva with feelings of peculiar veneration. The name of Calvin stands highest amongst the Reformers, Divines and Scholars of the sixteenth century... There is no man to whom I owe so much as a commentator...[38]

While he faulted the great reformer for 'carrying his acuteness too far...and having followed not the Episcopalian but the Presbyterian model', he made a point of visiting the Geneva public library to view at first hand the preserved sermons and letters of Calvin.[39]

With such affinities as these, what would Wilson make of the five-year history of religious dissidence in the city? He sampled the preaching of the city's Company of Pastors and found one sermon such that 'a

---

[36] John Owen, *Brief Extracts From Letters...On His Late Tour To France and Switzerland*, (London: 1819) 36, 37.

[37] Owen, *Brief Extracts*, 38-40. Robert Haldane would subsequently vilify this posture of Owen at Geneva in his *Second Review of the Conduct of the Directors of the British and Foreign Bible Society*, (Edinburgh: 1826), 108-111. Yet Haldane's recalcitrance was rooted in his unwillingness to grant the continuation of any significant orthodoxy in the Geneva Company of Pastors. Owen, with the majority of British observers, gladly recognized this.

[38] Daniel Wilson, *Letters of An Absent Brother*, 2 vols, (London: 1823, 3rd ed., 1825), II, 289.

[39] Wilson, *Letters*, II, 223, 290.

Socinian might have preached it'; yet another contained 'nothing contrary to sound doctrine'.[40] He deliberately heard the preaching of César Malan, whom the *Christian Observer* had been so careful not to endorse. His reaction to Malan is worth recording because it was so disparate. On the one hand Wilson could extol the fact that

> His manner was so pathetic, so calm, so persuasive, and his matter upon the whole so edifying that I have scarcely heard anything like it since I left London... [A] preacher of first-rate powers, there is an inexpressible unction in all he delivers.

Yet on the other hand, he cautioned that

> his doctrine is a little too high, in my opinion, to be quite scriptural or safe in the long run; he does not sufficiently unite the preceptive and cautionary parts of Holy Writ with the consolatory and elevatory—a fault not important in a single discourse, but momentous as extending over the whole system of a minister's instructions.[41]

Wilson, the former tutor of St. Edmund's Hall, Oxford, and a vastly experienced preacher, was no mean judge of these things. Yet more importantly still, his published analysis of the Genevan scene supported the existing 'party line' established for evangelical Anglicans by the *Observer*. Like the *Observer*, Wilson was forthright in condemning Geneva's pastoral regulation of May 1817 (which provoked the dissidence). In response to the prohibition of preaching upon the divinity of Christ, original sin, grace and predestination, he observed that

> the three former...contain the very sum and substance of the Gospel and the latter is undoubtedly an important scriptural doctrine. Thus from being the flower of the Reformed Churches, Geneva has (for the time) fallen into the gulf of Deism and Socinianism.[42]

Yet such a verdict did not bring Wilson to support the position of the Genevan dissidents. His sympathies were instead with those like Louis Gaussen of Satigny and the visiting Merle D'Aubigné (whom he encountered during the latter's visit to Geneva from Hamburg). Such men were evidently labouring to strengthen the position of a vital orthodoxy from within rather than allying themselves with separatism. Wilson was happy, therefore, to engage Gaussen to translate the English *Commentary on the Bible* (1792) by Thomas Scott and D'Aubigné to

---

[40] Wilson, *Letters*, II, 227.
[41] Wilson, *Letters*, II, 215.
[42] Wilson, *Letters*, II, 342, 343.

translate Joseph Milner's *History of the Church of Christ* (1797) into French in keeping with this aim.[43]

Although Wilson was unacquainted with Haldane, he praised the fervour and courage of the enterprising Scot:

> A gentleman of Scotland almost unacquainted with French, about seven years since and in a few months, by simply dwelling on the authority and manifest truths of the New Testament, was the means of attracting the attention and regard of a whole circle of young students and imbibing their minds with its evangelical doctrine.[44]

The steady stream of enthusiastic journalistic reports and published impressions soon made Geneva a major stopping-off place for sympathetic British Protestants. Among those who visited Geneva during the 1820s were James Haldane Stewart, Anglican rector of Percy Chapel, London,[45] the brothers Gerard and Baptist W. Noel (both Anglican clergymen),[46] and the Scots advocate and lay-theologian Thomas Erskine of Linlathen.[47] Several generalizations may be attempted about these visits.

As none of the visits resulted in the immediate publication of accounts, such as those of Owen and Wilson, they had no measurable impact upon the existing polarized opinion. Yet having said this, it is noteworthy that the attraction which Geneva held for all four (three of whom were ministers of the Church of England) lay definitely with the orthodox party within the National Church and with César Malan. The Genevan Established Church taken as a whole held no attraction for them; nor did

---

[43] Wilson, *Letters*, II, 214. J. Bateman, *Life of the Right Reverend Daniel Wilson, D.D.*, (London: 1861), 109, 110, explains that the commentary publication faltered after the release of Matthew, Acts and Romans for lack of demand. This factor apparently halted all thoughts of the publication of Milner. Yet D'Aubigné's involvement in the project no doubt assisted preparations for his own historical works in the next decades.

[44] Wilson, *Letters*, II, 328. Haldane's analysis of Wilson was not forthcoming until 1829. It was then issued at Edinburgh as *A Review of the Conduct of the Rev. Daniel Wilson On the Continent*. Haldane's concern seems to have been primarily that of the buttressing of his own bleak analysis of the Christianity of Europe against those who viewed it more pragmatically. In pursuit of such an end, Haldane did not hesitate to resort to hectoring and invective.

[45] David D. Stewart, *Memoirs of James Haldane Stewart*, (London: 1857), 87.

[46] Gerard Noel, *Arvendale, or Sketches in Italy and Switzerland*, (London: 1826), e.g. 66. Noel's visit evidently followed promptly on the heels of that of Stewart, whose ministerial 'locum' he was. Baptist W. Noel, *Notes of a Tour in Switzerland in the Summer of 1847*, (London: 1847), 1, indicates a first visit in 1821 followed by a second in the year of publication.

[47] W. Hannah, ed., *Letters of Thomas Erskine of Linlathen*, (Edinburgh: 1878). The letters indicate meetings with Merle D'Aubigné at Hamburg, p. 30, Gerard Noel at Paris, p. 37, and César Malan at Geneva, p. 36.

the dissidents gathered at their chapel named 'Bourg-de-Four'. Thus Gerard Noel could recall that 'the names Satigny, Pré L'Évêque, and Cologny return often with all the softness of a magic sound'.[48] Only of the involvement of Thomas Erskine may we speak of an enduring legacy. The future preacher of Lyons and Paris, Adolphe Monod, was in the final year of his theological course at Geneva when he had the pleasure of making Erskine's acquaintance. His own theological outlook was then extremely unsettled; he described his student outlook as 'Orthodox, Methodist, Arian—I am each of these in turn'.[49] He was permanently helped by extended exposure to Erskine's then relatively-orthodox views, of which he said

> his system is more moral and more philosophic than that of the orthodox party at Geneva... He has nothing of that narrow mindedness which is to be seen in some of our orthodox people nor of that hard and unyielding spirit which appears in others among them.[50]

Paris Replaces Geneva as the Focal Point of 'Réveil' Attention

We may justifiably speak of a diminution of British journalistic and personal attention to Genevan events and personalities after 1823.[51] There are several related explanations for this.

First, the appointment of the Rev. Mark Wilks as minister of the English Independent congregation at Paris meant that increasingly,

---

[48] Noel, *Arvendale*, 80. Satigny was the country parish within the canton of Geneva served by Gaussen, and Cologny that served by J.L. Peschier at the time of Noel's 1821 visit. Pré L'Évêque was the site of César Malan's home and chapel.

[49] [A. Monod], *Life and Letters of Adolphe Monod*, (London: 1885), 13. Some additional British visitors to Geneva are described in Stunt, *From Awakening*, 102-109.

[50] [Monod], *Life and Letters*, 13. Erskine would have further influence over Monod at Naples in 1827; cf. p. 39. A helpful modern review of Erskine's Continental visits and contacts is provided by N.R. Needham, *Thomas Erskine of Linlathen: His Life and Theology 1788-1837*, (Edinburgh: 1990).

[51] The English translation of Prof. J.J. Chenevière's 'Summary of Theological Controversies Which Have Lately Troubled Geneva' in *The Monthly Repository of Theological and General Literature*, 19 (1824), 1ff, and the rejoinders it drew from J. Pye Smith, 'Reply to Prof. Chenevière', in the same volume of that journal, 321ff, and Robert Haldane, *Letter to Prof. Chenevière*, (Edinburgh: 1824), were all essentially retrospective and concerned primarily with the issues of 1816-19. Allan Sell has identified the London journal in which Chenevière's material appeared as clearly Unitarian and Pye Smith's reply as an attempt to thwart Unitarianism in Britain by making an example of the Geneva theologian. See Allan P.F. Sell's 'Revival and Secession in Early Nineteenth Century Geneva' in *Commemorations: Studies in Christian Thought and History*, (University of Wales Press, Cardiff, 1993), 204.

religious developments in French Europe would be reported from his Parisian vantage point and not that of Geneva as in preceding years.[52] The greater part of Genevan missionary energy in the 1820s would itself be focused on France. Second, it was at Paris that British societies focused their efforts to establish affiliate Bible, tract, and missionary societies and a religious periodical, *Les Archives du Christianisme*.[53] Thus, increasingly, the promotion of evangelical religion in French-speaking Europe became the business of British societies working through French affiliates, on whose behalf funds were raised and news circulated. This tendency marked the decided escalation rather than diminution of British interest.[54]

Third, we may note in passing what will be developed below, i.e. the constitution in October 1818 of the 'Continental Society for the Diffusion of Religious Knowledge', which was, in effect, a specialist organization which made Francophone Europe its chief field of operations. Virtually all of the early principal workers of the Society were Genevans or persons otherwise connected with the Genevan dissidents now known as the 'Bourg-de-Four' congregation. Their labour in France was symptomatic of a shift of focus away from Geneva, which offered only restricted missionary opportunity. This shift in effect facilitated the diffusion of the Genevan 'réveil' into France under the Society's auspices. The Society, through its annual meetings, publications and speaking tours became, for more than a decade, the foremost vehicle for the marshalling of British religious efforts regarding Francophone Europe.

However, the unforeseen Genevan developments of 1831, in which Merle D'Aubigné, Louis Gaussen, and others would be thrust from the Genevan National Church in a second 'wave' of dissidence, would again

---

[52] The commencement of Wilks' Parisian ministry was noted by the *Evangelical Magazine*, 30 (1822), 288. Wilks had been a close acquaintance of César Malan since 1818. Wilks was a most capable correspondent on all Francophone evangelical affairs.

[53] The establishment of which was happily reported in the British religious press. E.g., 'The Paris Bible Society' in *Evangelical Magazine*, 27 (1819), 29, and *New Evangelical Magazine*, 5 (1819), 66. Also 'Les Archives du Christianisme' in *Evangelical Magazine*, 26 (1818), 121.

[54] In this context we may introduce the dramatic upsurge of British Protestant interest in the Waldensians of south-east France. The Rev. W.S. Gilly (1789-1855) made visits to the region in 1823 and on the basis of such travels wrote *Narrative of an Excursion to the Mountains of Piedmont and Researches Among the Vaudois or Waldenses*, (London: 1824). This led to the rise of relief efforts enjoying royal and wide public support. Gilly was later the author of the standard English biography of Continental Society worker among the Waldensians, Félix Neff, *Memoir of Félix Neff*, (London: 1832). Gilly's earlier writings influenced John Charles Beckwith (1789-1862), a decorated and disabled veteran of the Napoleonic Wars, to devote the final thirty-five years of his life to social and missionary work in the region. Both Gilly and Beckwith are well described in the *Dictionary of National Biography*.

bring British religious opinion to focus, with avid attention, upon Geneva itself.

The Rise and Fall of the Continental Society

British Protestants were quick to recognize that the stirring of Protestantism in French-speaking Europe deserved their moral and financial support. It had been appropriate to gather collections on behalf of the suffering Protestants of the Midi in 1815-16; how much more so was it appropriate now as gospel fortunes revived?

Yet, the immediate post-war years were financially difficult for most Britons. The cessation of hostilities left many British mills and factories over-committed to wartime production; these now faced shrinking markets. The military demobilization of some 300,000 men combined with the foregoing factors led to massive unemployment. While the price of food declined on account of good harvests and the free flow of imports, the fall of agricultural prices from record wartime levels seriously threatened agricultural landowners who had borrowed to expand during wartime. Income taxes, even when lowered to half their wartime levels, were a great but unavoidable burden for the heavily-in-debt victor nation. Even in 1818, almost two thirds of public expenditure was required to service the national debt accumulated over more than a decade of hostilities.[55] This being so, it is remarkable that evangelical agencies expanded their operations at the return of peace.

We have already noted that the Rev. John Owen strengthened the efforts of European Bible societies affiliated to the British and Foreign Bible Society by his visits and financial grants in 1818.[56] The Religious Tract Society disbursed funds through its agent, Dr Steinkopf, to eleven south German and Swiss tract concerns in 1815.[57] From 1816, the American export merchant based at Paris, Sampson V.S. Wilder, supervised the wide distribution of Religious Tract Society French-language materials. As it became clear that an undesirable stigma was attached to religious material of British origin, Wilder, with Tract Society financial assistance, began the indigenous production of tracts in Paris.[58] An American business associate fluent in French, Hillhouse of New Haven, translated many standard English Tract Society titles, and from

---

[55] See Elie Halévy, *A History of the English People in 1815-1830*, (London: 1926), 36; and Ashton, *The Industrial Revolution*, 122.

[56] See pp. 154, 155. The affiliate 'Société Biblique Protestante de Paris' was founded in 1819.

[57] W. Jones, *Jubilee Memorial of the Religious Tract Society*, (London: 1849), 86.

[58] See Sampson V.S. Wilder, *Records From the Life of Sampson V.S. Wilder*, (New York: 1865), 78, 80; and Jones, *Jubilee Memorial*, 283-84.

these informal beginnings emerged the Paris Tract Society in 1818.[59] The London Missionary Society, in addition to funding a handful of missionary agents in France and the printing of major English works in French translation, from 1820 assisted an affiliate, the Paris Missionary Society, to begin its operations.[60]

Yet these efforts, whether measured in terms of money or manpower, were relatively insignificant. The LMS, for instance, in the years 1817-19 committed £133, £199 and £115 to France respectively. The Religious Tract Society assisted the inauguration of its Paris affiliate with a grant of £110.10s.[61] These were not negligible sums but neither did they represent the giving of any special priority to Francophone Europe by societies with constantly widening global horizons. It was, therefore, no direct affront to existing agencies when an independent organization, the Continental Society, was launched in 1818.

It has been asserted that the 'Continental Society for the Diffusion of Religious Knowledge' came into being largely as a result of the efforts of Henry Drummond after Robert Haldane's 1817 departure for Montauban.[62] An older and more compelling view, originating with the Haldane biographer, is that Haldane and Drummond collaborated in launching the scheme during their brief overlap of itineraries at Geneva. Haldane, before departing, is said to have supplied ideas for the deployment of aspiring young Genevan students based on his earlier familiarity with itinerant schemes in the Society for the Propagation of the Gospel at Home. The execution of the ideas was left largely to Drummond.[63] The comprehensiveness of even this theory is challenged, however, by an independent account, almost certainly stemming from Drummond, which reports that,

In the year 1817, a plan was in agitation among some zealous Christians at Berlin, Petersburg, Basle, Berne and Geneva for forming a Society in aid of persons over the Continent of Europe; it was the intention of those persons to establish a branch also at Paris and another at London. The difficulty of carrying the design into effect without much personal communication retarded its execution until the spring of 1818, when a few religious persons being at Paris, determined no longer to delay the commencement of this important work and accordingly subscribed a sum nearly sufficient for one missionary immediately—which was done... In order to obtain

---

[59] Wilder, *Records*, 80. Hillhouse had advised Haldane at Paris in September 1816. See p. 72 *supra*.

[60] *L.M.S. Handlist: Disbursements to France 1800-1837*, n.p..

[61] See *L.M.S. Handlist*; and Jones, *Jubilee Memorial*, 284.

[62] See A.L. Drummond, 'Robert Haldane at Geneva', *Records of the Scottish Church History Society*, 9 (1946), 79-80; Wemyss, *Le Réveil*, 98; and Stunt, 'Geneva', 37.

[63] A. Haldane, *Lives of the Haldanes*, 426, 454, has been carefully followed by L. Froom, *The Prophetic Faith of Our Fathers*, 3 vols, (Washington, DC: 1949), III, 441-46.

sufficient funds to carry on what was already begun, the present Continental Society was formed in London.[64]

Granting the probable accuracy of such a report, many questions arise which are most difficult to answer. One might be the identity of the 'zealous Christians' who originally helped to 'agitate' the scheme. Here we may simply note that J.H. Merle D'Aubigné went from Geneva to Berlin in the latter half of 1817, that the chaplain of Mme Krüdener, Empeytaz, had been in the Baltic region in the same period, and that Haldane had made personal contact with A. Galland at Berne in late 1816.[65] The American merchant at Paris, Sampson Wilder, certainly knew Drummond by correspondence and hosted Haldane, homeward-bound fron Montauban in August 1819.[66] These names admittedly form mere hypotheses as to the make-up of the zealous circle within which the idea of a society was discussed.

It is also a matter of some curiosity that the discussions of 1817 envisioned a London connection. While Drummond as a banker and former Member of Parliament certainly had connections of his own in that city, we have seen that the first mention of his name in connection with religious affairs at Geneva had drawn a blank in the British evangelical press.[67] The historian, A.L. Drummond, suggested that the reason for this might be that the banker had only come under serious religious influences in the year 1817;[68] it was under these influences that he had embarked for Palestine only to be diverted to Geneva from Genoa. Now the very London evangelical connections which Drummond lacked, Robert Haldane certainly had from his eight-year term (1796-1804) as an LMS director and confidante of David Bogue. If Haldane was no longer a member of the London pan-evangelical elite on account

---

[64] *Report of the Continental Society For the Diffusion of Religious Knowledge*, 1 (London: 1819), 8. From 1822, the published 'reports' were styled 'proceedings'. Accounts in both the *New Evangelical Magazine*, 7 (1821), 122, and *Evangelical Magazine*, n.s. 4 (1826), 126, make plain that the spring 1818 meeting took place in May at Paris.

[65] A. Haldane, *Lives of the Haldanes*, 390.

[66] Wilder, *Records*, 122, 142.

[67] See p. 147 above. Considerable light has recently been shed on the character and activity of Drummond by Dr Grayson Carter in treatments in the *Blackwell Dictionary of Evangelical Biography* (Blackwell: 1996), and *Anglican Evangelicals: Protestant Secessions from the via Media, c.1800-1850* (Oxford: 2001), 111, 162, 164.

[68] A.L. Drummond, *Edward Irving and His Circle*, (London: 1937), 126. Carter, *Anglican Evangelicals*, 162, would concur, and adds that Drummond, just prior to his departure for the Continent in 1817, had been involved with members of the Baring banking family in what is termed the 'Western Schism', a west of England withdrawal from allegiance to the Church of England.

of his well-known advocacy of apostolic primitivism[69] and his autocratic hectoring of his former connexion of chapels and tabernacles, he was at least still well-connected and well-remembered.

It was on the strength of such long-standing bonds that the first London efforts were made to rally support for the proposed society in October 1818. The initial missionary, Pierre Méjanel, had been ratified by 'a few religious persons at Paris' in the spring of 1818.[70] In order that the envisioned society might undergo a metamorphosis from a circle of moneyed businessmen, operating on a 'handshake basis' to something public and expanding, Drummond made it his business on returning to London to assemble a group of supportive individuals. At least one such gathering took place prior to the first annual meeting of 28 April 1819.

In January 1819, the *London Christian Instructor or Congregational Magazine* could report that,

> A society has been formed in London whose object is to aid the progress of divine truth over the Continent of Europe by employing persons properly qualified, chiefly natives of the respective countries. We understand this society has emanated from those pious persons who have attempted the revival of evangelical principles at Geneva.[71]

More details are provided by one who attended the organizational meeting at London—the American and recent theological graduate, Matthias Bruen. Bruen, having earlier been present at Geneva to observe the influence of both Haldane and his own mentor, John Mason Mitchell, upon Geneva's divinity students,[72] was now in London as pastor-elect of an American congregation at Paris. Bruen was to be ordained at London's Homerton Chapel on 3 November 1818 in a service at which leading evangelical ministers, Alexander Waugh and Pye Smith, would preside.[73]

Significantly, it was while Bruen moved in the circle of such men—men whom we have already met as persons keen for the re-evangelization of Francophone Europe, that he attended a meeting on 21 October 1818 for the founding of the society. He confided in his diary,

---

[69] We have noted above, p. 150, the renewed raising of the question of Haldane's allegiance to the primitivistic 'Sandemanian hypothesis' at first report of his involvement at Geneva.

[70] We may surmise this group to have included Drummond, Haldane (by correspondence from Montauban), and the Americans Wilder and Hillhouse. Wilder's name appears as one of six society vice presidents in the *Report of the Continental Society*, 2, (London: 1820), i. He continued in this capacity until 1839.

[71] *London Christian Instructor*, 2, (1819), 62.

[72] Cf. p. 74 *supra*.

[73] Lundie, *Memoir of Bruen*, 117.

> The first object is to support and encourage all native ministers, everywhere over
> the continent in preaching the gospel... The thing they chiefly aim at, and indeed
> the principal difficulty, is to bring all the religious sects here to co-operate in the
> business. I was at a meeting last night of the principal persons...which augurs
> well.[74]

The early annual *Reports* of the society indicate that those 'principal persons' were persons with whom Robert Haldane had long been familiar—many of them numbered among the earliest supporters of the London Missionary Society. In such circles, Henry Drummond may still have been a novice, but this could have been remedied by some well-aimed letters of introduction from Haldane, still at Montauban. Drummond may also have gained entry into the LMS circles through his recently-formed acquaintance with Sampson Wilder of Paris, a close friend of key individuals in the London Missionary and Religious Tract societies since 1816.[75]

This substantial overlap between existing pan-evangelical societies and the Continental Society is further demonstrated in two main ways. First there are the explicit tributes paid to the memory of such senior stalwarts in the pages of the society's *Reports* and *Proceedings* at the times of their deaths. Thus, the 1826 annual meetings heard tributes paid to the Reverends David Bogue and John Townsend,

> the steady friends of this Institution from the beginnings of its operations to the
> period of their death... David Bogue was never absent from an anniversary when i n
> London.[76]

Townsend (1757-1826), minister of the Independent chapel, Jamaica Row, Bermondsey, from 1784, had been an LMS director at the 1802 sending to France of a four-man team of inquiry.[77] Speaking to the 1823 annual meeting of the Continental Society, he recalled those events of 1802 and saw them now being built upon by the new institution:

> When the L.M.S. was formed, the continent of Europe was contemplated as an
> object within the sphere of its operations. While it was formed for the heathen,
> there was added to the object, the words 'and other unenlightened countries'; that
> phrase was proposed by myself for the very purpose of carrying the operations of
> Christian benevolence into France and Germany... We sent a deputation consisting
> of Mr. Hardcastle and three others to see if churches could be opened at Paris and we

---

[74] Lundie, *Memoir of Bruen*, 109, 110.
[75] Wilder, *Records*, 76-78.
[76] *Continental Society Proceedings*, 8 (1826), 13, 14.
[77] Cf. pp. 58, 59 *supra*.

actually commenced the printing of New Testaments with a view to beginning operations there. War then interspersed. We now perceive the door opened...[78]

David Bogue (1750-1825), himself a member of that 1802 LMS delegation to France, and theological tutor at Gosport Academy, could inform the 1824 gathering of the Continental Society that

> I esteem it an honour to say that there were six students with me now preaching on the continent within the field of your labours; four of them were converted by a minister in this place.[79]

In a similar vein, the passing of another founder of the LMS, the Rev. Alexander Waugh (1754-1827), himself also a member of the 1802 delegation to France, was marked by a tribute from the Society president, Joseph Strutt, who stated that Waugh 'was one of the earliest and best friends of this Society. It received his countenance and aid as well through evil and good report.'[80] On the same occasion, Henry Drummond recorded the tribute, 'I cannot help remembering how much the society was indebted to him for powerful support at its first foundation.'[81] Such examples indicate that the launching of the society at London in October 1818 was heavily dependent upon the established credibility and influence of LMS founders, all of whom were Robert Haldane's former associates in that cause. From this same Nonconformist constituency, the Society's committee of management drew John Pye Smith of Homerton College, W. Anderson, the London-based Scot whose own visit to Geneva in 1817-18 had subsequently yielded such informative correspondence,[82] and William Jones, subsequently secretary of the Religious Tract Society.

Secondly, the young Society emphasized its continuity with the older one at its annual meetings. Thus, at the 1822 meeting, the Rev. Mark Wilks, only recently posted to Paris, declared,

> I am glad this society is formed on the principle of those great societies which have done so much good. When I see here the fathers and founders of the *Evangelical*

[78] *Proceedings*, 5 (1823), 76, 77. Townsend was an LMS director 1796-1825, and a Tract Society director, 1800-19.

[79] *Proceedings*, 6 (1824), 76. Bogue was an LMS director 1795-1825. The six students had been enrolled at Gosport at LMS expense. Bogue implies that the six now serve the Continental Society, though he may only mean that they laboured in the same region.

[80] *Proceedings*, 10 (1828), 8. Waugh, the minister of the Wells Street, London Secession Church, was an LMS director 1795-1827. As a London resident, he served the business committee of the Continental Society from 1818 until his death.

[81] *Proceedings*, 10 (1828), 31

[82] *Continental Society Report*, 1 (1819), 3. Anderson's correspondence from Geneva has been discussed above, pp, 150 fn. 15, 151 fn. 21.

Magazine and of the (London) Missionary Society...when I see such men, I cannot but view in them a pledge for that broad Christian charity which embraces the world.[83]

At the same gathering, the Rev. J. Pye Smith argued that the younger Society's concentration on nominally-Christian Europe was freeing the LMS to concentrate on evangelizing the heathen regions:

> The (London) Missionary Society has most honourably laboured in this field; but who can wish that any part of its funds should be diverted from the heathen world? Thus the existence of the Continental Society is a matter of the most pressing necessity. When the Continental Society was established, I felt it my duty to become a member of it.[84]

This argument was taken up in 1825 by a father-figure of the LMS, George Burder, who maintained, at the Continental Society annual meeting, that

> We have laboured many years to send the gospel to the remotest nations of the earth and we have done so, we thank God, not without success. But we are not to forget our neighbours nearer to home.[85]

This was a significant articulation of LMS-Continental Society solidarity.

The initial support of Bogue, Waugh, and Townsend, and later endorsements by such men as Burder, were simply part and parcel of a very extensive adoption of the new society by LMS supporters. Indeed, Bogue, Waugh, Townsend and Burder were but four of at least ten LMS founders committed to the support of the new society.[86] Of this number, one, Joseph Hardcastle, had been LMS treasurer 1795-1815. His successors in that office, William Alers Hankey (1816-32), and Thomas Wilson (1832-43), were also Continental Society supporters from its early years.

But would the new society transcend the Nonconformist constituency? Bruen, the eyewitness of the first organizational meeting had noted that

---

[83] *Proceedings*, 4 (1822), 18.

[84] *Proceedings*, 4 (1822), 21.

[85] *Proceedings*, 7 (1825), 49, 50.

[86] The ten formed a healthy proportion of the thirty-six founders treated in John Morison's *The Fathers and Founders of the London Missionary Society*, 2 vols, (London: 1844). Not all of these persons were still living at the founding of the junior society in 1818. Other such supporters were Joseph Hardcastle, the Rev. John Love (Paisley), the Rev. Rowland Hill (Surrey), the Rev. William Roby (Manchester), the Rev. Edward Parsons (Leeds), and Thomas Wilson (London). This information is garnered largely from the lists of donations printed in the *Proceedings* from 1822.

the great difficulty was to 'bring all the sects to co-operate'.[87] Behind the remark lay two obstacles, one of recent and one of older vintage. As recently as 1815-16, Anglican and Nonconformist evangelicals had found themselves in a stand-off over the issue of what ought to be done for the Protestants of southern France.[88] Nonconformists, convinced that Protestants were suffering for their religion, had gathered funds which were still being dispersed in the Midi in 1817. The Anglican *Christian Observer*, however, had cautioned against intervention into what it viewed as a purely political matter. In the more distant past, the Church Missionary Society had been founded in 1799 because of settled Anglican reservations over the agenda set by the co-operating Nonconformists who founded the London Missionary Society in 1795. Such had been the concern over Nonconformist political sympathies in that age of revolution and the espousal of a fundamental principle[89] (permitting each evangelized region to establish its own church order) that only Anglicans deemed 'irregular'[90] had given strong support to the London society. Could Anglicans, earlier so committed to the upholding of their own distinctives, now make common cause? An affirmative response was secured by two initiatives.

First, care was taken to draft what might be called a 'fundamental principle' for the Continental Society which would resolve in advance all questions about the form of Christianity to be propagated in Europe. This principle was, as stated in 1819,

The object of this society is to assist local native ministers in preaching the Gospel, and in distributing Bibles, Testaments and Religious publications over the

---

[87] Cf. p. 164 *supra*.

[88] Cf. p. 64 *supra*.

[89] The drafting of this policy is attributed by his biographers to Alexander Waugh. Cf. Hay and Belfrage, *Waugh*, 153. That policy stated, 'As the union of God's people of various denominations, in carrying on this great work, is a most desirable object; so, to prevent, if possible, any cause of future dissension, it is declared to be a fundamental principle of the Missionary Society, that our design is not to send Presbyterianism, Independency, Episcopacy, or any other form of church order and government (about which there may be a difference of opinion among serious persons) but the glorious Gospel of the blessed God, to the heathen; and it shall be left (as it ought to be left) to the minds of the persons whom God may call into the fellowship of his Son from among them, to assume for themselves such form of church government as to them shall appear most agreeable to the word of God.'

[90] Such were Rowland Hill, Thomas Haweis, and John Eyre, all numbered by Morison, *Founders*, vol. 2.

Continent of Europe, but without the design of establishing any distinct sect or party.[91]

Such a principle was adopted because of 'diversity of opinions among professing Christians'.

The Continental Society has therefore wisely determined to guard against the possibility of collision arising from the usual causes of dissension, by employing none but natives in the respective countries... No Englishman has been or can be employed by this society.[92]

David Bogue, long the advocate of co-operative enterprises, expressed himself content with such policies in the 1822 meeting:

It is a true principle of Christianity not to establish new sects among those people, but, to strengthen the hands of the true disciples of Christ and to give all the aid we can to the friends of the gospel in advancing religion.[93]

We shall have reason to note that these objectives were never perfectly achieved and were in fact frequently skirted. Yet they did serve initially to facilitate Establishment-Nonconformist co-operation in a way not characteristic of the LMS. Europe's existing churches were to be strengthened rather than scuttled.

Second, deliberate efforts were made to involve representatives of the Church of England in the leadership of the society. The presidency was entrusted from 1819-26 to Thomas Baring, MP (1790-1848), the heir of Sir Francis Baring, cloth merchant and East India Company director.[94] The hard-working secretary of the society 1820-25 was the Rev. Isaac Saunders, rector of St. Anne's Church, Blackfriars. The independently wealthy Rev. Lewis Way, associated with the London Society for Propagating Christianity Among the Jews, was one of six vice-presidents from 1820 until at least 1832.[95] Another Anglican, the Rev. S.R.

---

[91] *Continental Society Records*, 1 (1819), 4. The statement formed the first of eight objectives and regulations printed in each annual report.

[92] *Continental Society Records*, 1 (1819), 8, 9.

[93] *Proceedings*, 4 (1822), 19, 20

[94] The *DNB*, III, 192, indicates that Baring, Sr, accumulated a fortune of £7million. Grayson Carter indicates that Thomas Baring was a sympathetic participant in the 'Western Schism' movement in the south-west of England, c.1815, and that an acquaintance with Henry Drummond had been formed in that very movement. See *Anglican Evangelicals*, 111-13.

[95] Ernest R. Sandeen, *The Roots of Fundamentalism: British and American Millenarianism 1800-1930*, (Chicago: 1970), 9, indicates that Way had trained as a barrister and practised law until inheriting £300,000 from a John Way to whom he stood in fact unrelated. Thereafter ordained, he used his wealth to place the debt-ridden 'Jewish Mission' of the LMS on an Anglican footing. By 1825, he served a Paris congregation.

Drummond of Swarraton, gave vital assistance to Isaac Saunders in the important work of itinerating on behalf of the society as far afield as the major cities of Scotland.[96] Upon the secretarial duties becoming too demanding, Saunders withdrew in 1825 and was replaced as secretary by both Drummond and the Rev. Hugh McNeile, rector of Albury, Surrey. Only in 1827 was a Nonconformist secretary added to this team; this was the Rev. Henry F. Burder of London.[97] Such an arrangement strongly suggests that support was garnered most easily among the original LMS-oriented constituency.

The strategy bore fruit in so far as Anglican involvement markedly increased. By 1822 (the first year for which contributions are recorded in the annual *Proceedings*) prominent persons in the Church of England, such as the Rev. Charles Simeon of Cambridge and William Wilberforce, MP, could be found among the supporters.[98] The Rev. Josiah Pratt, long intimate of Simeon through the London Eclectic Society, and Zachary Macaulay, with Wilberforce reckoned part of the 'Clapham Sect', were both involved in the 1820s.[99] Daniel Wilson, rector of St. John's Chapel, Bedford Row, London, himself just returned from the Continent, also joined their number.[100] The Rev. Gerard Noel was added to the business committee in the same year (1826) as his travel sketches of Switzerland, entitled *Arvendale*, were published in London.[101] The Rev. Edward Bickersteth, itinerating secretary of the Church Missionary Society until 1830, was a supporter from 1827.[102] And we may add that the same assurances of non-sectarian activity which made the participation of 'regular' Anglicans feasible served equally well to warrant the participation of others. The prominent Methodist, Jabez Bunting, was present to give a supporting speech in 1823.[103]

Such a survey of the trans-denominational complexion of the society in its initial years does not disclose anything of the organization's growth and operations. The simple fact is that it was severely hampered by its

---

[96] *Reports*, 3 (1821), 9
[97] *Proceedings*, 9 (1827), ii. Henry F. Burder was the son of LMS and *Evangelical Magazine* founder, George Burder.
[98] *Proceedings*, 4 (1822), appendix. The records indicate that Simeon ceased contributions in 1825. Wiberforce was still a strong supporter in 1829.
[99] *Proceedings*, 9 (1827); 10 (1828), 11 (1829) appendices.
[100] *Proceedings*, 5 (1823), appendix.
[101] *Proceedings*, 8 (1826), 1. Other members of the Establishment who had been in Europe, such as James Haldane Stewart (cf. p. 157 *supra*) and Miss Anna Greaves (p. 73 *supra*) were steady supporters through the 1820s.
[102] *Proceedings*, 9 (1827), appendix. Bickersteth made a speech the following year *Proceedings*, 10 (1828), 34. A recent trip to the Continent had quickened his interest in the society.
[103] *Proceedings*, 5 (1823), 93.

small numbers concentrated in the England's south-east until 1821. Only those capable of paying the not-inconsiderable one guinea annual membership fee were eligible for membership.[104] Already at its first annual meeting (1819), four itinerants were under appointment in France on annual stipends ranging from £50 to £80;[105] it is highly unlikely that such expenses were being met by the number of one guinea subscriptions received. By 1820, the number of agents had doubled, largely on the basis of a few sizeable donations rather than increased subscriptions. The *Report* for the year indicated that, as regards funds,

> these are at present very low. The Society has been supported hitherto chiefly by large donations from a few individuals. No considerable efforts have yet been attempted to make it known, consequently the number of annual subscribers is still small.[106]

In 1821, the number of agents had risen drastically to fifteen. Yet the financial footing of the society had scarcely changed, for the *Report* could indicate that 'income does not at present exceed £200 whilst expenditure is nearly £1000. Heavy expenses have been met by donations'.[107] But there were now glimmers of hope. A promotional 'memoir' was prepared to publicize the society's existence. What is more, appeals from northern Britain for a tour by society representatives led to extensive itineration in March 1821 by Isaac Saunders and S.R. Drummond. Consequently, auxiliary societies were founded at Edinburgh and Glasgow with corresponding committees formed in Dundee, Perth, Stirling, and Paisley. Some £220 in offerings was received in the course of this promotional tour.[108]

From this period onward, the society underwent rapid expansion and saw its revenue dramatically increase. By the year 1822, income rose dramatically to £1,074, of which £700 was raised by the Scottish auxiliaries.[109] This surge of interest came on the heels of an extensive itineration by agent Pierre Méjanel. This colourful personality spoke in at least thirty-five communities in the north of England and Scotland and

---

[104] There were at that time 21 shillings to the guinea and 20 to the pound sterling.

[105] *Reports*, 1 (1819), 9.

[106] *Reports*, 2 (1820), 6. Agents were in that year labouring in Valenciennes, Rouen, Piedmont, Paris, Strasbourg, Geneva, Basle, and the Netherlands. In the preceding year (1819) there was circulated in Britain on the Society's behalf materials such as Henri Pyt's 'Address to British Christians', printed at volume end as Appendix C.

[107] *Reports*, 3 (1821), 8. The £200 figure would indicate not more than 190 members paying one guinea each.

[108] *Reports*, 3 (1821), 9-11.

[109] *Proceedings*, 4 (1822), 36. This would increase to £751 in the following year. Cf. *Proceedings* 5 (1823), appendix.

was often accompanied by Robert Haldane.[110] The same duo was successful in gathering the nucleus of an auxiliary society at Dublin, in which families of Huguenot descent figured most prominently.[111]

The cross-denominational alliance, achieved in London after considerable effort, seems to have manifested itself spontaneously among the Scots. The Edinburgh-Leith auxiliary was a microcosm of the entire Scottish constituency in this respect. Prominent in the organization were ministers of the Establishment such as Robert Gordon of Buccleuch Church and T.S. Jones of Lady Glenorchy's Chapel. The (now) United Associate Synod was represented by Dr Peddie of Rose Street Chapel and the Congregational Union by John Aikman of College Street Chapel (later Augustine Church). The Haldane brothers, William Innes, and the eccentric physician, Charles Stuart, represented Edinburgh Baptists.[112]

Promptly thereafter, the initiative for the forming of auxiliaries took hold among English sympathizers. The 1823 *Proceedings* reported the formation of committees of correspondence in Gloucestershire, Bristol, Liverpool, Leeds and Hull; income rose to a respectable £1,625. Twenty agents were now in the employ of the society.[113] The following year saw twelve new auxiliaries founded, total receipts of £2,014, and twenty-six agents in service.[114] Steady progress was registered through 1826 when income reached £2,733 and auxiliaries totalled thirty-nine; thereafter separate handling of accounts for English and Scottish auxiliaries made the plotting of aggregate progress impossible.

Even at its period of greatest financial strength, the Continental Society was a small concern when compared with endeavours such as the Religious Tract Society or the London Missionary Society. In the year (1826) of the Continental Society's highest income (£2,733) their own

---

[110] The itinerary can be largely reconstructed from the summary of collections received for the Society in connection with the tour. Cf. *Proceedings*, 5 (1823), appendix. The present writer is not prepared to accept that the bond joining Haldane and Méjanel in 1821-22 went beyond a common pursuit of the restorationism Haldane had advocated at Geneva. After 1830, Méjanel allied himself with clearly radical causes in both Britain and Francophone Europe, ultimately entering the service of the Drummond-inspired Catholic Apostolic Church. A letter of 1821, reflecting one of Méjanel's early itinerations in Britain is supplied at volume end as Appendix D.

[111] Names such as La Touche, Bissonet, and Metge figured prominently in this auxiliary. *Proceedings*, 4 (1822), 5.

[112] *Proceedings*, 4 (1822), 4. Co-operation on highly similar lines was evident in auxiliaries or corresponding committees at Glasgow, Dundee, Stirling, Paisley, and Aberdeen. Interestingly, Thomas Erskine of Linlathen supported the society from 1822 and served as president of the Dundee Auxiliary from 1826. Full reportage of the Edinburgh meeting was supplied in *The New Evangelical Magazine*, 7 (1821), 153-58. Robert Haldane played a major part.

[113] *Proceedings*, 5 (1823), 1, 45, 93.

[114] *Proceedings*, 6 (1824), preface, 4, appendix.

receipts were £12,568 and £38,860 respectively.[115] The number of agents, both part-time and full-time, reached thirty-one in 1829 and thereafter declined, for complex reasons which will be discussed below.[116] The Continental Society had been early advised that it would be indiscreet to circularize the names of its European agents and their stations of labour. Such self-imposed restraint must have been very difficult to maintain. The society's stated view was that

> the Continental Society labours under difficulties unknown to similar societies. It must maintain an unbroken silence on the part of your committee respecting names of persons and places. Any other line of conduct would subject agents to considerable danger.[117]

The need for such a policy was repeated by the well-informed pastor of the English Independent congregation at Paris, Mark Wilks, in the 1822 meeting. He warned that

> There is a universal dread of foreign agents. If you wish to destroy your Society in France, the best way is to make it known.[118]

In pursuit of this policy, the Continental Society seldom if ever named their agents or indicated their locations other than by region, when such details involved Francophone Europe. Claus Von Bülow, a Dane who served the society in coastal Norway in 1827-28, and J.G. Oncken, a German-born but Edinburgh-reared agent of the society at Hamburg from 1823-29, as non-Francophones, form clear exceptions to the policy.[119] Even the quarterly *Extracts of Correspondence* from society agents, issued by the management committee to members in an attempt to bridge the communication 'void', systematically deleted all names and places.[120]

---

[115] See Jones, *Jubilee Memorial*, Appendix 1; and Lovett, *History of the L.M.S.*, 2, 753.

[116] *Proceedings*, 11 (1829), 1. *Proceedings*, 14 (1832), 17, indicated a decline to thirty agents. By 1834 the number had been reduced to twenty-one. See *Appeal of the Continental Society of Dublin*, (1834), 3.

[117] *Report*, 2 (1820), 3. The air of secrecy necessary to the operations of the Society in France at this time was simply reflective of the awkward position of all Protestant agencies in France under the Bourbon regime.

[118] *Proceedings*, 4 (1822), 17.

[119] See *Proceedings*, 6 (1824), 49; and 9 (1827), 50-51.

[120] From approximately 1824 these were printed and bound with the *Proceedings*. The British Library holds a free-standing pamphlet, *Extracts of Correspondence* 58, April-November 1838. However, a clear lapse from this policy of secrecy was committed by the *Evangelical Magazine*, 4 (1826), 156-57, for it then gave names and details of all society agents known to it. This important report is reproduced at volume-end as Appendix E.

As a consequence of such a policy, supporters had to be content with knowing only generalities about the agents they supported. Thus, the *Report* for 1821 disclosed only that workers were distributed as follows: two at Paris, two at Orleans, one each in the Netherlands and the canton of Vaud, two in Piedmont, and the prospect (never realized) of placing an agent in Spain.[121] The following year, subscribers were simply informed that the fifteen agents had itinerated in France, Germany, Switzerland, Italy and the Rhine region.[122] While these secretive policies may not satisfy the modern observer, they do not appear to have caused friction or misunderstanding among the early society's supporters. For them, the published *Extracts of Correspondence* illustrated wonderfully (albeit without names and locations) the progress being made in Scripture distribution and village evangelism. The committee of management were themselves privy to much helpful information which was never published. When correspondence from abroad did not yield all necessary information, they were prepared to deputize one of their number to visit the European agents on their behalf. One such representative, vice-president Captain Cotton, visited every European mission station supported by the society to gather facts and to explain current society decisions and policies.[123]

Even when agents of the society visited Britain, either to itinerate on the society's behalf,[124] or to gain ordination at the hands of ministers supportive of the Continental Society in gatherings at Poultry Chapel, London,[125] care was taken not to unduly draw attention to them in the religious press.[126] Ironically, the general supporters of the society only learned the identities of some agents when tributes were paid following their untimely deaths. Such was the case as regards Ferdinand Caulier and Félix Neff.[127]

The London-based society, the distinctive of which was its employment of European agents 'to assist local native ministers in preaching the Gospel...without the design of establishing any sect or party',[128]

---

[121] *Report*, 3 (1821), 12.

[122] *Proceedings*, 4 (1822), 36.

[123] *Proceedings*, 9 (1827), 3.

[124] As did P. Méjanel in 1821-22; see p. 170 *supra*. Ami Bost itinerated extensively in England in 1822, *Memoires*, I, 310ff. Henri Pyt itinerated throughout Britain as late as 1832, *Vie de Pyt*, 290

[125] As with agents Henri Pyt and M. Falle in July 1821 (see Guers, *Vie de Pyt*, [1850], 130), and Félix Neff in May, 1823 (see Bost, *Life of Neff*, 99).

[126] The *Evangelical Magazine*, 29 (1821), 339, by contrast reported in full on the ordination at Poultry Chapel of dissident Genevan pastors Guers and Gonthier.

[127] *Proceedings*, 11 (1829), 4.

[128] I.e., the greater portion of the Society's first regulation, printed in each annual report or proceeding.

encountered some difficulty ensuring the application of this non-sectarian principle. As early as 1821, the officers of the society felt compelled to respond to the persistent questions of those who demanded to know 'what are the sentiments of the agents in doctrine and discipline?'[129] The question arose not because of sectarian bickering within the society's supporters but because of well-founded reports that some agents 'held the tenet of adult baptism and have been no less assiduous in making proselytes than in preaching the gospel'.[130] The agent, Henri Pyt, was himself the likely source of such disquieting reports. He had admitted as much in a letter of 7 March 1818 to 'Mr. A.',[131] that his own views, as well as those of Émile Guers, were unconventional on the doctrine of baptism. Then, later the same year, Pyt had been made the young society's second agent.[132] Shortly thereafter, Pyt's preference for believer's baptism and separatist church polity became public knowledge at Nomain and Bayonne.[133]

One suspects that some cracks were being 'papered over' when the society members were informed, at the 1821 annual meeting, that as to the sentiments of the eight agents,

> the majority are of the Reformed Church in France. Two are Baptists, two are former Catholics... The society acknowledges that two agents did introduce the subject (of baptism) into their ministry and that they did baptize a small number of individuals. The committee must positively declare that it was done without any knowledge, consent or connivance of the committee and that measures were immediately taken to prevent a recurrence.

> Your committee moreover explicitly assure you that the doctrines promulgated by the agents of this society are in strict accordance with the articles of the Church of England and those of the Assembly's catechism.[134]

---

[129] *Report*, 3 (1821), 15.

[130] *Report*, 3 (1821), 15.

[131] The Mr A. was surely Mr W. Anderson, involved later that year in founding the Continental Society. The letter was published in *Christian Repository and Religious Register*, 3 (1818), 309-11.

[132] Guers, *Vie de Pyt*, 59. Méjanel had been the first agent appointed.

[133] Wemyss, *Réveil*, 105, 127. Guers (himself of baptistic views) in his *Vie de Pyt*, 125, admits that Society agents Méjanel, Pyt and Porchat all held this outlook, yet maintains that only Méjanel propounded it. Correspondence was then received from Robert Haldane, who counselled, 'In speaking much about baptism, one makes people forget about their spiritual misery and love to the saviour; one seeks more to satisfy his proper judgement than to advance the edification of the church of God.'

[134] *Report*, 3 (1821), 15-16. Pyt had been present for the 1820 annual meeting.

In hindsight, it seems obvious that the two initial appointees, Méjanel and Pyt (the two Baptists alluded to), enjoyed their employment largely on the basis of personal agreement or accord with the two principals, Haldane and Drummond. This method of selecting agents, while it may have seemed satisfactory to the principal founders, raised serious questions in the mind of the chiefly paedobaptist society membership. Was there not a more even-handed method of selection? The society's vaunted non-sectarian character seemed to hang in the balance. To guard against any further unsettling developments, the committee reported to the 1822 meeting (by which time fifteen agents were serving): 'Two committees have been formed; one at G_____ and the other at M_____. By this method, we guard against a wrong choice of agents.'[135]

But this cannot have been the end of the matter, for the committee found it necessary in 1826 to provide six rules for agents in order to safeguard the original non-sectarian basis of 1818-19, i.e., 'the aiding of native preachers without the design of establishing any distinct sect or party'.

I. The agents shall confine themselves to the preaching of the Gospel... They shall not encourage a spirit of separation from the Protestant Churches nor establish churches under any form of government whatsoever.

II. They shall abstain from the administration of the sacraments of Baptism and the Lord's Supper altogether as the opinions of Christians concerning the proper mode and subjects of these ordinances are greatly divided... They are at liberty to partake of the latter.

III. Should an agent meet with an offer to become a stated pastor...he shall be at liberty to do so, but in that case he will no longer be considered an agent of the society.

IV. No agent shall be allowed to transact the business of any other society or to become an editor or author of any publication without the express permission of the committee; and it is recommended to the agents not to correspond with any society, church or individual on matters relating to ecclesiastical discipline.

V. The agents shall promote as much as possible the circulation of the Scripture, exclusive of the apocrypha, and religious tracts and consider themselves as cooperating with every religious institution which is formed for the purpose of advancing Christ's Kingdom in the world.

---

[135] *Proceedings*, 4 (1822), 36. The locations, as usual shrouded in secrecy, were likely Geneva and Montauban. Guers, *Le Premier Réveil*, 278, indicates that he served as central agent of the Geneva committee for many years before relinquishing the role to Henri Pyt. As both held to Baptist views, it is difficult to see how their appointment necessarily served to rectify the tensions of the early 1820s.

VI. The agents shall keep journals of their labours and transmit a copy of the same.[136]

Plainly, the mere existence of screening committees in two European cities for the purpose of selecting the right sort of agent was no panacea for the sectarian tensions of the time. If the society attracted some agents who entered the ministry of the French Reformed Church when the opportunity presented itself,[137] and others who sought entry without success,[138] there was always a sizeable third group within Francophone Europe and beyond which found the idea of such 'rapprochement' unpleasant in the extreme. Henri Pyt, from 1828 the 'central agent' of the society within France,[139] had sought employment in the society originally because he sensed that 'only in the work of itinerant evangelism could he avoid compromise with the national church'.[140] That Pyt, who shared convictions so similar to those of his mentor, Haldane, should have occupied such an influential place within the society suggests internal tension between the individual stance of some of its principle backers and agents *and* the organization's originally-stated non-sectarian posture.

The Continental Society and Contemporary Controversy

To its credit, the society did manage to steer clear of one of the two major issues serving to divide British evangelical Christians in the 1820s. The 'apocrypha controversy', pursued by Robert Haldane and Henry Drummond with the British and Foreign Bible Society over the constitutionality and propriety of the latter's including the Apocryphal books in bound copies of the Holy Scriptures supplied to Europe, did not bring estrangement between the two societies. One might have expected otherwise, given the prominence of Haldane and Drummond in the unfortunate debacle. While the Continental Society's 'rules for agents' of 1826 had urged circulation of Scriptures without the Apocrypha 'as much as possible' (a deliberately ambiguous phrase?), it is plain that the

---

[136] *Proceedings*, 8 (1826), 16.

[137] E.g., Laurent Cadoret and Philippe Falle, both graduates of Bogue's Gosport Academy.

[138] E.g., Félix Neff, whose lack of French citizenship served to bar his ratification by the government of the day.

[139] *Proceedings*, 10 (1828), 8.

[140] Guers, *Vie de Pyt*, 59. Characterizations of the Continental Society made by such recent writers as Stunt, *From Awakening*, 241-42, and Carter, *Anglican Evangelicals*, 161-64, show a willingness to suppose that agents in this third, separatist category were representative of the total number. On closer examination of the agents and their records, this interpretation will not stand.

society's agents were highly eclectic in their Scripture distribution. Repeated appreciative statements in the *Reports* and *Proceedings* indicate the Bible Society's unstinting help in providing the 'de Sacy' Catholic version of the New Testament for broad and enthusiastic distribution by Continental Society agents.[141] The time-honoured Martin version was also widely used. The agent, Félix Neff, recorded his displeasure that Scriptures with the Apocrypha were not widely enough available for distribution to the largely Catholic population of the High Alps.[142]

The charge of the Haldane biographer that 'the Bible Society was induced, by the dread of giving offence, to refuse to entrust Bibles for distribution to such able men as Bost, Pyt, or Neff',[143] finds no corroboration in the *Reports* or *Proceedings* or in the biographical records of society agents. At the 1827 annual meeting, the secretary, Hugh McNeile, repudiated in no uncertain terms the rumour, fed by the Apocrypha controversy, 'that the Continental Society is opposed to the Bible Society'. McNeile admitted that it was probably his own and Henry Drummond's purely personal opposition to the inclusion of the Apocrypha which had fed the rumour. Yet he rejoiced that the Bible Society itself had recently resolved that 'it is injudicious to add the Apocrypha to the volume of the Holy Scripture'. Now he was happy to state that 'the interests of the Bible Society are interests which ought to be sacred to the end of the world'.[144] Robert Haldane, meanwhile, carried on his own polemic with the Bible Society from Edinburgh.[145] But these machinations, leading to the estrangement of the Edinburgh Bible Society from the British and Foreign Bible Society and the inauguration of the Trinitarian Bible Society within England in 1831, were not Continental Society concerns.[146] Yet if the Apocrypha controversy passed this society

---

[141] *Report*, 2 (1820), 5; 3 (1821), 19; 4 (1822), 38, 39: 'The mainspring of the whole has been the B.F.B.S. of London'; 6 (1824), 15: 'Your agents have been regularly supplied with all they have required.'

[142] A. Bost, *Letters and Biography of Félix Neff*, (London: 1855), 251. Neff to M. Bonifas (1822): 'As it is useless to offer Bibles without the Apocrypha to the Roman Catholics, this good work of distribution must at present stand still.'

[143] A. Haldane, *Lives of the Haldanes*, 507. This misrepresentation is the more remarkable when it is recalled that Alexander Haldane, as one involved in and supportive of the Continental Society, would have had access to the very kinds of materials cited above demonstrating the emptiness of the charges he levelled.

[144] *Proceedings*, 9 (1827), 115.

[145] Some examples of this polemic are furnished by Stunt, *From Awakening*, 240-44.

[146] Cf. W.C. Somerville, *From Iona to Dunblane*, (Edinburgh: 1948), 21. They were, however, the concerns of his nephew and biographer, Alexander Haldane. The latter, resident in London from 1822, was a member of the Continental Society business committee from 1824. From 1828 he was the incisive editor of the ultra-Protestant *Record*. Cf. Balleine, *Evangelical Party*, 135. Alexander Haldane's role as editor has been

by, the same cannot be said for the second major issue of the 1820s facing evangelical Protestants: the sudden rise of premillennialism.[147] Premillennialism, in contrast to the established postmillennial outlook, did not expect the gospel to win more than marginal advances in the world prior to the second advent of Christ. Further, it predicted continual societal and ecclesiastical decline until the great event of the 'eschaton'. A strong feature of this movement in the 1820s was the attempt at intercalating contemporary historical events into the biblical teaching regarding the 'end'. Three of the most vocal advocates of this new system of prophetic interpretation were all officers of the Continental Society: Lewis Way, Henry Drummond and Edward Irving.

Lewis Way,[148] vice-president from 1820 until at least 1832, is credited by the leading contemporary historian of premillennialsm with having sparked the rise of the movement in post-war England.[149] In 1820, using the pen-name 'Basilicus', he wrote a series of articles in the journal of the London Society for the Propagation of Christianity Among the Jews arguing that the second advent of Jesus Christ would occur before the millennium.[150] Among the many evangelicals influenced was Henry Drummond, a principal figure, as we have seen, in the founding of the Continental Society.[151] Edward Irving, a member of the business committee of the society from 1826 (and anniversary preacher the year preceding), was by 1825 also an exponent of the new theology; he acknowledged himself the disciple not of Way but of another early writer on these subjects, J. Hatley Frere.[152]

The relative inaccessibility of the *Reports* and *Proceedings* of the society, when taken in combination with the known involvement of such

---

helpfully investigated by Joseph Atholz, 'Alexander Haldane, the *Record* and Religious Journalism', *Victorian Periodicals Review*, 20 (1987), 23-31.

[147] This issue has been briefly alluded to in ch. 1, pp. 38ff. The present writer has offered the material which follows in a somewhat compressed form in an essay, 'A Millennial Maelstrom: Controversy in the Continental Society in the 1820s', in Crawford Gribben and Timothy C.F. Stunt. eds, *Prisoners of Hope? Aspects of Evangelical Millennialism in Britain and Ireland, 1800-1880*, (Carlisle: 2004), 122-49.

[148] To whom reference has been made above, p. 168.

[149] Sandeen, *Roots*, 12. Way still apears as vice-president in the 1832 *Proceedings* but has vanished from the executive in the *Proceedings* of 1839.

[150] Sandeen, *Roots*, 12. Significantly, Way's preoccupation with the issue led to the termination of his connection with the LSPCJ, which was unsympathetic.

[151] We may safely surmise that Way was drawn into the Continental Society on the basis of Drummond's growing appreciation for this viewpoint and of Way's obvious wealth.

[152] Irving's controversial anniversary sermon of 1825, 'Babylon and Infidelity Foredoomed', was not published in its original form. The much expanded version published in 1826 at London gave, in its introduction, a declaration of clear indebtedness to Frere.

vocal advocates of the premillennial scheme, has left the field open for conjecture as to the relation of the one to the other. What is more, the only twentieth-century scholar to make extensive use of the extant society records was the Adventist historian, Leroy Froom, who examined the society as part of an over-arching attempt to demonstrate the persistence of premillennial interpretation across the Christian centuries. Froom tenuously equated the viewpoint of vocal individuals (e.g., Way, Drummond, and Irving) and that of the society;[153] his analysis has been adopted as definitive by more recent students of the society.[154]

A close examination of the records, however, indicates that it is an oversimplification to suggest, as does one writer dependent on Froom, that the society was 'very quickly dominated by millenarian concerns'.[155] The related judgement that 'the Genevan 'réveil' in general and César Malan in particular were associated with the circle of radicals around Drummond and Irving[156] is equally open to question. Both conjectures are largely dependent upon Froom's highly selective sifting of the records.

We may note initially that the new premillennial theology with its pessimism regarding the possibility of progress in this world, proved most attractive to ministers and laymen of the Established Churches of England and Scotland.[157] It was this constituency and not that of English or Scottish Dissent which recoiled most forcefully from the events and example of the French Revolution. It was this same constituency which had fastened upon the slightest evidence of Dissenting sympathy for that revolutionary cause as the basis for an estrangement of recent cordial relationships in the early 1790s. Post-war agitation over the price of corn, unemployment, Catholic emancipation, and extension of suffrage tended to be construed by the members of the Established Churches as symptoms of a great social upheaval. And in this respect, younger evangelical ministers and laymen within the Establishment Churches were far more likely to strike a volatile and strident posture than the older

---

[153] Leroy E. Froom, *The Prophetic Faith of Our Fathers*, 4 vols, (Washington DC: 1950-54). The relevant materials are found in vol. III, 435-60. Examples of this over-readiness to equate the view of one for all are found on pp. 446-47 where Froom speaks of 'the real purpose' and 'the unchanging keynote' of the Society.

[154] Cf. Sandeen, *Roots*; Iain Murray, *The Puritan Hope: Revival and the Interpretation of Prophecy*, (London: 1971); T.C.F. Stunt, 'Geneva and the British Evangelicals in the Early 19th Century', *Journal of Ecclesiastical History*, 32 (1981), 35-46. It is appropriate to add that such writers have not shared Froom's concern to commend the premillennial understanding.

[155] Sandeen, *Roots*, 16.

[156] Stunt, 'Geneva and the British Evangelicals', 41.

[157] A point effectively made by Sandeen, *Rise*, 19.

generation.[158] Yet Dissent, proliferating by leaps and bounds in this period, saw in the steady return of freedoms to French Protestants a harbinger of the restoration of its own political rights, and claimed to see in the successes of the Bible and missionary societies evidences of world conquest for the gospel.

We have noted that the founding of the Continental Society was greatly assisted by certain stalwarts who two decades earlier had been among the founders of the LMS.[159] This group was so characterized by evangelical optimism throughout the 1820-40 period it was virtually impervious to the appeal of the pessimistic premillennial emphases. The appointment of Lewis Way as vice-president in 1820,[160] just as Way was gaining a reputation for his novel premillennial views, might strike us as odd, given the existing consensus. But Way was not the spokesman for any premillennial 'movement' as such at this point.[161] Until 1826, premillennial writers such as Way, J.H. Frere, and William Cunningham,[162] were looked upon as eccentric individualists. Against the background of the early and sustained support for the society from the LMS constituency and the undeveloped state of premillennialism before 1826, the allegation that premillennialism provided the 'real purpose' and 'unchanging keynote'[163] of the society cannot be sustained.

Having set this tendentious hypothesis aside, we are now free to observe instead the gradual and increasing employment of the society's annual meetings for apocalyptic speculations, the spirited resistance to such speculation by representatives of the society's older (and probably larger) constituency, and the role played by this rise of apocalyptic controversy in the rapid decline of the society after 1830.

There can be little doubt that Lewis Way was sounding a very strange and unexpected note when, in 1822, moving the adoption of the committee's report at the society's fourth annual meeting, he intimated,

---

[158] See David Newsome, *The Parting of Friends*, (London: 1966), 10; and Sandeen, *Roots*, 41.

[159] See pp. 164ff *supra*.

[160] Note p. 149 *supra* and fn. 149.

[161] This cannot be said to have existed in any official sense until Henry Drummond hosted successive annual 'Albury conferences' for premillennial enthusiasts at his Surrey estate, commencing December 1826. Cf. Sandeen, *Roots*, 18ff.

[162] All of whom eventually supported the Continental Society. It may be surmised that the principal founder, Henry Drummond, once under the influence of Lewis Way in prophetic matters, certainly made it his business to propose the inclusion of persons holding these views to positions of influence within the Continental Society. A case in point was Hugh McNeile, who having received the living of Albury by Drummond's presentation in 1822 and similarly joined the business committee of the society in 1824, was soon joining his patron and Way in sounding the premillennial note within the society. *DNB* s.v. 'McNeile, Hugh', XXXV, 246; *Proceedings*, 6 (1824), i.

[163] Froom, *Prophetic Faith*, III, 446, 447.

There is a time for all things: and I think this is the very time marked out by prophecy and determined by the circumstances of Europe when this Society ought to commence a scriptural crusade under that sacred commission...to call its members out of the mystical Babylon. This is the foundation on which this Society ought to rest and if continued on this foundation, stand it must.[164]

Behind this cryptic statement lay Way's conviction, buttressed by his recent tour of Europe, that the national Churches of Europe were in an utterly ruinous state—a state so deplorable that they had become foes rather than allies of the Christian gospel. Way continued,

There is just no religion on the continent at all! I don't mean to exclude the thousands who have not bowed the knee to Baal; God has his people there—but they are so few that I could not find them.[165]

Way's contention, so utterly at odds with the society's position that Europe's existing churches were worthy of assistance in their present difficulties, was immediately challenged. Mark Wilks, a constant observer of the religious affairs of French Europe and from 1822 pastor to an English congregation at Paris, was promptly on his feet to insist that

the state of France is highly encouraging. There is a movement among the minds of men highly favourable to revealed truth. There is among the Catholics a disposition, perhaps not seen since the Reformation, to receive the truth and examine the truth. I shall neither therefore talk of the extent of infidelity nor of catholic superstition but tell you of the glorious appearance of divine goodness, truth and mercy in subduing infidelity by the gospel, and in dispelling all the shadows of superstition... [C]ertainly if there are encouragements anywhere in the world...it is on the Continent.[166]

Listeners might have been forgiven for wondering whether the two speakers had in fact visited the same continent! To be sure, they had. Yet to Way, a pessimistic minister of the Church of England, the frailty of the gospel cause in Europe had only served to reinforce his disposition to believe that the end of all things was at hand. Wilks, by contrast, saw in the same struggle being waged in France ample encouragements that the gospel was still a world-changing force. He had seen

a Bible Society formed in France with forty auxiliaries established. Almost all the large cities of France now possess ministers of the Gospel of Christ who all preach

---

[164] *Proceedings*, 4 (1822), 9. It is highly significant that no evidence of this apocalypticism is found in any of the preceding *Reports* or *Proceedings*. Without such antecedents, the new note can be judged to have been disturbingly innovative.

[165] *Proceedings*, 4 (1822), 10.

[166] *Proceedings*, 4 (1822), 15, 16.

the fall of man, the necessity of the sacrifice of Christ, and the doctrine of salvation by faith.[167]

The novel missionary pessimism had shown its head and been made to give place not only to the older view, but a view well buttressed by an abundance of encouraging current developments.

At the 1823 annual meeting, the extravagant utterances of the preceding year were restrained. The anniversary preacher, John Williams of Stroud, Gloucestershire, articulated the purpose of the society in a way acceptable to all by indicating that 'The Continental Society aims at nothing more and nothing less than a revival of spiritual religion on the Continent of Europe.'[168] Mark Wilks reported once more, in glowing terms, on the encouraging aspects of evangelical work in France, while a budding premillennialist Scot, William Cunningham of Lainshaw, spoke of how the missionary exertions of favoured Britain did not yet equal the measure of her responsibility in 'the wreck of Europe (there) in almost-Egyptian darkness'.[169]

The 1824 annual meeting featured sermons by both Hugh McNeile of Albury and Ralph Wardlaw, professor of theology at the Glasgow (Congregational) Theological Academy. There were no clashes of opinion. Henry Drummond cleverly made liberal use of extracts from Daniel Wilson's recently-published *Letters from an Absent Brother On the Continent* (1823) to 'demonstrate the true state of Europe and the validity of the society's enterprise'.[170]

Given the absence of apocalyptic expressions at society gatherings following the mild flare-up of 1822, the selection of Edward Irving as preacher for the 1825 annual meeting probably signified nothing more than the considerable esteem in which he was then held. On account of this same general regard he had been invited to preach the anniversary sermon of the LMS in May 1824.[171]

---

[167] *Proceedings*, 4 (1822), 17.

[168] *Proceedings*, 5 (1823), xivff. This aim was lauded by the Methodist, Jabez Bunting, see p. 93.

[169] *Proceedings*, 5 (1823), 83, 89.

[170] *Proceedings*, 6 (1824), 63. It is somewhat ironic that while Drummond quoted the work approvingly, Robert Haldane would speak disparagingly of the work in his *Review of the Conduct of Daniel Wilson On the Continent,* (Edinburgh: 1829). We have noted that Wilson supported the Continental Society in the early 1820s.

[171] *The Pulpit,* 2 (1824), 461, having printed the sermon in full, commented acerbically 'how far it was judicious to expose the errors of the missionary system to upwards of 3,000 persons, we do not now say. Neither are we competent to determine the propriety of engaging in any argument for three and a half hours.' The development of Irving's own apocalyptic thinking is helpfully explored by Tim Grass, 'Edward Irving: Eschatology, Ecclesiology and Spiritual Gifts', Gribben and Stunt, eds, *Prisoners of Hope?,* 95-121.

When Irving stood to unfold his theme of 'Babylon and Infidelity Foredoomed of God' before the Continental Society in May 1825, there was an instantaneous reaction. William Jones, the early biographer of Irving, records that

> it was attended with the effect of disturbing and disquieting the minds of those for whose edification it was written, and several of the leading members of the committee had neither Christian patience nor decorum enough to hear the preacher out, but abruptly left the place. From hints that were subsequently dropped, Mr. Irving found that his object in the discourse had been much misapprehended.[172]

Perhaps because of the instantaneous furore, the sermon was not printed for circulation.[173] Some consummate diplomacy must have been required to restore a sense of decorum to the annual meeting, the featured guest of which was Professor A. Tholuck of Halle, Prussia. Tholuck bluntly underlined the spiritual decline of the Christian Church in his homeland, but emphasized that pious young Prussian ministers were receptive to the evangelical emphasis of the society.[174]

In 1826, the guest preacher was César Malan of Geneva, no friend of millennialism.[175] Yet in the meeting, Henry Drummond further indicated the development of his own thinking by maintaining that

> the Bible, Jews [i.e. London Society for Propagating the Gospel Among the Jews] and Continental Societies, by their very existence, are indicative of the signs of the latter times.[176]

Lewis Way seized the opportunity to reiterate his theme of 1822, that the work of this society was 'to call the people out of Babylon';[177] by this

---

[172] William Jones, *Biographical Sketch of the Rev. Edward Irving, A.M.*, (London: 1835), 141. It is as likely, however, that this noticeable disapproval was rooted in a clear recognition of Irving's meaning, rather than a misjudging of it.

[173] Irving, however, filled this void by turning the sermon into a book-length treatise of the same name, published in 1826. In it, the author predicted that the second advent would occur in 1868.

[174] *Proceedings*, 7 (1825), 42. Tholuck was in 1827 to urge on a young George Müller the need for Continental Society workers in Bucharest, Romania. Müller was otherwise directed and eventually settled in the UK where he undertook the direction of Christian orphanages. See A.T. Pierson, *George Müller of Bristol*, (London: 1899), 52. I am indebted to Dr Kent Eaton of Bethel Seminary, San Diego, for this information.

[175] Malan, *Life of C. Malan*, 200, credits Alexander Haldane for this re-introduction into the London evangelical world after a lapse of seven years. Haldane was now a London barrister and committee member of the Society. Malan's antagonism to millennialism is made plain in the *Life*, 411.

[176] *Proceedings*, 8 (1826), 33.

[177] *Proceedings*, 8 (1826), 38.

terminology he represented all nominal Christianity in Europe, whether Catholic or Protestant, as idolatrous.

Having surveyed the first eight years of the society's existence, it is worth remarking that we find very little evidence that this society was 'very quickly dominated by millenarian concerns'.[178] In honesty, we may speak only of the manifestation of the new viewpoint by select persons in the face of an otherwise-minded membership.

Before the society would assemble again in an annual meeting, there occurred another meeting at the private residence and by the personal invitation of Henry Drummond. To his estate in Albury, Surrey, in December 1826, Drummond summoned approximately twenty ministers and laymen, chiefly of Established Churches, for a discussion about the fulfilment of biblical prophecies. Sandeen acutely remarks that

> As might be expected, many of those attending the conference had been previously associated in the work of the Continental Society and the London Society for the Propagation of Christianity Among the Jews. In addition to Drummond and Irving, there were Lewis Way, Joseph Wolff, and Charles Hawtrey, editor of the *Jewish Expositor* (of the L.S.P.C.J.). William Cunningham of Lainshaw amd James Hatley Frere, prophetic expositors. George Montagu, Lord Mandeville, and later Duke of Manchester and the Rev. William Marsh. Also the Rev. Hugh McNeile, rector of Albury, Daniel Wilson, later Bishop of Calcutta, John James Strutt, later Baron Rayleigh, Rev. Robert Story of Roseneath, the Rev. James Haldane Stewart, the Rev. James Stratton, the Rev. Edward T. Vaughan all Anglicans, and two laymen, John Bayford and John Tudor.[179]

It has now been possible to identify[180] no less than fourteen of these twenty-two persons as Continental Society supporters. The immediate result of this conference (repeated annually through 1830) for the society to which so many were affiliated, was that these persons began to be immediately identified with the pessimistic premillennial tenets and singled out for scorn. Thus Edward Irving, even when he rose in the 1827 meeting to give the conventional commendation of the efforts of the society against 'hollow Protestantism and superstitious popery', stopped to complain of the scurrilous treatment being shown him within the meeting:

> I would beg leave to suggest that those around me might be better employed than endeavouring to drown the sound of my voice in the acclamation of their own... It is

---

[178] Sandeen, *Roots*, 16.

[179] Sandeen, *Roots*, 18, 19.

[180] From the *Reports* and *Proceedings* of that decade.

not to be endured that on such occasions as these, a speaker should stand up and be overawed by the approbation or disapprobation of those that surround him.[181]

Hugh McNeile, himself a participant in the Albury conferences and society secretary since the preceding year, reflected the same defensiveness when he attempted to respond

> to an alarm that has sprung up among Continental Society members lest the society should be injured by the literal interpretation of the prophecies as understood by some of those connected with the society and the platform of the meeting should be made the arena of particular views. In reply, I have this to say, 'that it is by its *Report* that the Society must be judged, and not by the opinion of any particular member'... By such [attention to] prophecies, I do not feel that the dignity of any society is compromised.[182]

Yet it may be remarked that it was only the determined effort of the Albury circle to raise their novel perspective in the annual meetings which threatened to make the platform just such an arena. McNeile's remarks were therefore a clear case of special pleading for his own cause. The Albury circle must have taken courage from the fact that one of their number, John James Strutt, was named in that year as the new society president and Lord Mandeville as member of the committee. But they were still very far from dominating the society.

As though building upon a foundation laid by McNeile's remarks at the close of the annual meeting of 1827, Henry Drummond rose to his feet at the meeting of 1828 to maintain that the organization's purpose was primarily to 'send preachers into the heart of Christendom to tell the inhabitants that they are not Christian'. Further, Drummond presented a rambling and verbose defence of his premillennial scheme. Ostensibly careful to make it plain that he delivered only personal opinion, he drew both hisses from the hall and some cheering from the platform when he maintained

> that in my opinion it is the duty of the agents to declare to Babylon that she is not to be converted but destroyed... When I first perceived that the present dispensation was not to end in the conversion of the world but in judgements from God, I thought it so clear that I wondered I had never seen it before and I concluded that all my Scripture friends were previously aware of it... Those who oppose our views bring forward two texts of Scripture; the one is 'Go into all the world and preach the gospel', the other 'The knowledge of the Lord shall cover the earth' whence they

---

[181] *Proceedings*, 9 (1827), 103.
[182] *Proceedings*, 9 (1827), 116.

draw the unavoidable conclusion that their societies are to produce such a state of things. Their logic is bad, their theology worse.[183]

We need not wonder that Drummond found it necessary to pause and protest at the lack of decorum in the meeting; his comments seemed guaranteed to raise the ire of what in all likelihood was the majority of his hearers. Was he not making the platform 'the arena of particular views'? Curiously, a second premillennialist designated to second Drummond's motion, Edward Bickersteth of the Church Missionary Society, commenced by insisting that 'he did so without concurring in every remark which the preceding speaker had made'.[184] The reaction was not yet complete; J. Pye Smith of Homerton College (without mentioning Drummond by name) repudiated his apocalyptic sentiments in the strongest possible terms:

> When the kingdoms of this world should be declared to be the kingdoms of our Lord and of his Christ, it should be by an extraordinary blessing poured out upon those common means of grace which this society was engaged in sending among the Continental nations.[185]

With such goings-on in the annual meetings, surely it was an act of extraordinary honesty for Drummond to inform the following year's meeting that the press was now describing the gatherings of the Continental Society as 'the exhibitions of theological mountebanks'.[186] Yet such press reports did not seem to dampen the zeal of the Albury circle. John James Strutt, now society president, indicated in his opening remarks for 1829 the extent to which he was now a devotee of the new school:

> The political aspect of affairs seems to confirm the opinion that the sixth seal (of Revelation chap. 6) is nearly expired and we see the kingdom which formed the image of gold, silver, brass, and iron in Nebuchadnezzar's dream... The time is not distant when a terrible day of vengeance will come; the Lord Jesus will return, but he will return offended with those who have slighted his doctrines.[187]

As if the president's opening statement did not constitute a sufficient defence of the new theories, additional exhibits were provided by the Rev.

---

[183] *Proceedings*, 10 (1828), 31, 34.

[184] *Proceedings*, 10 (1828), 34. Interestingly, one of the very few identifiable Nonconformist ministers to sympathize openly with Drummond, Joseph Irons of Grove Chapel, Camberwell, stated that 'he concurred with Drummond's point that the return of Christ will be a day of vengeance'. See p. 43.

[185] *Proceedings*, 10 (1828), 37.

[186] *Proceedings*, 11 (1829), 35.

[187] *Proceedings*, 11 (1829), 23.

C.S. Hawtrey's attempt to show that 'the 14th chapter of Zechariah was the key chapter in reference to the millennial day', and the Rev. Horatio Montague's effort to demonstrate 'that Popery is the apocalyptic Babylon'.[188] Such zealous spokesmen for the cause seemed to proceed on the mistaken assumption that all and sundry listeners understood and agreed with the details of their apocalyptic argument.

All this proved too much for one listener to bear. Dr J. Pye Smith of Homerton, a clear proponent of the older prophetic view, had been due to speak in support of the anti-papal resolution. Like any robust Protestant of his day, he was profoundly distrustful of the papacy. Smith diplomatically indicated that he gave the anti-papal motion his 'cordial approbation', yet 'was concerned over sentiments which he could not but deem erroneous'.[189] He went on to insist that,

> This society was founded upon the great common principles in which all Christians agreed; therefore he deeply lamented that there had been an infusion of other opinions which to say the least were doubtful and which put those who conscientiously felt otherwise into the unwelcome alternative of seeming either to acquiesce by their silence or raising their voices... He begged to express his dissent from the dark and gloomy views which some of them took of the state and prospects of Christianity... On the contrary there was considerable ground for hope and rejoicing... He respectfully conceived that opinions which are not generally approved by serious and devoted Christians ought not to be introduced on these occasions. As one of the original members of that society...he begged to enter his humble protest against the introduction of these sentiments.[190]

Such a call brought the unprecedented interjection of the society's secretary, the premillennialist McNeile, that 'according to the Society's rules, the Society is not responsible for the sentiments of any individual'.[191] Smith graciously accepted this reminder and completed his speech on a note of Christian optimism regarding the future by claiming that 'never since the days of the primitive Christians was there so propitious an aspect for the growth of the Word of God'. Yet his speech ended to a 'combination of hisses, applause, and cries of "chair!"'[192]

It is perhaps significant that the records of the Continental Society have proved almost unobtainable beyond the year 1829.[193] The growing strife

---

[188] *Proceedings*, 11 (1829), 28.

[189] *Proceedings*, 11 (1829), 30

[190] *Proceedings*, 11 (1829), 29, 30.

[191] *Proceedings*, 11 (1829), 31

[192] *Proceedings*, 11 (1829), 31-34.

[193] The bound volume of the *Reports* and *Proceedings* at the Bodleian Library, Oxford, encompasses the years 1819-29 only. Some society supporter apparently terminated his support with the year 1829. The British Library can add only *Proceedings* for 1832 and 1839.

over the implications of biblical prophecies bearing on the denouement of history for the conduct of Christian mission, a strife engendered by the outspoken advocates of the newer pessimistic views, was working steadily to erode the spirit of goodwill originally recognized as vital to the society's existence. The champions of strident premillennialism, determined to have a platform for their views, had fastened upon the Continental Society—not least because that society was in a position of financial dependency upon Henry Drummond.[194]

The Society Overtaken by Events

Yet before this fissure could be further broadened, the society was overtaken by two developments—one domestic and the other foreign—which brought complete upheaval to the contemporary situation. The first was the growth of notoriety and suspicion surrounding the Rev. Edward Irving, minister of the National Scotch Church, Regent Square, London. Irving's connection with the society as an anniversary preacher in 1825, a charity sermon preacher in 1827,[195] and a committee member from 1826 raised awkward and unwelcome questions regarding the body when, in 1829, he was complained against by his congregation for his encouragement of 'prophecy' and 'glossolalia' in church services. The presbytery in the city not only took up the complaint and found it entirely justified but also moved to dissolve the pastoral tie between Irving and the congregation.[196] In early 1830, it also commenced its own investigation into the espousal by Edward Irving and A.J. Scott (another London minister) of the view that the Son of God had received a sinful human nature at his incarnation. A charge of heresy against Irving was sustained and remitted to his home presbytery of Annan.

The practical effect of Irving's aberrations for the society was one of confusion. The growing circle of society officers moving in the Albury circle of Henry Drummond (of which Irving had been one) suffered considerable discredit and inner division. Irving was himself promptly

---

[194] The *Reports* and *Proceedings* indicate Drummond to have been consistently the largest single donor to Society operations through the 1820s, with annual contributions in the region of £290.

[195] Irving preached a sermon entitled 'The Three Unclean Spirits' (Rev. 16.13, 14) at Hackney in 1827. The sermon is printed in Irving's *Sermons, Lectures, and Occasional Discourses*, 3 vols, (London: 1828) III, 847-92.

[196] Jones, *Sketch of Irving*, 274. The volume contains extensive documentation of this and subsequent proceedings. Owing to the fact that the 'presbytery' of Church of Scotland congregations in London had no legal standing in the eyes of the Scottish General Assembly its ability to adjudicate these complaints was contested by Irving, who renounced his connection with it. The dissolution was not finally enacted until 2 May 1832.

removed from the business committee of the Continental Society.[197] A dual exodus from the society followed; one of persons who supported Irving, and a second comprised of persons who unsuccessfully demanded the removal of Henry Drummond as well as Irving. Plainly, some papering over of cracks took place, for Drummond, who was as much as Irving the advocate of the restoration of the charismata, was permitted to remain on the business committee as a wealthy patron. He gave assurances that he would not seek to make his particular opinions prevail.[198] The premillennial faction within a straitened society was therefore a somewhat chastened group by the year 1832. Strains within the Drummond 'circle' were illustrated by the publication in 1832 of three sermons by Hugh McNeile contesting the claimed restoration of miracles.[199] The annual meeting of 1832 received sombre news of a troublesome year past. Total annual receipts had declined from an average of £2,400 to £1,909; some agents had by then been released for lack of funds.

The other and apparently larger development to overtake the society was the second wave of 'dissidence' in the Genevan Church.[200] The immediate outcome of these developments at Geneva was the creation in 1831 of the Geneva Evangelical Society, an evangelical agency committed to the provision of alternative religious services, itinerant home evangelism and colportage, foreign mission, and theological education. The Genevan society invited and received foreign assistance with the latter two tasks from a very early period.

From America, the returned Paris merchant, S.V.S. Wilder, organized financial assistance for the Geneva Society and disbursed it through a European agent, Robert Baird.[201] In London, concerned individual evangelicals within the Church of England responded as early as 1832 to

---

[197] Guers, *Vie de Pyt*, 296. The account of these developments provided by Guers represents the only known contemporary source. Guers acknowledges the sister of the deceased Pyt (himself central agent of the Society in France and visitor to the London annual meeting in 1832) as the person supplying these details.

[198] Guers, *Vie de Pyt*, 296. Drummond continued as major financial supporter of the Society as late as 1839, when he contributed £340. *Proceedings*, 21 (1839), appendix. Yet, as we shall see in the following chapter, Drummond, while continuing to support the budget of the Continental Society, felt free to recruit current Continental Society agents in Francophone Europe to be, instead, agents of the Catholic Apostolic Church which he was helping to found. See infra p. 199.

[199] *DNB*, XXXV, 246. See also Stunt, *From Awakening*, 267 note 107.

[200] Described in ch. 3, above.

[201] Significantly, Wilder continued as long-term vice president of the Continental Society 1820-1839 (by correspondence after 1823). This involvement did not preclude his generating quite distinctive New England responses to the needs for the evangelization of Francophone Europe, the best known of which was the Foreign Evangelical Society. Its *Reports* 1840-46 are available in the British Library.

the new state of affairs at Geneva by establishing a 'Central Committee in Aid' of the new Geneva Society.[202] Such new responses to French Europe may have been reflective of a lack of confidence in the stability and resolve of the Continental Society. Yet they were more certainly recognition that that body, beset with difficulties largely of its own making, had more responsibility than it could properly bear for the present in simply supporting its existing agents. The Continental Society was certainly unprepared for the escalation of evangelical opportunity created by the commencement of the Geneva Society.

The Continental Society made what was surely an overdue attempt to indigenize its French operations in late 1832. No doubt it was spurred to do this by the example of the indigenous society at Geneva, which aimed to support and direct its own colporteurs and evangelists. At the urging of Henri Pyt, the Continental Society agreed to the establishment of a committee of twelve persons at Paris which would give direction to all society agents working in the country.[203] Yet the beneficial scheme was scuttled by the proposal, printed that year in *Les Archives du Christianisme*, that a purely French evangelization society be created along the lines of that now begun at Geneva. The proposal was accompanied by the offer of 500 francs to assist. The London-linked society of French directors led by Pyt met only three times before its majority opted to found such a new, all-French society.[204] Pyt and the

---

[202] See Edward Bickersteth, ed., *A Voice From the Alps*, (London: 1838), 4. The new organization, as reflected in the 1838 publication, was supported by such notables as W.S. Gilly (biographer of Neff), brothers Gerard and Baptist Noel, and Richard Burgess, former Anglican minister at Geneva. Yet certain Church of England evangelicals such as Bickersteth, Hugh McNeile, and S.R. Drummond were still faithful supporters of the Continental Society as late as 1839. Bickersteth and the Noel brothers were obviously strong supporters of both.

[203] The Pyt proposal will have also reflected the increased liberty experienced by Christian societies in France under the July Monarchy commenced in 1830. Cf. ch. 3 *supra*.

[204] Guers, *Vie de Pyt*, 298. There is a very considerable likelihood that the initial backing for the indigenous Paris-based society was provided by the S.V.S. Wilder-linked American grouping then known as the 'French Committee'. If this surmise is correct, Wilder, linked also to the Continental Society, was outflanking that body by advancing an American-backed indigenization. Furthermore, Wilder will have known in detail the Continental Society's inability to expand to meet the increasing number of opportunities. See Robert Evans, 'The Contribution of Foreigners in the French "Réveil"', (Manchester University PhD dissertation, 1971), 398; and Wilder, *Records,* 273. It must, in honesty, be admitted that the Continental Society could hardly just 'fold' in light of the new Paris initiative. Even if it had favoured the Paris-based supervision of its agents, the Continental Society still had a proportion of its agents in Belgium, the Netherlands, German and Baltic regions in which supervision from Paris would have been impractical.

minority continued in connection with London. Thus began the 'Société Évangélique Française' and the Continental Society subsequently experienced serious marginalization in the country where it had most focused its agents and funds. The Church of England-related 'Central Committee' was happy to embrace the new indigenous Paris Society and a similar organization founded at Brussels in 1838,[205] as well as the pioneering Evangelical Society of Geneva. The 'Central Committee' existed simply to encourage moral and financial support of the European societies and left all selection and supervision of agents to these bodies. Increasingly, the beleaguered Continental Society sought to make a virtue out of its non-involvement in this process of indigenization. Under a new name, the European Missionary Society (perhaps chosen to shed unhappy associations from the past), its *Proceedings* now asserted that

> The committee is aware of the existence, and desires the success of societies with objects nearly similar, but as the operations of these societies are confined to particular localities, or the raising—not the distribution—of funds for such purposes, it is presumed that the duties and claims of the European Missionary Society are in no respect superseded by their efforts... Your committee see no sufficient reason why they should surrender to any body of persons on the continent the management of those funds entrusted to them by the people of Great Britain.[206]

But this was mere whistling in the dark. The society had never really recovered from the loss of goodwill generated by the activities of the strident premillennialists and the aberrations of Edward Irving. The untimely death of its mainstay in France, Henri Pyt in 1835, deprived it of a seasoned helmsman. By 1840, it was insolvent and was forced to submit to an inequitable merger with the Church of England-related 'Central Committee'. Henceforth known as the Foreign Aid Society, the merged organization conducted its business on strict Established Church lines, and would allow no Nonconformist to hold more than honorary office.[207]

---

[205] This was the Belgian Evangelical Society.

[206] *Proceedings of the European Missionary Society formerly designated the Continental Society*, 21 (1839), 5. The change of name had taken effect as early as 1836 for in that year E. Bickersteth preached for it a sermon later published as *The Religious State of Europe*, (Glasgow: 1836). See p. 1 *supra*. The present writer suspects that the British 'contributor' *most* likely to oppose this indigenization process was a donor rather like a Drummond or Haldane, who always reserved to himself the option of unilateral action in things of importance. It is by no means implausible to hold that the 'voice' behind the quoted argument against indigenization is that of Drummond himself.

[207] *Report of the Foreign Aid Society*, 1 (1841), 5. The person most responsible for the merger was the indefatigable Edward Bickersteth, active member of both. Ironically the Church of England-related society was not the richer but only the more solvent of the two. The receipts of the senior society for 1838-39 (the last year for which we have

The disappearance of the Continental Society brought about the end of that era of cross-denominational missionary effort in Europe.

Britain's Churches Respond to the 'Réveil'

The demise of the Continental Society might have been expected quite apart from the suspicion and mistrust sown by the Drummond 'circle', the advance of indigenous Protestant mission agencies within Switzerland and France, and the deaths of veteran agents such as Pyt; the era 1810-30 brought great change in Britain's own ecclesiastical landscape. Viscount Sidmouth, speaking to the House of Lords in 1811, had warned that the day was coming when Britain would be a nation with an 'Established Church and sectarian people.'[208] The prolific growth of evangelical Nonconformity which lay behind Sidmouth's warning now began to converge into denominational patterns not seen earlier.

Though temporarily destabilized by the death of John Wesley in 1791, his Methodist followers continued a strong connexional life through the annual conference of 'the one hundred' delegates from the regions where this form of evangelicalism had taken root. A Methodist Mission Society was then founded in 1813 and a theological college set up in 1837.[209] English Baptists, who had long maintained strong county associations and, under the impulse of the Evangelical Revival, used these as the framework for expansion through itinerant preaching, witnessed the formation of the Baptist Missionary Society in 1792. The Baptist General Union, formed in 1813, gradually expanded to encompass Wales and Ireland as well.[210] Congregational Independency in England similarly saw a progression from expansionary county associations to a national Union in 1832; Scottish Congregationalists had already federated in 1812.

It has recently been maintained that this heightening of denominationalism represents a retreat from the co-operative and non-denominational idealism of the 1790s—an idealism which gave rise to the

---

records) totalled £1,983, while for the 'Central Committee' in its last year of separate existence a mere £1,277. But the former left a bank deficit of £300 which the merged society kindly took upon itself to repay. The merged society continued a vigorous existence through the century before finally expiring on the eve of the First World War. Its annual *Reports* are found in the British and Bodleian libraries as are its magazines, *The Gospel on the Continent* and *The Watchfire*.

[208] In *Cobbett's Parliamentary Debates*, 19 (1811), 1131, quoted in D. Lovegrove, *Established Church, Sectarian People: Itinerancy and the Transformation of English Dissent, 1780-1830*, (Cambridge: 1988), vi.

[209] *ODCC* s.v. 'Methodist Churches'.

[210] *ODCC* s.v. 'Baptists'.

London Missionary, tract, and Bible societies.[211] However, such an analysis, while properly noting denominationalism's advance and the effect of this on co-operative enterprises, has neglected to note the fashion in which denominationalism was the indirect result of the success of domestic and foreign evangelical enterprises.

Baptist, Methodist, and Independent preachers and Sunday School workers may not have aimed at the direct creation of connexional churches by their labours. But the very success of their widespread efforts did create new congregations which customarily gravitated into the connexion from which preacher and workers had come.[212] Similarly, the support of the Baptist Missionary Society by non-federated Baptist congregations and the support of the LMS by non-federated Independents served cumulatively to commend the usefulness of the denominational unions which followed.[213] Thus conceived, denominationalism was the offspring of evangelical expansion.

Thus, by the 1820s and 1830s there had developed a considerable expectation that denominations ought to be active in organizing their own foreign endeavours and placing their own agents. We have seen[214] that British Methodists had been active in France on this basis since 1792 and afresh after the peace of 1815. From that period commenced several decades of working to assist the French Reformed Church in locales where assistance was welcomed. Charles Cook became the most prominent British Methodist working in France. Yet, by mid-century such collaborative efforts on the part of the Methodists began to give way to the foundation of self-consciously Methodist congregations.[215]

The opportunity for such European activity was inadvertently thrust upon the newly-configured United Secession Church of Scotland[216] in he spring of 1825 by the written request of the Genevan minister, César

---

[211]Martin, *Evangelicals United*, 196.

[212] David M. Thompson, *Denominationalism and Dissent, 1795-1835: A Question of Identity*, (London: 1985), 13.

[213] Thompson, *Denominationalism and Dissent*, 12.

[214] Ch. 2 *supra*.

[215] The missionary career of Charles Cook and the issues raised by it are helpfully treated in Maury, *Le Réveil*, I, 416-42. Recent work has been carried out on the involvement of Methodism in nineteenth-century France. See, James C. Deming and Michael S. Hamilton, 'Methodist Revivalism in France, Canada, and the United States', in George A. Rawlyk, and Mark Noll, eds., *Amazing Grace: Evangelicalism in Australia, Britian, Canada, and the United States* (Montreal: 1994), 124-56. Deming, the co-author responsible for the portions of the essay dealing with France, found that after 1830 Methodists in France became the competitors rather than the colleagues of the French Reformed among whom they had earlier worked. See pp. 142-43.

[216] Founded in 1821 by the re-union of the majorities of the Burgher and Anti-Burgher Secession Churches. We have noted the 'Réveil' interests of each church as reflected in their respective magazines in the first section of this chapter.

Malan, for ministerial reception. The latter had sought reception unsuccessfully from the Assembly of the Church of Scotland the previous year, but had fallen afoul of a regulation of 1799 requiring ministers to have trained in a Scottish university. The United Secession Church, being happily without any such bar, granted Malan the status he sought, both on the basis of his declaration of doctrinal affinity and the widespread familiarity of Synod ministers with his case. M'Kerrow, the Secession historian, could record that

> the expulsion of Mr. Malan from his church, in the city of Geneva, and the persecution to which he had otherwise been subjected...had excited a lively interest in him among the friends of religion in this country. And those ministers of the Secession who were acquainted with his history were ready to hold out to him the right hand of fellowship and to hail him as a fellow labourer.[217]

The Secession Church went so far as to offer Malan financial aid in the following year; while this was accepted towards the cost of Malan's newly-built chapel, it was declined as regards his personal subsistence.[218] With the impetus provided by the linkage with Malan, the Secession gradually opened itself to further involvements in Europe. By 1838, the Synod of the Secession was prepared to ordain a Genevan, John Monnard, upon completion of his studies at Edinburgh University and the Synod Divinity Hall. Commissioned for an evangelistic ministry in France, Monnard tragically died in the first month of his labour at Vadencourt, near Amiens. Another worker, Charles F. Major, was received by the Secession in 1839 for similar labour at Strasbourg; he had undergone examination by Secession ministers serving at London.[219] The continuing vitality of Secession interest in French Europe was demonstrated by the 1843 travels of senior minister, Hugh Heugh; his volume published the following year bore the name *Notes of the State of Religion in Geneva and Belgium.*[220]

We have noticed, above, the commencement of organized independent Anglican effort in aid of the 'réveil' in the 1832 launching of the 'Central Committee'. No comparable response was forthcoming at that time among the ministers and members of the Church of Scotland, even though a considerable number of persons from this communion had

---

[217] John M'Kerrow, *History of the Secession Church*, (Glasgow: 1841), 679, 680; and Malan, *Life of C. Malan*, 102.

[218] Malan, *Life of C. Malan*, 102, 116.

[219] M'Kerrow, *History*, 714. It is apparent that at least in the case of Monnard, C. Malan would have played a decisive role in orienting him to the Secession.

[220] (Glasgow: 1844). The Rev. Hugh Heugh had earlier been active as treasurer of the Stirling auxiliary association of the Continental Society. See *Proceedings*, 4 (1822), 5.

supported the Continental Society in the 1820s.[221] What did occur however is that the continental interests of Dr Thomas Chalmers, professor of divinity in the University from 1828, and a patron to the University Missionary Association, served to encourage many future ministers to take note of the 'réveil' movement. Chalmers' own *Tron Church Sermons* and *Christian and Civic Economy* were then available in French translation at Paris. Leading French Protestants had secured for Chalmers the distinction of membership, by correspondence, in the prestigious Royal Institute of France in 1834. His visit to Paris in June 1838 to lecture before that Institute brought him into personal contact with the leading crown minister and 'réveil' activist, François Guizot.[222]

In the period of the 1830s, the Edinburgh University Mission Association showed an observable growth in interest in French Europe accompanying the growth of the patron's influence there. The association heard a student essay on 'The State of Protestantism in France' and began a subscription to the main French Protestant journal, *Les Archives du Christianisme*.[223] From the academic year 1836-37 to 1840-41 the association made grants, sometimes amounting to one third of the total disbursed in a year, to the Evangelical Society of Geneva and the Society for the Printing of Religious Books at Toulouse.[224] Further, a very extensive correspondence was carried on by the students with European figures such as Merle D'Aubigné of the Evangelical School of Theology, Geneva (and the student body there), Louis Courtois of the Toulouse Religious Book Society, and the students of the theological college at Montauban.[225] Such eager contacts were maintained right up to the eve of the Disruption of 1843 and laid the foundation of a more enduring internationalism, of which more will be said below.

---

[221] This interest in the Continental Society had extended to the student members of the Edinburgh University Missionary Association. One sixth of their subscribed funds were given to this cause in 1827 and one fourth in 1828. Active members of later note included W. Cunningham, Andrew and Horatius Bonar, Robert Murray McCheyne, John Cairns, and J.G. Lorimer. The latter would later write *A Historical Sketch of the Protestant Church in France*, (Edinburgh: 1841). See 'Minutes of the Edinburgh University Missionary Association 1826-1842', in New College Library, Edinburgh. I am indebted to Dr David Currie for this reference.
[222] S.J. Brown, *Thomas Chalmers*, (Oxford: 1982), 272, 273.
[223] *Minutes of the E.U.M.A.*, entries for 3 March and 28 March 1835.
[224] *Minutes of the E.U.M.A.*, entries for 3 March and 28 March 1835. See entries for the annual general meetings in March of these years.
[225] 'E.U.M.A. Correspondence', Box 1 (1826-45), New College Library, Edinburgh. Items 48, 49, 62, 65, 71, 73, 78, 99, 108, show Edinburgh students were also corresponding with their counterparts at Glasgow, Aberdeen, St. Andrews, Princeton, and Andover in this period. Item 108, received from Geneva students, indicates that the EUMA had successfully urged similar correspondence to Geneva from mission associations at Aberdeen and Glasgow.

Considerable awareness of the developing situation on the Continent was also shown by the Kirk's General Assembly of May 1835. When the Geneva Company of Pastors invited the General Assembly to send a deputation to their city's ter-centenary Reformation celebration on 23 August, the Assembly was not inclined to accept. The immediate past moderator, Dr Patrick McFarlane, rose to oppose acceptance of any such invitation:

> He was sorry to say, that he could not propose to the General Assembly that they should express, even in the feeblest terms, their approbation of that Church, which had become deplorably corrupted in its doctrine. Still, he thought it was the duty of the Assembly to answer the letter, certainly in all the mildness and gentleness of Christianity, but at the same time with the firmness of men who held the principles of the Reformation... The reverend doctor concluded by proposing the appointment of a small committee to draw up an answer to the letter. After a few words from Dr. Stewart of Erskine, Dr. Smythe of Glasgow, Principal Dewar and Dr. Welsh corroborative of Dr. McFarlane's statements, the motion was agreed to and the committee appointed.[226]

Yet despite such a militant stance based on current knowledge of the European situation, the Church of Scotland involvement in the 'réveil' did not then advance. It may be that the links formed between the Edinburgh Bible Society and the Geneva Evangelical Society from the latter's formation in 1831[227] provided both an outlet for the concern of ministers and members of the Kirk and a channel for their contributions. But the failure of the Kirk officially to involve itself seemed puzzling to 'réveil' leaders in Europe who looked for its support.

When a circle of French 'réveil' pastors wrote directly to the Church of Scotland Assembly in May 1836, appealing for direct communication and encouragement, their letter was noted but never pursued.[228] William Meston, who called for a reversal of this seeming neglect, both pointed out that American Presbyterians were already corresponding directly with the Protestant Consistory of Paris and supplied a number of feasible

---

[226] *Acts of the General Assembly, Church of Scotland*, Friday, 22 May 1835, 52; and *Edinburgh Christian Instructor*, 4 n.s. (1835), 407. The *Instructor* had been, since the 1831 creation of the Geneva Evangelical Society, an excellent source of news regarding Genevan events.

[227] Somerville, *Iona to Dunblane*, 27

[228] *Acts of the General Assembly of the Church of Scotland* (1836), 30 May, 66. Admittedly, the letter reached the hands of the moderator, Norman MacLeod, on the morning of the final day of the Assembly. The failure to respond to the letter was cited by William Meston in his *Observations On the Present State of Religion in France...*, (London: 1839), 55, 56. Meston printed the letter of 1836 in full in French. It is signed by Juillerat Chasseur, founding editor of *Les Archives*, Martin Rollin, Frédéric and Adolphe Monod, J.J. Audebez and D.L. La Place, all pastors.

proposals for greater Church of Scotland involvement. Meston then proposed the creation of a Scottish equivalent to the London 'Central Committee', the bringing of select Montauban students to Edinburgh or Glasgow for one or more sessions of study, and the direct Scottish funding of colporteurs in definable districts.[229] Only the first of these was taken up.

A somewhat ambivalent outlook was reflected in an article published in 1840 by the *Scottish Christian Herald* entitled 'The Claims of France Upon British Christians'. The article described the demanding work and financial needs of the Evangelical Societies of Geneva and Paris without so much as indicating where a donation might be sent.[230] Yet by the following year, the same magazine could publish a two-part report from the newly-founded 'Edinburgh Continental Association' which was filling the very role Meston had outlined in 1839.[231]

That the Disruption of 1843 was being monitored in Europe with intense interest was made plain by the presence in the first Free Church Assembly of a Prussian delegate and receipt of a written expression of solidarity from the 'Free Dissenters' of Holland.[232] The autumn Assembly of that Disruption year gave prominence to the visit of César Malan, who was invited to speak at length.[233] In 1845, both Merle D'Aubigné and Frédéric Monod were present in and addressed the General Assembly.[234] A committee appointed the year previous under the convenorship of J.G. Lorimer 'for corresponding with foreign churches and aiding them in their evangelical operations and trials' reported that £2,034 had been collected in the intervening months for the needs of the

---

[229] Meston, *Observations*, 55-57. Meston is a somewhat elusive figure. He plainly was known to the Church of Scotland readership which he addressed. Yet, though self-identified as a preacher, he is nowhere mentioned in *Fasti Ecclesiae Scoticanae*, (1866). Long a schoolmaster at Caen, France, he was from 1848 agent of the Edinburgh Bible Society at Lille. See Somerville, *Iona to Dunblane*, 27.

[230] *Scottish Christian Herald*, 2 n.s. (1840), 641-44.

[231] *Scottish Christian Herald*, 8 second series, (1841), 726-29, 765-68. The Association secretaries were Charles J. Brown, D.T.K. Drummond, and Aeneas M. Rate. The account, 766, indicated that the 1840 General Assembly had received delegates from the Evangelical Societies of Geneva and Paris.

[232] *Free Church Assembly Proceedings*, (1843) [Spring], 107, 117. The effects of the 'réveil' in Holland have been detailed in ch. 3. The 'free dissenters' were very likely the seceders who had departed from the Netherlands Reformed Church in 1834, now formally organized as the 'Christlikje Gereformeerde Kerken'. Some elaboration on the Dutch-Free Church affinity is provided in Johannes Van den Berg, 'The Evangelical Revival in Scotland and the nineteenth century Réveil in the Netherlands', *Records of the Scottish Church History Society*, 25.2 (1994), 309-37. The Dutch seceders in time found that they had the greatest affinity with Scotland's United Presbyterian Church.

[233] *Free Church Assembly Proceedings*, (1843) [Autumn], 40.

[234] *Free Church Assembly Proceedings*, (1845), 128-40.

Waldensian Church, Evangelical Societies of Paris, Toulouse and Lyons, and the similar societies in Geneva and Belgium.[235] The committee, under Lorimer's lead, was conscious of having to make up for lost time:

> The committee rejoices to think that greatly as the continent has been neglected in its religious interests by the churches in Britain, some assistance has long been rendered. Besides the labours of the European Missionary Society of London (afterwards the Foreign Aid Society)...the Wesleyan Methodists have for fifty years carried forward important operations on the continent... And within these few years, our American brethren have come forward in behalf of the same cause with great liberty and zeal. Three years ago, they supported above fifty religious agents in one form or another... Surely if, with the wide waters of the Atlantic in between, they cherish so lively an interest in behalf of their brethren, we, separated from them by only the British Channel should share in a zeal at least as devoted.[236]

With the leadership of persons such as Lorimer, Robert Candlish and Patrick McFarlane, this committee rapidly made the affairs of continental Protestants the business of Free Church families and individuals. Addresses given in Glasgow and Edinburgh in 1845-46 and published as *Lectures on Foreign Churches*[237] soon provided the whole church with information about affairs at Geneva, Paris, Leghorn and Budapest. Thus, in the space of a very few years, the Free Church of Scotland became as deeply involved in support of the 'réveil' as any of the British Churches.

The London Baptist Society had sought to organize its own missionary endeavour in Switzerland from as early as 1831.[238] Concerned individuals within the young Congregational Union of England and Wales were galvanized into a similar, though more modest involvement in the same period, as was the Free Church. Many of the individuals involved, centring around former Continental Society stalwarts W. Alers Hankey,

---

[235] *Free Church Assembly Proceedings*, (1845), 121. The significance of this sum will be better appreciated when it is noted that the total receipts for the same year of the recently amalgamated Foreign Aid Society were £2,408. The Free Church's denominational collections were, therefore, from the outset almost on a par with those of a long-standing voluntary society.

[236] *Free Church Assembly Proceedings*, (1845), 124.

[237] Robert Candlish, ed., *Lectures on Foreign Churches*, 2 vols, (Edinburgh: 1845-46). W. Wilson, *Memoir of Candlish*, (Edinburgh: 1880), 337, 353, makes plain that his subject advocated the creation of the committee and was an eager fundraiser for the Continental Churches at the presbytery level.

[238] Former 'Bourg-de-Four' pastor and Continental Society agent Ami Bost served this denominational society in 1831-32. Bost, *Mémoires*, II, 127-30. An article in *Evangelical Magazine*, 12 n.s. (1834), 158, 159, reports the creation of the Baptist Continental Society in May 1831. Its short-lived existence has recently been described by Sébastien Fath: 'A Forgotten Missionary Link: The Baptist Continental Society in France (1831-1836)', *Baptist Quarterly*, 40.3 (2003), 133-150.

Mark Wilks, J. Pye Smith and Sir Culling Eardley Smith, rallied afresh to the needs of the continental evangelicals in conjunction with the July 1845 visit to England of Merle D'Aubigné; they formed themselves into the Evangelical Continental Society. The members, all Congregationalists, having been prohibited from sharing in the governance of the Foreign Aid Society after its 1840 absorption of the European Missionary Society, had then been reduced to supporting a small 'corresponding committee' of their own. But for this bar to their deep involvement, they would gladly have thrown their efforts behind the latter.[239] In the same period, the Calvinistic Methodist Churches of Wales began a missionary effort in the French coastal region of Brittany.[240]

An unsavoury aspect of this heightening of British denominational involvement on the Continent was the intentionally divisive influence of two nascent groups. The Continental 'pioneer' for the Christian Brethren, J.N. Darby, was deeply involved in propagating his own particular tenets at Lausanne and Geneva in the period following 1837.[241] Darby's activity, which focused on and divided the dissident evangelical communities of these cantons, prompted one of the earliest critiques of his peculiar theological system. J.J. Herzog, professor of theology at Lausanne, to publish *Les Frères de Plymouth et J.N.D., Leur Doctrine et Leur Histoire* (Lausanne: 1845).

A similar tendency and strategy was demonstrated in French Europe by the Catholic Apostolic Church. The latter, established in England in 1832 under the influence of the now-familiar Henry Drummond, secured the services of former Continental Society agent, Pierre Méjanel as European agent. Another former agent, Ami Bost, declined the offer of this employment after careful investigation of the new movement.[242]

---

[239] *Continental Echo and Protestant Witness*, 1 (1845), 242. £517 was raised in the first year.

[240] *ODCC* s.v. 'Calvinistic Methodists'.

[241] A. Christopher Smith, 'J.N. Darby in Switzerland: At the Crossroads of Brethren History and European Evangelicalism', *The Christian Brethren Review Journal*, 34 (1983), 53-94. W. Lindsay Alexander, *Switzerland and the Swiss Churches*, (Edinburgh: 1846), 278. E. Guers, *Le Prémier Réveil*, 335-41; T.C.F. Stunt, *From Awakening to Secession*, 299ff.

[242] The standard history by P.E. Shaw, *The Catholic Apostolic Church*, (New York: 1946), fails to trace this European aspect of the movement. Brief coverage is provided in R.A. Davenport, *The Albury Apostles*, (London: 1970, reprinted 1973), 153-60. 'Réveil' historians customarily describe the divisive and disruptive influence of this teaching in France and Switzerland, see Guers, *Le Prémier Réveil*, 328, 329 ; Bost. *Mémoires*, I, 93, 95, and II, 166-99. Wemyss, *Le Réveil*, 166 ; Maury, *Le Réveil*, 1, 184ff. Behind the European and British activities of the Catholic Apostolic Church was Henry Drummond, who simultaneously continued to support the endeavours of the Continental Society. Drummond was not above soliciting current Continental Society workers to become

Division and confusion followed in the wake of its arrival in European centres of evangelical activity.

The Continental Society had initially attempted to influence French Europe for the gospel in a non-sectarian manner; in this it achieved a limited success. Subsequent efforts, such as that of the 'Central Committee' of London, and the Free Church of Scotland, attempted to guard against sectarianism by making European societies (which they profusely supported) the administrators of evangelistic activity. But a third phase sadly saw British agencies employ their own agents to replicate their own British forms and notions of the Christian gospel and Church on the Continent.

---

agents of the Catholic Apostolic Church. Some details are provided by Stunt, *From Awakening*, 306.

CHAPTER 5

Geneva and Early Nineteenth-Century Britain

The British Veneration of Geneva

'I approach Geneva with feelings of peculiar veneration. The name of Calvin stands highest among the reformers'. So confided the touring Daniel Wilson to his diary in 1823.[1] The Englishman's visit to the Swiss city clearly represented the fulfilment of a longstanding aspiration and he made sure to allow time for an excursion to the city library where he examined Calvin's sermon manuscripts. Yet in Georgian and early Victorian Britain, the magnetism of Geneva was felt by many who were never privileged, as was Wilson, to tour the Continent. They venerated Geneva from afar and thronged to hear representatives of the Swiss churches when they came to Britain.

Though Genevan preacher and mission agent Ami Bost sensed the emotive power of his connection with Geneva during a speaking tour through England on behalf of the Continental Society in 1822, he could scarcely have understood the lineage of the attraction.

> A foreign minister was then a rarity. Arriving in a town I would see, to my great surprise, my name affixed to a wall-poster. The adjoined words, 'of Geneva' were by themselves a powerful recommendation.[2]

What Bost attributed to the mysterious appeal of the foreign visitor was in fact something far deeper. In the 'collective memory' of the British Protestant population, Geneva had many positive associations.

---

[1] Wilson, *Letters of An Absent Brother*, II, 289.

[2] Bost, *Memoires*, I, 315. Modern Reformation scholarship's insistence that Geneva was but *one* of a constellation of Reformation cities, each with an international radiating influence suggests that the Georgian evangelicals had been swept along by a 'legend' of Geneva's predominating influence that did not quite square with historical realities. Only later, through the nineteenth-century efforts of the Parker Society and such authors as Edward Arber (1836-1912), would British Protestants be reminded of similar Reformation-era ties with Zurich, Strasbourg, Frankfurt, and Emden. Modern treatments of these inter-relationships are provided by Philip Benedict, *Christ's Churches Purely Reformed,* (New Haven, CT: 2002), chs 1 and 2; and Graeme Murdock, *Beyond Calvin: The Intellectual, Political and Cultural World of Europe's Reformed Churches*, (London: 2004), chs 1 and 2.

In the sixteenth century, it was believed, Geneva had been the centre of a Protestant 'solar system' of which England and Scotland, like France and the Low Countries, had been orbiting planets. The city had been one of several safe havens in which English Protestant refugees had found safety during the period of Catholic persecution under Mary Tudor (1553-58). From this Geneva had come that most influential of Reformation-era English translations of Scripture, the Geneva Bible (1560), which was only displaced with difficulty by the subsequent Authorized Version (1611). Geneva had been the primary initial destination of the Huguenot refugees after 1685 and, not least important to British minds, the powerful symbol of resistance to Continental Roman Catholicism and political absolutism.

British evangelicals in the late Georgian and early Victorian period were under no illusions that such halcyon days still existed at Geneva. We have noted that evangelical leaders had repeatedly lamented that Geneva was now a place where all had changed.[3] But it remained true that Geneva, considered in its legendary character as the seat of Calvin, had lost nothing of its old power to evoke strong Protestant sentiment. Evangelical Protestants longed for Geneva's return to scriptural Christianity as assuredly as medieval Christians had longed for the liberation of Jerusalem from Muslim control.

Thus, when Genevan evangelical Protestants came calling in early nineteenth-century Britain, they were afforded no ordinary welcome; it soon dawned on such Genevans that they were religious celebrities merely by virtue of their city of residence and employment. The Continental Society knew this instinctively and 'traded' on it by inviting the Swiss to come at intervals and meet the religious public on its behalf. César Malan, though never the agent of the Continental Society, also grasped this principle and resorted to England and Scotland with a regularity which played into the hands of his detractors.[4] Henri Pyt, principal agent of the Continental Society, Frederic Monod in his capacity as representative of the Evangelical Society of Paris, and J.H. Merle D'Aubigne representing the Evangelical Society and theological

---

[3] Thomas Haweis, quoted at ch. 2, p. 58, had expressed the opinion in 1800 that he doubted whether there remained a single professor or pastor at Geneva who adhered to Calvin. John Pye Smith, quoted in the same chapter, p. 65, had observed in 1816 that 'Geneva stands in need of a reformation and reformer scarcely less than she did in the sixteenth century'.

[4] A nameless contributor to the *Evangelical Magazine*, 6 n.s. (1828), 477, emphasized that Malan's theological eccentricities were to be taken the more seriously just because 'he repairs almost every year to this metropolis and gives all possible currency to these views'. This was an exaggeration, to be sure, but the exaggeration of a truth. Malan was certainly a celebrity in Britain, and one who used that celebrity status to garner British support for his Geneva ministry.

school of Geneva were all Protestant notables in Britain of the 1830s primarily because they all had the 'Geneva connection'. Geneva, when taken as a whole, might still be far from scriptural Christianity and this was to be lamented; but there was now at least a restored 'evangelical Geneva' in whose orbit Britain might once more rotate.

It was this same Geneva connection which made the heroic missionary labours of Félix Neff in the High Alps of eastern France of compelling interest to British evangelicals. In a somewhat hyperbolic strain, the French church historian, Guillaume de Felice, observed of the now-deceased Neff in 1849,

> No name of the French Reformation in our day has been so famous as his; numerous original writings and a host of translations have been published concerning his life. In the heart of Germany, in the most distant valleys of Scotland, on the banks of the Orinoco and the Ohio, the name of Félix Neff is pronounced...[5]

But such rhapsodic praise would scarcely have exaggerated the interest of the English in Neff. A mere three years following his untimely death in 1829, the Church of England clergyman, W.S. Gilly, hastened into print a *Memoir* of the Alpine missionary; the book was an immediate success and proved highly influential. The Religious Tract Society quickly followed suit with a *Memoir* of its own. Ami Bost, compatriot and friend of the deceased, composed a fuller *Letters and Biography of Félix Neff* which appeared in two separate translations and many English editions.[6] Within a decade of Neff's death, the Religious Tract Society published a translation of the biography of F.A.A. Gonthier (1773-1834) whom it mistakenly identified as the human means of the conversion of Neff at Geneva.[7] This editorial blunder only bore unwitting testimony to the fascination the English-speaking world had with the career of Neff, who much like the still-revered American missionary of the previous century, David Brainerd (1718-47), had literally spent himself in missionary service to a remote region.

Neff's life was not without additional uses for the reading public of the 1830s. Gilly, his first biographer, was a loyal and temperate Church of England cleric who for his English readers (many of whom were Nonconformists) took pains to point out that Neff, though from a dissident background at Geneva, had served loyally in the state-regulated

---

[5] de Felice, *History of Protestantism*, 495.

[6] W.S. Gilly, *Memoir of Félix Neff*, (London: 1832); *Memoir of Félix Neff*, (London, n.d.); Ami Bost, *Letters and Biography of Félix Neff*, M.A. Wyatt, translator (London: 1843), and his *The Life of Félix Neff*, (London: 1855).

[7] L. and C. Vullieman, *Some Account of the Life of the Rev. F.A.A. Gonthier*, (London: 1837), 176. The true instrument of Neff's conversion had been César Malan, cf. Stunt, *From Awakening*, 42 n.72.

Church of France. Moreover, Neff, though a staunch Protestant who revered the Reformation confessions, was no extremist. According to Gilly,

> The broad distinctions and uncompromising truths of Protestantism were matters of awful sanctity with Neff; and yet though he was the pastor of a flock opposed to Popery by all the strong prejudices of hereditary separation...nevertheless with dogmatical and polemical Protestantism he would have nothing to do.[8]

Gilly had once supported the Continental Society which had subsidized Neff's Alpine ministry. Yet the biographer seemed to suggest that Neff had been nobler than the agency which had assisted him; that agency had come by 1832 to be known for the very types of intemperate and extreme views now cautioned against.[9]

Again, in the same decade William Jones, second biographer of the late Rowland Hill (1744-1833) seized on the current fascination with Neff. He made extensive quotation from the *Memoir* then being circulated by the Religious Tract Society in order to illustrate the life of his own subject. Hill, he maintained, had been as ideally suited to his own work of preaching at the Surrey Tabernacle and itinerating throughout Britain as had the missionary to the High Alps been suited to his sphere; both, moreover, had been just as much given to the use of striking pulpit illustrations.[10] That the life of the Alpine missionary should have been estimated to shed this light on the long career of Hill—who was surely the 'old soldier' of the Evangelical Revival—provides striking evidence of the place which Neff then held in the mind of the Protestant public.

Now in all this British veneration of persons and things Genevan there was very considerable irony. On all sides British evangelicals would have admitted that the segment of current Genevan Protestantism which they so venerated was something rather modest when compared with the whole.[11] Yet, for the purpose of rekindling the 'legend' of Protestant Geneva set amidst the constellation of its Christian allies, it was sufficient that there be at Geneva only a vigorous evangelical presence. However,

---

[8] Gilly, *Life of Neff*, 314.

[9] We have shown in the preceding chapter that the Continental Society suffered considerable loss of usefulness and support by reason of internal agitations over millennialism and Irvingism.

[10] A first and most substantial biography by Edwin Sidney, *The Life of the Rev. Rowland Hill*, (London: 1835), remains the standard work. The second, William Jones' *Memoir of the Rev. Rowland Hill*, (London: 1837), 20, 189, sought to correct deficiencies in the first. We have alluded to remarks in the latter.

[11] Thus, for instance, the Church of Scotland had admitted as much when it declined to join with the National Church of Geneva in celebrating the tercentenary anniversary of the coming of the Reformation to that city, on account of the National Church's departure from orthodoxy. See the preceding chapter p. 196.

the truth of the matter was that, even allowing for the substantially indigenous genesis of the Francophone evangelical revival, the momentum of the new Geneva was being supported and financed largely from without. British evangelicals were venerating a 'new' Geneva which they had largely bankrolled themselves; in truth the 'new' Geneva was in the orbit of London and Edinburgh rather than the reverse.[12] Geneva's numerous emissaries to Britain, honoured as they were on arrival, were nevertheless there to encourage the flow of support which, if discontinued, could easily endanger the continuance of the Geneva 'legend'. But this was not perceived or admitted at the time within Britain.

This fascination with the Geneva of legend was but a symptom of the Romantic Movement, by which heroic persons and struggles of the past were being recalled from obscurity—often for the benefit of the newly-moneyed artisan and business classes which now read, assembled home libraries, and conversed about the bearing of the past on the present. It was true in the world of fiction. Sir Walter Scott wrote forty historical novels for such a readership; among them was *Old Mortality*, a tale of the Covenanting times of the seventeenth century.[13] The same appetite for the past was manifested by the many, predominantly young, ministers who devoured the twin biographies of John Knox (1514-72) and Andrew Melville (1545-1622) authored by the Scottish clergyman, Thomas McCrie, in 1811 and 1819. Here biographies of heroic sixteenth-century figures were being written with an eye to the Church-state questions vexing the early nineteenth century; the lessons were not being lost on a rising generation.[14]

What McCrie did to bring Scotland's sixteenth century to bear on contemporary questions was only performed on a larger scale and a larger canvas by Merle D'Aubigné, whose multi-volume *History of the Reformation in the Sixteenth Century* began to be available in English

---

[12] Merle D'Aubigné indicated his grasp of this fact when he wrote in 1842, 'God has given the dominion of the seas to nations who bear everywhere with them the Gospel of Jesus Christ. But if, instead of good news of salvation, England carries to the heathen a mere human and priestly religion, God will deprive her of her power.' 'Geneva and Oxford', in Merle D'Aubigné, *Discourses and Essays*, (Glasgow: 1846), 202.

[13] Bruce Lenman, *Integration, Enlightenment and Industrialization: Scotland 1746-1832*, (London: 1981), 130.

[14] Halévy, *A History*, 465; Lenman, *Integration, Enlightenment*, 147; John Campbell, *Memoir of John Angell James*, (London: 1860), 6; Robert Rainy and James MacKenzie, *Life of William Cunningham*, (London: 1871), 64. W. Wilson, *Memorials of R.S. Candlish*, (Edinburgh: 1880), 27, notes 'the biographies carried the mind back to Reformation views and principles and were a very effective protest against the Moderation which had so long cramped and stifled the religious life of Scotland...[by them] many apprehended the doctrine of the Church's autonomy'.

from 1838. This 'magnum opus' delighted British readers by its extensive treatment of the Reformation in England; that the treatment of the theme was provided by a trusted Genevan narrator was all that could be asked for in that period which was so susceptible to the city's legendary influence. And of his treatment of the Swiss Reformation, no less a judge than Thomas Chalmers wrote to the historian to say that

> The Swiss Reformation was very much unknown in its details to the people of this country, and I never was more riveted in my life to any book than when engaged in the perusal of it. But while the latter half of (this) your (fourth) volume is full of interest on the subject of the Church's spiritual independence, and the danger of mixing up the secular with the spiritual, I should hold that the former half of your volume will be still more prized by the theologians. The Confession of Augsburg and the conference between Luther and Zwingle at Marburg are truly splendid and memorable passages.[15]

Evangelical Geneva, when considered numerically, financially, and educationally, was but a modest force which was in perpetual dependency on foreign financial aid. But when considered as the epicentre of that 'second Reformation'[16] which British evangelicals agreed Francophone Europe desperately needed, Geneva seemed as potent a centre in the nineteenth century as the sixteenth. Just how susceptible evangelicalism in the English-speaking world was to the allure of this Geneva of legend is hinted at in the introduction to the British edition of Merle D'Aubigné's *Discourses and Essays*:

> Of all the men of this age, it may safely be said, Dr. Merle D'Aubigné is the most thoroughly imbued with the spirit of the Reformers. In fact, he hardly lives in the present era, though he does move bodily about among the men of our times. Sure I

---

[15] 'Thomas Chalmers to J.H. Merle D'Aubigné 14 Feb. 1846', in W. Hannah, ed., *A Selection From the Correspondence of the Late Thomas Chalmers, D.D., L.L.D.*, (Edinburgh: 1853), 447. The present writer takes the statement of Chalmers to mean that British Christians, at least of his own generation, were at this time largely uninformed about the Reformation in Switzerland. Yet while the evangelical adulation of Geneva was stoked to a hotter pitch by the availability of D'Aubigné's volumes, it predated the release of his series, and ensured a readership for it upon its release. Interestingly, the late Gordon Rupp suggested that Britons were similarly unfamiliar with Luther until Erasmus Middleton's re-translation of Luther's *Lectures on Galatians* (rep. 1836), the 1820s translation of Luther's *Select* Works by Henry Cole, and the release of Julius Hare's *A Vindication of Luther against his recent English Assailants* (1854). See his *The Righteousness of God*, (London: 1953), 46-50. Rupp suggests that while Cole was motivated by the agitation for Catholic Emancipation, Hare was motivated by John Henry Newman's attack on the Protestant doctrine of justification.

[16] The phrase was used by Merle D'Aubigné to describe events at Geneva since 1816. Cf. the quotation in A. Haldane, *Lives of the Haldanes*, 402.

am, his whole spiritual man is at least as much conversant with the events and spirit of the age of the Reformers, as with those of our own day.[17]

Recognizing that this veneration of Geneva was a potent force within British evangelicalism in the early nineteenth century, we may now consider how British religion and church life was influenced by Genevan preachers and theologians. We will consider three main representatives of the 'réveil' at Geneva and their contributions: César Malan and British evangelism; Louis Gaussen and British attitudes towards the Bible; and J.H. Merle D'Aubigné and the growth of evangelical ecumenism.

Genevan Evangelism in Britain

César Malan was not the only foreign-born evangelist to have an impact in early nineteenth-century Britain, but he was surely one of the most colourful.[18] A 'news item' in the British evangelical press even before his first visit, he seemed to be the living refutation of the common surmise that rigorous Calvinistic theology could not be successfully wedded to aggressive evangelism.[19] By the 1830s, evangelicalism's fascination with the modified theology and methodology of Charles Finney, fresh from his campaigns in New York and Ohio, would illustrate the degree to which a new generation of ministers was experiencing a loss of nerve in attempting to evangelize from the traditional theological base. Malan, by contrast, provided proof enough that an unashamed Calvinistic presentation of the gospel could still be compelling.

At least nine times between 1819 and 1853, Malan was in Britain to address public meetings, preach in churches and evangelize through house gatherings.[20] He himself provided records of two of these visits.[21]

---

[17] Robert Baird, introduction to Merle D'Aubigné, *Discourses and Essays*, (Glasgow: 1846), iv. D'Aubigné received the honorary DD from both Princeton Seminary and Edinburgh University as a testimonial of this esteem.

[18] R.J. Carwardine, *Transatlantic Revivalism*, (Westport, CT: 1978), has described the visits to Britain of American evangelists Asahel Nettleton (1783-1844) and Charles Finney (1792-1875) in this period. While Finney did not visit Britain until 1849, his influential work, *Lectures on Revival of Religion*, was available in a British edition, with forward by John Angel James, by 1840.

[19] In fact, we have tried to demonstrate in ch. 1 that a very large segment of the Evangelical Revival had stood on this theological footing.

[20] The computations of such visits provided in Good, *History of the Reformed Church*, 389, and David Brown, *Life of John Duncan*, (Edinburgh: 1872), 124ff, are both incomplete. We believe Malan to have been in Britain in 1819, 1822, 1826, 1828, 1833, 1834, 1839, 1843, and 1853. Cf. Malan, *Life of Malan*, 200, and *supra.* pp. 152-154. Malan received the Glasgow University DD in 1826 in recognition of his preaching in Britain.

After his reception in 1825 as a minister by the United Secession Church of Scotland, he found most, but not all, of his public Scottish preaching opportunities in that communion.[22] We have noted above that due to the numerical decline of his Geneva congregation after 1830, he increasingly gave himself to itinerant preaching tours; in the 1830s this was not a common habit as most preachers did almost all their preaching in one place.

Even now, the sermon summaries from the period of his visits make stirring reading; the texts themselves were often most apposite to the occasion.[23] We will comment on some of the sermon subject matter below. Here we can allude to the striking fact that the records of two conversions under the ministry of Malan both attribute great significance to the Genevan's effectiveness in personal interviews. Both John Duncan (1796-1870), later professor of Hebrew at New College, Edinburgh, and John Adam, later LMS missionary to India, attributed their Christian conversions to Malan's methodical use of this technique in homes where he was entertained.

> He requested that each guest be sent to him alone, one by one... He would insist that the state of matters between the soul he was dealing with and God should be brought to a point then and there.[24]

Malan was, to be sure, a powerful preacher.[25] But he excelled with individuals every bit as much as with congregations. In England also, much of his preaching and evangelistic work was done in private homes.[26]

John Duncan may have believed that Malan's habit of pressing for a response to the gospel without delay was novel; it is likely that it was only novel to him and the circles of the United Secession Church in which he then moved. The belief in sudden conversion was, in fact, quite

---

[21] César Malan, Jr, *Recollections of the Rev. Caesar Malan of Geneva, D.D. being notes of sermons preached by him in May and June 1826*, (London: 1827). These sermons were recorded by a journalist. See also his *A Visit to Scotland in 1843*, (Edinburgh: 1843).

[22] This focus is reflected in the churches named in *Recollections*, (London: 1827). In *A Visit*, (Edinburgh: 1843), he noted sermons preached in that communion as well as Free St. Georges and the Haldane Tabernacle, both in Edinburgh.

[23] As when on 11 June 1826 at the Floating Chapel, Leith, he preached from John 6.16 regarding Jesus walking on the water.

[24] Brown, *Life of John Duncan*, 129, 130, 142. See also Adam, *Memoir of John Adam*, (London: 1833), 14. The method was somewhat reminiscent of Haldane's method of student interviews at Geneva in 1816-17.

[25] Adam, *Memoir*, 9, confided to his diary, 'never did I hear a preacher who came so near to my idea of what a minister ought to be'.

[26] Stunt, 'Geneva and the British Evangelicals', 43, 44.

widespread throughout the regions affected by the Evangelical Revival—although it never enjoyed universal approbation among evangelicals.[27] Older evangelicalism had often emphasized the preparation of the hearer to receive the gospel by a stress on the exacting standards of the divine moral law. It was the distinguishing trait of the New England evangelist, Asahel Nettleton, that he defended and utilized this traditional approach in Britain just as in America.[28] Even the great and unsettling innovator, Charles Finney, had used the 'anxious seat' below the pulpit in America and Britain not as the guarantor of sudden conversion, but only as a device to assist in 'breaking the pride' of the sinner and helping them to seek conversion. This was, in fact, but a variation on the older preparationism.

The aged Rowland Hill had heard Malan preach in England and proclaimed thereafter 'this day I have heard George Whitefield preach'.[29] In all likelihood, it was the call to decision, to conversion without delay which the old soldier of the Evangelical Revival saw as the common factor uniting Whitefield and this Swiss pastor. Yet, in the case of Malan there were highly unique theological presuppositions beneath the emphasis upon sudden conversion and those presuppositions were regularly made the subject of British debate. Complaints were made against Malan's supposed antinomianism (stemming from a lack of emphasis upon repentance), his undue emphasis upon the Christian believer's enjoyment of Christian assurance, and his unsatisfactory description of the sinner's experiential transfer from being under the divine displeasure to the divine favour.[30] All such complaints were ultimately traceable back to the prominence of predestination, construed in supralapsarian fashion, in Malan's dogmatic thought. Malan evidently held, in a way quite uncommon among evangelical Calvinists of his day, that the election of individuals to eternal life through Christ was an election of persons who were considered in the mind of God as not yet

---

[27] Cf. the helpful discussions of the question in Bebbington's *Evangelicalism in Modern Britain*, 5-10; and Bernard Citroen, *The New Birth*, (Edinburgh: 1950), 67-75. Bebbington returned to the subject with an essay, 'Evangelical Conversion, c.1740-1850', *Scottish Bulletin of Evangelical Theology*, 18.2 (2000), 202-27.

[28] Andrew Bonar (1810-92), prominent Free Church of Scotland minister, indicated his approbation for this older approach by editing Nettleton's biography for British readers in an edition published at Edinburgh in 1854.

[29] Malan, *Life*, 283.

[30] We find these complaints reflected in the *Christian Observer*, 27 (1828), 73-77, where Malan's *Conventicle of Rolle* (1821, ET 1865), is under review. They are also made in the *Evangelical Magazine*, 6 n.s. (1828), 477-81, where Malan's *Theogenes* (1828), is under consideration. See also McKerrow, *History of the Secession Church*, 681, for evidence that Malan's adoptive denomination took note of his eccentricities.

fallen into sin. Two major consequences followed for those who shared Malan's understanding of Christian salvation.

First, the incarnation, atonement and resurrected life of the Son of God were understood to have no reference whatsoever to whatever portion of humanity was passed over in election. In Malan's case, this viewpoint was articulated in terms of an ultra-particularism that quite out of vogue among contemporary British Calvinists. Before the special meeting of the General Assembly of the fledgling Free Church of Scotland in the autumn of 1843, Malan implored the preachers present to

> Keep to the standards of your faith—preach Christ the Saviour and his atonement solely for the Church—solely for the Church—solely for the Church [emphasis his]; for Popery says that his atonement is for all men, which is a lie. Christ is a saviour and not a helper. He has not two wives—he has only one, which is the Church. He has not two bodies—he has but one beloved one, chosen for him of the Father. Oh ye ministers of Scotland, have you some men among you who would listen to the doctrines of Arminianism? God Almighty forbid! The truth which has made the Church of Scotland conspicuous is the truth that Christ is God indeed—that he is a Saviour indeed, that he never died for those who are lost—that those for whom he died he has saved fully and forever.[31]

Malan's remarks, part of a deeply emotive speech which marked the first personal recognition of the Disruption by a Francophone, were warmly received. He had been introduced as 'the delegate from Geneva'. But this variety of high-Calvinism, while it was keen to preach the gospel to all who would hear, was also suspect in that it deduced all the gospel's breadth, scope and efficacy 'backwards' from the terms of its eventual accomplishment (i.e. the salvation of the elect). This was not the strain of Calvinism being taught in those very years by the reigning theologian of the Free Church, Thomas Chalmers. As his lectures, posthumously published as his *Institutes of Theology*, make plain, Chalmers was earnest in attempting to place all possible distance between his young preachers-in-training and this outlook. (Chalmers also gave a workmanlike and orthodox treatment of predestination in volume 2 of his *Institutes*.[32])

---

[31] *Records of the Assembly of the Free Church of Scotland*, (Autumn, 1843), 40, 41. Malan's keen interest in extirpating all traces of 'Arminianism' in Scotland was likely fuelled by the atonement controversies then engulfing his own adoptive denomination, the United Secession Church. The latter's efforts to maintain both a universal and particular reference in the atonement of Christ in this period is well-documented in the work of Ian Hamilton, *The Erosion of Calvinist Orthodoxy*, (Edinburgh: 1990). Malan delivered similar admonitions in 1843 sermons delivered during that visit; these are recorded in his *A Visit to Scotland in 1843*, (Edinburgh: 1843), ix, 38.

[32] Chalmers, in lecturing on the proper framing of the gospel offer, had warned against ultra-particularistic formulations of Calvinist theology. Such formulations he designated as belonging to the 'middle ages' of theology. Cf. his *Institutes*, II, 403-405.

César Malan could not have been accused of denying the universal offer of the gospel. But his attempts to bolster up the tenets of high-Calvinism were likely construed in ways that would restrain other, impressionable preachers from proclaiming the freeness of the gospel themselves. Second, Malan's extreme Calvinist particularism, rooted in a supralapsarian understanding of predestination, manifested itself in an implicit over-emphasis upon the eternal divine purposes and a de-emphasis upon the individual's conscious experience of and entering into the saving favour of God in history. In a sermon preached in Edinburgh in June 1826, Malan urged his listeners,

Suppose one of you was guilty of a crime against your king, worthy of the gibbet. You run and hide. You are in pain and fear. Well, but the King has been so good as to determine in his heart, to give you grace; *that moment* [italics his] you are saved; the king has given you a pardon. But hear this. As the law and the king's justice cannot be disregarded, he has said, 'I cannot save him without fulfilling the law; the law requires the death of the guilty'. The King then has determined to give himself for you...to transfer on his own son your crime. The letter of pardon is written out for you. You are safe. But I seek after you and only after two years am I able to find you. I read you your letter of pardon. You believe and are at peace. Now believe Christ. He is saying this very thing to you.[33]

It is not difficult to understand how such a strain of preaching alarmed discerning hearers. By the analogy employed by the evangelist, as-yet unconverted hearers were being invited to contemplate themselves as being the object of the ancient saving purposes of God which reckoned them saved and safe quite apart from the exercise of any faith, repentance or response on their own part. The elect sinner's only lack or deficiency was that of an awareness of the divine favour. Malan's emphasis was not here universalistic (though at first sight it might appear so), but actually deterministic; the divine favour was understood by him to be so fixed on elect sinners that their experiential transition from a state of sin to that of salvation was all but eclipsed by the actualization of the eternal divine purpose. It would not misrepresent his position to characterize it as teaching the salvation of the elect from eternity.

Under such a scheme, we need not wonder that contemporaries listened in vain for evangelical admonition to repentance from known sin, appeals to place conscious faith in Christ as sin-bearer, and instructions to the converted to walk in holiness of life. The future professor, John Duncan, recalled that Malan attempted to resolve his doubts as to whether he was a genuine Christian or not by a mere form of syllogistic reasoning based

---

Suggestive remarks regarding the correlation between the populist spirit of that era and its bearing on some theological questions of the period are made in N.L. Walker, *Robert Buchanan*, (Edinburgh: 1877), 23.

[33] Malan, *Recollections of Sermons Preached in Edinburgh*, (London: 1827), 63.

on a Scripture verse, 1 John 5.1: 'Everyone who believes that Jesus is the Christ is born of God.' When the troubled Duncan gave satisfactory answer to the question of Jesus' identity, the Swiss evangelist gave him the strongest assurances of his standing in grace. The impressionable Duncan at first thought Malan's whole manner both 'reasonable and apostolic', but on more mature reflection came to see that his method was based upon a defective understanding of the interior work of the Holy Spirit.[34] Orthodox reviewers of Malan's writings in the *Christian Observer* and *Evangelical Magazine* appraised him similarly. The latter writer concluded his remarks with the expressed hope

that the sentiments contained [in the work] may never disturb the peace, tarnish the purity, or dishonour the profession of the churches in Great Britain.[35]

Most British evangelicals rejected Malan's theology and methods not because they rejected predestination but because they believed that the doctrine could not be given this degree of prominence without eclipsing equally important biblical teachings. Here was one important respect in which a popular and revered representative of the Geneva of legend clashed with British evangelicalism; that he felt authorized to denounce what he—by his high-Calvinist outlook—termed Arminianism, would not have endeared him to the many evangelical Calvinists who found his doctrinal formulations severe in the extreme. In this instance, 'legendary Geneva'—at least as refracted through Malan the preacher-evangelist—was viewed with disdain. And this was not an isolated case.

Genevan Theology in Britain

British theology in the late Georgian and early Victorian era was neither well-informed about nor concerned to know the state of theology in Europe. H.P. Liddon, the biographer of E.B. Pusey (1800-82), was one who did gain a knowledge of the European theological scene in the mid-1820s, wrote that

German politics and German editions of the classics were welcomed in England; but the history, the results, the temper and the tendencies of German protestant theology were as little understood as though they had belonged to another and a distinct continent far beyond the pale of Christendom and civilization.[36]

---

[34] Brown, *Life of Duncan*, 129, 216. Ironically, this had been the criticism made by the Swiss réveil converts of the older generation of Swiss ministers. See ch. 3 *supra*.

[35] Cf. footnote 29 above. Also, *Evangelical Magazine*, 6 n.s. (1828), 481.

[36] H.P. Liddon, *Life of E.B. Pusey*, 4 vols, (London: 1891). I, 147. Similar sentiments are recorded by A.R. MacEwen, *Life of John Cairns*, (Edinburgh, 1895), 148, in connection with Cairns' continental study two decades later.

Professor August Tholuck of Halle (1799-1877), who had served as a close advisor to Pusey in the latter's German sojourn, was one of a select few European theologians considered worthy of general trust by the English Protestant public. Yet, though invited to be the guest speaker at the London annual meeting of the 'Continental Society' in May 1825, he was not considered to be beyond criticism by Robert Haldane. In the following decade the Scottish polemicist penned a scathing review of the theologian's translated writings.[37]

By 1842, and in the context of a proposed joint Anglican-Lutheran action to establish a Protestant bishopric at Jerusalem, Pusey wrote a public *Letter to the Archbishop of Canterbury*.[38] The letter warned both of the decidedly rationalistic character of European Church life and theology and of the way in which this degenerate approach to the Christian faith was now so much a part of the life of the Church of England as to make large scale internal conflict necessary. Pusey judged that one magnetic 'pole' towards which a substantial segment of Anglican opinion leaned was Geneva. In his mind, Geneva, the city of Calvin, was now the epitome of the Reformation run to rationalistic ruin.

> Two schemes of doctrine, the Genevan (i.e. the rationalistic) and the Catholic, are probably for the last time struggling within our Church; the contest which has been carried on ever since the Reformation, between the Church and those who parted from her has now been permitted to be transferred to the Church itself; on the issue hangs the destiny of our church...[39]

In just such a setting, when all things to do with continental theology were held suspect by the vast majority of British Christians, there came forward the preachers and theologians associated with the evangelical 'réveil' emanating from Geneva. That trusted Protestant leaders in Britain such as Edward Bickersteth, John Pye Smith, Thomas Chalmers and

---

[37] R. Haldane, *Two Pamphlets for the Consideration of the Church of Scotland on Professor Tholuck's Neologian Opinions*, (Edinburgh: 1837), 38. The kindest interpretation that can be placed on Robert Haldane's denunciation of Tholuck in the late 1830s is that Tholuck had become theologically concessive in the interim. But a harsh interpretation would no doubt find in this activity of Haldane yet another example of his self-referential activity. The first interpretation is supported by the article, 'Tholuck' in the Donald M. Lewis, ed., *Blackwell Dictionary of Evangelical Biography: 1730-1860*, 2 vols, (Oxford: 1995), II, 1092.

[38] Oxford: 1842.

[39] Pusey, *Letter to the Archbishop*, 70. Pusey had likely chosen Geneva as the 'type' of rationalistic Christianity in the light of the publication in the previous year of fellow High Churchman William Palmer's *Aids to Reflection on the Seemingly Double Character of the National Church*, (Oxford: 1841). Palmer had visited Geneva in 1835-36 and recorded in graphic detail the heterodox views of the official theological faculty, cf. pp. 38, 39.

Robert Haldane could vouch for the trustworthiness of the foreigners made them rapidly the 'toast' of many Protestants. Here were Europeans who could be found emphasizing as emphatically and unambiguously as any native Protestant the themes of Christ and Scripture, human ruin and redemption. Here was positive reassurance that the evangelicalism and biblicism which the British shared with other Anglo-Saxon peoples were not unique to them.

We may note in passing that the 1830s had ushered in a period when, not only the writings of the 'réveil' leaders themselves, but the writings which had first influenced them had become widely available in Britain. It cannot be attributed to coincidence that Edward Bickersteth, acting in his capacity as advisory editor for the London publisher, Seeley and Co., included the *Christian Theology* of Benedict Pictet of Geneva (d.1724) in his series the 'Christian Family Library'.[40] Similarly, there appeared in print in London in 1838 the work which the Genevan dissidents, Émile Guers among them, credited with delivering them from an unbalanced preoccupation with the work of sanctification, David Hollaz's *The Order of Grace in the Economy of Salvation*.[41]

As for the writings of the 'réveil' men themselves, we have mentioned already the approbation given to the historical writings of Merle D'Aubigné.[42] Here we may simply note that within a decade of is first release in French dress in 1838, the multi-volumed history had been published by *five* separate British publishing houses, each utilizing a fresh translator.[43] César Malan proved himself an able commentator on Swiss theological affairs for the British evangelical public in the same period. In 1839, the *Scottish Christian Herald* published his acounts both of the abolition of the *Helvetic Confession of Faith* within the neighbouring canton of Vaud and the successful popular opposition at Zurich of the now-notorious David Friedrich Strauss when the latter was named to a theological chair in the university.[44]

---

[40] Pictet had been reckoned by the evangelicals at Geneva as the last orthodox theologian to teach in their city's academy. Malan clearly was indebted to Pictet for assistance in his own formative period. Malan, Jr, *Life of Malan*, 45. The translation was published by Seeley at London in 1834.

[41] The translator of Hollaz from the French edition of 1825 was clearly an enthusiast for the book. He had the work published at his own expense.

[42] *Supra* pp. 205, 206.

[43] An interesting review provided by the *Eclectic Review*, 11 n.s. (1842), 652-73, weighed the merits of the translations published by Walther and Whitaker (both of London) and Blackie of Glasgow. A second Glasgow edition by Collins and one at Edinburgh by Oliver and Boyd followed in mid-decade.

[44] *Scottish Christian Herald*, 1 n.s. (1839), supplement, 27, 36, 37. The latter material was reprinted by the *Herald* from the *Record*, the strident Church of England newspaper published at London. The *Record*'s editor was Alexander Haldane.

Gaussen's Theopneustia *and British Evangelicalism*

Among purely theological (as distinct from historical) writings, no work emanating from the Genevan 'réveil' had such a noticeable impact on Britain as that of F.S.L. Gaussen's *Theopneustia*; the volume was published in Paris and in London in 1841.[45] Gaussen, following partially in the footsteps of his Scottish mentor, Robert Haldane,[46] was keen to emphasize that according to Scripture's self-description all parts of the biblical canon enjoyed an equally pervasive inspiration and consequent authority in matters of faith. Gaussen was disarmingly candid in admitting that he was utterly at a loss to explain the process or 'psychology' of inspiration and could only concern himself with the resultant authoritative volume. He defined inspiration as being

> that inexplicable power which the Divine Spirit exercised, aforetime, upon the authors of Holy Scripture, to guide them even to the words which they have employed and to preserve them from all error, as well as from any omission.[47]

The author's purpose was a rather restricted one. He did not seek to convince the sceptic or agnostic that humanity stood in need of a revelation from God, or that the Scriptures provide the record of just such a revelation; he left all such argument to others. His concern was primarily for those within the Christianity of Western Europe who accepted that the Scriptures were a book from God—but who were without fixed views about the way in which the Scriptures had come from God. Maury, a considerable authority on the theology of the 'réveil', indicated that Gaussen had been provoked to write his treatise by the teaching of Étienne de Chastel (1801-86), professor of ecclesiastical history in the Academy of Geneva from 1831, and J.E. Cellérier (1785-1862), honorary professor of biblical criticism in the same institution. The two, who had in common a pious upbringing and the earlier confidence of the 'réveil' circle, combined forces in the 1830s to

---

[45] A separate translation and edition was issued at New York in 1842. The present writer has published an enlarged version of this section regarding Gaussen's twentieth century influence. Cf. Kenneth J. Stewart, 'A Bombshell of a Book: Gaussen's *Theopneustia* and its Influence on Subsequent Evangelical Theology', *Evangelical Quarterly*, 75.3, (2003), 235-57. Belatedly drawn to my attention is another study, that of Jean Decorvet, 'F.S.R. Gaussen. Sa vie, son oeuvre et le débat sur la théopneustie', *Hokhma*, 70 (1999), 24-55.

[46] His views on the inspiration of Scripture have been detailed in ch. 2 above. The Gaussen-Haldane indebtedness is officially recorded in correspondence of Gaussen printed in A. Haldane, *Lives of the Haldanes*, 515, 516.

[47] Gaussen, *Theopneustia*, (London: 1841), 37.

introduce the latest German critical views about the Bible to Genevan theology.[48]

Against such a backdrop, Gaussen was eager to maintain that all Scripture was uniformly and equally inspired:

> Our object is to establish, by the word of God, that the Scriptures are from God, that they are in every part from God, and they are as a whole, entirely from God.[49]

The consequence of such a uniform inspiration was that the books of Scripture 'contained no error, their entire contents are inspired of God... Not one of these words ought to be neglected'.[50]

Some contemporary observers, while not unsympathetic to Gaussen, found the work unconvincing. Adolphe Monod, then teaching in the theological college of Montauban, wrote to the author to suggest that

> this absolute doctrine of inspiration has been formed, I believe, 'a priori', to meet the needs of theology more than on the teachings of the Bible. I myself need to conceive of inspiration more broadly.[51]

The daughter and biographer of Merle D'Aubigné saw illustrated in Gaussen's views 'the fatal law of spiritual tides'[52]—an excessive reaction to earlier opposite excesses.

There were major weaknesses in Gaussen's volume. For one, his eagerness to maintain an all-embracing inspiration for every part of Scripture prevented him from addressing the problem posed by the inclusion of material in the Bible which are plainly meant to be understood as deficient. The faulty counsel of the friends of Job, for instance, may have been painstakingly recorded and included in Scripture by inspiration, but nevertheless represent something far less than divine wisdom. Some writers criticized by Gaussen dealt with such nuances far more adequately.[53] Again, Gaussen aimed to achieve his all-embracing and absolute doctrine of inspiration by an insistence that all Scripture writers functioned as prophets—subject to the immediate promptings of the divine spirit. But even if such a construction fit the case of the Old Testament writings[54] (and we would maintain that it did so imperfectly), it seemed to comport poorly with the various literary forms

---

[48] Maury, *Le Réveil Religieux*, II, 44.

[49] Gaussen, *Theopneustia*, 30.

[50] Gaussen, *Theopneustia*, 37.

[51] Quoted in Maury, Maury, *Le Réveil Religieux*, II, 35.

[52] Biéler, *Une Famille*, 112. A similar view was later maintained in Gretillat, 'Movements of Theological Thought', 424, 425.

[53] So for instance John Dick, *The Inspiration of Scripture*, (Glasgow: 1803), 30-33.

[54] The argument of Gaussen, *Theopneustia*, 382ff.

of the New Testament and the admissions of some New Testament writers as to their methods of compilation and composition.[55] Though Gaussen was then understood, and continues to be understood, as an innovator both in the high doctrine of inspiration he espoused and the methodology employed in asserting this view, the first judgement is much less certain than the last. Benedict Pictet, the last trusted theologian of Geneva, the republication of whose work we have noted above, had himself maintained that the Scripture writers

> wrote nothing without the Spirit either inspiring them, or influencing them to write, or directing them, so as not to suffer them while writing to commit even the least error or mistake.[56]

The notion of a comprehensive inspiration, embracing the different genres and stylistic variations in Scripture, and guaranteeing freedom from error was plainly much older than Gaussen or his Scottish mentor, Haldane.

This fact was underlined by the generally enthusiastic reception given the book by evangelicalism in Britain. The reviewer for the *Evangelical Magazine* concluded his thorough overview of the work, spread across two monthly instalments, by stating that

> It is a work which will repay the reader. It is the work of a man of considerable ability, extensive scholarship, and deep piety. It embraces a full, comprehensive and interesting discussion of an important and agitated question. It is written in a clear, forcible and elegant style, containing passages of much beauty and eloquence in which there are 'thoughts that breathe and words that burn' and above all, an unction from above that renders its perusal truly edifying.[57]

The *Eclectic Review*, though somewhat more restrained, was also full of praise. Though its reviewer noted features of the work which were not exactly to his taste, nevertheless he maintained that

> we do not the less readily hail him as a fellow labourer in the great field of European evangelization. We have been edified by his glowing appeals to the heart. We go entirely with him in his reverential homage to the authority of Scripture... We

---

[55] The argument of Gaussen, *Theopneustia*, 410.

[56] Pictet, *Christian Theology*, 33.

[57] *Evangelical Magazine*, 20, n.s. (1842), 177. In New England, similarly laudatory views of the book were set down in the *American Biblical Repository*, 6, 2nd series (1841), 113. which claimed, 'all in all, we think it decidedly the best work on the subject which we have ever read'. The *Princeton Review*, 14 (1842), 525, declared, 'it establishes and vindicates the thorough going, old school doctrine of the plenary inspiration of the scriptures. Though this doctrine has never, so far as we know, been formally denied among ourselves, it has been neglected and derided on the continent of Europe'.

strongly recommend the study of it to those who are tempted by the freedom of German rationalism and to those also, who are fettered by the servitude which is spreading so widely through the land under the high pretensions of Anglican theology.[58]

But Gaussen's work did raise nationalistic concerns and test the bounds of Christian charity when appearing in English dress.

As to the former, Gaussen showed himself just as ready as Malan[59] to subject British evangelical theology to criticism. While Malan had done this in defense of his particular version of high-Calvinism, Gaussen—now defending a still more central theme in contemporary theology—had gone so far as to name those British theologians whom he believed had abandoned the ramparts of a full and absolute inspiration. To be sure, these British divines were not the only theologians named as falling below Gaussen's standard of acceptability. A first group, comprised of the Germans F.D.E. Schleiermacher and W.M.L. De Wette, were charged with rejecting all miraculous inspiration. A second, represented by the German, J.D. Michaelis, was faulted for acknowledging only the inspiration of some of the sacred books. But the Britons, Drs John Pye Smith, Daniel Wilson and John Dick, along with the contemporary German, Augustus Twesten, formed a third group charged with denying that inspiration was in evidence in equal degree in all portions of Scripture.[60]

Here was an attack on the view popularly known as the 'degrees of inspiration' theory. It had been adopted by many Christian thinkers a century earlier in the face of the deistic allegation that the purported miraculous element in Christianity and the Bible had been highly exaggerated. From Philip Doddridge forward, many British Reformed theologians had responded to this criticism by adopting the view that the supernatural or miraculous element necessary to the composition of the Bible had varied in degree from book to book. The supposed variation was correlated with the method of biblical composition employed (were extant documents relied upon?), the subject matter under discussion (was the material sublime and otherwise concealed from humanity, or simply everyday?), and the question of whether prediction of the future was involved. The 'degrees of inspiration' stance had seemed attractive in that it took note of the observable genres in Scripture and hints as to composition found within the Bible itself. It also guarded the orthodox writers who employed it against the charge of 'over-belief'—the claim of

---

[58] *Eclectic Review*, 11, n.s. (1842), 382, 383.
[59] *Supra* p. 210.
[60] Gaussen, *Theopneustia*, 27, 28. Daniel Wilson, *Lectures On the Evidences of Christianity*, (London: 1828); John Dick, *Inspiration*, (Glasgow: 1803).

the operation of a miraculous inspiration in a manner more widespread than seemed necessary to account for the Bible's existence.

Gaussen was not the first early nineteenth-century writer to protest against this stance. We have seen that his mentor, Haldane, had made the criticism as early as 1816.[61] Yet Gaussen did not deny that there may have been a manifold and diverse divine activity in superintending the writing of the books of Scripture. He simply maintained that

> The power which then operated in those men of God, and which they themselves experienced in very different degrees has not been defined to us. There is not any thing to authorize our explaining it. Scripture never presents to us either its mode or its measure as an object of study. It is spoken of only incidentally and is not associated with our devotion.[62]

The matter was not peripheral, but central, maintained Gaussen; the 'degrees' of inspiration schema was, in fact, a dangerous concession.

This protest was noted and acted upon, not least because of the author's connection with the Geneva of legend.[63] In short, it assisted in the launching of a kind of revisionist treatment of Britain's past century of Reformed theology. Such revisionism seemed necessary to the reviewer in the *Evangelical Magazine* because at the present day, biblical infallibility was under attack in light of the critical ideas of Samuel Taylor Coleridge (enunciated in *Confessions of an Inquiring Spirit* (1840)) and the rise of Tractarianism. The writer believed that

> there are many who entertain doubts on the subject, partly in consequence of their having been accustomed to follow Doddridge's unscriptural distinctions on inspiration and partly for their having too easily abandoned the true and ancient doctrine.[64]

The reviewer for the *Eclectic Review* demurred, however. Although acknowledging the overall value of Gaussen's volume, he objected to seeing the evangelical theologians of his country denigrated by a foreigner. He believed that the 'main design of M. Gaussen's volume is to impugn some opinions of those who acknowledge the inspiration of

---

[61] See the discussion above, ch. 2, p. 76.

[62] Gaussen, *Theopneustia*, 24, 25.

[63] The *Princeton Review*, 14 (1842), 525, suggestively commented, 'It will be read, understood, and felt by those who would throw aside with a sneer the productions of a Scottish or American author.'

[64] *Evangelical Magazine*, 20, n.s. (1842), 173. It was one of the ironies of the controversy that the 'degrees of inspiration' view, emanating from Doddridge, was as widely known in Europe as in Britain, because the Religious Tract Society had been circulating Doddridge's *Lectures* in translation since 1807. Thus the new attack on Doddridge was, by extension, an attack on the Tract Society.

the Scripture'; he believed that such tactics were but an example of 'dogmatic harshness'.[65] He furthermore believed that the Swiss writer had been guilty of sowing the seeds of mischief by seriously exaggerating the differences of opinion between him and the British theologians named.

> Of our own writers we will say, with M. Gaussen's permission, that they have taught an inspiration of the Scriptures as plenary as that for which he contends and that in teaching it they display a calmness of thought, a sagacity of discrimination, and a strength of argument which we are tempted to claim as the national characteristics of English theology on this, as on every other question.[66]

The *Eclectic*'s charge that Gaussen had treated the British evangelicals unfairly appears well justified. Pye Smith, Wilson and Dick had contended for a plenary inspiration of Scripture; but they did not all use the term in an identical sense.[67]

The argument of Gaussen not only cut across the grain of British nationalism, but of Christian charity. There can be no doubt that Gaussen knew both Pye Smith and Wilson by reason of their earlier sojourns in Geneva. Wilson had actually commissioned Gaussen in 1823 to translate Scott's *Commentary on the Bible* into French.[68] Gaussen must have known that both Smith and Wilson had also been keen supporters of the Continental Society.[69] And as for John Dick, he had been the honoured theologian of the Associate Synod, which, when re-united in 1820 as the United Associate Synod, had been prepared to receive César Malan as minister and support young men referred to them for service in French Europe. Of course, Gaussen may have sincerely believed that these British writers were gravely in error and worthy of being exposed to the religious public. But we can endorse neither the questionable theological judgement nor the faulty diplomacy which caused him to turn on his evangelical allies; his polemic only served to exacerbate existing tensions within British evangelicalism. At Geneva, Gaussen had long gained a reputation as an evangelical 'concordist'—drawing the different strands

---

[65] *Eclectic Review*, 11, n.s. (1842), 379, 373.

[66] *Eclectic Review*, 11, n.s. (1842), 377.

[67] Dick, for example, maintained a plenary inspiration which involved dictation, extended to the words as well as ideas of Scripture, and included judicious conceptions of varying degrees of divine involvement required in the process of inscripturation. It is difficult to see that this position, reflected in his *Inspiration*, (Glasgow: 1803), 1, 3, 20-27, 34, differed significantly from that of Gaussen. We have noted in ch. 2 above, that Dick's position on this has been vindicated afresh in recent times, see s.v. 'Systematic Theology', de S. Cameron, ed., *Scottish Dictionary of Church History and Theology*.

[68] Wilson, *Letters from an Absent Brother*, II, 214.

[69] The involvement of both Pye Smith and Wilson in British schemes supportive of the Francophone 'réveil' has been indicated in the previous chapter.

of evangelicalism together to co-operate with one another.[70] His writings on inspiration played no such role in British evangelicalism. It has been claimed that Gaussen 'provided, for the first time, a carefully argued defence of the inerrancy of the Bible'.[71] The evidence we have marshalled would suggest a somewhat modified appraisal of his significance. He may at least be said to have been the early nineteenth-century theologian most responsible for rehabilitating the views of biblical inspiration postulated in the period of high Protestant orthodoxy; it must be added that these views had never ceased to be held in segments of the Reformed theological tradition.

The 'Formula Consensus Helvetica' of 1675, composed at Zurich by theologians of that canton, Geneva and Basle, had maintained that the text of the Hebrew Bible is

> not only in its consonants, but in its vowels—either the points themselves, or at least the power of the points—not only in its matter, but in its words, inspired of God, thus forming with the New Testament, the sole and complete rule of our faith and life.[72]

We have noted already that Benedict Pictet of Geneva, writing in the following generation, had not hesitated to speak of the Scriptures as being 'free from even the least error or mistake' by virtue of inspiration. Among the Scottish Presbyterians, there were those such as Thomas Boston (1676-1732) who approximated the views of the 'Formula Consensus Helvetica' and wrote in defence of the inspiration of the Hebrew vowel points.[73] John Dick, to whom we have referred already, held views hardly distinguishable from those of Gaussen, while Andrew Thomson (1779-1831), minister of St. George's Church, Edinburgh, and editor of the *Christian Instructor*, stood beside Robert Haldane in these matters. The same could be said of Robert Gordon (1786-1853), minister of the High Church, Edinburgh.

The prominent United Presbyterian theologian, John Cairns, read Gaussen while a theological student in the period 1840-44 and even

---

[70] Cf. ch. 3, pp. 98, 107.

[71] Bebbington, *Evangelicalism in Modern Britain*, 90. The helpful thesis of Bebbington, that an evangelicalism influenced by the outlook of the Romantic era challenged its predecessor, influenced by the Enlightenment, is in fact supported by the evidence put forward here. It is only suggested, by way of modification, that many 'Romantics' (Gaussen among them) were quite consciously returning to pre-Enlightenment theological views or joining forces with those who had never relinquished them.

[72] Article II. The twenty-six articles are printed as an appendix to A.A. Hodge, *Outlines of Theology*, (London: 1886), 656-63.

[73] Andrew Thomson, *Thomas Boston of Ettrick: His Life and Times*, (London: 1895), 178-80.

twenty years later, when known for his somewhat broadened views, could recall for a correspondent,

> You ask about inspiration. I do not know a perfectly satisfactory work on the subject. Gaussen is a little too rigid for me, but contains many fine things.[74]

Seen in this light, Gaussen did not originate but merely lent his considerable weight to the re-assertion of an older view of biblical inspiration in a time of flux. But this flux was in such progress at the time he wrote, that neither the view identified with Gaussen's volume nor the moderating British view which he criticized could long hold the field. The release of *Essays and Reviews* in 1860 would upstage both. By late century, Gaussen's stance had come to be identified with Anglican clergyman J.C. Ryle (1816-1900) and the London Baptist preacher, C.H. Spurgeon (1834-92).[75]

The Réveil and Evangelical Ecumenism in the Victorian Era

We have alluded above to the fact that the 1830s witnessed an upsurge in denominational identity and activity; this tendency was in contrast to the preceding quarter-century of extensive inter-church co-operation.[76] Now we will argue both that the decade of the 1840s contained its own counter-thrust in pursuit of evangelical Protestant ecumenism and that the personalities of the 'réveil' had their own significant role to play in this movement.

In May 1842, the Rev. John Angell James of Birmingham stood before the annual meeting of the Congregational Union to advocate a union among churches committed to the voluntary principle with the object of combating infidelity and opposing 'Popery, Puseyism and Plymouth

---

[74] MacEwen, *Life of Cairns*, 485. The quotation indicates that Cairns, having read Gaussen, was still awaiting a work which maintained its strengths while making up its deficiencies.

[75] Nigel M. de S. Cameron, *Biblical Higher Criticism and the Defense of Infallibilism in 19th Century Britain*, (Lewiston, NY: 1987), has identified Gaussen's contribution in the context of that century; cf. 136, 261, 351. See also J.C. Ryle, *Old Paths: Being Some Plain Statements On Some of the Weightier Matters of Christianity*, (London: 1877). C.H. Spurgeon contributed a Foreward to a new and revised edition of *Theopneustia*, B.W. Carr, ed., (London, 1888). It is also worthy of note that Gaussen's volume has been repeatedly reprinted in the USA during the twentieth century.

[76] Cf. p. 192 *supra*. We have there accepted the hypothesis of D.M. Thompson, *Denominationalism and Dissent* (London: 1985), that the rise in denominationalism was the natural outgrowth of evangelical expansion rather than a lapse from earlier charitable relations.

Brethrenism'.[77] The moving force behind the call for a new ecumenism could not have been made clearer. British evangelicals were all too keenly aware of seismic changes which were underway, and found themselves in reaction to these forces. From 1841, the summarized argument of D.F. Strauss's unsettling *Das Leben Jesu* had begun to circulate in England[78] and this served, as it were, as a harbinger of things to come. The massive influx of Irish immigrants into Lancashire and the West Midlands, especially as a result of the potato famine, fed latent fears of the spread of Catholicism. The publication from Oxford of the series of *Tracts for the Times* convinced the same constituency that Britain faced a Catholicizing 'fifth column' from within the Established Church of England. Such was the evangelical Protestant perception of affairs, and that perception, however partial or blurred, was the stimulus to action. The proposals made by James won favour with the Congregational Union and led to a massive rally at Exeter Hall, London, in the following June; however, the rally was frustrated in taking any action beyond its own confines by the lack of any formal ongoing organization.[79]

Similar concerns for Protestant unity were aired in a co-operative gathering of Scottish Presbyterians meeting at Edinburgh in July 1843 to celebrate the bi-centenary of the meeting of the Westminster Assembly (1643-47). A speech given in that setting by Dr Robert Balmer, professor of theology of the United Secession Church, called for 'co-operation in the things in which we are agreed' in the expectation that 'our incorporation would be ripened and would come in due time'.[80] This speech served in turn to incite a Christian philanthropist, John Henderson of Glasgow, to sponsor the writing of a volume of *Essays on Christian Union*;[81] the essays uniformly called for a visible unity. A letter from the

---

[77] The turbulent context of that period in which Catholic Emancipation, the Maynooth Grant, and the Oxford Movement combined to set evangelical Protestants such as James on an alarm footing is provided by Stewart J. Brown's *The Established Churches of England, Ireland and Scotland: 1801-1846*, (Oxford: 2001). The quotation of John Angel James is provided in R. Rouse and S.C. Neill, *A History of the Ecumenical Movement*, vol. 1, (London: 1954), 318.

[78] The full English translation did not appear until 1846 at the hands of Marian Evans, better known to us as the novelist George Eliot. Cf. Daniel L. Pals, *The Victorian 'Lives' of Jesus*, (San Antonio, TX: 1982), 25ff. It is worth noting that the warning notes sounded by César Malan regarding Strauss, alluded to at fn. 44 above, actually preceded by two years the appearance of Strauss's arguments in any English dress.

[79] J.B.A. Kessler, *A Study of the Evangelical Alliance in Great Britain*, (Goes, Netherlands: 1968), 17.

[80] J.W. Massie, *The Evangelical Alliance: Its Origin and Development*, (London: 1847), 98.

[81] David King, ed., *Essays on Christian Union*, (Edinburgh and London: 1845). The contributors were Drs Thomas Chalmers, Robert Balmer, Robert Candlish, David King, Ralph Wardlaw, Gavin Struthers, Andrew Symington and the Rev. John Angell James.

American minister, Dr Patten, placed in the published volume at the close of the essay by J.A. James, went so far as to call for an international planning convention to be held in July 1845.[82] This sentiment James heartily endorsed, but it was eventually agreed that the conference should be held not in London but in Liverpool, and that the Scots should take the initiative in calling for British and foreign delegates.[83]

There was, simultaneous with these British stirrings, another initiative launched by Merle D'Aubigné at St. Gall, Switzerland, in August 1844. There, while addressing an all-Switzerland conference of Protestant pastors, the historian had issued a summons for the preparation of a unified pan-Protestant confession of faith. He articulated the resolutions:

1. That it is highly desirable for all Evangelical Christians, Reformed and Lutheran, Presbyterian and Episcopalian and generally all who believe in the fundamental truths of the gospel to unite for the purpose of making an open confession of their common faith in opposition to the unity, purely material, of the Romish Church and thus proclaim their own true spiritual unity.

2. The conference resolves to put itself in communication with some of the pastoral conferences recently founded in Germany, particularly with that of Berlin, which has very recently occupied itself on the same question and this may eventually lead to a similar union with the pastoral conferences of other countries, namely France, Great Britain, Holland, and America and to the re-establishment of an ecumenical confession of the Christian faith.

3. It appoints a commission, authorized to fix the basis of an evangelical confession of the 19th century and which shall contain all the truths embodied in all the existing Protestant confessions and arranged in a form adapted to the wants of the present age. This commission should likewise be authorized to take the necessary steps to attain the end pointed out in the preceding articles.[84]

To this initiative of Merle D'Aubigné and its being reported in Britain we may legitimately trace the extension of the then-current Anglo-Saxon Protestant ecumenical initiative into the pan-Protestant scheme it soon became.[85]

---

[82] King, ed., *Essays on Christian Union*, 223-225.

[83] Kessler, *A Study*, 23.

[84] The initiative was reported in the new periodical *The Continental Echo and Protestant Witness*, 1, (1845), 29. In May 1845, Merle D'Aubigné spoke of the St. Gall initiative in his speech to the General Assembly of the Free Church of Scotland, cf. *Proceedings of the Free General Assembly*, (1845), 139.

[85] In this wider sense, it was proper for the *Continental Echo*, 2 (1846), preface, to attribute the creation of the Evangelical Alliance to this Swiss initiative: 'The institution of the Evangelical Alliance is the greatest historical fact, not merely of the year, of the era—not merely of Britain, but of the world... In being really effected by the British churches, though originally suggested by a continental divine...'

The fact was that the formerly Protestant cantons of Switzerland had had their own exclusively Protestant constitutions altered under the Napoleonic policy of granting freedom of religion throughout the lands of the Empire. Merle D'Aubigné now publicly claimed that Geneva was 'half Catholic'. He was, moreover, fully abreast of those developments in Britain which tended to corroborate the conviction that a large-scale Roman advance was now underway and that only a united Protestantism could maintain its position.

To his Genevan students in the autumn of 1842 he had delivered a rousing address entitled *Geneva and Oxford*[86] in which he reviewed and confuted the claims of E.B. Pusey's *Letter to the Archbishop of Canterbury* (1842). When in the spring of 1845 he embarked on a speaking tour in Britain, he was ready to inveigh against the proposed 'Maynooth Bill' (which would increase the state grant to the Catholic seminary at Maynooth, Ireland) and the larger issue which he believed to underlie it:

> The present state of things shows us that the Church has nothing more to expect from the State. The Maynooth Bill is a bill of divorce which the State sends to the Church. During three centuries, Protestantism expected much from its union with the State; it has now no longer anything to expect from it... The State is disconnecting itself from the Church.[87]

All this was the result of the gradual 'disappearance of the Protestant State'. What was now called for in its place was 'the manifestation of the spiritual unity of all Protestants', and a 'great Christian union against the Roman league'.[88] The historian called on the Free Church of Scotland, just freed from State interference, to be ' a special engine for that great work of Christian union'.[89] Whether or not the Swiss visitor knew it to be the case, this was the very role being urged upon the Free Churches in the previous year by John Angell James. The James initiative would eventuate

---

[86] The address was promptly translated into English and published at Edinburgh and London. We have utilized the edition included in D'Aubigné's *Discourses and Essays*, (Glasgow: 1846).

[87] *Proceedings of the Free Church General Assembly*, (1845), 137. It is highly ironic that such sentiments regarding the state's failure in it duties towards established Protestantism had also been expressed by John Keble in his 1833 *Sermon On National Apostasy*; the latter is generally regarded as the warning shot which marked the inauguration of Tractarianism which Merle D'Aubigné was concerned to warn against. Keble had asked, 'How may a man best reconcile his allegiance to God and his Church with his duty to his country, that country, which now by the supposition, is fast becoming hostile to the Church and cannot long be the friend of God?' See *National Apostasy*, (Oxford: 1833 reprinted, Steventon: 1983), 21.

[88] *Proceedings of the Free Church*, (1845), 138, 140.

[89] *Proceedings of the Free Church*, (1845), 139.

in a conference at Liverpool in October of 1845 preparatory to the launching of the Evangelical Alliance the followng year.

Here it is not our purpose to re-tell the story of the founding of that Alliance,[90] but only to emphasize the part played by Merle D'Aubigné in convincing the evangelical public of the need for such an expression of unity. We may also rightly stress that the significant European (and more particularly Francophone) participation in the inaugural conference at London in August 1846 could never have materialized were it not for the events of the preceding thirty years described above. Of the 800 representatives present, forty-eight were from various continental countries.[91] Internationalized Protestantism was the thing sought in that age when state Protestantism had proven itself obstructive because it was unable or unwilling to meet the challenges posed by a new era in Western Europe.

Merle D'Aubigné and César Malan's attendance had been anticipated at London in August 1846, as had been that of Alexandre Vinet of Lausanne; all were temporarily indisposed and kept from attending.[92] Yet among those present were numerous Francophones with whom we have become familiar: Adolphe Monod, professor at Montauban, Louis La Harpe, of the Evangelical Theological College of Geneva, Georges Fisch, minister of 'L'Église Évangélique de Lyons', J.J. Audebez of 'La Chapelle Taitbout' in Paris. Antoine Vermeil of Paris, Émile Froissard of Nimes, and D.D. Duvivier of Saumur were also present. Ami Bost was present, as was a delegate of 'L'Église Évangélique de Vaud', Charles Baup. From what would shortly be constituted as the 'L'Église Missionaire de Belge' came Louis Panchaud.[93]

---

[90] A work which has been adequately performed by Kessler, *A Study*, and Massie, *The Evangelical Alliance*.

[91] Kessler, *A Study*, 35. Eighty were American delegates and the balance British. We cannot dwell here on the various European representations.

[92] Massie, *The Evangelical Alliance*, 379.

[93] Massie, *The Evangelical Alliance*, 392-96. Bost has left a record of his impressions at the inaugural meetings in his *Mémoires*, II, 388ff, as has the biographer of *Adolphe Monod*, 152ff. Both men indicated misgivings at the Alliance's efforts to be exclusive of some currently unpopular views. Biéler, *Une Famille*, 218, indicates that La Harpe of Geneva took with him the written support of 130 ministers and laymen to the inauguration of the Alliance. The recent history of the Evangelical Alliance by Ian Randall and David Hilborn, *One Body in Christ*, (Carlisle: 2001), disappointingly shows no awareness of the network of relationships provided by the Francophone 'réveil' over the preceding thirty years which made this substantial European representation possible. It is the more remarkable when their work makes use of Nicholas Railton's study, *No North Sea: The Anglo-German Network in the Middle of the Nineteenth Century*, (Leiden: 2000), which, while primarily about Anglo-German evangelical relationships in this period, still evidences an impressive awareness of similar Anglo-Francophone relations, fostered through the 'réveil'. Randall and Hilborn record only the involvement of

These persons, when taken in combination with early supporters of the Continental Society who were now deeply active in the launching of the Alliance,[94] suggests something of the way in which the Alliance was able to draw on a fund of international good will built up over time. These long-standing co-operative links also go some way to explain the facility with which affiliates of the Alliance were rapidly established in France and Switzerland, among other places. And these same international links, by then extending back more than half a century, made the European involvement in another ecumenical scheme originating in the English speaking world—the World Presbyterian Alliance (f.1875)—seem desirable and natural.[95] We have noted in our third chapter how common it was that new denominations emerging in the Francophone regions affected by the 'réveil' sought affiliation to this Alliance at its foundation. 'Free churches' they might be, in contradistinction to the national Churches from which they had separated; but it seems fair to say that their reflexive action after separation from these national Churches was to seek wider and international fellowship.

This 'ecumenical tendency' of the 'réveil' has been remarked upon, especially as the roots and antecedents of the twentieth-century ecumenical movement were being probed. However, it is not evident that Rouse and Neill judged the matter accurately when they suggested of the 'réveil' that its tendency was *initially* towards division and only *ultimately* towards union:

> The unpalatable conclusion must be accepted that one feature of the Evangelical Awakening, as of other dynamic spiritual awakenings, was a tendency to create divisions or new denominations... The 'réveil' in Switzerland and France played its part in leading to the formation of the Free Churches in several Swiss cantons and in France... Yet all this reaction against Christian unity led to a counter action in its favour.[96]

What is lacking in this analysis is a recognition that the regions affected by the 'réveil' *rapidly* found an alternate, international unity to replace the unsatisfactory ecclesiastical unity which they believed to have failed them in their home cantons and countries. The story which has unfolded here is not of Francophone Christians finding a new Christian

---

individual Francophone leaders in the formative period of the Alliance and provide no explanation as to why a reported 7% of the 800 initial delegates at Liverpool (p. 53) were representing continental churches and agencies.

[94] We might mention Edward Bickersteth, W. Alers Hankey, J. Pye Smith, James Haldane Stewart, Baptist Noel and Hugh McNeile.

[95] However, the roots of this linkage in the 'réveil' go undocumented in Pradervand, *A Century of Service*, yet this author nevertheless records the expanse of the initial cooperation.

[96] Rouse and Neill, eds, *History of the Ecumenical Movement*, 316, 318.

unity after half-a-century of ambivalent, unattached existence. It is rather that of how spiritual awakening in Francophone Europe, assisted on the one hand by European Moravian influences and on the other by British evangelical agencies and individuals, created new ecumenical relations which took the tangible form of assistance in building churches, funding home missionaries, and assisting in the establishment of tract and Scripture distribution agencies. These trans-national and cross-Channel relationships, which sprang up almost instantly in the post-Napoleonic era performed excellent work and only, in time, gave way to the formal ecumenical bodies which came into existence in 1846 and 1875. The earlier, less formal, ecumenical relationships were in fact the building blocks on which the later structures were constructed.

British evangelicals found in the events and personalities of the 'réveil' much to stir their imagination and to invigorate their interest in the heritage of the Protestant Reformation. Yet the Francophone influence was, as we have seen, sometimes at odds with British evangelicalism. The theology of evangelism of César Malan represented a form of Calvinistic thought perhaps harking back to a previous era; thus such ideas were widely perceived as retrograde by British persons no less at home in the Reformed tradition than Malan. Louis Gaussen's writings on inspiration had commanded respect for their learning and strength of argument, but had fallen far short of securing the comprehensive support he had sought; by their polemical character, they served to fragment rather than consolidate British evangelical conviction. J.H. Merle D'Aubigné's speeches and writings in advocacy of international Protestant solidarity against perceived Roman Catholic advance materially assisted the advance of evangelical ecumenism. His advocacy of these ideas was rooted in convictions about the demise of European state Protestantism which were somewhat more developed than those of many of his closest supporters in the Established Churches of Britain.

CHAPTER 6

Conclusion

Some reassessment of our subject is plainly called for in the light of the researches reflected in the preceding pages. It seems best that these reassessments be set out as a series of modifications to our understanding. It is plain that we must cease to draw our major impressions about the 'réveil' era from the tendentious *Lives of the Haldanes*. The latter was penned by a loyal son and nephew who was eager to secure for his own father, James, and uncle, Robert, a kind of respectability such as he himself had gained by forsaking their sectarian evangelicalism in favor of Anglicanism. As pugilistic in his conservative Anglicanism as they had been in their evangelical restorationism, Alexander Haldane succeeded in establishing the Haldane family-version of the 'réveil' as 'gospel' for more than a century. Still in print,[1] the *Lives of the Haldanes* continues to impress on its readers the notion that without Robert Haldane's presence in Geneva and France the movement with which he was indeed associated could never have unfolded.

It is now clear that pan-evangelical organizations and individuals with which Robert Haldane was familiar through his 1796-1804 involvement with the London Missionary Society were themselves active in the Swiss cantons, France, and the Low Countries in advance of and following his journey there in 1816-19. Indeed, some of his own earliest impressions of Europe had been gained in the company of an individual, David Bogue, who eventually was sent on a European fact-finding mission by the LMS in 1802. Haldane thus went to Europe quite aware of what the various London pan-evangelical agencies were currently doing in the region; his distinctive hallmark there was the championing of private initiative. German and American evangelical Christian leaders already present in Geneva were active in ministering to theological students during the very weeks and months of Haldane's own activity there. Previous Moravian missionary activity in and around Geneva had already led to the conversion of theological students who had graduated prior to Haldane's arrival as well as some whose studies were still in process.

Partly because he was poorly advised by an American merchant at Paris, and partly because he carried with him from Scotland a thorough

---

[1] The volume was reprinted at Edinburgh in 1990.

disdain for Established or national Churches, Haldane's Geneva ministry
was carried out on the supposition that little or no support for the
evangelical message could be expected from the Reformed clergy of the
canton. However, the very students whom Haldane influenced while there
had a much more reliable grasp of the extent of evangelical support
within the Company of Pastors; Haldane might have learned by listening
to them. That so many of them did complete their studies at the Geneva
Academy and proceed to pastoral assignments in Huguenot diaspora
congregations across north-west Europe (whereas only a minority
withdrew from the Academy and commenced Independent ministry) is an
interesting indication that Haldane was not deferred to on every question.

While it may be pointed out that select individuals from among the
number Haldane influenced at Geneva were later quick to insist that he
had played an indispensable role while there, it is interesting to reflect on
the fact that those who reiterated this theme—whether in writing, or in a
guest appearance before a British audience—were consistently those
whose work in Francophone Europe was carried on in greatest
dependence on British generosity. Thus, when they praised the memory
of Haldane's ministry at Geneva or at Montauban, they were signaling to
other Britons that their own involvement and support was also
indispensable. We will return to this problem below.

Robert Haldane's undoubted legacy at Geneva included the coaching
of certain young men whose theological studies had been disrupted in
advance of his own labor there, regarding his understanding of
Independent church order. In spite of what the family biographer has
insisted regarding Haldane's restraint in speaking on sensitive subjects,
these very Christian workers were themselves candid in relating how the
order of their church at Geneva was remarkably consistent with the
principles Robert and James Haldane had introduced, with destructive
consequences, into their connexion in Scotland in 1808. Robert Haldane,
working in league with Henry Drummond, knowingly advanced these
young men—now imbued with his own restorationist principles—as the
earliest agents of the fledgling Continental Society. It was never disclosed
to the membership of that Society that these men were not simply
evangelical and Reformed Christians, but separatists and restorationists.

Yet to admit that such persons were among the circle of students
influenced by Haldane is to stop short of proposing that radicalism or
separatism was the dominant characteristic among this young generation
of 'réveil' enthusiasts. While young men of such an outlook did in fact
have similarities and links with persons of similar disposition and outlook
in Lausanne, France, and Britain,[2] they were, in fact, out-numbered by a

---

[2] These affinities have been highlighted in the impressive works of Stunt, *From
Awakening to Secession*, and Carter, *Anglican Evangelicals*.

much larger group of Swiss and French ordinands who worked at spreading the new earnestness *within* their Reformed Churches.

Haldane's approaching Geneva with the presupposition that most resident ministers were untrustworthy, was his general approach also in approaching Montauban in the fall of 1817. He insisted on holding suspect Christian leaders in that city and seminary who his old acquaintances in the London Missionary Society and *Evangelical Magazine* trusted implicitly. Consistently self-referential, he had already determined as he journeyed homeward from Montauban in 1819 that he would fund independent theological training at Paris under tutors responsible to him.[3] It was his determined wish that France, just as Geneva, should have the option of evangelical Independency[4] beyond the reach of the national Churches.

Thankfully, Haldane's self-referential plan was not the only strategy employed by British evangelicals in this period. Both in advance of the foundation of the Continental Society, and of Haldane's personal return from France in 1819, the Bible, Tract, and London Missionary societies had been busy establishing working relationships with sympathetic ministers and churches in Francophone Europe. Promptly, these London organizations had affiliates in numerous European centers, affiliates which were increasingly able to develop expanding circles of influence for the gospel where they were, and under local leadership. While, over a twenty-year period, the London-based Continental Society did have up to thirty Francophone agents in France, Switzerland and the Low Countries, in the larger picture of things it was the Tract, Bible and Missionary societies which—through their affiliates—would have the larger impact. Especially from 1831 onwards, there came to be organized first at Geneva, then at Paris, indigenous home mission agencies which, when assisted by British and American donors, carried out effective evangelization and biblical literacy efforts.

In these indigenous efforts of the 1830s, Francophone evangelicals were building upon what had been principally true all along: there had been, prior to Haldane, an indigenous spiritual awakening unfolding in their region. They grasped that it was of the utmost urgency that it be directed and administered by thoroughly indigenized local leadership. However, this Francophone evangelical enterprise, having begun in the

---

[3] François Olivier, the Vaudois separatist appointed by Haldane as his first Paris theological tutor would, in the 1830s, align himself with the Plymouth Brethren as an extension of his original restorationist perspective. See Nicholas Railton, *No North Sea* (Leiden: 2000), 24.

[4] An attitude which might have, but did not, characterize the London pan-evangelicals known to Haldane for another generation. Though Independents, Congregationalists and Seceding Presbyterians, they supported joint labor with the Reformed Church of France until at least 1849.

post-Revolutionary period with a financial dependency on British evangelicalism,[5] found it difficult to learn to do without this. It was not that Britons no longer wished to give; it was that this financial dependency, when spread across decades, perpetuated harmful attitudes in both those Britons who gave and the Francophone agencies which received. British donors only gradually relinquished to Francophones the direction and administration of funds designated for Europe. And appeals from Europe for funding, while on the whole following a natural and justifiable rationale, nevertheless left open the possibility that the availability of this foreign generosity would unintentionally tip the scales in the direction of precipitous and separatist action. One can only be astonished at the rapidity with which ecclesiastically independent causes raised church edifices and paid stipends once a conduit to foreign funding was opened.[6] Only in the late-nineteenth and early-twentieth century was there wide inter-church consultation aimed at eliminating unwholesome patterns of dependency on foreign funding in cross-cultural mission.[7]

Further, though it was the original intention of the London pan-evangelical societies that British denominational patterns be kept out of Francophone Europe, there was also, implicit in the early efforts of the Methodist Churches[8] and of Robert Haldane, the intention that distinct types of British evangelicalism replicate themselves across the Channel. And sadly, it was this mindset, rather than the earlier pan-evangelical attitude, which was to prevail after 1830. Very soon, British Baptists, Methodists, Darbyists and Irvingites all replicated themselves in France, Switzerland and beyond.

Francophone evangelicals not only appealed to Britons for assistance to build churches, to fund Bible societies, and for help in training missionaries and pastors, but visited them in the process. And this interaction was itself the means of knitting together in the 1820s and 1830s an international evangelicalism which would be a powerful influence throughout the nineteenth century and beyond. This was the

---

[5] And eventually, American, as Robert Evans' '*The Influence of Foreigners*' made plain.

[6] The rapidity with which buildings were provided for the 'Bourg-de-Four' and 'Église du Témoignage' congregations at Geneva and the 'Église Évangélique de Lyon' in reliance on foreign donors illustrate this problem clearly. At what point did the availability of foreign generosity actually serve to enhance the possibility of ecclesiastical division and independency?

[7] Cf. Stephen Neill, *A History of Christian Mission,* (London: 1986), ch. 12, 'From Mission to Church'.

[8] Here it is worth noting that this more narrow concern that we can identify in Haldane was in fact present in the Methodist attempt to open a chapel at Paris in 1792. See ch. 2 *supra.*

soil out of which would grow both the Evangelical Alliance (1846) and the World Presbyterian Alliance (1875). Neither movement could have been the trans-national successes that they were without the preparation provided by the 'réveil' after 1816. Such alliances were made necessary both by the unraveling of European state Protestantism in that age of political liberalism and the resurgence of an ultra montane Catholicism.

Yet as Britons encountered Francophone evangelicalism—whether through its visiting emissaries, Malan and D'Aubigné, or through its theologians—its self-understanding of the Reformed and Protestant tradition was challenged. British Protestantism was confronted with how little it knew, and how much it had merely supposed to be true about Reformed Christianity in Geneva, Lausanne, Montauban and Paris. The theologies of the two Protestant cultures, while overlapping, were not strictly identical. From this period of reciprocal discovery—Britons of Francophones, and Francophones of Britons—have been passed down many of the hardiest notions of what the Reformed and Protestant tradition is and means. Whatever modern reverence we may have for historic Geneva is as much the product of this era of the nineteenth century as of any earlier period. The veneration of the 'Geneva of legend', which was so characteristic of the generation of British evangelicals described in this study, still grips the imagination of many Protestants today—and with as little actual warrant.

Did the British evangelicals indeed 'restore the Reformation' in Francophone Europe? We may say that they saw more ground gained than they did in their contemporaneous attempts to see the Reformation take root in Ireland,[9] where just as energetic schemes of itineration and Scripture distribution were used as in France. Yet, what the British evangelicals could not properly see (and we cannot fault them here) is that their greatest declared successes in Europe would prove, over time, to have helped to constitute only minority evangelical cultures in a progressively secularizing Europe. And before the nineteenth century was out, the progressive marginalization of evangelical Protestantism in a secularizing Europe was almost as fully in force in Britain.

---

[9] The British attempts at the 'reformation' of nineteenth-century Ireland are detailed in Stewart J. Brown's *The National Churches of England, Ireland and Scotland 1801-1846*, (Oxford: 2001). Note particularly the chapter, 'Second Reformation: Ireland 1822-33'.

France:
Report Concerning the State of Religion There[1]
(The *Evangelical Magazine* 10 [1802], 462-67)

The Members composing the Deputation[2] formed by the Directors of the Missionary Society, for the purpose of visiting France, in order to the publication of the New Testament, and the *Essay* on its Divine authority; and also to procure such information of the actual state of religion in that country, as may assist the Society to form a discreet judgment respecting the most eligible means of promoting the interests of pure Christianity therein, have the satisfaction to submit to them the process and result of their Mission.

They deem it, however, incumbent on them, in the first place, to record their grateful testimony to the goodness of God, not only for their safe preservation, but also for having prospered their way by preparing and disposing suitable instruments to promote their object, whose friendship has proved of considerable advantage, particularly as it has been the medium of introducing them to persons of respectable station and influence, who have received them with cordiality, highly approved the benevolence and utility of their design, greatly encouraged them by assurances of its probable success, and their co-operation to promote it.

Bearing in their minds the immediate object of their mission, which was the Translation of the *Essay*,[3] and its Circulation with the New Testament through France, they have taken measures for its accomplishment, and have the pleasure to inform the Directors, that they have succeeded beyond their expectations, it will afford them satisfaction to learn that God has graciously disposed the heart of a respectable member of the legislative assembly to take a lively interest in our cause; in consequence of which he voluntarily offered his services to translate the *Essay*; and is now assiduously engaged therein, receiving, according to his own

---

[1] This is the Report made to the Committee of the London Missionary Society after it delegated a committee to visit the Continent on its behalf. We have referred to this visit and its findings in ch. 2, above.

[2] Ch. 2, above indicates that the four members of this committee, appointed by the LMS were David Bogue, Joseph Hardcastle, Matthew Wilks, and Alexander Waugh.

[3] This was the *Essay On the Divine Authority of the N.T.* authored by Bogue.

declaration, increasing edification as he proceeds. The Society, we believe, may calculate on the future services of this gentleman, and proper measures to promote the Protestant cause; and he feels so much animated by the account of the design and proceedings of our institution, as to have formed the intention of being present at our next annual solemnities.

But it is not in the French language only that the Society is likely to be instrumental in the circulation of the New Testament and of the *Essay*: —it is highly probable that at the present moment the latter is under translation into the Italian language, by another individual, whom God has raised up and filled with zeal against the errors of the Popish Communion. The Directors will learn with pleasure, that an Italian Bishop has expressed his disinterested desire to serve their cause in this way; and it waits only on their own determination to give full effect to his zealous disposition. This dignitary of the Roman See, in the early periods of the revolution, directed his enlightened efforts against the pretensions of the Papacy, and for three years suffered imprisonment, as well as the loss of his worldly substance. Feeling strongly on account of the abominations of Popery, he appears ready to lend his utmost assistance to diffuse the purer Principles of the Protestant faith.

Another member of the legislative body, a zealous Protestant, and who appears eminently devoted to the Lord Jesus Christ, entered most cordially into our views. He lamented the want of faithful and zealous ministers; and on our expressing a hope that our Society might be disposed to educate some truly devoted and zealous young men for the exercise of the ministry in France, said 'that he thought he could find out, in the south, six young men truly devoted and spiritual, whom he would send over to England to be trained up there for the service of the Protestants in France;' and he waits the direction of the Society for the accomplishment of this purpose.

The resolution of the Society was limited to the New Testament; because, it was concluded that the addition of the Old, would occasion an inconvenient expenditure of its funds, it being understood that they were to be distributed gratuitously; but on this subject, as well as others, the minds of the deputation were every day receiving more just and comprehensive information; and they have now the satisfaction to say, that the Directors are likely to have the opportunity of printing and circulating the whole Scriptures, as well as the *Essay*, and other Protestant works, to a very great extent, without any eventual expense to the Society: and although we would not too strongly indulge this expectation, yet the following circumstance, among others, may in some degree encourage it.

In Paris, it required a search among the booksellers of four days, to find a single Bible: —we fear this is also the awful situation of the greater part of France, and other countries formerly connected with the

See of Rome. —The report of an intention to publish it, produced an application from one bookseller, for 1,500 copies; and we found on calculation that the sale of 1,000 copies on his terms, would leave some advantage to the Society. This bookseller being a Catholic, it was supposed, that he might be inquiring for their edition of the Scriptures: but he stated, that it was the Protestant Scriptures that he wanted, and for the purpose of selling them to the Catholics, who were eager to procure them, in preference to their own.

That the Directors may form a judgment, as to the probable extent in which the Scriptures and the works of the best Protestant Authors may be circulated, it may be necessary to state to them the information received from a gentleman who was formerly in one of the highest departments of state in Sardinia. Prompted by his approbation of the object, and desirous to prompt its success, he communicated the following intelligence: —That in Piedmont, and other Popish countries, the Bible was prohibited, under the penalty of eternal damnation; but that since their union with France, Protestantism is not only tolerated, but its worship is public; and that the benevolent views of the Society would meet with the greatest success, if prosecuted with order and wisdom. In Piedmont, and especially at Turin, there are a considerable numbers of Genevans who would assist it, as well as most of the literary characters of the country. Besides books, he recommends, that well instructed, prudent and discerning Missionaries be sent. There will be an equal opportunity of spreading instruction into the Cisalpine republic; and from thence into Tuscany. Books and Missionaries would also, he states, be received with enthusiasm at Naples; and this would prepare the way to Rome itself. —Without entering into further detail of the immense scope which Divine Providence has prepared for the exertions of Christian benevolence, in the cause of the blessed Redeemer: indeed, the moral effects produced over a very extensive and populous part of Europe, by the late conflict of the nations, are so evident and important, as not to be overlooked without impiety; and the facilities for the introduction of the Gospel, are so greatly increased, as to invite, and even demand, the earnest prayers and unwearied efforts of the disciples of Christ, to improve to the utmost so interesting a dispensation. It is extremely manifest, that a wide door is opened for the Gospel; and it will be a great privilege and honour, if the Missionary Society should, in any degree, become instrumental in making it an effectual one. The operations of Divine Providence, in rendering the political convulsions of the world subservient to his superior plan of wisdom and grace, in relation to the kingdom of the Messiah, has seldom been more apparent than in the public events which have lately occurred; yet, it is not by great political arrangements only, but also by moral impressions upon the minds of those who authority controls the affairs of nations that the duty of Christian Societies is pointed out and enforced. This observation admits of an appropriate application.

The Protestant cause is considered by the present government of France to be favourable to its stability: the apprehension of danger is from the party attached to Popery; the government, therefore, is on its guard with respect to the latter; but is well disposed to the former: this is demonstrated by its appointments to stations of political importance, or to offices of magistracy. An occurrence which happened on the return of the deputation, will illustrate this remark. They had been informed that, in one of the departments through which they had to pass, there were a number of their Protestant Brethren destitute of a pastor; conceiving to be their duty to visit them, in order to rouse and animate them, they stayed for one day in that district. The useful friend who accompanied them, being acquainted with the prefect, called on him, and informed him of their design in coming to France: this great officer entered with much zeal into the subject, highly approved of the measure, strongly recommended the Protestants to exert themselves, and promised them a church and a house, both well repaired, for the use of the minister whom they might get appointed. This circumstance being made known to two of the Protestants residing there, whose minds had previously been filled with gloomy apprehensions as to the state of religion, it had such an enlivening influence upon them, as to induce them to pledge themselves to furnish a very liberal support to any Protestant minister who would settle among them; and expressed their undoubting persuasion, that the church would soon be filled with such Catholics as would willingly contribute to the support of a Protestant ministry. This last sentiment, which is of very great importance, appears to be well founded. It is highly probable, that an energetic ministry, in which the great principles of the Gospel should be powerfully inculcated, would be numerously attended by the Catholics in various, if not in all parts of France. Indeed, the religion of Rome, unsupported by extensive funds, and destitute of civil power, seems fast verging towards its fall: the activity of its priests, who, by writings and other means, are endeavouring to revive its interests, may, however, succeed if no proper attempts are made to introduce into its place a purer system; because the intellectual principle in men, conscious of its immortal destiny, feels the necessity of some religion whereon its anxieties may repose; and will therefore lean upon a false one in the absence of the true. This anxious feeling of the mind after the true religion seems to be increasing in France. Disgusted with the superstitions of Popery, they betook themselves to the principles of infidelity, and have proved *them* to be insufficient for their happiness, as well as pernicious in their tendency. The day of infidelity and of superstition is closing; and as soon as the Sun of Righteousness arises, they will be chased into eternal darkness, their native region. It may be added also, that the Protestant religion would be supported by a considerable portion of the people, who being friendly to the principles of civil liberty, conceive that a natural alliance subsists between these, whilst that of the Papalists is supposed to be in hostility thereto. This is therefore that political and moral state of things in France and its dependencies, which the Directors will probably consider as a distinguishing character of a dispensation favourable to the interest of true religion; and therefore designed to be a signal to Christians, and especially to Christian societies, in order to engage their utmost energies to improve it.

The Members of the Deputation now proceed to state, that God has been pleased to render their visit to France the occasion of exciting already a very considerable impulse in the minds of many in favour of genuine Christianity. The objects of the institution, and the disinterested philanthropy, to which they attributed their visit, had a powerful effect on them, and awakened a train of ideas which were either entirely new, or had long lain dormant in their minds. They soon formed the project of communicating their views and feelings to others; and we believe that, at this time, a correspondence is opening with the Protestants in every part of France, with a view to form a general and useful organization of the whole body, in order to revive the long-persecuted interest of true religion, and extend them on every side; but they feel their need of the advice and assistance of the Society in the commencement of their efforts; and are disposed, in return, to co-operate in all the measures which may be recommended as likely to promote our great object. What these measures ought to be becomes therefore an important subject to be considered. Probably the Directors will coincide in the conviction which this visit to France has produced in our minds, —That, depending on the blessing of God, the bible, and an Evangelical Ministry, are the principal things requisite to promote the Cause of the Redeemer in that country; and it will probably be the distinguished honour of the Missionary Society to be the means of distributing the word of God, in a very extensive degree, through France and its dependencies, which appear to be now nearly destitute thereof: and this one circumstance will impress upon it a character of usefulness, which will afford to the mind a source of perpetual joy and thanksgiving. It is also hoped, it will be in their power to find out and recommend to the Brothers in France, some ministers whose knowledge of the peculiar doctrines of the Gospel, and experience of their power, may fit them for eminent usefulness; but so great is the want of suitable ministers in these populous and extensive regions, that, without an interposition of Providence in a way at present unknown, there must long remain a great deficiency in this respect. To lay the foundation of supplying this, as far as circumstances permit, it may probably be of essential service to select a few young men of the French nation, whose hearts may be inclined to the service of God, for the purpose of giving them such full and appropriate instructions as may fit them for the Christian ministry in their native country. It appears, moreover, to be a matter of great importance, that a member of the Society, or a friend in close connexion with it, should reside in Paris, for the exercise of his ministry among the Protestants there; whose number is estimated at from 30 to 40,000; and who it is feared are deplorably ignorant, as to the nature and effects of the religion which they profess. It may be necessary, in the first instance, to conduct the service in the English language; but the principal design is, to preach eventually in that of the French; not only to Protestants, but to Catholics also. This measure appeared so important in its nature, so honourable to the Society, and so essential in various views to the interests of religion through France, that the persuasion has been indulged, that the friends of the Society in England, would cheerfully extend their liberal aid to support it; and on this ground, the Members of the Deputation have instituted an enquiry concerning the price of one of the churches, well adapted for this purpose; the result of which, we expect very shortly to lay before the Directors.

Another means for promoting the success of the Gospel in France, we conceive would be the circulation of various Protestant works, explaining and impressing the leading principles, and beneficial effects of Christianity; and especially by a Publication of the nature of the *Evangelical Magazine*; the profits whereof should be applied to the Relief of the Widows of Protestant Ministers in that country; or to the education of young men for the ministry; as may appear best. On these grounds the adoption of the following Resolutions is recommended to the Directors:

1. That the measures already taken for the Translation of the *Essay*, and its Circulation by Sale, as well as the Printing and Sale of the New Testament, be confirmed.

N.B. 2,000 of each are ordered; the cost of which will be about £115

2. That the Committee be authorized to direct the following Books to be printed and circulated by Sale, for account of the Missionary Society; *viz.*

5,000 Bibles and Testaments, which will cost about	£625
5,000 Watts 1st Catechisms which will cost about	8
5,000 Watts 2nd Catechisms which will cost about	20
5,000 Assembly's Catechisms	25
4,000 New Testaments in the Italian language	100
2,000 Of the *Essay*	70
	£848

3. That a Committee be formed for taking into consideration the best means by which a periodical publication, similar to the *Evangelical Magazine*, could be formed and conducted in France.[4]

4. That an Application be made for Six Suitable Persons to be sent over to England, to receive Instructions under the patronage of our Society, with a view to the Exercise of the Protestant Ministry in France.[5]

5. That an Address from our Society to the Protestants in France, tending to call forth their Exertions in the Cause of the Redeemer, be formed by the Committee of Correspondence.

6. That the Rev. Samuel Tracy be appointed the Agent of our Society in Paris, for six months to come; and that he be considered as having acted in that capacity from the commencement of his arrival in that city.[6]

(Signed by the Committee)

The Editors are informed, that the above Resolutions were unanimously passed; and they partake of the satisfaction which the prospect of extending the interests of pure Christianity into France, and its dependencies, will undoubtedly diffuse among Christians in every part of our highly favoured country.

---

[4] As described in ch. 3, above, the magazine was eventually begun at Geneva in 1819, rather than at Paris. The LMS could not have known in approving the resolution, that the resumption of war with France would make the pursuit of this objective impractical until the return of peace.

[5] This objective was rapidly acted upon, with David Bogue's Gosport Academy being utilized for the purpose.

[6] The resumption of hostilities with France by 1803 seems to have interfered with pursuit of this objective. By 1819, this role was filled at Paris not by Samuel Tracy, but by Mark Wilks.

An Account of the Worship of the Genevan Dissidents in Nov. 1817

(A communication of Henry Pyt published in the *New Evangelical Magazine* 4 [1817], 96)

Geneva, Nov. 4, 1817
Sir,[1] and Dear Brothers in Christ:
  After a long but vain expectation of your return through Geneva, I have at last made up my mind to write to you, though uncertain if my letter will not reach London before you; notwithstanding this I am too desirous of having some news from you, not to attempt every means of obtaining it.
  Whilst you were among us, though our little Society was not yet very well organized, we felt all the necessity of taking no steps in church-order but according to the word of God; but now that it has pleased the Lord, to give us the desire of being united as a church, separated from the prejudices and the evil-walk of the outward church, we feel more than ever the urgent necessity of not taking a single step without being enlightened, directed and conducted by the word of God; since we have taken it as the sole foundation of our hopes, we must also draw from it alone the principles of our conduct and Christian walk. These are also your principles; we know your church has the same object in view as ours, and it is that which has engaged me to communicate with you, and to beg of you to impart to me all that you have learned from the Holy Scriptures concerning the order of the church. Permit me to tell you how our church walks, that if we be wrong upon any point, you may shew us from the Scriptures wherein we err.
  What I ask you, I ask you in the name of the Lord, that through modesty, you may not refuse us your advice, and that of your brethren. First, the members of our church have chosen three Pastors,[2] or

---

[1] The *New Evangelical Magazine* discloses only that the recipient of the letter is 'a gentleman here, who is lately returned from Geneva'. A likely candidate would be the Scottish Secession Presbyterian, W. Anderson, who had visited the dissidents at Geneva in the aftermath of the departure of Robert Haldane.
[2] It is the view of the present writer that we are seeing here in Pyt's description very strong evidences of Robert Haldane's having instilled in the fledgling dissident

Presidents, elected from among the brethren, who are brother Gonthier, brother Méjanel, whom perhaps you have known in London;[3] and myself. The church has also chosen a Deacon. We meet every Evening at 8 o'Clock. He who presides, prays, gives out a hymn, reads the word of God, and after the reading invites the brethren to speak upon some verse of the chapter which has been read; then those who have to speak do it by turns, and in general the President finishes by an exhortation, and with a hymn of thanksgiving, after which the church separates.

On Thursday evening at 7 o'Clock, one of the three Pastors, or another brother gives an exhortation, the principle design of which is to call those who are without the knowledge of Christ; and on that day there are more people than on the other days, because many are attracted by the desire of hearing the preaching. On the Lord's Day we meet three times; at 11, at half-past 4 and at 7. At 11, we exhort each other as on the other days of the week; at half-past 4, we take the Lord's Supper after this manner; one of the Pastors presides, he prays, and afterwards gives an exhortation suitable to the circumstance; he reads in the Holy Scriptures the institution of the Lord's Supper by the Lord himself, and before he breaks the bread, he offers up a short prayer of thanksgiving, afterwards he breaks it, repeating the last part of 1 Cor. X.16, he eats of it, and after him every one of the brethren; afterwards, before he takes the cup, he again gives thanks, he blesses it, repeating the first part of the above verse, he drinks of it, and each of the brethren after him; he then reads some part of the Scriptures, and closes with a prayer, and the singing of a hymn.

On Sunday at 7 o'Clock in the Evening, there is, as on Thursday, a Sermon preached which is designed in great measure for those who do not yet know the salvation of Christ; the day terminates with a collection. Thus our church has walked unto this time. As we find directions in the Scriptures, we follow them if it be the Lord's will to give us strength so to do.

Henry Pyt.

---

congregation at Geneva the very principles insisted on in the Haldane connexion in Scotland c.1808.

[3] This can only refer to a London visit by Méjanel prior to the time of writing, November 1817. In Appendix C is provided a report of an English itineration tour undertaken by Méjanel for the Continental Society in 1821. Therefore, Méjanel was known to some persons in England *prior to* the organization of the Continental Society.

Henri Pyt's 1819 'Address to British Christians, in Behalf of the Continental Society'[1]

(From the *New Evangelical Magazine* 6 [1820], 24-26)

To all who expect the advancement of the kingdom of the Lord Jesus.
Beloved!
What a scene does the world at this moment present to the observation of the Christian! Like one whose eyes are turned towards the signs which precede the rising of the day, he expects some great event, even the appearance of Him who is called 'The Bright and Morning Star'. Already the fig tree has budded, its leaves appear, the fields of the Lord are ripening, and seem to call for the reapers: the harvest is approaching. But all things are not quite ready: many portions of these fields require to be vivified by the rays of the sun, to be watered with fertilizing showers, and cultivated with care: immense plains are still untilled, or to speak without a figure, many countries of the earth have received the gospel, others are ready to receive it, whilst some again have not yet heard the voice of the messengers of peace.

England seems to have been chosen to provide for these labours. She is become the centre, from which the glad tidings go forth, and the heralds who proclaim them.[2]

But who will not be astonished, that these labours have not been first of all directed towards their neighbouring countries? Whilst the messengers of the glad tidings have gone forth like a great army, to subdue the most distant and the most savage nations with the gentle yoke of the Saviour; whilst the generous servants of Jesus, bidding a lasting adieu to the land of their birth, have banished themselves into distinct climes, France, which

---

[1] Pyt had left the pastorate of the 'Bourg-de-Four' independent church at Geneva in 1818 to become the agent of the Continental Society. He would, in the late 1820s, become the chief agent for the society's operations in Francophone Europe. He here gives his impressions of the spiritual state of France after one year's service of the Society.

[2] This kind of fulsome praise of Britain (and it is repeated near the end of this document) might suggest that the writer was an Anglophile. But such remarks are not hard to find from European evangelicals in this period. Just as Britain had led the way in restoring European liberties through the defeat of Napoleon, so there was an expectation that Britain would similarly lead the way in gospel concerns.

ought, as it would seem, to have been the first object of their exertions, on account of its proximity and its necessities, has remained without culture, for want of labourers. Since the exertions of missions first began, a whole generation has passed away without having known the true gospel. The Lord has permitted it, and blessed be his holy name!

Shall this country be any longer deprived of the light of the gospel? Ought it not also to become one day a province in the kingdom of the Lord? Yes it will, for it is included in the promise: 'The whole earth shall be filled with the knowledge of the Lord, as the waters cover the sea'.[3] Oh my brethren, were you but eye witnesses of all the spiritual misery of this people, in whose favour I am now about to plead with you; could you but observe this future portion of the inheritance of your master, now made desolate by the impiety, ignorance, or prevarication of those, who ought to cultivate it, your charity would be excited, and I should have gained my cause.

Many of you, dear brethren, have been witnesses of this, but it is hardly possible that you should have known the extent of the evil. You may have some *general knowledge* of it from seeing the Lord's Day openly profaned, the name of God taken in vain, and blasphemed, the country covered with altars erected to idols, that is to say, chapels dedicated to the Virgin, and to saints, the people hastening in crowds to render homage to these false gods; but what would your concern have been if, entering into the interior of the families of the most numerous class of this people—that of the poor—you had seen every where by the side of the deepest distress, the most profound ignorance of the only way to escape from eternal misery? What would it have been if you had heard every where persons, whom the stagnation of trade had reduced to poverty, mourning over their present evils, whilst the danger in which they are of falling into interminable misery does not affect them? What could you have thought while seeing, among devout families, the unhappy people seeking consolations in superstitious observances, invoking the help of the Virgin, calling on the saints, devoutly opening books written in an unknown tongue, and neglecting the gospel of salvation, which they hardly know by name? Wretched creatures! After having contended with temporal misery, and earnestly sought for consolation where it was not to be found, they die—but alas! Death does not terminate their misfortunes, since they die without having savingly known Christ. Such is the lot of the immense majority of the French people of the poorer class.

---

[3] Pyt's invoking of this biblical imagery (found in the prophets Isaiah [11.9] and Habakkuk [2.14]) suggests that at this stage he still endorsed the optimistic postmillennial eschatology common among British Nonconformists. His biographer indicates, however, that by the 1830s, he embraced the far-less optimistic premillennial outlook associated with Henry Drummond, with whom he had been acquainted since 1817.

Let us now consider the religious state of the next most numerous class to that of which we have just spoken. It is composed of a crowd of people of every kind, commonly included in the general term 'persons of easy circumstances'. Here are found the careless and indifferent; Catholics by custom; deists, become such from disgust at superstition. The distinctive character of these three orders is frivolity, love of the world, and indifference about their salvation. These are they who fill the play-houses, public places, & c. Nothing can better express their religious state than those words of the prophet, 'the harp, the viol, and wine is in their feasts, but they consider not the work of the Lord, neither do they regard the operations of his hand'. Seldom will you see them troubled by the thoughts of a judgment, of a hell, or of an eternity; these concerns, so important, are never alluded to in their conversation but as matters of jest. Seldom perhaps has the voice of a faithful servant of Christ arrested them in their worldly career. If now and then they have cast an eye upon their conduct, if they have had some lucid moments in the midst of their delirium, they may have seen that they were sinners, but Christ crucified has not been presented to them as a Saviour who will freely save the unjust, the enemies of God: they have been brought up to believe that salvation is only obtained by mortifications, and by acts of penitence, which revolts them: ignorant therefore of the grace of God, they hasten to reject every serious thought, and replunge into vortex of vanities, if haply they may forget themselves. Thus passes the life of the multitudes, who rush carelessly to encounter the wrath to come.

There is also a third class, that of the 'Great'. Surrounded by the pomp of grandeur, they are almost inaccessible to the retired observation of the Christian. He only sees them afar off: but what reasons are there to fear that the state of this class is as deplorable, to say the least of it, as that of the preceding ones!

Hitherto, I have spoken only of the Catholics; let us now consider the Protestants, who as far as respects their members, are lost in the multitude of the others.

The state of religion among the Protestants is not uniform. Thus those of the North do not resemble those in the South; neither do these latter resemble those of the West. Simplicity characterizes those of the North; indifference and worldly-mindedness those of the West; whilst they in the South partake of both.

It is amongst the Reformed in the North that the least corruption in doctrine is found. They profess to believe that which is generally unknown among others, that 'salvation is by grace, through faith, and not of works.' The greater part is composed of proselytes, i.e. of Catholics, who from conviction have abandoned the worship of their fathers. Discussion upon the errors of the Romish church, and particularly the reading of the word of God, have effected this change. Being Protestants by conviction, they are more attached to the doctrines of the reformation than those, who are Protestants only by birth.

The Reformed are more numerous in the South, but they are more indifferent, and more ignorant of sound doctrine. The gospel, however, is preached there: some faithful servants courageously proclaim Christ crucified; but besides that they are few in number, they are almost all denounced as innovators, Moravians, sectarians, & c. so that their efforts are not crowned with all the success that might be expected. The Lord however does not fail to bear witness to his word: the South can reckon even among the great, a few persons firmly attached to Jesus as their only Saviour.

How melancholy is it not to be able to bear as good a testimony to the great mass of the Reformed! With some exceptions, their indifference to the Saviour, their ignorance of the gospel, and their worldly mindedness are almost as great as among the middling class of Catholics. The greater part of their pastors preached a mixed doctrine; some among them go still farther. Self-righteousness is enthroned; the 'righteousness of God by faith' is despised, or openly rejected. The flocks are led into dry and barren pastures, far from the wells of water springing up to everlasting life. The consequence of which is, that the greater number of the Reformed walk with the Catholics in the ways of death, and go on to perdition without hesitation.

About twenty faithful pastors[4] exerting their influence over 15 or 20,000 souls is all that France can offer us as a set-off to the melancholy picture here presented. But what are 15 or 20,000 souls among a population of at least 27 millions? More than 26 millions then live in France, exposed to the most terrible of all dangers, that of eternal death! Are you not moved, my dear brethren, at so great a calamity? The Lord has given you the means to aid this people. Your zeal sends preachers of glad tidings over all the countries of the globe: embrace France also in the extent of your charity. The invitations, the appeals of savage nations, who ask the gospel from you have touched you; but will you not be still more moved by the awful silence which reigns over the inhabitants of this

---

[4] This estimate, while meagre, is still a more optimistic estimate than the one which characterized Robert Haldane as he left Geneva for Montauban in 1817. However, what is truly striking about Pyt's survey is the highly disparaging way in which he speaks about the membership of France's Reformed Church. Supporters of the Continental Society would not have been shocked to hear that the Protestant Church of France had a very 'mixed' membership; such realities cross national boundaries. But Pyt can hardly have helped himself here by his using the language of destitution so freely. What is most truly disclosed here is Pyt's settled aversion to collaboration with national or Established Churches. The constituency of the Continental Society would here have found legitimate grounds for questioning his suitability for the work that the Society professed to be undertaking.

country respecting their eternal interests, since this silence betrays their ignorance of the danger which threatens them? What, —whilst you possess the treasure of the gospel, will you suffer your neighbours to perish through poverty? While your happy country seems ready to be completely subjected to the Saviour; while you rejoice in this glorious hope, will you leave the god of this world in peaceable possession of this land, connected with you by so many ties?

But if these motives are not sufficient, I will present one of a superior order to you: the love which you owe to Christ. Can you in fact see *Him* forgotten, unknown and rejected, and not make some effort that He may be glorified among the multitudes who dishonour Him?

There has lately been formed in your country a Society, whose object is to propagate the gospel on the Continent: already the Lord has crowned by his blessing their generous intentions. Join your effort to theirs, O Christians of England, you whom the Lord has chosen by his grace to be every where the heralds of his glorious gospel. Support it by your prayers, by your liberality: it will administer your donations to the glory of God, for the advancement of the kingdom of Christ in these countries desolated by infidelity.

May he who gives seed to the sower, and bread to the eater, multiply your seed sown, and increase the fruits of your righteousness.

(Signed) H_____ P_____
Minister of the Gospel
France, Nov. 12, 1819.

Pierre Méjanel: A Francophone Itinerant in Britain[1]

(Extract of a letter of 23 Aug, 1821 published in the *New Evangelical Magazine*, 7 [1821], 340)

My dear friend and brother:[2]

As you do not understand the French, I am obliged to write you in bad English. Before I left London I could not pay you another visit, to take leave of you and of your family for good. Since I arrived in Paris, I wrote to Mr. Stennett,[3] and desired he would have the kindness to express, especially to you and to some other friends, my affectionate regards, and to remember me to your church; but I fear the letter was not properly directed.

My journey from London to Gosport was very pleasant, we had a fine country, fine weather, and good books; I enjoyed the favours of Creation and of grace. The good tutor[4] and his family were to me, at Gosport, another means of consolation, edification and pleasure, as were other friends there. But I saw more of Dr. Bogue; I was in his house. I went to the Isle of Wight. They made me preach and address, once in French and six times in English; I feared much at first to speak in English to so many people, but soon after I commenced, I was almost as free as I am in French. I saw much of your good friend Mr. A. and his good wife, and was edified with them. Those preachings did me good. Happy is the soul that the Lord employs as an instrument of mercy, and by whom the Holy Spirit runs, as it were, as in a channel, in order to refresh others souls by the preaching of the glorious gospel! Happy the vessel that the hand of the Lord dips in the living water to cause those who are thirsty to drink! I do not mean to say, that I have been such a channel and such a vessel; for there are, on the contrary, many dry places in me; but the rain of the former season will be followed, I hope, by that of the latter; and my great desire is that the mouth of your friend may be made a fountain of life. My little exertions at Newport, attracted the attention of the good people

---

[1] Pierre Méjanel was frequently in Britain in the 1820s, making appearances on behalf of the Continental Society, whose agent he then was. In the year following (1822), he journeyed extensively in the north of England, Scotland, and Ireland in company with Robert Haldane.

[2] The recipient of this letter is not disclosed by the *New Evangelical Magazine*.

[3] Samuel Stennett was at this time secretary of the Continental Society.

[4] A reference to Dr David Bogue, tutor of the theological academy at Gosport.

in that town, and interested them much. I was invited to speak in the pulpits of the three denominations. Mr. A. was the means of calling me into the chapel of the Methodists. It is very edifying to see all those that love the Lord, united by the same love. I intended to stay two days at Newport and I was there ten! At last I went away blessing and being blessed—even thanked as if I had been useful. At Ride I preached again, I hope with some degree of success. At Gosport, I preached on the Thursday for Dr. Bogue. I was glad to see he was gratified; he said that such preaching was calculated to do much good. Thus, my dear brother, if I have the pleasure of ever returning among you, perhaps I shall not be so obstinate as I was, in refusing to preach in English; but every thing must have a beginning. I embarked on the 13th of July for the Havre, and arrived there on the evening of the next day; it was Saturday. There are a few Protestants whose pastor had left them; almost all of them were gone into the country. I could not preach to them, and endeavouring to gather them, I lost, in a great measure, my Sabbath. What a melancholy thing is the loss of a Sabbath! The Sabbath is the time of gathering spiritual riches. The loss of a Sabbath is like the loss of a harvest destroyed by storm, or of a vineyard desolated by wild beasts, such make us poorer for all the week, and sometimes for the whole of life.

At Bolbec I saw two ministers who are well disposed. At Rouen I preached to the Protestant congregation; the minister is a good man, very kind, but timid. I told him we must not be afraid to preach the gospel, because the gospel is the voice of the good Shepherd, it gathers the sheep and turns away the wolves. He feared lest I should say too strong things to his congregation; but I did not. I spoke very plainly upon the sacrifices of Abel and Cain. The hearers were exceedingly attentive; the elders, some of whom were decorated with red ribbons, thanked me very kindly. As for the minister, his fears made room for his edification and satisfaction.

My poor little flock in Paris, were, as it might be expected, like sheep without a shepherd. Notwithstanding every kind of opposition, the work may be continued here, I hope with success.

We have very good news from Geneva, from Switzerland, and from Spain. France is advancing. In a village near Lyons they have found Christians—they say many hundreds. You may have read the particulars in an English Magazine.

I expect, next week, to set off to pay my visit to my parents in the South of France.

God be with you, dear friend.

I am,

Your sincere friend and brother.

Passy near Paris,

August 23, 1821.

The Continental Society as at 1826

(As reported in the *Evangelical Magazine* [1826], 155-156)

Brief History of the Continental Society

The Continental Society, exclusive of the claim which it has upon the attention of the friends to the advancement of the Redeemer's kingdom, in common with all other institutions, whose object it is to spread the gospel in the world, has characteristics of a very distinct kind, which are highly interesting to every pious mind. It is its professed design to attempt the spiritual improvement of Christendom, to convert nominal Christians to the saving knowledge of the truth, and rekindle the light of the gospel among the churches of the continent, which had been nearly extinguished. Its intention is the establishment of no sect or party, the setting up of no distinct or separate form of church order or discipline, but the revival of that vital godliness which is essential to true religion, and without which the clearest creed and the purest discipline are but the form of godliness without the power.

Not only is the progress of the gospel on the Continent opposed by a debasing superstition, as among Catholics, but a dreadful species of infidelity almost everywhere prevails among the Protestants in Germany, called Neology, which, while it professes to acknowledge the Christian doctrine, and appeals to the Christian records, does every thing to reason away the one, and to deprive the other of their infallibility, denying their most important facts and miracles. (See Statement, 1st and 4th Rep. at the beginning; 6th Rep. p. 8; Extracts, No. 15).[1] In France and Switzerland, until lately, almost all the Protestant pastors were Socinians, or Arians at the best, preaching mere dry morality instead of the gospel of Christ; and the populace, led by them, entertain the most inveterate prejudices, and have frequently manifested the most persecuting spirit against the preachers of the gospel, and those who followed them.[2] (See 1st Rep. p. 9

---

[1] Here the writer is directing readers to the annual published *Reports* (sometimes *Proceedings*) issued by the Society, as well as occasional *Extracts* of missionary correspondence. The former have been drawn on regularly in the body of the present work.

[2] The unidentified author of this summary is one who is choosing to emphasize the somber aspect of European Christianity rather than encouraging signs of change for the better. Both kinds of analysis were found among Society members and contributors.

and 10; beginning of 4th Rep; 6th Rep. p. 9, 10, 13; 5th Rep. App. No. 1; 6th Rep. App. Nos. 6, 8, 9; 7th Rep. App. Nos. 2, 8 & c.)

At the time of its formation in Paris, in the month of May, 1818, the Society began its operations by employing one Missionary, (a native, for such only are employed) to whom others were soon added, all of them preachers and most of them ordained ministers of the French and Swiss reformed churches; so that during more than seven years, not fewer than forty persons have been at different times labouring on the continent under its auspices. At present the number of its agents is twenty-four, who are engaged in preaching the gospel and distributing the Scriptures in the following countries: —

Two ministers in Paris, one of whom was banished from the Pays de Vaud not long since, for his adherence to the doctrines of the gospel, are preaching the truth with some success to both Protestants and Catholics. One of them, Mr. Mejanil (sic) has made very extensive and useful tours through different parts of France; the other is Mr. F. Olivier, an ordained minister of the Swiss church. (See 7th Rep. App. No. 14; Extract, No. 22, p. 202.)

In the north of France, at Léme, a worthy pastor, Mr. Colany Née, is assisted by the Society with a small annual grant, to enable him to preach in the villages round his numerous parishes, — at least fifteen or sixteen, and some of them eight or ten leagues distant from others. Since his conversion, he has been blessed to several hundreds of souls. (See 5th Rep. p. 42, 43.; Extracts, No. 13, p. 149; No. 24, p. 225, 226; No. 25, p. 234, c.)

In Flanders, Mr. De Faye, pastor of the reformed church at Tournay, by the aid of a small annual grant, is enabled to make excursions in the villages round, and in the adjacent parts of Frances. (For the success of his labors see 7th rep. App. No. 12; Extracts, No. 24, p. 224; c; No. 25, p. 233, 234.)

In the neighbourhood of Orleans one of the Society's agents is stationed, who was some time one of the colporteurs (a description of agents employed now for several years in distributing the Scriptures and conversing with people about them), and now a very useful preacher of the gospel. His name is F. Caulier. In these countries there is a great need of such exertions, as there are many protestant churches altogether without pastors; and a great number of the Catholic population are desirous of hearing the gospel (See 4th Rep. p. 38, 39; 7th Rep. App. No. 1; Extracts No. 16, p. 161, 162; No. 21, p. 193, 194; No. 22, p. 205; No. 21, p. 299; No. 25, p. 237.)

One of the Society's agents, Mr. Falle, labours with diligence and success at Calmont, a town 24 miles south of Toulouse, as suffragan to an aged minister there, and under the eye of the venerable Chabrand, pastor of Toulouse. (See Extracts, No. 9, p. 119; No. 10, p. 128, 129; No. 22, p. 203, 204.)

The Society has an agent very successfully employed in the valley of the Piedmont, preaching the gospel, and endeavouring to revive the almost extinguished zeal of the Waldensian churches. His name is Neff; he is a man of remarkable energy and self-denial. (See 7th Rep. p. 29, 30; Extract no. 25, p. 236 & c.)

Another of the Society's agents, Mr. Barbey, one of the exiled ministers of the Canton de Vaud, is now labouring in the neighborhood of Lyons, a very interesting district, where recently great numbers have been brought to renounce the Roman Catholic, and publicly to profess the Protestant faith. He succeeds, in this work, a most valuable man, lately an agent, but who left the Society in consequence of becoming a stated pastor. (See Extract, No. 21, p. 228, 229.)

At Colmar, and the neighboring towns and villages, the Society has an active young preacher stationed, named Louis Bott, who from time to time sends very interesting accounts of his success, and of the revivals the Lord is accomplishing through his means. (See Extracts, No. 10, p.126, 127; No. 12; p. 145, 146; No. 21, p. 197, 198.)

Another is stationed at Strasburg, on the Rhine, Martin Fuchs, and labours in the surrounding villages. He is an unlettered man, but mighty in the Scriptures, and has been a powerful instrument in the hands of God in producing a great revival of religion in those parts. These two last agents have been recommended to the Society by a most laborious, intrepid, and successful minister, who was in the Society's employ from the beginning of its operations until very lately, when he took charge of a church at Geneva. His name is Ami Bast (sic), and he is well known to many friends in this country. (See 3d. Rep. p. 6, 7, 8; 7th Rep. App. p. 29; Extracts, No. 10, p. 135, 135; No. 11, p. 141; No. 15, p. 157; No. 17, p. 167; No. 22. p. 204.)

In the north of Germany, the Society has in its employ at Hamburgh, a young man, Mr. Oncken, who is extremely diligent, and his ministry is crowned with considerable success. (See 6th Report, App. 49, & c.; 7th Re. p. 16, 17 & c.; Extracts, No. 21, p. 196; No. 22, p. 206, & c; No. 25, p. 244, &c.)

Besides these, the Society has other labourers (colporteurs) who are employed in selling the holy Scriptures, and distributing them gratis, and conversing with those who receive them. Most of the ministers above mentioned have a colporteur under their direction; and in the north of France, two or three are labouring, who often furnish the Committee with very interesting journals of their proceedings and success, particularly Ladam and Wacquier. (See 3rd Rep. p. 17, & c.; 7th Rep. App. p. 25c; Extracts, No. 9. p. 114, & c.; No. 10, p. 133.)

The Society has also an agent traveling through parts of the Continent not yet visited, who watches the openings that may occur for making known the gospel, and forming a correspondence with truly pious Christians, wherever they are to be found. His name is Mayers. (See Extracts, No. 23, p. 211, & c; No. 24. p. 219, & c; No. 25, p. 241.)

The Committee has engaged a gentleman of high respectability, a doctor of medicine, recently converted to the Protestant faith, Dr. Naudl, of Malta, to visit Italy, and other parts where the same languages is spoken. (See extract, No. 25, p. 241.)

The have also agreed to undertake a mission to the coast of Norway, under the direction of a Danish baron, named Von Bülow. (See beginning of Extracts No. 23, 124, 125.)

One agent more should be mentioned, whom the Committee have recently engaged, a learned professor in one of the northern universities, (Göttingen)[3] who, for a small annual sum, has promised to devote a great portion of his time to preaching and lecturing among the students and others in order to check the progress of the Neological infidelity, that so awfully prevails in those seats of literature.

The Society's income has been gradually increasing every year; but owing to the numerous calls on its funds, it has never been able to make any reserve; the large donations, on which it subsisted during its first years, could not be husbanded. It is therefore still called to go forward, trusting, that the resources it has always found the hearts of a generous public will never fail it.

The documents referred to in the above paper may be had by application at the Society's office.

---

[3] We have elsewhere learned of the support given to the Continental Society by August Tholuck, who served the University of Berlin from 1824 as extraordinary professor of Oriental Languages and the University of Halle from 1826 as professor of theology. We are completely left to guess at the identity of this second German academic, sympathetic to the Continental Society.

Bibliography

Manuscript Materials

Council for World Mission (formerly London Missionary Society) Archive, London, University School of Oriental and African Studies

Europe Handlist, 'Disbursements to France' (1800 -1837)
European Correspondence (France), 1799-1849, Box 3

Edinburgh University Missionary Association. New College Library, University of Edinburgh

Minutebook, 1825-1842
Correspondence, 1825-1842, Box 1

Contemporary Periodicals and Published Reports

Acts and Proceedings of the General Assembly of the Church of Scotland
The American Biblical Repository, (New York: 1836ff.)
Appeal of the Continental Society of Dublin, (Dublin: 1834)
Les Archives du Christianisme, (Paris: 1818ff)
The Christian Magazine or Evangelical Repository, (Glasgow: 1807ff)
The Christian Observer (London: 1801ff)
The Christian Repository and Religious Register, (Edinburgh: 1816ff)
The Continental Echo and Protestant Witness, (London: 1845ff)
The Edinburgh Christian Instructor, (Edinburgh: 1805 ff.)
The Eclectic Review, (London: 1792ff)
The Evangelical Magazine, (London: 1793ff)
Extracts of Correspondence of the Continental Society, later the European Missionary Society, (London) Nos. 42, 45-7, 58
Free Church of Scotland General Assembly Reports, (Edinburgh: 1843ff)
The London Congregational Magazine (formerly London Christian Instructor), (London: 1818ff)
The New Evangelical Magazine, (London: 1815ff)
The Princeton Review, (Princeton, NJ, 1829ff)
Proceedings of the European Missionary Society, Formerly Designated the Continental Society, (London: 1839)
The Pulpit (London: 1823ff)
Die Reformatie, (Amsterdam: 1837ff)
Reports (later Proceedings) of the Continental Society, (London: 1819-29, 1832)
Reports of the Foreign Aid Society, (London: 1841ff)
Reports of the Foreign Evangelical Society, (New York,1840 ff.).

Reports of the London Missionary Society. (London: 1796-98)
The Scottish Christian Herald, (Edinburgh: 1835ff)

Select Bibliography

Adam, *Memoir of John Adam* (London: 1833)
Alexander, W.L., *Switzerland and the Swiss Churches*, (Glasgow: 1846)
Altholz, Josef L., 'Alexander Haldane, the *Record*, and Religious Journalism',
     Victorian Periodicals Review, 20 (1987), 23-31
Anderson, Hugh, *The Life and Letters of Christopher Anderson*, (London: 1854)
Anet, Leonard, *Histoire des Trente Prémieres Années de la Societé Évangélique   ou
     Église Missionaire Belge*, (Brussels: 1875)
Ashton, T.S., *The Industrial Revolution: 1760-1830*, (Oxford: 1948. reprinted
     1986)
Baker, Derek, ed., *Reform and Reformation: England and the Continent 1500-1750*,
     Studies in Church History, Subsidia 2 (Oxford: 1979)
Baker, Frank, *William Grimshaw: 1708-1763*, (London: 1963)
Balleine, G.R., *A History of the Evangelical Party in the Church of England*,
     (London: 1911)
Balmer, Randall and Catherine Randall, '"Her Duty to Canada": Henriette Feller and
     French Protestantism in Quebec', *Church History*, 70.1 (2001), 49-72
Bateman, John. *The Life of the Right Reverend Daniel Wilson, D.D.*, (London:
     1861)
Beales, Derek, and Geoffrey Best, eds, *History, Society, and the Churches: Essays in
     Honour of Owen Chadwick*, (Cambridge: 1985)
Bebb, E.R. *Nonconformity and Social and Economic Life; 1600-1800*, (London:
     1935)
Bebbington, D.W., ed., *The Baptists in Scotland: A History*, (Glasgow: 1988)
—, *Evangelicalism in Modern Britain* (London: 1989)
—, 'The Life of Baptist Noel: Its Setting and Significance', *The Baptist
     Quarterly*, 24.8 (1972), 389-411
Beattie, James, *Memoir of Robert Haldane and James Alexander Haldane*, (New
     York: 1858)
Bellenger, Dominic, 'The Emigré Clergy and the English Church, 1789-1815',
     Journal of Ecclesiastical History, 34. No.3 (1983), 392-410
Benedict, Philip, *Christ's Churches Purely Reformed: A Social History of
     Calvinism*, (New Haven, CT: 2002)
Bennett, G.V. and J.D. Walsh, eds., *Essays in Modern English Church History*,
     (London: 1966)
Bennett, James, *Memoirs of the Life of the Rev. David Bogue*, (London:1827)
Benson, Louis F., *The English Hymn*, (Atlanta: 1964)
Best, G.F.A., 'The Evangelicals and the Established Church in the early 19th
     Century', *Journal of Theological Studies*, 10, (1959), 71-78

Bickersteth, Edward, *The Religious State of Europe Considered*, (Glasgow: 1836)
—, ed., *A Voice From the Alps*, (London: 1838)
Biéler, Blanche, *Une Famille du Refuge*, (Paris: 1930)
Birks, T.R., *Memoir of the Rev. Edward Bickersteth*, 2 vols, (London: 1851)
Black, Robert Merrill, 'Anglicans and French-Canadian Evangelism 1839- 1848',
    Journal of the Canadian Church History Society, 26.1 (1984), 18-33
Blaikie, W.G., *John Campbell, Founder of the Tract Society*, (Edinburgh, 1886)
Bogue, David, *An Essay On the Divine Authority of the New Testament*, (Portsea:
    1801)
Bogue, David, and James Bennett, *History of Dissenters From the Revolution Under
    King William to the Year 1808*, (London: 1808)
Bogue, David, *Theological Lectures*, edited by J.S.C. Frey, (New York: 1849)
Bonjour, E., H.S. Offler, and G.R. Potter, *A Short History of Switzerland*, (Oxford:
    1952)
Bonnet, Jules, 'Notice sur la vie et sur les écrits de M. Merle D'Aubigné', *Bulletin
    de le Société d'Histoire du Protestantisme Française*, Vol. 23, (Paris: 1874), 158-
    184
Bost, Ami, *Genève Religieuse en Mars 1819*, (Geneva: 1819)
—, *The Life of Félix Neff*, (London: 1855)
—, *Mémoires Pouvant Servir a l'Histoire du Réveil Religieux*, 3 vols, (Paris: 1854)
Boudin, H.R., 'Einige Aspekte des Reveils in Belgien', in Van den Berg, J., and
    J.P. Van Dooren, eds., *Pietismus und Reveil*, (Leiden: 1978), 289-299
Bratt, James, *Dutch Calvinism in Modern America*, (Grand Rapids, MI: 1984)
Brown, Calum G., *The Social History of Religion in Scotland Since 1730*,
    (London: 1987)
Brown, David, *Life of John Duncan*, (Edinburgh: 1872)
Brown, Stewart J., *The National Churches of England, Ireland and Scotland 1801-
    1846*, (Oxford: 2001)
Brown, Stewart J., *Thomas Chalmers and the Godly Commonwealth in Scotland*,
    (Oxford: 1982)
Bundy, David, 'Between the Réveil and Pentecostalism: The American
    Wesleyan/Holiness Traditions in Belgium and the Netherlands', *Asbury
    Theological Journal*, 51 (1996), 105-113
Burder, Henry F., *Memoir of the Rev. George Burder*, (London: 1833)
Burleigh, J.H.S., *A Church History of Scotland*, (Oxford: 1960)
Burns, Robert, *Memoir of the Rev. Stevenson Macgill D.D.*, (Edinburgh: 1842)
Cadier, Jean, 'La Tradition Calviniste dans le Réveil du XIX siécle', *Études
    Theologique et Religieuses*, 22 (1952), 9-28
Calder, R.G., 'Robert Haldane's Theological Seminary', *Transactions of the
    Congregational Historical Society*, 13 (1937-39), 59-63
Cameron, Nigel M. de. S., et al, eds., *Scottish Dictionary of Church History and
    Theology*, (Edinburgh: 1993)
Campbell, John, *African Light Thrown On a Selection of Scripture Texts, With a
    Biographical Sketch*, (Edinburgh: 1842)

Campbell, John, *John Angell James: A Review of His History, Character, Eloquence and Literary Labours*, (London: 1860)

Candlish, Robert S., ed., *Lectures On Foreign Churches*, 2 vols, (Edinburgh: 1845-46)

Canton, William, *The History of the British and Foreign Bible Society*, Vol. 1, (London: 1904)

Cart, Jacques, *Histoire du Mouvement Religieux et Écclesiastique dans le Canton de Vaud Pendant la Première Moitie du XIX siécle*, 3 vols, (Lausanne: 1890)

Carter, Grayson, *Anglican Evangelicals: Protestant Secessions from the Via Media, c.1800-1850*, (Oxford: 2001)

Carwardine, R.J., *Transatlantic Revivalism* (Westport, CT: 1978)

Chadwick, Owen, *The Mind of the Oxford Movement*, (London: 1960)

Chalmers, Thomas, *Institutes of Theology*, 2 vols, (Edinburgh: 1849)

Chenevière, J.J.C., 'A Summary of Theological Controversies Which Of Late Years Have Agitated the City of Geneva', *Monthly Repository of Theology and General Literature*, 19 (1824), pp. 1ff, 65ff, 129ff

Cheyne, A.C., *The Transforming of the Kirk: Victorian Scotland's Religious Revolution*, (Edinburgh: 1983)

Clipsham, E.F., 'Andrew Fuller and Fullerism: a Study in Evangelical Calvinism', *Baptist Quarterly*, 20 (1963-64), 99ff, 146ff, 214ff, 268ff

Coad, Roy, *A History of the Brethren Movement*, (Exeter: 1968)

Cowan, Henry, *The Influence of the Scottish Church in Christendom*, (London: 1896)

Crawford, Michael J., 'Origins of the Eighteenth-Century Evangelical Revival: England and New England Compared', *Journal of British Studies*, 26.4 (1987), 361-397

Cross, F.L. and E.A. Livingstone, eds., *The Oxford Dictionary of the Christian Church*, (Oxford: 1974)

Cuming, G.J. Derek and Baker, eds, *Popular Belief and Practice*, Studies in Church History, Vol. 8, (Cambridge: 1972)

Curtat, L.A., *De L'Établissement des Conventicules dans le Canton de Vaud*, (Lausanne: 1821)

Dallimore, Arnold, *George Whitefield*, 2 vols, (Edinburgh: 1970, 1978)

Davenport, R.A., *The Albury Apostles*, (London: 1970, reprinted 1973)

Davies, G.C.B., *The Early Cornish Evangelicals, 1735-1760*, (London: 1951)

Davies, R.E. and E.G. Rupp, eds., *A History of the Methodist Church in Great Britain*, 4 vols, (London: 1965ff)

De Felice, Guillaume, *History of the Protestants of France From the Commencement of the Reformation to the Present Time*, translated by P.E. Barnes, (London: 1853)

De Jong, P.Y., ed., *Crisis in the Reformed Churches*, (Grand Rapids, MI: 1968)

Deacon, Malcolm, *Philip Doddridge of Northampton: 1702-1751*, (Northampton: 1980)

Decorvet, Jean, 'F.S.R. Gaussen. Sa vie, son oeuvre et le débat sur la théopneustie', *Hokhma*, 70 (1999), 24-55

Deming, James C., 'The Threat of Revival to a Minority Protestant Community: The French Reformed Church in the Department of the Gard, 1830-1859', *Fides et Historia*, 21.3 (1989), 68-77

Dick, John, *The Inspiration of Scripture*, 2nd edition, (Glasgow: 1803)

Ditchfield, G.R., *The Evangelical Revival*, (London: 1998)

Dodwell, C.R., ed., *The English Church and the Continent*, (London: 1959)

Douen, O., *Histoire de la Société Biblique Protestant de Paris*, (Paris: 1868)

Drew, Samuel, *The Life of Dr. Coke*, (London: 1817)

Drummond, A.L., *Edward Irving and His Circle*, (London: 1937)

—, *The Kirk and the Continent*, (Edinburgh: 1956)

—, 'Robert Haldane at Geneva', *Records of the Scottish Church History Society*, 9 (1947), 69-82

Dubief, Henri, 'Reflexions Sur Quelques Aspects du Prémier Réveil', *Bulletin de la Société d'Histoire Protestantisme Française*, 114 (1968), 373-402

Douglas, J.D., ed., *The New International Dictionary of the Christian Church*, (Grand Rapids, MI: 1974)

Escott, Harry, *A History of Scottish Congregationalism*, (Glasgow: 1960)

Evans, Robert, 'The Contribution of Foreigners in the French 'Réveil', (University of Manchester PhD dissertation, 1971)

Ewing, J.W., *Goodly Fellowship; A Centenary Tribute to the World's Evangelical Alliance*, (London: 1946)

Fath, Sébastien, 'A Forgotten Missionary Link: The Baptist Continental Society in France, 1831-36', *Baptist Quarterly*, 40.3 (2003), 133-150

—, 'Deux Siècles d'Histoire des Églises Évangéliques en France (1802-2002)', *Hokhma*, 81 (2002), 1-51

Fawcett, Arthur, 'Scottish Lay Preachers in the Eighteenth Century', *Records of the Scottish Church History Society*, 12 (1955), 97-119

Ferguson, William, *Scotland: 1689 to the Present*, (Edinburgh: 1968)

Fleming, J.R., *A History of the Church in Scotland 1843-74*, (Edinburgh: 1927)

Ford, Clarence, *Life and Letters of Madame de Krüdener*, (London: 1893)

Ford, Franklin L., *Europe: 1780-1830*, (London: 1970)

Foster, Charles I, *An Errand of Mercy: The United Evangelical Front, 1790-1837*, (Chapel Hill, NC: 1960)

Froom, Charles Leroy, *The Prophetic Faith of Our Fathers*, 3 vols, (Washington, DC: 1949)

Gaussen, F.S.L., *Theopneustia*, (London: 1841)

Gee, Henry and W.J. Hardy, eds, *Documents Illustrative of English Church History* (London: 1896)

Genevray, P., 'L'État Français et la Propagation du Réveil', *Bulletin de le Société de l'Histoire du Protestantisme Française*, 95-96 (1946-7), 12-39

Gilbert, A.D., *Religion and Society in Industrial England*, (London: 1976)

Gilbert, Joseph, *Memoir of the Life and Writings of the late Edward Williams*, (London: 1825)

Gilley, Sheridan, 'Edward Irving: Prophet of the Millennium', in Jane Garnet and Colin Matthews, eds, *Revival and Religion Since 1700*, (London: 1993), 95-110

Gilly, William Stephen, *Memoir of Félix Neff*, (London: 1832)

Good, James I., *History of the Swiss Reformed Church Since the Reformation*, (Philadelphia, PA: 1913)

Gretillat, August, 'Movements of Theological Thought Among French-Speaking Protestants From the Revival of 1820 to the end of 1891', *Presbyterian and Reformed Review*, 3 (1892), 421-447

Gribben, Crawford and Timothy C.F. Stunt, eds, *Prisoners of Hope: Evangelical Millennialism in Britain and Ireland, 1800-1880*, (Carlisle, 2004)

Guers, Émile, *Notice Historique de L'Église Évangélique Libre de Genève*, (Geneva: 1875)

—, *Le Premier Réveil et la Premier Église Independent à Genève*, (Geneva: 1872)

—, *Vie de Henri Pyt*, (Toulouse: 1850)

Guthrie, David K. and J. Charles, eds, *Autobiography and Memoir of Thomas Guthrie, D.D.*, (London: 1874)

Gwynn, Robin D., *Huguenot Heritage: The History and Contribution of the Huguenots in Britain*, (London: 1985)

Haldane, Alexander, *The Lives of Robert Haldane of Airthrey and of his brother, James Alexander Haldane*, (Edinburgh: 1855)

Haldane, Robert, *The Evidence and Authority of Divine Revelation*, 2 vols, (Edinburgh: 1816)

—, *Exposition of the Epistle to theRomans*, 2 vols, (London: 1835)

—, *Letter to Edward Bickersteth*, (London: 1839)

—, *Letter from Robert Haldane, Esq. to M.J.J. Chenevière, Pastor and Professor of Divinity at Geneva*, (Edinburgh: 1824)

—, *A Review of the Conduct of the Rev. Daniel Wilson on the Continent*, (Edinburgh: 1829)

—, *Second Review of the Conduct of the Directors of the British and Foreign Bible Society*, (Edinburgh: 1826)

Halévy, Elie, *The Birth of Methodism in England*, translation and introduction by Bernard Semmel, (Chicago, IL: 1971)

—, *A History of the English People in 1815*, (London: 1924)

—, *A History of the English People 1815-1830*, (London: 1926)

Hamilton, Ian, *The Erosion of Calvinist Orthodoxy*, (Edinburgh: 1990)

Hamilton, J. Taylor, *A History of the Church Known as the Moravian Church*, (Bethlehem, PA: 1900)

Hannah, William, ed., *A Selection from the Correspondence of the late Thomas Chalmers*, (Edinburgh: 1853)

—, ed., *Letters of Thomas Erskine of Linlathen*, (Edinburgh: 1878)

Haweis, Thomas, *An Impartial History of the Church of Christ*, 3 vols, (London: 1800)

Hay, James and Henry Belfrage, *Memoir of the Rev. Alexander Waugh, D.D.*, (Edinburgh: 1839)

Hearder, Henry, *Europe in the 19th Century*, (London: 1970)

Hempton, D.N., 'Evangelicalism and Eschatology' *Journal of Ecclesiastical History*, 31.2 (1980), 179-194

Henderson, W. O., *Britain and Industrial Europe*, (Liverpool: 1957)

Hennell, Michael, *John Venn and the Clapham Sect*, (London: 1958)

—, *Sons of the Prophets: Evangelical Leaders of the Victorian Church*, (London: 1979)

Heron, Alasdair I.C., ed., *The Westminster Confession in the Church Today*, (Edinburgh: 1982)

Heugh, Hugh, *Notices of the State of Religion in Geneva and Belgium*, (Glasgow: 1844)

Heyer, Henri, *L'Église de Genève*, (Geneva: 1909)

Holmes, R.F.G., 'United Irishmen and Unionists', in W.J. Shiels and Diana Woods, eds, *The Churches, Ireland and the Irish*, Studies in Church History, Vol. 25, (Oxford: 1988), 171-190

Hordern, F., 'Les Moraves en France Sous L'Empire', *Bulletin de le Société d'Histoire du Protestantisme Française*, 112 (1966), 48-57

Hutton, William H., *The English Church from the Accession of Charles I to the death of Anne: 1625-1714*, (London: 1903)

Hylson-Smith, Kenneth, *Evangelicals in the Church of England 1734-1984*, (Edinburgh: 1988)

Innes, William, *Reasons for Separating From the Church of Scotland*, (Dundee: 1804)

Itzkin, E.S., 'The Halévy Thesis - a Working Hypothesis? English Revivalism: Antidote for Revolution and Radicalism 1795-1815', *Church History*, 44 (1975), 47-56

Jay, William, *Autobiography*, (London: 1854)

—, ed., *Memoir of Cornelius Winter*, (London: 1809)

Jones, R. Tudor, *Congregationalism in England 1662-1962*, (London: 1962)

—, 'The Evangelical Revival in Wales: A Study in Spirituality', in James P. Mackey, ed., *An Introduction to Celtic Christianity*, (Edinburgh: 1990), 237-267

Jones, Thomas Snell, *The Life of the Right Honourable Willielma, Viscountess Glenorchy*, (Edinburgh: 1824)

Jones, William, *Biographical Sketch of the Rev. Edward Irving, A.M.*, (London: 1835)

—, *Jubilee Memorial of the Religious Tract Society 1799-1849*, (London: 1849)

—, *Memoir of the Rev. Rowland Hill*, (London: 1837)

Juillerat-Chasseur, M., 'Notice Sur La Vie et Les Écrits de Daniel Encontre, Professeur de dogme à la Faculté de Théologie protestante de Montauban', *Archives du Christianisme*, 3 (1820), 406-445

Keble, John, *Assize Sermon on National Apostasy*, (Oxford, 1833, reprint edition, Abingdon, 1983)

Kent, John, *Holding the Fort; Studies in Victorian Revivalism*, (London: 1978)
—, *Wesley and the Wesleyans*, (Cambridge: 2002)
Kessler, J.B.A., *A Study of the Evangelical Alliance in Great Britain*, (Goes, Netherlands: 1968)
Kiernan, V., 'Evangelicalism and the French Revolution', *Past and Present*, 1 (1952), 44-56
King, David, ed., *Essays on Christian Union*, (Edinburgh and London: 1845)
Kinniburgh, Robert, *Fathers of Independency in Scotland*, (Edinburgh: 1851)
Klauber, Martin I., 'Family Loyalty and Theological Transition in Post-Reformation Geneva: The Case of Benedict Pictet (1655-1724)', *Fides et Historia*, 24.1 (1992), 54-67
Kluit, Elisabeth, 'Internationale Invloeden in de Voorgeschiedenis van het Réveil in Nederland', *Nederlands Archief Voor Kerkgeschiedenis*, 44-45 (1961-63), 33-52
—, 'Wenselijkheiden Voor de Studie Van Het Réveil', *Nederlands Theologisch Tijdschrift*, 11 (1956-67), 360-67
Krummacher, F.W., *Autobiography*, (Edinburgh: 1869)
Kuhn, Félix, 'La Vie Interieur du Protestantism Sous le Premier Empire', *Bulletin de le Société d' Histoire du Protestantisme Française*, 51 (1902), 57-73
Lane, Laura M., *The Life and Writings of Alexandre Vinet*, (Edinburgh: 1890)
Lecerf, August, 'The Reformed Faith in France', *Evangelical Quarterly*, 4.4 (1932), 391-98
Lenman, Bruce, *Integration, Enlightenment and Industrialization; Scotland 1746-1832*, (London: 1981)
Lewis, A.J., *Zinzendorf, Ecumenical Pioneer*, (London: 1962)
Lewis, Donald M., ed., *The Blackwell Dictionary of Evangelical Biography 1730-1860*, 2 vols, (Oxford: 1996)
Lewis, Glyn, 'British Nonconformist Reactions to the "Terreur Blanche"', *Proceedings of the Huguenot Society of London*, 20 (1964), 510-527
—, 'The White Terror and the Persecution of Protestants in the South of France in 1815', *Proceedings of the Huguenot Society of London*, 20 (1964), 419-439
Liddon, H.P., *The Life of E.B. Pusey*, 4 vols, (Oxford: 1893)
Lindsay, T.M., et al., *Religious Life in Scotland from the Reformation to the Present Day*, (London: 1883)
Lods, Armand, 'Bonaparte et les Églises Protestantes de France', *Bulletin de le Société d'Histoire Protestantisme Française*, 46 (1897), 393-417
Lovegrove, D.W., 'English Evangelical Dissent and the European Conflict', in W.J. Sheils, ed., *Studies in Church History*, 20 (1983), 263-76
—, *Established Church, Sectarian People*, (Cambridge: 1988)
—, ed., *The Rise of the Laity in Evangelical Protestantism*, (London: 2002)
—, 'Unity and Separation: Contrasting Elements in the Thought and Practice of Robert and James Haldane', in K. Robbins, ed., *Studies in Church History*, Subsidia 7, (1990), 153-177

—, 'The Voice of Reproach and Outrage: The Impact of Robert Haldane on French-speaking Protestantism', in D.W.D. Shaw, ed., *In Divers Manners*, (St. Andrews: 1990), 74-84

Lovett, Richard, *The History of the London Missionary Society*, 2 vols, (London: 1898-99)

Lundie, Mary Duncan, *Memoir of the Life of the Rev. Matthias Bruen of New York*, (Edinburgh: 1832)

MacEwen, A.R., *Life of John Cairns*, (London: 1895)

McKee, Elsie Ann, 'Alexandre Vinet on Religious Liberty and Separation of Church and State', *Journal of Church and State*, 28.1 (1986), 95-106

MacInnes, John, *The Evangelical Movement in the Highlands of Scotland*, (Aberdeen: 1951)

McIntosh, John R., *Church and Theology in Enlightenment Scotland: The Popular Party, 1740-1800*, (East Linton: 1998)

McKerrow, John, *History of the Secession Church*, (Glasgow: 1841)

McLachlan, Henry, *English Education under the Test Acts*, (Manchester: 1931)

McLeod, Hugh, *Religion and the People of Western Europe, 1789-1970*, (Oxford: 1981)

McManners, John, *The French Revolution and the Church*, (London: 1969)

McNaughton, William D., 'Revival and Reality: Congregationalists and Religious Revival in Nineteenth Century Scotland', *Records of the Scottish Church History Society*, 33 (2003), 165-216

McNeill, John T., *History and Character of Calvinism*, (New York: 1954)

Macpherson, John, *Christian Dogmatics*, (Edinburgh: 1898)

MacWhirter, A., 'The Early Days of the Independents and Congregationalists in the Northern Islands', *Records of the Scottish Church History Society*, 16 (1966), 63-87

Malan, César, *The Conventicle of Rolle*, (Geneva: 1821; ET London: 1865)

—, *Documents Relative to the Deposition of the Rev. Caesar Malan from his office in the College of Geneva*, (London: 1820)

—, *Recollections of the Rev. Caesar Malan of Geneva, D.D. being notes of sermons preached by him in Edinburgh in May and June, 1826*, (London: 1827)

—, *Sermons Translated from the French, to which is prefixed a sketch of the religious discussions which have recently taken place at Geneva*, (London: 1819)

—, *Theogenes*, (London: 1828)

—, *A Visit to Scotland in 1843*, (Edinburgh: 1843)

Malan, César, Jr, *The Life, Labour and Writings of César Malan*, (London: 1869)

Martin, Roger H., 'The Bible Society and the French Connection', *Journal of the United Reformed Church History Society*, 3.7 (1985), 285-291

—, *Evangelicals United: Ecumenical Stirrings in Pre-Victorian Britain, 1795-1830*, (Metuchen, NJ: 1983)

Mason, John M., *Sermons, Lectures, Orations, with a memoir by John Eadie*, (Edinburgh: 1860)

Massie, J.W., *The Evangelical Alliance: Its Origin and Development*, (London: 1847)

Matheson, Janet J., *Memoir of Greville Ewing*, (London: 1843)

Maury, Leon, *Le Réveil Religieux a Genève et de France*, 2 vols, (Paris: 1892)

Mechie, Stewart, *The Church and Scottish Social Development 1780-1870*, (London: 1960)

Medway, John, *Memoir of the Life and Writings of John Pye Smith, D.D.*, (London: 1853)

Meek, Donald, 'Evangelical Missionaries in the Nineteenth Century Highlands', *Scottish Studies*, 28 (1987), 1-34

—, 'The Doctrinal Basis of Christopher Anderson', (privately circulated essay, 1989)

Merle D'Aubigné, J.H., *Discourses and Essays*, (Glasgow: 1846).

—, *Geneva and Oxford*, (London: 1843)

Meston, William, *Observations On the Present State of Religion in France; and on the Duty of the Church of Scotland to aid the Cause of the Reformation in that country*, (London: 1839)

Mitchell, A.F. and J. Struthers, *Minutes of the Sessions of the Westminster Assembly*, (Edinburgh: 1890)

Monod, *The Life and Letters of Adolphe Monod* (London: 1885)

Monod, Adolphe, *Appel aux Chretiens de France et de l'Etranger en faveur de l'église Évangélique de Lyon*, (Paris: 1833)

Monod, Frédéric, *Memorial of Jules Charles Rieu*, (Edinburgh: 1854)

Morison, John, *The Fathers and Founders of the London Missionary Society*, 2 vols, (London: 1844)

Morris, J.W., *Memoirs of the Life and Writings of the Rev. Andrew Fuller* (London: 1816)

Mours, Samuel, *Les Églises Reformées En France*, (Paris: 1958)

Murdock, Graeme, *Beyond Calvin: The Intellectual, Political and Cultural World of Europe's Reformed Churches*, (London: 2004)

Murray, Ian H., *The Puritan Hope; Revival and the Interpretation of Prophecy*, (London: 1971)

Needham, N. R., *Thomas Erskine of Linlathen; His Life and Theology 1788-1837*, (Edinburgh: 1990)

Neill, Stephen, *A History of Missions*, (London: 1986)

Newsome, David, *The Parting of Friends: A Study of the Wilberforces and Henry Manning*, (London: 1966)

Nichols, J.H., *A History of Christianity 1650-1950*, (New York: 1956)

Noel, Baptist W., *Notes of a Tour in Switzerland in the Summer of 1847*, (London: 1847)

Noel, Gerard, *Arvendale, or Sketches in Italy and Switzerland*, (London: 1826)

Noll, Mark, David Bebbington, and George Rawlyk, eds, *Evangelicalism: Comparative Studies of Popular Protestantism in North America, the British Isles, and Beyond, 1700-1990*, (New York: 1994)

Noll, Mark A., *The Rise of Evangelicalism: The Age of Edwards, Whitefield, and the Wesleys*, (Downers Grove, IL, and Leicester: 2004)

Nuttall, Geoffrey F., 'Assembly and Association in Dissent 1689-1831', in J.G. Cuming and Derek Baker, eds, *Councils and Assemblies*, Studies in Church History, 7, (Cambridge: 1971), 289-309

—, 'Calvinism in Free Church History', *Baptist Quarterly*, 22 (1967-68), 418-428

—, 'Continental Pietism and the Evangelical Movement in Britain', in J. Van Den Berg and J.P. Van Dooren, eds, *Pietismus und Reveil*, (Leiden: 1978), 207-236

—, 'George Whitefield's Curate: Gloucester Dissent and the Evangelical Revival'. *Journal of Ecclesiastical History*, 27 (1976), 369-86

—, 'Methodism and the Older Dissent: Some Perspectives', *Journal of the United Reformed Church Historical Society*, 2.8 (1981), 259-274

—, 'Northamptonshire and *The Modern Question*', *Journal of Theological Studies*, 16 (1965), 101-123

O'Brien, Susan, 'A Transatlantic Community of Saints: The Great Awakening and the First Evangelical Network, 1735-1755', *The American Historical Review*, 91.4 (1986), 811-832

Oliphant, Margaret, *The Life of Edward Irving*, 2 vols, (London, 1864)

Ollard, S.L., *A Short History of the Oxford Movement*, (London: 1915, reprinted 1963)

Orchard, Stephen, 'Evangelical Eschatology and the Missionary Awakening', *Journal of Religious History*, 22.2 (1998), 132-158

Orr, J. Edwin, *The Eager Feet*, (Chicago, IL: 1975)

Osen, J. Lynn, 'The Theological Revival in the French Reformed Church, 1830-1852', *Church History*, 37.1 ((1968), 36-49

Owen, John, *Brief Extracts From Letters...On His Late Tour to France and Switzerland*, (London: 1819)

—, *The History of the Origin and First Ten Years of the British and Foreign Bible Society*, 3 vols, (London: 1816-20)

Palmer, William, *Aids to Reflection On the Seemingly Double Character of the Established Church With Reference to the Foundation of a Protestant Bishopric at Jerusalem*, (Oxford: 1841)

Pals, Daniel L., *The Victorian 'Lives' of Jesus*, (San Antonio. TX: 1982)

Payne, Ernest A., *The Free Church Tradition in the Life of England*, (London: 1944)

Philip, Robert, *The Life, Times and Missionary Enterprises of the Rev. John Campbell*, (London: 1841)

Poland, Burdette C., *French Protestantism and the French Revolution*, (Princeton, NJ: 1957)

Poole, Reginald Lane, *A History of the Huguenots of the Dispersion at the Recall of the Edict of Nantes*, (London: 1880)

Pradervand, Marcel, *A Century of Service: A History of the World Alliance of Reformed Churches 1875-1975*, (Edinburgh: 1975)

Pratt, John H., *The Thought of the Evangelical Leaders*, (London: 1856, reprint Edinburgh: 1978)

Prestwich, Menna, ed., *International Calvinism 1541-1715*, (Oxford: 1985)

Prickett, Stephen, *England and the French Revolution*, (London: 1989)

Pusey, E.B., *A Letter to His Grace, the Archbishop of Canterbury on some circumstances connected with the Present Crisis in the English Church*, (Oxford: 1842)

Railton, Nicholas, *No North Sea: The Anglo-German Evangelical Network in the Middle of the Nineteenth Century*, (Leiden: 2000)

Rainy, Robert, and James Mackenzie, *Life of William Cunningham*, (London: 1871)

Randall, Ian and David Hillborn, eds, *One in Christ: The History and Significance of the Evangelical Alliance*, (Carlisle: 2001)

Rawlyk, George and Mark Noll, eds, *Amazing Grace: Evangelicalism in Australia,Canada and the United States*, (Montreal: 1994)

Reeves, Dudley R., 'The Interaction of Scottish and English Evangelicals 1790-1810', (Glasgow University MLitt Thesis, 1973)

Reynolds, John S., *The Evangelicals at Oxford 1735-1871*, (Appleford: 1975)

Rieu, Charles, 'Aux genereuse bienfaiteurs de l'église et colonie reformée de Frederica (Jutland)', *Archives du Christianisme*, 3 (1820), 330-332

Robert, Daniel, *Les Églises Reformées En France 1800 -1830*, (Paris: 1961)

—, *Genève et les Églises Reformées de France de la Réunion (1798) aux Environs de 1830*, (Paris: 1961)

—, *Textes et Documents Relatifs à L'Histoire des Églises Reformées en France 1800 -1830*, (Paris: 1961)

Roney, John B. and Martin Klauber, eds, *The Identity of Geneva: The Christian Commonwealth, 1564-1864*, (Westport, CT: 1998)

Roney, John B., 'Romantic Historiography and the European Réveil, 1815-1850', *Fides et Historia*, 30.1 (1998), 3-14

Ross, Andrew, *John Philip (1775-1851)*, (Aberdeen: 1986)

Ross, James. W., *Lindsay Alexander, D.D. His Life and Work*, (London: 1887)

Rouse, Ruth and Stephen Neill, eds, *A History of the Ecumenical Movement 1517-1948*, (London: 1954)

Roxburgh, Kenneth B.E., *Thomas Gillespie and the Origins of the Relief Church in Eighteenth Century Scotland*, (Bern: 1999)

Rupp, Ernest Gordon, *Religion in England 1688-1791*, (Oxford: 1986)

Ryland, John, *The Life and Death of the Rev. Andrew Fuller*, (London: 1816)

Sell, Allan P.F., 'Revival and Secession in Early Nineteenth Century Geneva', in *Commemorations: Studies in Christian Thought and History*, (Cardiff, University of Wales Press: 1994)

Schaff, Philip, ed., *The Creeds of Christendom*, 3 vols, (London: 1877)

Scherer, Edmond, *On the Present State of the Reformed Church of France*, (Paris: 1844; ET London: 1845)

Schmidt, Leigh Eric, *Holy Fairs: Scotland and the Making of the American Revolution*, (Princeton, NJ: 1989)

Scorgie, Glenn, 'The French Canadian Mission Society: A Study in Evangelistic Zeal and Civic Ambition', *Fides et* Historia, 36.1 (2004), 67-81

Scouloudi, Irene, ed., *The Huguenots in Britain and Their French Background 1550-1800*, (London: 1987)

Shaw, Duncan, ed., *Reformation and Revolution*, (Edinburgh: 1967)

Shaw, Ian, *High Calvinists in Action: Calvinism and the City 1810-1860*, (Oxford: 2003)

Shaw, P.E., *The Catholic Apostolic Church*, (New York: 1846)

Sherwig, J.M., *Guineas and Gunpowder*, (Boston, MA: 1969)

Sidney, Edwin, *The Life of the Rev. Rowland Hill, A.M.*, (London: 1835)

Sitoy, Valentino S., 'British Evangelical Missions to Spain in the 19th Century', (University of Edinburgh, PhD Thesis, 1971)

Smith, A. Christopher, 'British Nonconformists and the Swiss "Ancienne Dissidence": The Role of Foreign Evangelicals and J.N. Darby in the Rise and Fall of the "Ancienne Dissidence" in French-Speaking Switzerland' (International Baptist Theological Seminary, Rüschlikon, BD Thesis, 1979)

—, 'J.N. Darby in Switzerland: at the Crossroads of Brethren History and European Evangelicalism', *Christian Brethren Review Journal*, 34 (1983), 53-94

Smith, John Pye, *A Reply to Professor Chenevière's 'Summary of Theological Controversies'*, (London: 1825)

Smyth, C.H., *Simeon and Church Order*, (Cambridge: 1940)

Somerville, W.C., *From Iona to Dunblane; The Story of the National Bible Society of Scotland to 1948*, (Edinburgh: 1948)

Sorkin, David, 'Geneva's "Enlightened Orthodoxy": The Middle Way of Jacob Vernet (1689-1789)', *Church History*, 74.2 (2005) 286-305

Spangenburg, August Gottlieb, *An Exposition of Christian Doctrine as Taught in the Protestant Church of the United Brethren* (Barby: 1778; ET 1796)

Sprague, William B., *Letters from Europe in 1828*, (New York: 1828)

Stephan, Raoul, 'Les Origines du Réveil au XIX siécle', *Bulletin de le Societé de l'Histoire du Protestantisme Française*, 8 (1961), 21-28

Stephen, Leslie, ed., *The Dictionary of National Biography*, 65 vols, (London: 1885ff)

Stewart, David D., *Memoir of James Haldane Stewart*, (London: 1857)

Stewart, Kenneth J., 'A Bombshell of a Book: Gaussen's *Theopneustia* (1841) and its influence on subsequent Evangelical Theology', *Evangelical Quarterly, 75.3* (2003), 235-257

—, 'Did Evangelicalism Predate the Eighteenth Century? An Examination of David Bebbington's Thesis', *Evangelical Quarterly*, 77.2 (2005), 135-154

—, 'A Millennial Maelstrom: Controversy in the Continental Society in the 1820s', in Crawford Gribben and T.C.F. Stunt, eds, *Prisoners of Hope? Aspects of British Millennialism 1800-1850*, (Carlisle: 2004), 122-149

Stoeffler, F. Ernest, *The Rise of Evangelical Pietism*, (Leiden: 1965)

—, *German Pietism During the Eighteenth Century*, (Leiden: 1973)

Stoughton, John, *Religion in England Under Queen Anne and the Georges, 1702-1800*, 2 vols, (London: 1878)

Stoughton, John, *Religion in England from 1800 to 1850*, Vol. 1, (London: 1884)

Stunt, Timothy C.F., *From Awakening to Secession: Radical Evangelicals in Switzerland and Britain 1815-1835*, (Edinburgh: 2000)

—, 'Geneva and the British Evangelicals in the Early Nineteenth Century', *Journal of Ecclesiastical History*, 32.1 (1981), 35-46

—, 'John Henry Newman and the Evangelicals', *Journal of Ecclesiastical History*, 21.1, 65-74

tenZythoff, Gerrit J., *Sources of Secession: The Netherlands Hervormde Kerk on the Eve of the Dutch Immigration to the Midwest*, (Grand Rapids, MI: 1987)

Terpstra, C., 'David Bogue, D.D. 1750-1825; Pioneer and Missionary Educator', (Edinburgh University, PhD Thesis, 1959)

Thompson, David M., *Denominationalism and Dissent, 1795-1835: A Question of Identity*, (London: 1985)

Thompson, E.P., *The Making of the English Working Class*, (Harmondsworth: 1963, reprinted 1978)

Toase, William, *The Wesleyan Mission in France*, (London: 1835)

—, *Memorials of the Rev. Wm Toase*, (London: 1874)

[Unattributed], *L'Union des églises évangéliques libres de France; Ses Origines, son Histoire, son oeuvre*, (Paris: 1899)

Van den Berg, Johannes, *Constrained by Jesus Love*, (Kampen, Netherlands: 1956)

—, 'The Evangelical Revival in Scotland and the nineteenth century Réveil in the Netherlands', *Records of the Scottish Church History Society*, 25.2 (1994), 309-337

Vickers, John, *Thomas Coke, Apostle of Methodism*, (London: 1969)

Vidler, Alec R., *The Church in an Age of Revolution: 1789 to the present day*, (Harmondsworth: 1974)

Vulliemin, L. and C. Vulliemin, *Some Account of the Life of the Rev. F.A.A. Gonthier*, (London: 1837)

Walker, Norman L., *Dr. Robert Buchanan: An Ecclesiastical Biography*, (Edinburgh: 1877)

Ward, W. Reginald, 'John Wesley and His Evangelical Past', *Asbury Seminary Journal*, 59.1-2 (2004), 5-16

—, *Religion and Society in England 1790-1850*, (London: 1972)

—, *The Protestant Evangelical Awakening*, (Cambridge: 1992)

Watt, Hugh, 'Thomas Gillespie', *Records of the Scottish Church History Society*, 15 (1964), 89-101

Watts, Malcolm R., *The Dissenters*, (Oxford: 1978)

Wellwood, Henry Moncrieff, *An Account of the Life and Writings of John Erskine, D.D.*, (Edinburgh: 1818)

Wemyss, Alice, *Le Réveil; 1790-1849*, (Toulouse: 1977)

Wernle, Paul, *Der Schweizerische Protestismus im XVIII. Jahrhundert*, 3 vols, (Tübingen: 1923)

Westin, Gunnar, *The Free Church Through the Ages*, (Nashville, TN: 1958)

Wilder, Sampson, V.S., *Records From the Life of S.V.S.W.*, (New York: 1865)

Wilks, Mark, *History of the Persecutions Endured by the Protestants of the South of France...During 1814, 1815, 1816*, (London: 1821)

Williams, Basil, *The Whig Supremacy*, (Oxford: 1962)

Williams, Edward, *A Defense of Modern Calvinism*, (London: 1812)

Wilson, Daniel, *Letters From an Absent Brother Containing Some Account of a Tour in 1823*, (London: 1823, reprinted 1825)

Wilson, William, *Memorials of Robert Smith Candlish, D.D.*, (Edinburgh: 1880)

Wintle, Michael, *Pillars of Piety: Religion in the Netherlands in the 19th Century*, (Hull: 1987)

Wolffe, John, 'The Evangelical Alliance in the 1840s: An Attempt to Institutionalise Christian Unity', in W.J. Sheils and Diana Woods, eds, *Voluntary Religion*, Studies in Church History 23, (Oxford: 1986)

—, *The Protestant Crusade in Great Britain*, (Oxford: 1991)

Wood, A. Skevington, *The Inextinguishable Blaze*, (London: 1960)

—, *Thomas Haweis*, (London: 1957)

General Index

Studies in Evangelical History and Thought
(All titles uniform with this volume)
Dates in bold are of projected publication

Andrew Atherstone
Oxford's Protestant Spy
The Controversial Career of Charles Golightly
Charles Golightly (1807–85) was a notorious Protestant polemicist. His life was dedicated to resisting the spread of ritualism and liberalism within the Church of England and the University of Oxford. For half a century he led many memorable campaigns, such as building a martyr's memorial and attempting to close a theological college. John Henry Newman, Samuel Wilberforce and Benjamin Jowett were among his adversaries. This is the first study of Golightly's controversial career.
2006 / 1-84227-364-7 / approx. 324pp

Clyde Binfield
Victorian Nonconformity in Eastern England
Studies of Victorian religion and society often concentrate on cities, suburbs, and industrialisation. This study provides a contrast. Victorian Eastern England—Essex, Suffolk, Norfolk, Cambridgeshire, and Huntingdonshire—was rural, traditional, relatively unchanging. That is nonetheless a caricature which discounts the industry in Norwich and Ipswich (as well as in Haverhill, Stowmarket and Leiston) and ignores the impact of London on Essex, of railways throughout the region, and of an ancient but changing university (Cambridge) on the county town which housed it. It also entirely ignores the political implications of such changes in a region noted for the variety of its religious Dissent since the seventeenth century. This book explores Victorian Eastern England and its Nonconformity. It brings to a wider readership a pioneering thesis which has made a major contribution to a fresh evolution of English religion and society.
2006 / 1-84227-216-0 / approx. 274pp

John Brencher
Martyn Lloyd-Jones (1899–1981) and Twentieth-Century Evangelicalism
This study critically demonstrates the significance of the life and ministry of Martyn Lloyd-Jones for post-war British evangelicalism and demonstrates that his preaching was his greatest influence on twentieth-century Christianity. The factors which shaped his view of the church are examined, as is the way his reformed evangelicalism led to a separatist ecclesiology which divided evangelicals.
2002 / 1-84227-051-6 / xvi + 268pp

Jonathan D. Burnham
A Story of Conflict
The Controversial Relationship between Benjamin Wills Newton and John Nelson Darby

Burnham explores the controversial relationship between the two principal leaders of the early Brethren movement. In many ways Newton and Darby were products of their times, and this study of their relationship provides insight not only into the dynamics of early Brethrenism, but also into the progress of nineteenth-century English and Irish evangelicalism.

2004 / 1-84227-191-1 / xxiv + 268pp

Grayson Carter
Anglican Evangelicals
Protestant Secessions from the Via Media, c.1800–1850

This study examines, within a chronological framework, the major themes and personalities which influenced the outbreak of a number of Evangelical clerical and lay secessions from the Church of England and Ireland during the first half of the nineteenth century. Though the number of secessions was relatively small—between a hundred and two hundred of the 'Gospel' clergy abandoned the Church during this period—their influence was considerable, especially in highlighting in embarrassing fashion the tensions between the evangelical conversionist imperative and the principles of a national religious establishment. Moreover, through much of this period there remained, just beneath the surface, the potential threat of a large Evangelical disruption similar to that which occurred in Scotland in 1843. Consequently, these secessions provoked great consternation within the Church and within Evangelicalism itself, they contributed to the outbreak of millennial speculation following the 'constitutional revolution' of 1828–32, they led to the formation of several new denominations, and they sparked off a major Church–State crisis over the legal right of a clergyman to secede and begin a new ministry within Protestant Dissent.

2007 / 1-84227-401-5 / xvi + 470pp

J.N. Ian Dickson
Beyond Religious Discourse
Sermons, Preaching and Evangelical Protestants in Nineteenth-Century Irish Society
Drawing extensively on primary sources, this pioneer work in modern religious history explores the training of preachers, the construction of sermons and how Irish evangelicalism and the wider movement in Great Britain and the United States shaped the preaching event. Evangelical preaching and politics, sectarianism, denominations, education, class, social reform, gender, and revival are examined to advance the argument that evangelical sermons and preaching went significantly beyond religious discourse. The result is a book for those with interests in Irish history, culture and belief, popular religion and society, evangelicalism, preaching and communication.
2005 / 1-84227-217-9 / approx. 324pp

Neil T.R. Dickson
Brethren in Scotland 1838–2000
A Social Study of an Evangelical Movement
The Brethren were remarkably pervasive throughout Scottish society. This study of the Open Brethren in Scotland places them in their social context and examines their growth, development and relationship to society.
2003 / 1-84227-113-X / xxviii + 510pp

Crawford Gribben and Timothy C.F. Stunt (eds)
Prisoners of Hope?
Aspects of Evangelical Millennialism in Britain and Ireland, 1800–1880
This volume of essays offers a comprehensive account of the impact of evangelical millennialism in nineteenth-century Britain and Ireland.
2004 / 1-84227-224-1 / xiv + 208pp

Khim Harris
Evangelicals and Education
Evangelical Anglicans and Middle-Class Education in Nineteenth-Century England
This ground breaking study investigates the history of English public schools founded by nineteenth-century Evangelicals. It documents the rise of middle-class education and Evangelical societies such as the influential Church Association, and includes a useful biographical survey of prominent Evangelicals of the period.
2004 / 1-84227-250-0 / xviii + 422pp

Mark Hopkins
Nonconformity's Romantic Generation
Evangelical and Liberal Theologies in Victorian England
A study of the theological development of key leaders of the Baptist and Congregational denominations at their period of greatest influence, including C.H. Spurgeon and R.W. Dale, and of the controversies in which those among them who embraced and rejected the liberal transformation of their evangelical heritage opposed each other.
2004 / 1-84227-150-4 / xvi + 284pp

Don Horrocks
Laws of the Spiritual Order
Innovation and Reconstruction in the Soteriology of Thomas Erskine of Linlathen
Don Horrocks argues that Thomas Erskine's unique historical and theological significance as a soteriological innovator has been neglected. This timely reassessment reveals Erskine as a creative, radical theologian of central and enduring importance in Scottish nineteenth-century theology, perhaps equivalent in significance to that of S.T. Coleridge in England.
2004 / 1-84227-192-X / xx + 362pp

Kenneth S. Jeffrey
When the Lord Walked the Land
The 1858–62 Revival in the North East of Scotland
Previous studies of revivals have tended to approach religious movements from either a broad, national or a strictly local level. This study of the multifaceted nature of the 1859 revival as it appeared in three distinct social contexts within a single region reveals the heterogeneous nature of simultaneous religious movements in the same vicinity.
2002 / 1-84227-057-5 / xxiv + 304pp

John Kenneth Lander
Itinerant Temples
Tent Methodism, 1814–1832
Tent preaching began in 1814 and the Tent Methodist sect resulted from disputes with Bristol Wesleyan Methodists in 1820. The movement spread to parts of Gloucestershire, Wiltshire, London and Liverpool, among other places. Its demise started in 1826 after which one leader returned to the Wesleyans and others became ministers in the Congregational and Baptist denominations.
2003 / 1-84227-151-2 / xx + 268pp

Donald M. Lewis
Lighten Their Darkness
The Evangelical Mission to Working-Class London, 1828–1860
This is a comprehensive and compelling study of the Church and the complexities of nineteenth-century London. Challenging our understanding of the culture in working London at this time, Lewis presents a well-structured and illustrated work that contributes substantially to the study of evangelicalism and mission in nineteenth-century Britain.
2001 / 1-84227-074-5 / xviii + 372pp

Herbert McGonigle
'Sufficient Saving Grace'
John Wesley's Evangelical Arminianism
A thorough investigation of the theological roots of John Wesley's evangelical Arminianism and how these convictions were hammered out in controversies on predestination, limited atonement and the perseverance of the saints.
2001 / 1-84227-045-1 / xvi + 350pp

Lisa S. Nolland
A Victorian Feminist Christian
Josephine Butler, the Prostitutes and God
Josephine Butler was an unlikely candidate for taking up the cause of prostitutes, as she did, with a fierce and self-disregarding passion. This book explores the particular mix of perspectives and experiences that came together to envision and empower her remarkable achievements. It highlights the vital role of her spirituality and the tragic loss of her daughter.
2004 / 1-84227-225-X / xxiv + 328pp

Don J. Payne
The Theology of the Christian Life in J.I. Packer's Thought
Theological Anthropology, Theological Method, and the Doctrine of Sanctification
J.I. Packer has wielded widespread influence on evangelicalism for more than three decades. This study pursues a nuanced understanding of Packer's theology of sanctification by tracing the development of his thought, showing how he reflects a particular version of Reformed theology, and examining the unique influence of theological anthropology and theological method on this area of his theology.
2005 / 1-84227-397-3 / approx. 374pp

Ian M. Randall
Evangelical Experiences
A Study in the Spirituality of English Evangelicalism 1918–1939
This book makes a detailed historical examination of evangelical spirituality between the First and Second World Wars. It shows how patterns of devotion led to tensions and divisions. In a wide-ranging study, Anglican, Wesleyan, Reformed and Pentecostal-charismatic spiritualities are analysed.
1999 / 0-85364-919-7 / xii + 310pp

Ian M. Randall
Spirituality and Social Change
The Contribution of F.B. Meyer (1847–1929)
This is a fresh appraisal of F.B. Meyer (1847–1929), a leading Free Church minister. Having been deeply affected by holiness spirituality, Meyer became the Keswick Convention's foremost international speaker. He combined spirituality with effective evangelism and socio-political activity. This study shows Meyer's significant contribution to spiritual renewal and social change.
2003 / 1-84227-195-4 / xx + 184pp

James Robinson
Pentecostal Origins
Early Pentecostalism in Ireland in the Context of the British Isles
Harvey Cox describes Pentecostalism as 'the fascinating spiritual child of our time' that has the potential, at the global scale, to contribute to the 'reshaping of religion in the twenty-first century'. This study grounds such sentiments by examining at the local scale the origin, development and nature of Pentecostalism in Ireland in its first twenty years. Illustrative, in a paradigmatic way, of how Pentecostalism became established within one region of the British Isles, it sets the story within the wider context of formative influences emanating from America, Europe and, in particular, other parts of the British Isles. As a synoptic regional study in Pentecostal history it is the first survey of its kind.
2005 / 1-84227-329-1 / xxviii + 378pp

Geoffrey Robson
Dark Satanic Mills?
Religion and Irreligion in Birmingham and the Black Country
This book analyses and interprets the nature and extent of popular Christian belief and practice in Birmingham and the Black Country during the first half of the nineteenth century, with particular reference to the impact of cholera epidemics and evangelism on church extension programmes.
2002 / 1-84227-102-4 / xiv + 294pp

Roger Shuff
Searching for the True Church
Brethren and Evangelicals in Mid-Twentieth-Century England
Roger Shuff holds that the influence of the Brethren movement on wider
evangelical life in England in the twentieth century is often underrated. This
book records and accounts for the fact that Brethren reached the peak of their
strength at the time when evangelicalism was at it lowest ebb, immediately
before World War II. However, the movement then moved into persistent
decline as evangelicalism regained ground in the post war period.
Accompanying this downward trend has been a sharp accentuation of the
contrast between Brethren congregations who engage constructively with the
non-Brethren scene and, at the other end of the spectrum, the isolationist group
commonly referred to as 'Exclusive Brethren'.
2005 / 1-84227-254-3 / xviii+ 296pp

James H.S. Steven
Worship in the Spirit
Charismatic Worship in the Church of England
This book explores the nature and function of worship in six Church of England
churches influenced by the Charismatic Movement, focusing on congregational
singing and public prayer ministry. The theological adequacy of such ritual is
discussed in relation to pneumatological and christological understandings in
Christian worship.
2002 / 1-84227-103-2 / xvi + 238pp

Peter K. Stevenson
God in Our Nature
The Incarnational Theology of John McLeod Campbell
This radical reassessment of Campbell's thought arises from a comprehensive
study of his preaching and theology. Previous accounts have overlooked both his
sermons and his Christology. This study examines the distinctive Christology
evident in his sermons and shows that it sheds new light on Campbell's much
debated views about atonement.
2004 / 1-84227-218-7 / xxiv + 458pp

Kenneth J. Stewart
Restoring the Reformation
British Evangelicalism and the Réveil at Geneva 1816–1849
Restoring the Reformation traces British missionary initiative in post-Revolutionary Francophone Europe from the genesis of the London Missionary Society, the visits of Robert Haldane and Henry Drummond, and the founding of the Continental Society. While British Evangelicals aimed at the reviving of a foreign Protestant cause of momentous legend, they received unforeseen reciprocating emphases from the Continent which forced self-reflection on Evangelicalism's own relationship to the Reformation.
2006 / 1-84227-392-2 / approx. 190pp

Martin Wellings
Evangelicals Embattled
Responses of Evangelicals in the Church of England to Ritualism, Darwinism and Theological Liberalism 1890–1930
In the closing years of the nineteenth century and the first decades of the twentieth century Anglican Evangelicals faced a series of challenges. In responding to Anglo-Catholicism, liberal theology, Darwinism and biblical criticism, the unity and identity of the Evangelical school were severely tested.
2003 / 1-84227-049-4 / xviii + 352pp

James Whisenant
A Fragile Unity
Anti-Ritualism and the Division of Anglican Evangelicalism in the Nineteenth Century
This book deals with the ritualist controversy (approximately 1850–1900) from the perspective of its evangelical participants and considers the divisive effects it had on the party.
2003 / 1-84227-105-9 / xvi + 530pp

Haddon Willmer
Evangelicalism 1785–1835: An Essay (1962) and Reflections (2004)
Awarded the Hulsean Prize in the University of Cambridge in 1962, this interpretation of a classic period of English Evangelicalism, by a young church historian, is now supplemented by reflections on Evangelicalism from the vantage point of a retired Professor of Theology.
2006 / 1-84227-219-5 / approx. 350pp

Linda Wilson
Constrained by Zeal
Female Spirituality amongst Nonconformists 1825–1875
Constrained by Zeal investigates the neglected area of Nonconformist female spirituality. Against the background of separate spheres, it analyses the experience of women from four denominations, and argues that the churches provided a 'third sphere' in which they could find opportunities for participation.

2000 / 0-85364-972-3 / xvi + 294pp

Paternoster
9 Holdom Avenue,
Bletchley,
Milton Keynes MK1 1QR,
United Kingdom
Web: www.authenticmedia.co.uk/paternoster

ND - #0069 - 270225 - C0 - 229/152/17 - PB - 9781842273920 - Gloss Lamination